JERUSALEM:
WHAT MAKES FOR PEACE!

*A Palestinian Christian Contribution
to Peacemaking*

JERUSALEM:
WHAT MAKES FOR PEACE!

*A Palestinian Christian Contribution
to Peacemaking*

edited by

Naim Ateek, Cedar Duaybis
and Marla Schrader

MELISENDE
London

First published 1997 by Melisende
An imprint of
Fox Communications and Publications
London, England

ISBN 1 901764 00 1

General editor: Leonard Harrow
Assistant editor: Alan Ball
Origination by Walden Litho Plates
Printed and bound in England by The Balkerne Press, Colchester

CONTENTS

Contributors   viii
Sponsors   xi
Acknowledgements   xii
Preface   xiii
Introduction   xv
    Naim Ateek
Conference Message   xviii
Jerusalem in the Greek Orthodox Tradition   xx
    Aristarchos Peristeris
Keynote Address: xxiv
    The Significance of Jerusalem for Christians
    and of Christians for Jerusalem
    Patriarch Michel Sabbah

Worship Meditations
1   Conference Invocation   1
    Salpy Eskidjian
2   A Dream from Jerusalem   2
    Samir Kafity
3   Pentecost and Jerusalem   5
    Atallah Hanna
4   The Prophet Micah and Jerusalem   8
    Mitri Raheb
5   Vision of a New Jerusalem   11
    Eileen W Lindner
6   Empty Tomb and Risen Lord   13
    Elias Chacour

Christian Presence and Unity
7   The Continuity of the Christian Presence in Jerusalem   17
    Maroun Lahham
8   Pathways to Christian Unity I   23
    Kevork Hintilian
9   Pathways to Christian Unity II   28
    Jean Zaru

Christian–Muslim Relations
10   Christian-Muslim Relations in Historic Perspective   31
    John L Esposito

11   A Vision for Christian-Muslim Relations   38
      Geries Khoury
12   The Significance of Jerusalem for Muslims   45
      Antonie Wessels

Theologies of Jerusalem
13   Jesus and Jerusalem: New Testament Perspectives   61
      Peter Walker
14   Marching to Zion: Western Evangelicals and Jerusalem
      Approaching the Year 2000   73
      Don Wagner
15   A Palestinian Theology of Jerusalem   94
      Naim Ateek

Pilgrimage and Spirituality
16   The Spirituality of Christian Pilgrimage   107
      Anba Abraham
17   Local Community and Tourism   111
      Zoughbi Zoughbi
18   A Perspective on Pilgrimage to the Holy Land   114
      Michael Prior

The Christian Community and Current Realities
19   Profile of the Christian Communities: Challenges and Hopes   132
      Bernard Sabella
20   The Separation of Jerusalem from the West Bank and Gaza   141
      Lynda Brayer
21   The Changing Face of Jerusalem   154
      Ibrahim Matar
22   The Message of Jerusalem Today   167
      Munir Fasheh

Archaeology, Environment and Heritage
23   The Effect of Politics on Archaeology   176
      Nazmi Al-Jubeh
24   Political Conflict and Environmental Degradation in Jerusalem   182
      Jad Isaac and Leonardo Hosh
25   A Bi-millennial Celebration in Jerusalem:
      The House of Christian Heritage   195
      Ruth Hummel

Legal Requirements for a Just Resolution
26   Applicability of Israeli Law Over East Jerusalem:
      Concept and Dimensions   200
      Usama Halabi

27 Jerusalem: International Law and Proposed Solutions   209
    Camille Mansour

Galilee Christians and Jerusalem
28 Who are the Christians in Galilee?   213
    Sami Geraisy
29 Factors Affecting the Palestinian Christian Presence in Israel 217
    Ibtisam Mu'allem
30 The Importance of Jerusalem to the Christians of Galilee   221
    Boulus Marcuzzo
31 The Perspective of a Lay Christian from Galilee on
    the City of Jerusalem   226
    Johnny Mansour

Conference Overview
32 The Holy City as an Image of a New Creation   230
    Salpy Eskidjian
33 The Mosaic of Jerusalem   233
    Harry Hagopian

Appendix
Significance of Jerusalem for Christians
    Memorandum of the Patriarchs and Heads
    of the Christian Communities in Jerusalem   236

CONTRIBUTORS

Abraham, Dr Anba
Metropolitan of the Coptic Orthodox Church in Jerusalem and the Middle East

Al-Jubeh, Dr Nazmi
MA in Islamic Studies, Iranian Studies and Biblical Archaeology
Ph.D. in Oriental Studies

Ateek, Revd Dr Naim
Canon, St George's Episcopal Cathedral and Pastor of the Palestinian
Congregation, Jerusalem. President, Board of Directors, *Sabeel*

Brayer, Attorney Lynda
Israeli Lawyer, Executive Legal Director of the Society of St Yves, a Catholic
Human Rights Centre for Legal Resources and Development.

Chacour, Revd Dr Elias
President and founder of Mar Elias College, Ibillin
Vice President, *Sabeel*

Eskidjian, Ms Salpy
Executive Secretary, International Affairs, World Council of Churches (WCC)

Esposito, Dr John
Director, Centre for Christian-Muslim Dialogue
Georgetown University, USA

Fasheh, Dr Munir
Mathematician, educator
Board Member, *Sabeel*

Geraisy, Dr Sami
Chairman of the International Christian Committee in Israel (ICCI)

Hagopian, Dr Harry
Executive Director of the Jerusalem Liaison Office of the Middle East Council of
Churches

Halabi, Attorney Usama
Quaker Legal Aid, Jerusalem

Hanna, Archmandrite Dr Atallah
Greek Orthodox Patriarchate, Jerusalem

Hintilian, Mr Kevork
Armenian Scholar and Author, Jerusalem

Hosh, Mr Leonardo
Director, Environmental Resource, Planning and Assessment Unit
Applied Research Institute (ARIJ), Bethlehem

Hummel, Mrs Ruth
Co-author of: *Patterns of the Sacred: English Protestant and Russian Orthodox Pilgrims of the Nineteenth Century* and contributor to the volume *The Christian Heritage in the Holy Land*

Isaac, Dr Jad
General Director-Applied Research Institute (ARIJ), Bethlehem

Kafity, The Rt Revd Samir
Bishop, Jerusalem Diocese, Episcopal Church in Jerusalem and the Middle East

Khoury, Dr Geries
Director of Al-Liqa Centre
Head of Local Council, Fassouta, Galilee

Lahham, Revd Dr Maroun
Rector, Latin Seminary, Beit Jala

Lindner, Revd Dr Eileen
Associate General Secretary for Christian Unity of the National Council of the Churches of Christ in the USA

Mansour, Dr Camille
Dean, Law Department, Bir Zeit University

Mansour, Mr Johnny
Author, Ph.D candidate in history, Haifa University

Marcuzzo, Msgr Boulus
Bishop, Latin Church, Nazareth

Matar, Mr Ibrahim
Economist. Working in development with American Near East Refugee Aid (ANERA), Jerusalem

Mu'allem, Attorney Ibtisam
Lawyer, Member of the executive committee of the Arab Association for Human Rights

Peristeris, Archmandrite Aristarchos
Greek Orthodox Patriarchate, Jerusalem

Prior, Revd Dr Michael CM
Visiting Professor in Bethlehem University
Head of the Department of Theology and Religious Studies in St Mary's University College, England

Raheb, Revd Dr Mitri
Pastor of the Evangelical Lutheran Christmas Church in Bethlehem
General Director of the International Centre of Bethlehem

Sabbah, Msgr Michel
Latin Patriarch of Jerusalem, President, Middle East Council of Churches

Sabella, Dr Bernard
Associate Professor of Sociology, Bethlehem University
Co-author: *A Date with Democracy*

Wagner, Revd Dr Donald
Director, Centre for Middle Eastern Studies, North Park College, Chicago
Co-ordinator for Evangelicals for Middle East Understanding, USA

Walker, Revd Dr Peter
Research Fellow, Tyndale House, UK

Wessels, Dr Antonie
Professor for History of Religion and Mission at the Free University in Amsterdam

Zaru, Mrs Jean
Presiding Clerk, Society of Friends, Ramallah
Vice President, *Sabeel*

Zoughbi, Mr Zoughbi
Director, Palestinian Centre for Conflict Resolution, Wi'am, Bethlehem
Board Member, *Sabeel*

SPONSORS

Celebration 2000 Commission
Centre for Muslim-Christian Dialogue, Georgetown University
Church of Sweden Mission
Commission on Interchurch Aid of the Netherlands Reformed Church
Diakonia
Episcopal Peace and Justice Network
Revd Elizabeth Knott
Mission and World Service of the Reformed Churches in the Netherlands
Philanthropic Ventures
Pontifical Mission for Palestine
Presbyterian Church USA
Haseeb Sabbagh, Consolidated Contractors Corporation
St. Andrew's Scots Memorial Church
United Church Board for World Ministries
World Council of Churches
World Vision

ACKNOWLEDGEMENTS

It would not have been possible to hold the conference that led to this volume, without the help and support of many people who served on the various committees. *Sabeel Liberation Theology Centre* would like to express deep gratitude and appreciation for all those who made the conference possible, including: the patriarchs, archbishops, bishops and clergy in the Holy Land and the local Palestinian and international Christian community.

A special mention goes to Sabeel's staff, volunteers and friends, local and international, who worked tirelessly to bring this project to fruition: Nora Carmi, Marla Schrader, Cedar Duaybis, Dan Richards, Maha Misleh, Stephen Remsen, Ashlee Wiest-Laird, Lance Laird, Leonard and Julia Shaheen, Kathy Dixon, Sylvia Greenwood, Maha and Nevart Ateek and the Accord Foundation volunteers.

Our gratitude and appreciation go to Dr Khaled Tucktuck and Samia Zaru for designing the conference emblem which also features on the cover of this book. Thanks also to: Khalil Touma who did the translation from Arabic to English and to those who, very patiently, typed the manuscript: Anne Maclean, Rula Qumri, Salwa Duaybis and Maha Mikhail.

PREFACE

On January 22-29 1996 an International Conference on the *Significance of Jerusalem for Christians and of Christians for Jerusalem* was held in East Jerusalem. Over 400 people participated from 23 countries. These included clergy and lay, university and seminary professors, Palestinians and expatriates, Europeans and Asians, from the north and the south.

The conference was organised by Sabeel Liberation Theology Center. The best way to describe Sabeel is to quote its purpose statement:

> *Sabeel,* Arabic for 'the way' and also 'a channel' or 'spring' of life-giving water, is an ecumenical grassroots liberation theology movement among Palestinian Christians which encourages women, men, and youth to discern what God is saying to them as their faith connects with the hard realities of their daily life: occupation, violence, discrimination and human rights violations. Inspired by the life and teaching of Jesus Christ, Sabeel strives to develop a spirituality based on justice, peace, non-violence, liberation, and reconciliation for the different national and faith communities.
>
> *Sabeel* strives to promote a more accurate international awareness regarding the identity, presence, and witness of Palestinian Christians as well as their contemporary concerns. It encourages individuals and groups from around the world to work for a just, comprehensive, and enduring peace informed by truth and empowered by prayer and action.

The programme of the conference included lectures, discussions, and alternative tours to the Old City of Jerusalem as well as to the Israeli settlements that have been built on confiscated Palestinian land around the city. It also included a night of Palestinian folklore where the participants were exposed to Palestinian songs, dance, art, and culture.

Since many Palestinian Christians were not able to enter Jerusalem and participate in the conference due to the Israeli closure since March 1993, the participants were divided into smaller groups, each spending an evening with Palestinian Christians on the West Bank in the towns of Beit Sahur, Beit Jala, Bethlehem, Ramallah, and Taibeh. In addition, one group went to Ramla, Israel, in order to have an experience with Israeli Palestinian Arabs.

In order to offer the participants a comprehensive experience, a tour was arranged to Galilee. The morning was spent visiting some of the historical Christian places around the Sea of Galilee. The afternoon was spent in Haifa and Nazareth discussing and experiencing the life and concerns of the Christian Arab Palestinians in Israel.

The conference included times of worship and prayer on topics that related directly to the theme of the conference. The entire conference was, therefore, set within the framework of songs and worship as the participants sought God's guidance in their deliberations and in praying for Palestinians and Israelis, for Muslims, Jews, and Christians. They promoted a just peace for all the people of Palestine and Israel.

INTRODUCTION
Naim Ateek

The conflict over Palestine has been simmering for almost a hundred years, at times reaching boiling point and vacillating continuously between low and high intensity strife. Since the Madrid Conference in October 1991, Palestinians and the Israelis have been attempting to achieve a settlement to the conflict through peaceful negotiations.

The negotiations between the two sides have also gone through a number of stages with interim agreements marking important milestones in their journey on the road to peace. Some of the most critical and difficult issues were postponed to the final status negotiations. Chief among them are the final demarcation of borders, Palestinian refugees, water resources, Jewish settlements and Jerusalem. Final status negotiations were supposed to commence in May 1996 and span a three-year period. A perfunctory meeting was held towards the beginning of May but due to the impending Israeli elections no substantial progress was expected and the meetings were postponed until after the elections held 29 May 1996.

Jerusalem has become a microcosm of the whole conflict. Both Palestinians and Israelis consider Jerusalem to be the heart of the conflict. Each side is doing its utmost to substantiate its claim over the city. What becomes of Jerusalem, therefore, will determine whether the whole conflict will be resolved on the basis of justice or injustice. In turn this will determine whether the region will enjoy peace and security or not.

For a number of years, it has been evident that the Israeli government has intensified its efforts to Judaise and Israelise Jerusalem. Over 27,000 *dunums* (a *dunum*, 1000 square metres, is approximately one quarter of an acre) of land have been confiscated from Palestinians. Over 50,000 settlement housing units have been built for the exclusive benefit of Jews. More than 160,000 Jews have been placed in these settlements which are actually colonies referred to by Israel as neighbourhoods. These demographic changes have been carried out by Israel in defiance of international law. Moreover, Israel has insisted all along that Jerusalem remain the united eternal capital of Israel and the Jewish people.

In light of these facts and the approaching final status negotiations, Sabeel Liberation Theology Center decided to call for an international conference to discuss a Christian approach and a Christian contribution to the peace of Jerusalem.

This Christian approach must be placed in its broader matrix. The Christian community in Palestine and Israel has decreased numerically due to a number of reasons, chief of which is the political instability in the region. Other reasons include economic, educational, and social factors most of which are the ramifications of political circumstances. Palestinian Christians are currently 2 percent of the population of the land. This fact has caused many people to underestimate their significance politically and religiously. Furthermore, it has caused some people locally and abroad to marginalise and peripherise their role. Indeed, many people in the world, including Western Christians are not even aware of their very presence. Their invisibility has contributed to the rise of a modern myth that the conflict is really between Islam and Judaism, or more precisely between Muslims and Jews, as if the Christian voice does not really matter or that Christians should *ipso facto* take the side of Jews against Muslims. In light of these myths and misconceptions, it was important for Sabeel to clarify the stance of Palestinian Christians, to show them their true name and face, to allow them to speak for themselves, and to make their prophetic voice heard throughout the world. It is important to emphasise that the identity of indigenous Christians is both Arab and Palestinian. At the same time, they are authentically Christian and are proud of Christian faith and heritage that was handed down to them from their ancestors ever since the first Pentecost in Jerusalem 2000 years ago. These Christians wanted a platform from which to raise their voice and make themselves clearly heard and understood. They stand for justice. Without justice for the Palestinians there will never be peace or security for Israel. Justice today is determined basically by the establishment of a Palestinian state on the whole of the Gaza Strip, the West Bank, including East Jerusalem, alongside the State of Israel.

Palestinian Christians, though numerically small, have played a significant role in the past and will continue to do so in the future. Their dedication and commitment to truth and justice have been exemplary. Their influence and impact has exceeded their ratio in society. In the conference they capitalised on another source of strength. Palestinian Christians are aware that they are a part of a much larger community that spans the globe. They are surrounded by a great cloud of witnesses (Hebrew 12: 1). Their call to the conference was heeded by a good number of their brothers and sisters from all over the world. Christians of different nationalities stood in solidarity together for truth, justice, and peace. Indeed, we are called to be God's witnesses in this God's world as we work for justice and peace. It has to do with keeping our baptismal vows, 'to strive for justice and peace among all people, and respect the dignity of every human being.' It is all about our faithfulness to God.

Most of the speakers in the conference were Palestinian Christians along with a number of internationals. We were also joined by a few Muslims and Jews who introduced their own community's perspectives. Sabeel, however, was not hesitant to emphasise that the conference was intended to be by and for Christians. Admittedly, Palestinian Christians and Muslims stand together in solidarity as one Palestinian people in the struggle for a just peace in Palestine. They are also joined by a number of Jews who work for a just peace. The conference, however, was meant to raise the Christian voice to people in power whether in Israel and Palestine or abroad. It was to send a message to Christian brothers and sisters inside and outside Palestine so that they might know what Palestinians themselves believe and say regarding the conflict.

We, therefore, humbly submit the fruit of this international conference to our readers. It is our contribution in a continuous process that aims at saving the Palestinians and Israelis from unnecessary pain by basing the future peace on a firm foundation of justice. We plead for open eyes to see the impending dangers of injustice and for open ears to hear and listen to the cry of our people for justice. We plead for hearts and minds that are ready to commit themselves to work for a better world. We invite you to share with us this ministry for peace through justice.

CONFERENCE MESSAGE

In Jerusalem, on 22-27 January 1996, over 400 Christians—Palestinians and international participants from more than 25 countries, lay people and clergy, including church leaders or their representatives—met to consider the theme 'The Significance of Jerusalem for Christians and of Christians for Jerusalem'. We gathered under the auspices of Sabeel Liberation Theology Centre.

We, the conference participants, discussed the theological, spiritual, legal, political, social and cultural aspects of Jerusalem. We reaffirmed that Jerusalem should serve as the capital for two sovereign and independent states, Israel and Palestine.

Furthermore, the Palestinian Christians gathered stressed their unity with Palestinian Muslims in striving for peace and the establishment of a sovereign state in their homeland, with Jerusalem as its capital.

We worshipped together in Jerusalem, and visited a number of villages in the West Bank, so that we could meet and pray with Palestinian Christians who are prevented from entering Jerusalem. We witnessed the effects of 29 years of occupation on Palestinian society: land expropriation, new settlements and the expansion of existing ones, roadblocks preventing free movement of Palestinians, and continued detention of political prisoners (especially women, the sick and the elderly). We were appalled by the effects of the closure of Jerusalem on Palestinian life. As a result of its illegal annexation by Israel, East Jerusalem has been cut off from its natural surrounding environment and access to it has been denied to Palestinian Christians and Muslims of the West Bank and Gaza. This closure has been strictly enforced since 1993, strangling normal life in East Jerusalem itself and depriving Palestinians of its rich spiritual, cultural, medical and economic resources.

In the light of these discussions and experiences, we insist on the following:

1   The government of Israel should remove forthwith all roadblocks and obstacles preventing free access to Jerusalem for Palestinians.
2   There should be an immediate cessation of all land expropriation in the West Bank, including East Jerusalem and of the building and expansion of Jewish settlements there, notably the Jabal Abu Ghneim (Har Homa) settlement.
3   The government of Israel should change its planning policies so that Palestinians have equal rights to build housing in Jerusalem and develop their institutions which have been restricted since 1967.
4   East Jerusalem, as an integral part of the occupied territories, should be included in all political arrangements relating to these territories, including self determination, release of prisoners, right of return and eventual sovereignty.

The participants visited with Palestinian Arab Christians in Israel, especially Galilee, and affirmed their demand that equal rights and opportunities for Palestinian Arabs living in the state of Israel be granted.

The conference participants commit themselves to respect the noble ideals of all religions and dissociate themselves from all fundamentalist tendencies which subvert the dignity of people under the pretext of an alleged divine mandate. The participants repudiate the ideology and activities of Christian Zionist groups and others who seek to sanctify exclusive Israeli control over the Holy City through such campaigns as 'Jerusalem 3000'.

Palestinian Christians affirm their essential attachment to the Holy City and acknowledge its significance for Muslims, Christians and Jews. The international participants affirm their attachment to the Holy City and the Church of Jerusalem, the Mother Church of all Christian believers, and express their concern for the welfare of Palestinian Christians (the Living Stones, 1 Peter 2: 5). In this light, we pledge to do all we can to maintain a vital Christian presence in the Holy Land. Moreover, we call on all peoples involved in the current Middle East peace talks to seriously consider this conference message.

We, both local and international Christians, recognise our responsibility to witness to the Lord Jesus Christ in the land of his birth, death and resurrection. We pray for the Peace of Jerusalem.

28 January 1996

JERUSALEM IN THE GREEK ORTHODOX TRADITION

Aristarchos Peristeris

It is indisputable that Jerusalem is a city of great significance for all Jews and Muslims, as well as Christians.

However, insofar as Christians are concerned, how do they feel about Jerusalem? What does Jerusalem mean to them? There are a variety of aspects which could be expressed in the following: first, the majority of Christians attribute a great deal of significance to Jerusalem; they prefer Jerusalem above their chief joy (Psalm 137: 6). Jerusalem is for them a Holy City (Matthew 27: 53), the holiest of three cities, unique in lifestyle, a city for pilgrimage and prayer. Secondly, there is the perspective of those Christians who look at Jerusalem relatively; for them ' . . . Jerusalem is the city that kills the prophets' (Matthew 23: 37). For them 'God is spirit', and ' . . . those who worship him must worship in spirit and truth', 'neither on [Garizim] nor in Jerusalem' (John 4: 21-24).

In spite of these contrasting attitudes, I will try to present the position of Jerusalem within the theology of my own church.

It is true that Jerusalem is the mother of all Christians, since Jerusalem is the city where those events which marked the history of humanity and signified the birth of Christianity took place.

In Jerusalem, the New Covenant of God with all peoples was written; the fact of the Last Supper constitutes for all ages the deepest existential experience in the Church towards an understanding of the sense of life, the forgiveness of sins and life eternal. In Jerusalem, during the days of Pontius Pilatus, the mediator of this Covenant was crucified and resurrected.

Moreover, in Jerusalem and through the Pentecost, those who believed in Christ received the Holy Spirit and formed the Church—the mother of the Churches—with the mission 'to be [His] witnesses [both] in Jerusalem [and] in all Judaea and Samaria and to the ends of the earth' (Acts 1: 8).

In Jerusalem the first Apostolic Church saw itself as a Christian community with equal possibilities for its members to participate in the mystery of salvation and in material benefits (Acts 4: 32-37).

In Jerusalem, in the year 49 AD the first Apostolic Synod was convened, which since has been the model for all synods, as the authentic way of ruling the church.

The 'little flock' (Luke 12: 32) in Jerusalem kept in its memory the holy sites, the shell of the revealed truth of God, during the next three centuries of Roman idolatry. And those places, Calvary, the Tomb of Christ, etc., were delivered to the whole Church when she made her exodus from captivity, from secret places and catacombs to freedom of worship. At that time, Jerusalem became the first city to have the first great church of Christianity, the Church of the Resurrection. Already at the first Ecumenical Council of Nicaea (325 AD) Jerusalem was characterised as the seat of the King of the Centuries. Her bishop is entitled to a special honour due to the holy shrines. Later their safeguarding was especially undertaken by an Order of Monks of the Holy Sepulchre, the *Spoudaei* ('industrious'), dwelling on Mount Zion, from where their second name, *Hagiossionitai* (Holy Zionists) came.

Since the Fourth Ecumenical Council of (451 AD), Jerusalem has been promoted to the highest ecclesiastical degree of Patriarchate, the fifth in order of eminence, with jurisdiction over the whole of Palestine.

In the centuries immediately following, with the support of the Byzantine emperors, Christian life flourished in Jerusalem. Extraordinarily beautiful churches and monasteries were built, as were schools and philanthropical organisations; contributions to Orthodox theology and to the rite of the ceremonies, iconography, classical ecclesiastical poesy, hesychastic monastical life in the desert and mystical prayer were all important products of this period. It is enough to name St Sabas, John of Damascus and Cosmas of Maiouma of Gaza.

This flourishing of Christianity was stopped by the Persians (614 AD). From the existing sources related to this invasion, I chose some verses of a poem of Sophronios, a monk of St Theodossios Convent, in which is shown, very clearly, how a Christian is attached to the city and pained at its destruction:

> Holy City of God,
> the best seat of the saints . . .
> the greatest,
> which kind of mourning
> shall I offer you?
>
> The cheating Persian came
> to the Holy Land
> aiming at destroying even
> Jerusalem the city of God.
>
> Children of holy Christians
> come and participate in the
> woeful mourning of Jerusalem!
> There were in Jerusalem servants of Christ
> from every nation
> and when they saw the Persian coming
> they fled from the city.[1]

The same poet who deplored the destruction of Jerusalem in 614 as a monk, delivered her to 'Umar ibn al-Khattab in 638 as a patriarch. However, this was a prudent gesture, worthy of his name, in order to avoid bloodshed and to safeguard

---

[1] Taken from Chryss. Papadopoulos, *History of the Church of Jerusalem,* pp. 263-264.

the right of life and freedom of religion in the framework of the new Muslim state. On the Mount of Olives the historical agreement (*Actinamê*) regarding the delivery of the city was signed. This agreement is the basis of the later more widely developed *Status Quo* which became the criterion of relations between Christians and the political authorities of the Holy Land and later between the different Christian sects.

Since Byzantine rule, Jerusalem has not had a Christian political authority, with the exception of the short period of the Crusaders (1099-1187) who unfortunately deviated from their original mandate and created an ecclesiastical situation in the Holy Land which did not comply with the decisions of the ecumenical councils.

It is a historically proven fact that during both fortunate and unfortunate circumstances, the patriarchs of Jerusalem, with their respective Christian congregations have struggled to support, defend and guarantee their rights of existence, religion and property in the Holy Land. Their main effort was not to leave Jerusalem, because in such a case the holy shrines could be neglected, demolished and obliterated. Such a situation, of course, would question the historicity of Christianity.

The Christian communities of Jerusalem, having suffered a long period of dispute and struggle, especially during Ottoman sovereignty, have found themselves since the end of the last and the beginning of the present century, in a situation of coexistence, mutual acceptance, understanding and co-operation within the framework of the *Status Quo*. For them Jerusalem means a lot, since an essential part of the Christian heritage from the beginning until today is bound to Jerusalem. For her sake and for her Christian holy sites, Jerusalem is in need of local Christians for witness, preservation and support. The Christians are natural witnesses of the events of the Christian revelation. Monuments without Christians can witness about a glorious past, not about a vital present. Jerusalem also needs the moral, legal and material support of Christians all over the world. This is their obligation towards their spiritual mother. In this context let us remember that the poor among the saints of Jerusalem were the object of interest concerning the *logia* (collection) of St Paul who argued that if the nations participated in the spiritual blessing of the Jerusalemites, then they should serve them in their material needs: '. . . for if the gentiles have come to share in their spiritual blessings, they ought also to be of service to them in material things' (Romans 15: 27).

The Christians, whose desire is to be in such a close relationship with Jerusalem, do not ignore the fact that their Holy City is also the Holy City of Judaism and of Islam. They recognise that in Jerusalem, and over the centuries, a situation has developed which should be respected by all sides. It is not a coincidence that most of the respected holy sites of the three great religions, Judaism, Christianity and Islam, are in Jerusalem: the Western Wall, the Church of Resurrection and the Dome of the Rock. In these three monuments are reflected the faith, the feelings, the desires and the dreams of the peoples of Jerusalem. This reality should be respected. Any attempt to act independently of this reality touches the rights of others in life, property, peace and freedom.

Concerning the resolution of the issue over Jerusalem between Israel and the

Palestinian Authority, the Church of Jerusalem prays eagerly for a peaceful and just solution. It urges the two interested parties to practise tolerance and mutual acceptance. It leaves the resolution to the political discernment of the two sides with an appeal for respect and the guarantee of personal and historical rights of all, regardless of creed. The peace and welfare of Christians and of every citizen of Jerusalem and the Holy Land is the object of prayer and effort of the Church in Jerusalem.

KEYNOTE ADDRESS
The Significance of Jerusalem for Christians and of Christians for Jerusalem
Michel Sabbah

The Sabeel Center, initiated by Canon Naim Ateek and a team of Christian thinkers both lay people and clergy, has invited us this week to reflect upon 'The Significance of Jerusalem for Christians'. Of course, we do know, and we insist upon, the fact that Jerusalem is holy for all three monotheistic religions: Judaism, Islam and Christianity. However, in this conference, during this week, we are invited to look upon one of Jerusalem's three aspects: the Christian one.

I hope that the reflections and discussions of this week will lead us as Christians to formulate an objective and clear vision for Jerusalem, a vision compatible with the nature of the city, a city of God and for God's people. This vision will be the enrichment of the Memorandum of the Patriarchs and Heads of Christian Churches in Jerusalem, and in this capacity, it will be a reference for Christians, Muslims, and Jews when the question of Jerusalem is discussed and its final status decided.

The Memorandum of the Patriarchs and Christian Heads of Churches in Jerusalem was published in November 1994.[1] It first gives basic historical and religious characteristics indicating the Christian significance of Jerusalem and then in its conclusion, it gives some essential elements for any possible solution. The definitive and concrete solution remains the task of both political leaders and specialists who are invited to take into consideration this document of Christian leaders, in which they will find the Christian position on Jerusalem.

Basic characteristics of Jerusalem, historical and religious:

1   [Jerusalem] has known numerous wars and conquests . . . religious motivations have always gone hand in hand with political and cultural aspirations, and has often played a predominant role. This motivation has often led to exclusivism or at least to the supremacy of one people over the others. But every form of exclusivity, every human supremacy is against the prophetic character of Jerusalem: Its universal vocation and appeal is to be a city of peace and harmony among all who dwell therein.[2]

2   Jerusalem is a holy city for the three religions: Judaism, Islam and Christianity.

---

[1] Memorandum of their Beatitudes the Patriarchs and of the Heads of Christian Communities in Jerusalem On *The Significance of Jerusalem for Christians.*
[2] *Ibid.,* memo 5, p. 2.

3   For almost two thousand years, through so many hardships and the succession of so many powers the local Church with its faithful, has always been actively present in Jerusalem. Across the centuries, the local Church has witnessed the life and preaching, the death and resurrection of Jesus Christ, in the same Holy Places its faithful have received other brothers and sisters in the faith as pilgrims, residents, or in transit, inviting them to be re-immersed into the refreshing, ever living ecclesiastical sources. That continuing presence of a living Christian community is inseparable from the historical sites. Through the living stones the holy archaeological sites take on life.[3]

In answer to the question often asked, 'Who are the Christians of Jerusalem and the Holy Land today?', I would say, they are the heirs of the first Church of Jerusalem and the guarantors of its continuity for centuries and through the vicissitudes and changes of states, peoples and languages, biblical Hebrew, Syrian-Aramaic, Latin, Greek, Armenian, Coptic and finally Arabic. These have been the common languages since the 7th century, while other languages remained and survived until today, as liturgical, ethnic and national languages.

4   The Christian attachment to Jerusalem is based on the Holy Scriptures, both Old and New Testaments: 'Through the prayerful reading of the Bible, Christians recognise in faith that the long history of the people of God, with Jerusalem as its centre, is the history of salvation which fulfils God's design in and through Jesus of Nazareth, the Christ.'[4]

In the Gospels, Jerusalem rejects the One sent by God, the Saviour; and He weeps over it, because this city of prophets, that is also the city of the essential salvific events, has completely lost sight of the path to peace (Luke 19: 42).[5]

The mystery of Redemption was accomplished in Jerusalem, and in it Jesus taught, died on the Cross, resurrected in glory from the dead, and ascended to heaven. In it, the Holy Spirit came upon the apostles and sent them to proclaim the good news of salvation to Jerusalem and to the whole world, and so the first Church was born in Jerusalem. Until today, Jerusalem remains the Mother Church for all the Churches in the world, and the Mother City for every Christian.

Jerusalem soon became a source of spiritual and deep significance: it is the image of the Church, the New Jerusalem (Revelations 3: 12 and 12: 2).

> This Holy City is the image of the new creation and aspirations of all peoples, where God will wipe away all tears and 'there shall be no more death or mourning, crying or pain, for the former world has passed away' (Revelations 21: 4).[6]

---

[3] *Ibid.*, memo 9, p. 3.
[4] *Ibid.*, memo 6, p. 2.
[5] *Ibid.*
[6] *Ibid.*, memo 6, p. 3.

The pilgrimage slowly developed an understanding of the need to unify the sanctification of space through celebrations at the Holy Places, with the sanctification in time through the calendered celebrations of the holy events of salvation.[7]

Local Christians and their relation with the Universal Church: as local Christians, we are aware that Jerusalem belongs to us for two reasons, religious and civil, while all other Christians of the world have concerns in Jerusalem on religious grounds only. We have the duty and the right to welcome all the Christians of the world in Jerusalem, and to serve them in their pilgrimage and in their faith relation to the same Mother City.

This relation between local Churches and the Universal Church is a normal and vital one, and it conforms with the nature of the Church. If it is well understood and well practised, it cannot lead to any contradiction between the double loyalty to the Church and to the nation. It is normal, that from time to time, these relations between local and Universal Church are questioned. Confusion can indeed easily arise in this field, as has happened in these last years concerning relations of the Roman Catholic Church, represented by the Holy See, with the State of Israel.

As far as our subject is concerned, the position of the Catholic Universal Church regarding Jerusalem is the following:

First, the Universal Church expresses the global concern of all Catholics regarding Jerusalem. This global concern implies no political claims, but addresses itself to all responsible political authorities. It requires from them the guarantee of free access for all believers, and the freedom of worship with all that it entails. It leaves to the local Church the task of giving more precision, and of taking a clearer and more concrete position, regarding questions which concern it in its daily life, such as the Church and the people who have rights and duties, as well as claims concerning those rights and duties.

Second, as a world moral authority, it supports the right of peoples and nations, in conflictual circumstances, but it does not take the place of any people or nation, and cannot talk in their name, except if it is formally called or invited to do so by one or by both parties, which is not the case for Jerusalem.

The position of the Holy See regarding Jerusalem is the following: the sovereignty over Jerusalem concerns two parties, Palestinians and Israelis, both of whom are responsible for defining their own respective positions and reaching a mutual agreement. When such agreement is reached, the Holy See requires from both parties to respect the attachment of all Christians to the Holy City, and to respect the duties and rights of local Christians. But local Christians have first the responsibility to define their own rights and duties themselves.

Necessary elements mentioned by the Memorandum for any possible solution to the question of Jerusalem:

1   Jerusalem has two essential and inseparable dimensions. First it is a holy city. Second, it is a city where local Christians live to this day.

---

[7] *Ibid.,* memo 8, p. 3.

[It is] *their native city where they live, hence their right to continue to live there freely, with all the rights which obtain from that.*[8] This means equality to all its citizens without any distinction or discrimination. Some rights are general, and concern their participation in all institutions and public affairs of the state. Others are special, and concern the Church as a religious institution, with all its requirements for religious and spiritual development and growth. This spiritual growth is the source of their strength, and underlies their participation in civil and public life.

Therefore, when we call upon our local Christians to live up to the requirements of their faith, we do not call them to a sterile and narrow-minded confessionalism, but to a faith full of spiritual riches which is rooted in their respective biblical and religious traditions. To demonstrate agnosticism or indifference is to deprive one's people and country of the richness of this heritage which they need in order to live as loyal citizens.

2   Christians recognise the same rights and duties for all believers, Muslims and Jews, and share with them in claiming these rights within the city, and in whatever status is decided upon by its own children.
3   Jerusalem is a holy city for all Christians, local and world-wide. Therefore, as already mentioned, freedom of access should be guaranteed. The local Church should be rendered able to welcome the Universal Church and fulfil its needs, concerning pilgrimage, worship and studies. Political authority should guarantee the required freedom for that.
4   Historic rights of different local Churches should be respected by any political power as defined and stated by the *Status Quo.*
5   Jerusalem requires a special status, given its pluralistic and religious importance. The memorandum says:

In order to satisfy the national aspirations of all its inhabitants, and in order that Jews, Christians and Muslims can be 'at home' in Jerusalem and at peace with one another, representatives from the three monotheistic religions, in addition to local political powers, ought to be associated in the elaboration and application of such a special statute.[9]

The guiding principle in this elaboration is the following: to give Jerusalem a lasting stability, so that it will not remain a cause for war between peoples and religions.

Because three religions are represented in Jerusalem, Judaism, Islam and Christianity, and two peoples, Israeli and Palestinian, these five components should

[8] *Ibid.,* memo 10, p. 4.
[9] *Ibid.,* memo 14 (1), p. 5.

be taken into consideration in order to find the suitable, final and definitive status for the Holy City. If one of these five elements is neglected, no stability could be reached, nor peace, or reconciliation. For that reason, political leaders and religious leaders should make common efforts to find their way in this delicate and sensitive question.

The memorandum goes on:

> Because of the universal significance of Jerusalem, the international community ought to be engaged in the stability and permanence of this statute. Jerusalem is too precious to be dependent solely on municipal or national political authorities, whoever they may be. Experience shows that an international guarantee is necessary.[10]

This clause of the memorandum was misunderstood by many. Some understood it as an invitation for a kind of internationalisation. This is not the true meaning. The dignity and the destiny of Jerusalem remains in the hands of its children, its sovereignty also and its government. It is up to the local political forces, Israelis and Palestinians, to come to an agreement and to define the definitive status of Jerusalem. Then, as any nation hastens to stabilise its own existence through recognition and guarantees by the international community, so it will be for Jerusalem. As soon as its new and definitive status is born, it will require to be stabilised by guarantees given by the international community.

Moreover, there is a special vision which derives from the nature of Jerusalem as the Holy City, which should always be open in all circumstances of war or peace. Accordingly, this vision should be above all hostilities and wars. Historic experience shows that it is impossible for any government to isolate any of its towns from general security circumstances. Therefore borders are closed in time of war, in the face of all enemies, and opened for friends only. This happened and happens, until today. Regarding the Holy City of Jerusalem, it is open to friends from all over the world, but closed for security reasons, in the face if its children and even from the nearest of its Palestinian towns and villages.

The fact requires its children, who run its affairs and are the guardians of its dignity and holy character, to give it a special status which will conform with its dignity and holiness in all circumstances, whether in peace or in war. God has put in our hands a city he has chosen and made unique among all cities of the world. Therefore, it needs a unique status which will distinguish it from all cities of the world, and put it above all security circumstances. So it will remain an oasis, a city of stable and lasting peace, for the good and the peace of the region and the world.

When Israelis and Palestinians agree to this vision, when believers of the three religions agree on this vision, they will have made a historical and decisive step, which will introduce the region and the world to a new historical phase.

In past history, in all its periods, Jerusalem was in the hands of one political power corresponding to, or supported by, one religion. We will not judge these

[10] *Ibid.*, memo 14 (2), p. 5.

periods, they are history, our common history. Rather, we learn from the lessons of the past, negative or positive, to reconsider our present and prepare for our future. From our past we take the spirit which supports justice and love, in order to build the new society of the Holy Land.

Exclusivism nourishes wars and hostility, today and tomorrow, as it was in the past. In order to reach a position of stable peace, a unique status for Jerusalem is the solution. Each one of its children, Israelis and Palestinians, Jews, Christians and Muslims, should feel at home and should enjoy the same freedom and the same duties and rights. No one should feel a guest or stranger in their own city. No one should be put in the situation of asking for protection from anyone else, and no one in his or her own home and city is willing to be only the guest, or submit to another. For all of us, children of Jerusalem, despite national and religious differences, our future is to be one family of the Holy Land. Many purifications and rectifications have to be done in order to reach that stage.

Jerusalem today is a disputed city, because of its sanctity and religious character. All three concerned religions agree that this city is the city of God and of his prophets. What God wants for believers is not war, although we find human history full of religious wars, and we find the spirit of war even in Holy Scripture in its human and linguistic expression. Despite that, the commandment of God to humankind is: know each other, love each other and collaborate for the good of all. Therefore human and linguistic expression should be correctly understood and interpreted, in order to reach the authentic meaning of the Revelation of God. The criterion for this purification of mind and heart is to be found in the conformity between our understanding of Holy Scripture and the attributes of God who is love, who is merciful, and holy, and who invites all humankind to be liberated from all forms of evil, as persons and peoples.

So Holy Scripture will help to explain the true nature of Jerusalem. With true understanding we will be able to find the convenient solution for our common Jerusalem, the city of God and all God's children who desire to live in it. Two peoples, Israeli and Palestinian, and three religions, Judaism, Christianity and Islam.

We ask God to help us find the right solution for the Holy City, to help us walk in love and justice, so that we will be able to make Jerusalem the city of reconciliation for us, for the region and for all humankind.

1
CONFERENCE INVOCATION
Salpy Eskidjian

Let us invoke the presence of the Holy Spirit
Let us pray

Most Holy God, we who gather here from many nations to consider the future of this Holy City offer you praise, for you have remained ever faithful to the Covenant you made with Abraham. We kneel before you, for despite our lack of faith, you have renewed your Covenant through your son, Jesus the Christ.

In this spirit of love, as a manifestation of the unity we have as a gift from you—the One True God—and in hope that the peace you will for this city, its people and for the whole world may be realised in our time, we gather here in your name.

Send your Holy Spirit into our midst, we humbly pray, that our tongues may speak words which can be understood by all as a call for peace expressed in unbounded love; that our ears may hear the expressions of others' hearts. Fill us with the wisdom that only you can give, with the compassion which you have taught through Christ.

In invoking your presence now, we praise you and give thanks for the millennial witness of Christians in this city. May what we do here honour, strengthen and increase the unity of these Christian communities and of the Church Universal. May our deliberations be seen by the people of the three faiths who share devotion to this Holy City as the expression of our will to build together a peace founded on justice, love and compassion for all.

In the name of Jesus, the Christ, the Prince of Peace,

Amen

2
A DREAM FROM JERUSALEM
Samir Kafity

Martin Luther King had a dream, a dream of liberation. He knew in his conscience and his sub-conscience mind that all people are equal under God. No different pricing of people according to colour was to be tolerated. Dr King's dream was inspired by people like Abraham Lincoln and Woodrow Wilson. His dream derived from a major article of the United States' Constitution. It was a translation of the Qur'anic teaching that all people are equals like the teeth of the comb. His dream was based on the content of the angelic hymn:

> Glory to God in the Highest
> On earth peace
> Good will among peoples.
> A dream of good will.

We in Jerusalem, descendants of apostolic Christianity, born in the Universal Church at the first Pentecost here in the Holy City, have been dreaming. Jerusalem, the abode of God, creates the natural profound atmosphere of dreaming. We dream with St Paul of a free Jerusalem. We dream with St John in revelation of a new Jerusalem. In his book, entitled *This Year in Jerusalem*, Bishop Kenneth Cragg writes: 'The road to Jerusalem is in the heart: and whether present or absent, its passionate history absorbs the spirit.'

It certainly does absorb the spirit, the spirit of all its past residents, its present residents, and all of the pilgrims of all three monotheistic faiths. It is a very special spiritual focus, a symbol that could perhaps change our present world. It could be the starter of the new order. One cannot forget Jerusalem even though Bethlehem is the natural focus of Christmas. At 2,500 feet above the sea level, the psalmist viewed this city as a unity in itself, as the abode of God, as the house of peace. When speaking of Jerusalem, the language of the heart supersedes that of the mind, the religious significance overrules the secular, and the universal factors cannot be sacrificed to the local or national interest of any single group. Perhaps this is what St John meant when he spoke of the new Jerusalem. St Paul in Galatians 4: 26 speaks of the Jerusalem which is above, which is free and is the mother of us all.

The motherhood of Jerusalem—rather than the old Jerusalem, the city which was ignorant of the things that belonged to its peace and over which our Lord wept—is the correct view of the city, both as a mother and as a symbol. The significance of the motherhood of Jerusalem to Judaism, Christianity, and Islam, lies in the fact that true motherhood does not discriminate or have any preferences. Jerusalem is a mother who loves all her children equally and alike. She loves her three children, the Jews, the Christians and the Muslims. She has no preference.

This symbol of motherhood, of love, and peace, is what Jerusalem has offered to humanity across the ages. We pray that it may regain this eternal symbolism and may once again be the answer to the quest for peace. May it be a city completely shared in every respect and at every level by Jews, Muslims and Christians, including a sharing of sovereignty. Jerusalem is more than courtesy access to the holy sites. Even free access could become subject to street checkpoints.

Jerusalem the mother, not the city, is the abode of God. The birth of Christ took place in Bethlehem, but His rebirth, His new life, His resurrection to life took place in Jerusalem.

Christianity was born in this region not in a secular society, nor in a democracy. The Christian faith was not formed by voting. It was given and revealed, not in a vacuum, but right here in Jerusalem where people have lived and existed since its birth.

Two other sister religions, Judaism and Islam were also born here. All three have common roots together and many points of understanding. For many years in the history of the area, co-existence, mutuality and close relations have been in evidence among the local people of all three faiths. Dialogue had been known in its own form in the area. It was an empirical day-to-day experience of dialogue among average people. We hardly need remind ourselves, for example, that the keys to the Holy Sepulchre are still kept by Muslims, the Joudeh and Nusseibeh families.

Blessed are the peacemakers. Peace is made. Peace is something done, produced. It is a way to follow, to walk in, as Zachariah and Bendictus put it, 'to guide our feet into the way of peace.' The cross of our Lord is the perfect model for the ministry of peace. He made peace by giving himself on the cross. Even the centurion, who was one of those who mocked him and used violence against him, was changed. The peace of the cross caused him to declare: 'truly this was the son of God.' The professional thief was changed by the ministry of peace at the cross. The resurrection then changed all and transformed all. Jerusalem was changed. St John saw Jerusalem as heavenly, coming down from above. The peace of Jerusalem means a new life for the individual and for the people—Jews, Muslims, and Christians— making us all to be seen as being of one blood dwelling on the face of the earth. Neither Jew nor gentile, Greek nor Roman, male nor female, but all one family of love.

Christians are peacemakers. This is a full-time vocation and a comprehensive calling. We are not meant to be peace negotiators or peace keepers, but peacemakers. The blessing and call is to be peacemakers. The identity granted to us is to be the children of God. This is our eternal identity card and passport. 'The child of God', peacemakers, may we be used as permanent instruments of peace. Amen.

President Woodrow Wilson said in his address to the Senate in January 1917, during World War I: 'It must be peace without victory.' Peace without victory so that all parties feel that they are victorious. There must be no victor nor victim, triumphant or defeated, but all must feel justly treated. This is the victory of peace.

3

As Milton in his sonnet to the Lord General Cromwell said: 'Peace hath her victories no less renown'd than war.'

This is the dream of Jerusalem, the city of peace. The victory of peace must be the only option for all parties in the Israeli-Palestinian conflict. The peace of Jerusalem consists of it being shared equally by all three religions at every level, including the level of sovereignty.

Cicero in his letters to Atticus says: 'I prefer the most unjust peace, to the justliest war that was ever waged.' The dream of no more war. Arnold Toynbee in his last, and twelfth, volume of history says: 'Finally, the salvation of the world is by returning to religion, to morals, to ethics.' The dream of returning to God even in and for Jerusalem. All are saying to us: 'Peace and only peace is God's way of renewing the world together, and of cementing the peace process.' Peace and only peace is our dreaming.

3

PENTECOST AND JERUSALEM

Atallah Hanna

In the name of the Father, the Son and the Holy Spirit one God, Amen

Dear brothers and sisters,

We thank God Almighty for enabling us to meet here to discuss matters that are important to all of us. The subject under discussion is 'The Significance of Jerusalem for Christians'. Let us thank God for his great blessings, and for opportunities such as this that bring us closer to each other.

When we talk about the Holy City of Jerusalem, we talk about a city that is closely connected to our Christian faith, our creed and our religious and national affiliation. Our Lord Jesus Christ chose this city for the incarnation of his boundless love for human kind, for whose redemption, he became flesh and took the form of man. In this city he performed miracles and endured his redemptive suffering. In this city he was crucified, died and rose again from the dead. Forty days after his resurrection he ascended into heaven, promising his disciples, as he bade them farewell, to send the comforter, which is the Holy Spirit. On the 50th day, his promise was fulfilled and the Holy Spirit descended on the disciples and they set forth spreading the Word of God to the whole world. That day is the birthday of the Church.

Dear brothers and sisters,

Let us together contemplate some matters connected with Pentecost and the outpouring of the Holy Spirit on the disciples in the upper room on Mt Zion. This event is narrated in the book of the Acts of the Apostles at the beginning of chapter 2.

1   If any country can boast about technological or scientific progress or new inventions, we too, the people of this Holy Land, can be proud that our country is the land of divine revelation and the birthplace of the prophets. There is no country in the world that can match what this country, Palestine, has witnessed of the mysteries of heaven. Let us remember how after Pentecost and the outpouring of the Holy Spirit on the disciples, the first Christian Church in the world was formed and the number of believers increased everyday. All this is due to the preaching and struggle of the apostles. They never tired, they never gave up their mission to humankind. Divine will and providence desired that this faith should not be limited to this tiny spot of the world, but that the saintly apostles should spread the Gospel

around the world.

The Holy Spirit descended on the apostles while they were all together in one place. There came a noise from the sky like that of a strong wind, which filled the whole house where they were gathered. And there appeared to them tongues like flames of fire and rested on each one of them. They were filled with the Holy Spirit which gave them the power to talk in different tongues. At that time there were many Jews and others gathered in the Holy City. At the sound, the crowd gathered at the house where the disciples were meeting. The disciples started to preach to them and tell them the Good News. They spoke in different languages but everyone was able to understand. Peter asked them to repent and be baptised. Many did, they were 3000 in number. From that day on the apostles preached openly about salvation through Jesus Christ. They preached in the temple and in private homes. Their success was great and many people joined the Church everyday. They performed many miracles, something that helped to convince the people of the authenticity of their faith. Many sick and suffering came to Jerusalem and were cured of their ailments. Thus we see that Pentecost was a historical turning point for humankind, the beginning of mission and the spreading of the Christian faith. It is the day that marks the founding of the Church and the day God's word of salvation began to spread throughout the world.

2   St John Chrysostom, one of the great saints of our Church, says: 'The Church will be no more, if the Holy Spirit does not dwell in it'. This means that at Pentecost the power of the Holy Spirit was revealed. On that day the mystery of the Holy Trinity, equal and indivisible, was revealed. We only need to ponder upon the hymns of the Church in order to uncover those aspects relating to the way the Holy Spirit takes care of the Church. They tell of the gifts of the Holy Spirit, like speaking in different tongues, and other gifts that the Spirit bestows upon the believers. This connection between the mystery of the Church and the mystery of the Holy Spirit is made clear as it reminds us of the substance of Church life, a life of love, a new commandment that our Saviour introduced to the world: 'I give you a new commandment: love one another; as I have loved you, so you are to love one another' (John 13: 34). Doing God's will and keeping his commandments can only be accomplished through the Church and with the Church, not outside it or far from it. The fruit of this love is true faith. During the celebration of Mass the priest says: 'Let us love one another so that, with one will, we can affirm and confess [our belief] in the Father, the Son and the Holy Spirit, three in One, equal and indivisible.' Jesus prayed to his heavenly Father for this same unity in the Church: 'Holy Father, protect by the power of thy name those whom thou hast given me, that they may be one, as we are one.' (John 17: 11)

The mystery of the Holy Trinity which was revealed to the apostles on Pentecost and which preserved the Church for almost 2000 years, is an integral part of every aspect of the Church and its activity. The Church calls the Trinity 'giver of life', why is that? The reason is that the Church considers it the source of its life; everything in the Church lives and breathes in the Trinity. Everything revolves around it: the creed, the sacraments, prayers, repentance and other things. St

Gregory, the theologian, tells those who come forward to holy baptism: 'Keep and proclaim your faith in the Holy Trinity—the Father, the Son and the Holy Spirit. I entrust this faith to you. In this faith I immerse you in this font, and in this faith I lift you up.'

The importance of the Holy Trinity in the life of the Church is great, for the believer does nothing except in the name of the Father, the Son and the Holy Spirit. At the beginning of the celebration of Mass the priest says: 'Blessed is the kingdom of the Father, the Son and the Holy Spirit.' During Lent and fast days as well as in our prayers of repentance we offer praise to the Holy Trinity.

3   Jerusalem is the city of Pentecost and the city of our faith. The Church of Jerusalem is rightly called 'the Mother of all Churches' because the first Church was established in Jerusalem. It is the city of redemption and salvation, and its name is mentioned several times in the Old and New Testaments. Today, its Holy Places witness to its purity and its historical, religious and spiritual importance for us Christians, as well as its association with the two other monotheistic religions, Judaism and Islam. For these reasons we absolutely refuse attempts by any party to impose its unilateral control over Jerusalem without taking into consideration the rights, the needs and feelings of others. We, the Christians of Palestine, regard ourselves as an integral and inseparable part of the city of Jerusalem. Jerusalem is in our hearts and conscience and we refuse the distortion of its image and character.

The closure of the Holy City to Palestinians (and I would like to mention here, that some of our brethren in Ramallah, Bethlehem, Beit Sahour and other places could not get to this conference because of the roadblocks of the occupation authorities) increases the feelings of contention and deepens the gap between the two peoples, at a time when we ought to pursue the path of good relations and reconciliation. I wonder, is it right that the Palestinians should only be passers-by or visitors in Jerusalem? Jerusalem will only be Jerusalem when the city unites with the people. There can be no city without its people, nor any people without their city. The genuine peace that we seek and pray for, can only be achieved when the problem of Jerusalem is solved, the city of faith, to which the hearts of millions of believers in one God, from all over the world yearn. Jerusalem is the heart of the conflict in our region. Its problem can only be solved by giving its residents equal rights. This is what we hope and pray for.

I wish to thank the *'Sabeel'* family for this blessed initiative, and for inviting our good friends to discuss the problem of Jerusalem and the relationship of Christians to it. I would also like to thank, in particular, our brother in Christ, Revd Naim Ateek. Thank you all.

7

4
THE PROPHET MICAH AND JERUSALEM
Micah 3: 1–4; 3: 9–4: 4
Bible Study
Mitri Raheb

Despite the fact that this text is very complex and requires a more comprehensive treatment, I wish to restrict myself in this bible study to three main points. As I am a pastor in Bethlehem myself, it is a particular pleasure for me to give attention to the prophet Micah. Micah devotes numerous, long passages to Jerusalem; he says some good things and some less than complimentary things about this city. But in the end, it seems that he has had enough of it. He eventually breaks off the discourse about Jerusalem and retires completely to Bethlehem. For him, the Messiah did not come from Jerusalem, but from Bethlehem, the least of all the cities (Micah 5). Somehow it is a pleasure for a Bethlehemite to read this. Let us now go back to the time of the prophet Micah.

First, in reading the Micah text, one notices a strong tension within the passage. In chapter 3: 1–4, 9–12, we find words of judgement on Jerusalem, which testify to the lack of justice. In chapter 4, however, there is a vision of the pilgrimage of the nations to Zion, as well as a beautiful song of peace. This tension is striking. Exegetes tend to down-play the tension by identifying chapter 4 as secondary and thus not originally from Micah. Nevertheless I think that we shouldn't make it so easy for ourselves. It is precisely this tension, produced by the two chapters, that today we Christians—presumably along with Muslims and Jews—experience daily in Jerusalem. The issue is the tension between the reality which we experience and the promise whose fulfilment we await. It is noteworthy that the words of judgement in chapter 3 speak of actual reality; for this reason the grammatical present tense is mostly used. Chapter 4, by contrast, is dealing with promise; here, mostly future tense is used. The present of Jerusalem is characterised by injustice, and yet we long and hope for a completely different scenario. This tension is something I think we should not let go of, because it is just this tension that people here in Jerusalem experience. It is the tension between the unjust building of Israeli settlements which we experience, and the simultaneous hope for a future of Jerusalem characterised by plurality and equal rights for all its peoples in all their diversity.

Second, in chapter 3, Micah addresses the 'rulers of the house of Jacob and the chiefs of the house of Israel.' The addressees here are not only from political but also religious leadership. Both the political and the religious leaders are subjected to a fundamental critique, as they promise the people security, both religious and political security. They promise security at a time of insecurity and promise peace at a time when there is no peace. We should also call this critique to mind today at a time when, throughout the world, people are talking of peace in the Middle East. News media reports cover virtually nothing which would disrupt the image of the peace process. Yet, we should bear in mind that we stand under God's judgement when we promise others too much security and a too-perfect peace. Moreover, we should note the remarkable interplay between economics and theology in our biblical passage. The prophet says 'Its rulers give judgement for a bribe, its priests teach for a price, its prophets give oracles for money.'

This leads to my third point, which I would like to make via an examination of chapter 4. It deals with a pilgrimage of the nations to Jerusalem, which is a vision that occurs two times in this particular form in the Bible; the other is in Isaiah 2. Theologically, this means that the text probably didn't originate with either Isaiah or Micah, but I do not wish to pursue this point any further in this context. Instead, I would prefer to concentrate on the differences between the two forms of the hymn in Isaiah and Micah. They are almost identical, with the exception of the last verse (Micah 4: 4), which appears only in Micah and not in Isaiah. It seems to me that this verse is very important, and all the more so, as we don't generally devote much attention to it when we study the hymn. Let me remind you of it. Isaiah's text concludes with:

> He shall judge between many peoples, and shall arbitrate between strong nations far away; they shall beat their swords into ploughshares, and their spears into pruning hooks; nation shall not lift up sword against nation, neither shall they learn war any more (Isaiah 2: 4).

Micah continues, and declares:

> but they shall all sit under their own vines and under their own fig trees, and no one shall make them afraid (Micah 4: 4).

This verse occurs only here in such a context. In Isaiah it does not appear until chapter 65 (Isaiah 65: 21-22), at the end of the book of tetra-Isaiah. For Micah, however, it was important to include this verse at this point. We can recognise why it was so important for him if we look at our contemporary situation.

There are people of the opinion that one can see the fulfilment of the promise given in this hymn in the peace process which we are experiencing today; namely the pilgrimage of the nations to Jerusalem and the sealing of peace between the nations. Of course, to a certain extent there is a beating of swords into ploughshares actually taking place, primarily because the driving force behind the peace process is economic development. Or to turn it around the other way, if we speak of economic development, then both politicians and non-politicians tend to entertain the 'grand ideas' of beating swords into ploughshares. It is clear to me that this phrase tends to foster very positive associations. During the cold war this verse played an important role in the efforts of the peace movement. For this reason I must apologise if I now rearrange this beautiful image somewhat.

For me it is too big a picture. It is too powerful a scenario that we conjure up if we speak via these images of transforming the Middle East into an 'Oasis of Peace'. For in doing so we tend to forget who those people really are who are supposed to sit under their own vines and fig trees; the people to whom this very thing is being denied. It seems as though Micah wants to say here: Please, if you intend to paint yourselves such great scenes of development, then don't forget the most important thing, namely that 'they shall *all* sit under *their own* vine and fig tree.' In the last analysis this is the only symbol of peace in the Bible and in reality for today. Isaiah makes it plain that no peace can reign when one plants the trees but another sits under them. This is the situation that we find for instance in Canada Park just outside Jerusalem: the trees were once planted by the Palestinians, but today, tourists, pilgrims and Israeli visitors sit under them and pick their fruits. The true symbol of peace stands over against this: 'they shall *all* sit under *their own* vine and fig tree.'

If we are to speak of this all-transforming experience, then it is important that it is experienced by each person, for otherwise, I think, we cannot speak of peace. For this reason, I also believe that our greatest challenge for the future is not a political one, but a socio-economic one. For what we are experiencing in the 'new' Middle East at present is a polarisation of society. On the one hand, there are the few, very wealthy people, whilst on the other are the great majority who are ever more profoundly impoverished. Those in the middle are disappearing, and with them, the living memory of those people who are *not* sitting under their own vines and fig trees. This is the challenge for us as Christians, and it still lies ahead of us.

(Transcribed into German by Uwe Gräbe and translated from German to English by Vicky and Peter Balabanski.)

5

VISION OF A NEW JERUSALEM
A Bible Study
Eileen W Lindner

The Lord Be With You!

Our text this morning comes from the difficult, perhaps even enigmatic, Revelation of John, and confronts us with the theme of 'A Vision of a New Jerusalem'. This passage, of course, owes its origins to the prophetic literature of Hebrew scriptures and especially to Isaiah 65. Its New Testament context derives more immediately from the strident persecutions of the 1st century and John's own exile from Jerusalem.

As a starting point, we might locate this passage within the larger theme of eschatological regeneration, which dominates the Book of Revelation. This stirring account of 'a new heaven and a new earth' defines and describes 'the holy city, the new Jerusalem.' In its bold hope and bright promise this is to be a place, first of all, of God's indwelling. By God's own hand the tears will be swept away, and mourning and crying and pain will no longer visit themselves upon God's children. What comfort, confidence, succour and hope these words must have given. With their antecedent in ancient Israel, we know that this holy hope for a new Jerusalem has continued to this day to symbolise the inchoate hopes and longings of both Jews and Christians throughout history and for us today.

Indeed, like other texts treating Jerusalem, this text is seen by a good many Christians today to provide a virtual schedule and culmination of events for the soon-to-be apocalyptic return of Christ. Yet, a reflective reading, I believe, calls us to great caution and care in any such reading. The 1st century Church did seek to reconcile their experience of the Risen Christ with the inherited expectation of the Messiah and the restoration of Israel. Nonetheless, there is a profound discontinuity between Jesus' own description of his own role in this might deed and the yet-to-be predictions of those who place such a restoration in the near future, whether those predictions are from the 1st or the 20th century.

If this passage is not about the end of time in Jerusalem, what is it about? Perhaps, like the 1st century Church, we might take this text as an explication of the resurrection's meaning for the life of the world. Taken within the larger corpus of the Book of Revelation we see this text as calling for the renovation of the old world, not an entirely new creation. Through faith and faithful deeds there is to be a great transformation of the heartsick and weary world—not a new creation, a redemption.

It is through the revelation of God's love in the resurrection of the Christ, that the eschatological regeneration is to come about. In Leonardo Boff's terms, 'The resurrection which began with Jesus continues to take place whenever injustice is overturned.'

If this is how the passage is to be understood, then God's word to us in our reflections on this passage might well be challenging us to redouble our efforts in fidelity to God's longing for the new humanity's unfettered rejoicing in the lives for which we were created. As the hometown of the new humanity, Jerusalem must not only be a place where proximate justice or egalitarian rights are achieved. By this scripture we are challenged to lift our sights and our goals not only for Jerusalem, which assures safe passage to peoples of all faiths to draw nigh to God, but, also for a vision of a Jerusalem in which the issues of race, gender, class and caste release their death grip on the peoples of God.

Enmity is to be banished beyond the town limits as the gospel love of the Risen Christ takes root. Understood this way, this passage renews our vocation in proclaiming love and rejecting enmity and hatred in service to the new Jerusalem. The passage then gives us not only a direction for our striving, but the reminder that God beckons us to act in faith and reliance on grace.

A brief story of Semitic origin illustrates the point. It seems there once was a man who had done an exceedingly great deed. The Lord of the Universe wished to reward the man for his good deed and thus sent an angel to him to offer him a gift of great value. But the Lord of the Universe was concerned because the man had a long-standing enemy, a long-standing relationship of enmity and envy. Thus, the angel came to the man and in God's name promised him any gift he should like to choose, with one stipulation: that whatever he chose for himself as a gift would be given twofold to that one he called the enemy.

For the next several days the man considered his options. First he thought, 'I could have a sack of gold.' But then, on reflection, he thought, 'No, no, then my enemy would have two sacks of gold.' Then he thought about land and a farm. 'No, no, then my enemy will have a farm twice as large with twice as many animals.' He considered offspring. 'Perhaps I should have two sons; no, no then my enemy would have four fine sons.'

Finally, the day of reckoning came and the angel appeared, telling the man it was time to make his decision. The angel pointed out that the man could choose anything of his heart's desire, if only he could let go of the enmity. Still the man wavered between grace and enmity, goodness and evil. He struggled to make himself free of the enmity but, in the end, its attractiveness seemed to strong. Finally, sadly, he turned to the angel and giving up all his dreams, he said to the angel, 'I have selected my gift: make me blind in one eye.'

In its tortured enmity and tangled hatreds the world is caught between enmity and grace. A vision of a new Jerusalem demands that we choose grace and reject enmity. The new Jerusalem is the longing of God's heart, God's hope and promise for the whole of creation, for God is still 'making all things new!'

6
EMPTY TOMB AND RISEN LORD
Elias Chacour

This is a special moment in our conference to reflect on the Bible here in Jerusalem, and especially on the Mount of Olives.

Jerusalem is strongly linked to three major events: the Crucifixion, the Resurrection of the Lord, and the coming down of the Holy Spirit promised by the Son and sent by the Father. This is Good News for the whole world.

For those of us from Galilee, Jerusalem has a unique significance. It has a central place in our lives, in our faith, and in our hope. It is the city of the empty tomb and of the risen Lord. That is why the first message we give you today is of peace. Peace be to you ! Be no more afraid; peace be to you! Why are you frightened and why do doubts arise in your heart? People of little faith, listen and understand: Palestine is alive, all the time Palestinians are alive.

Empty tomb and Risen Lord: he does not live in the tomb; he is not there anymore. He is risen, go to Galilee if you want to see him. Do not stay in the tomb, it is empty, the marble of the Holy Sepulchre cannot witness to his resurrection, it has been imported from Italy. Get up and go to Galilee, to the Galilee of the nations—not to my Galilee, we have enough problems together, Jews and Palestinians in Galilee—rather you should go to your own Galilee, in Europe, America, Africa, Australia. Go back into your own Galilee in Gaza, Nablus, Ramallah. Go back into your own Galilee, East or West Jerusalem, Palestine, Israel and proclaim the very unique Good News.

The Lord is risen: the banquet is set, ready for all and for everyone. There is an abundance of places. There are enough places for everyone. I mean there are many places for Christians, Muslims and Jews but no place for institutions: no place for Judaism, Christianity or Islam. No more Jew, no more gentile, as all are equal in the sight of God. I thank God for not being created Christian, Jew or Muslim. I was not born a Christian. I was born a baby. We all are born babies with the same identity, in the image and with the likeness of God.

The Good News from the Risen Lord is that we have renewed our vision of humanity. We have a new understanding of chosenness, of election. We have sharpened our understanding of God's message: to be called, means for us, to be responsible. God, who has risen Christ from death, is no more conceived as a tribal or regional God. To be called means to accept the challenge of getting up, of moving, of going ahead, of getting your hands dirty for the cause of righteousness. We do not need to extinguish the fire but to shed even more light. 'You are the salt of the earth . . . You are the light of the world' (Matthew 5: 2-14).[1]

> You men of Galilee, why do you stand looking up towards heaven?
> This Jesus, who has been taken from you into heaven, will come
> back in the same way as you saw him go into heaven (Acts 1: 11).

It is on this very Mount of Olives that they were conversing with the Risen
Lord exactly as were the two other disciples on the way to Emmaus. They stood
there amazed saying to each other, 'Were not our hearts burning within us while he
was talking to us on the road . . .' (Luke 24: 32).

Peace be with you. Why are you frightened and why do doubts arise in your
minds? The major solution to our problem is repentance and forgiveness. This is the
topic of our proclamation and of our witness. When we have accepted that with
serious commitment, then we can return to Jerusalem, to our own Jerusalem, with
great joy.

God is the universal and compassionate God. The famous answer given to
the Samaritan Woman is fundamental to our faith. This is the new theology:

> Woman, believe me, the hour is coming when you will worship the
> Father, neither on this mountain nor in Jerusalem . . . the hour is
> coming and is now here, when the true worshippers will worship the
> Father in spirit and in truth, for the Father seeks such as these to
> worship him (John 4: 21).

Brothers and sisters, this is a theology, not so much as a theology of liberation
as a liberation of theology. Don't we need to set God free? Yes, let us set God free
and dare to proclaim to the whole world the simple naked reality: God is not a
Christian! I hope and pray there will come a time in the future when men and
women of God would be proclaiming and confessing like Christ to the Samaritan
Woman: truly I say to you the hour is coming and it is now here, when the true
worshippers will worship the Father, neither in the church nor in the synagogue or
in the mosque, but in spirit and in truth. For Christ came to free us from institutional
theology. Set God free: God does not kill. Set God free from our own crimes against
each other. God has no party. God is the universal and compassionate God.

Yes, we are the guardians of our brothers and sisters. We are responsible for
being God's deputies on earth: to love, develop and protect his cosmos whether the
macro-cosmos (i.e. the universe) or the micro-cosmos (i.e. every human being).
Responsibility for the world before God does not mean to feel guilty for the evil
others have done or are doing.

Jerusalem would then be ready to welcome once more the stranger, the
foreigner, the vagabond and the sojourner like Abraham who came from Iraq,
Mesopotamia. Jerusalem would then be ready to welcome the stranger but only if the

---

[1] All biblical references taken from New Revised Standard Version.

'king' of Jerusalem is a righteous one like Melchizedek (Genesis 14). A Melchizedek, a 'king' of justice. Only he is able to make of this city the city of peace (*Urusalem*).

Jerusalem will suffocate if it is not liberated from exclusiveness, religious or political. Jerusalem will only prosper and flourish when it opens its gates and its arms to become inclusive. Then, only then, would Melchizedek welcome again Abraham; and similarly today the Jew would consider the Palestinian a partner. To exclude the one or the other would result in reducing Jerusalem, the city of peace, into a bloody city of hatred. If inclusiveness is rejected, Jerusalem will continue to ignore God's gift and continue killing those who are sent to bring it peace.

Empty tomb and Risen Lord: this is the core of our proclamation as Palestinian Christians. Therefore we cannot focus only on Catholicism, Orthodoxy or Reform, etc. Here in Jerusalem, our focal point of attention is as it was in the beginning: the empty tomb and the risen Lord.

I call on you, brothers and sisters—Catholics and non-Catholics from overseas—please stop asking Palestinian Christians whether they are or are not in communion with Rome, or with Geneva, or with Constantinople, or with the 'born-again' Christians at the Crystal Cathedral. Nothing started in those places but confessions and denominations. Everything started here in Palestine, in Galilee, and in Jerusalem. Set us free, please, and start asking whether you are in communion with us! In Rome it was only the death of Peter and of Paul. Nothing started in Geneva but the separation of Christians. Elsewhere it is the split of the church or some similar acts of separation. Here in Jerusalem, Christianity started, the Good News started, the divine economy for the salvation of humanity started. Yes, we want to ask you, and all of Christianity, if you are in communion with your own roots, with Palestinian Christianity? We proclaim our credo in an empty tomb and a risen Lord. We confess that we are brothers and sisters. Our God has no favourite. Our task is to jointly spread, all over the world, the unique generosity brought to us by our own compatriot. You are all born babies and are therefore entitled to call the God in heaven . . . Our Father who art in heaven . . .'

My dear brothers and sisters, listen to me from this Mount of Olives. Get up, go back home, carry with you the Good News from the Holy Land: no more Jew, no more gentile, but all of us children of God, all of God, in a human child from Galilee. The liberation of theology is the only urgent theology of liberation. Here we start. From here we march, each in one's own direction, but all of us towards the same kingdom of God.

We have been transfigured during this Sabeel Conference. We cannot pretend we do not know. Let us get up, go down from our mountain to meet our brothers and sisters who are still fighting for possessions and prestige, power and oppressive might. Let us get down to them, even if we run the risk of being crucified. We are not afraid. Yes, we need to live the crucifixion in it fullness. The intensity of Friday of the Crucifixion is only a passage, a step towards something else. Good Friday is the way to the Sunday of the Resurrection. No matter how arrogant we might be, no matter how gloomy the darkness, no matter how deep and real the suffering of Good Friday, it starts ripening and maturing us so we can enjoy the unavoidable Sunday of the Resurrection.

Brothers and sisters, no matter where we are, no matter how much persecution, deprivation, humiliation and oppression we endure, no matter how long is Good Friday, sad Friday, we shall overcome. That is why, amidst our turmoil, we sing our hope and our conviction:

Christ is risen—He is truly risen!
Christ is risen—He is truly risen!
Christ is risen—He is truly risen!

7
THE CONTINUITY OF THE CHRISTIAN PRESENCE IN JERUSALEM

Maroun Lahham

It pleases me to talk about the continuity of the Christian presence in Jerusalem and honours me to be a member of the Church of Jerusalem. I will try to present the stages of the history of this Church, which is long and full of the adventures of the Spirit, that '. . . blows where it chooses, . . .' The history of the Church of Jerusalem is no less painful than the history of its founder and redeemer.

From the start, I will make it clear that speaking about Jerusalem is allegoric; it deals with the part rather than the whole. It is like one who talks about the heart to discuss the entire person. So when I talk about Jerusalem I mean the Holy Land.

My speech is organised simply: past, present and future. The past will have the lion's share, because it is the heart of the matter I am dealing with, then I will deal briefly with the present that looms over the horizon. I will end with the future, especially the questions about our future asked by others.

The Past

The birth certificate of the Church of the Holy Land bears the following information:

> *Place of birth:* Jerusalem
> *Date of birth:* Pentecost 33 AD
> *Family members:* 3,000

When the Church was persecuted in Jerusalem it spread to Judea and Samaria. Then it crossed Palestine's geographical boundaries to East Jordan, Cyprus and Antakia.[1] Although the first Church originated from the Jewish community that existed before Jesus, it also accepted non-Jews (such as Cornelius). By the beginning of the 2nd century, large numbers of pagans entered the faith. This is especially true after the resolutions of the Council of Jerusalem when the Romans quelled the revolution of Barkochba the Jew in the year 135, and when the gentile Church carried the banner. Mark was the first bishop of the Holy City to come from a gentile origin.

---

1 Acts 11, 19-20.

The golden age of the Church began with the conversion of Constantine to Christianity. Churches were built in all the places that witnessed gospel events. Most of the people of the Holy City became Christians, and the Bishop of Jerusalem was given the title of Patriarch (451). He had 49 bishops working with him across the Patriarchate. This golden age lasted until the Arab conquest of the Holy City in 638 at the hands of 'Umar Ibn al-Khattab.

The Christian presence in Jerusalem continued during the Arab rule. It was marked by a high level of culture which I will discuss later, and was able to continue in its faithful procession by its own strength and local members. It gradually lost many of its faithful for various reasons: war, the *jizya* tax (imposed by Islam on Christians and Jews), fear and difficulties in everyday life. When the Crusaders occupied Jerusalem, they found an existing Church, Church authority, priests and people. But the Christians of the Holy Land had become a minority over time. The Crusaders tried to re-establish a majority status for Christianity by bringing Franks into the country and inviting Christians from neighbouring countries to settle in Jerusalem, but all their attempts failed. The Church of Jerusalem was able to continue in its faith journey by its own strength and its local membership.

The Mamluk and Turkish eras were the most difficult in the history of Jerusalem. The Christian presence reached its lowest levels, and the Christians suffered from abuse, poverty, low morale, confiscation of land, property and livestock, in order to appease the greed of the Turkish governmental officials.

The surprise renaissance of the Church took place in the second half of the 19th century. An unexpected renaissance took place in the Church. An Anglican bishopric was established in Jerusalem in 1843 and the Latin Patriarchate was re-established (1847). The Greek Orthodox Patriarch returned to reside in Jerusalem, whereas before that time he was elected and resided in Constantinople. The three churches worked simultaneously, with equal energy, and according to the mentality of the time competed with each other. At the same time the churches, through their priests and delegates, were able to protect the local Christians from the greed and oppression of the Turks. They were also able to establish their official presence within the state (which I will get into later). They helped to raise their cultural and material status, and prepared them suitably to enter the world of the 20th century.

The beginning of the 20th century of the Church in Jerusalem saw a continuation of the Turkish presence, which ended with the First World War, and was followed by the British Mandate and later the Jordanian era. After that came the series of Arab-Israeli wars.

This was a quick presentation of the most important stages of the history of the Church of Jerusalem, by which I intended to point out that the local Christian presence in Jerusalem was not interrupted once, even in the darkest conditions.

The current situation of the continued Christian presence in terms of: numbers, culture, ethnic and legal status.

Numbers

Numerically speaking, the Church has been a minority for eighteen out of the twenty centuries of its history. It had a majority from the 5th to 7th centuries, after which its majority status began to decline. Some historians put the number of Christians at the beginning of the Crusades at 50 percent of the population. At the turn of the 20th century it was 20 to 30 percent. Today's statistics are in agreement that only 2.5-3 percent of the population of Palestine, Jordan and Israel are Christians.

Education

The cultural role of the Christians of Jerusalem has been much larger than their numbers, except during the Mamluk and Turkish periods (until the middle of the 19th century) which was a period of general decadence for Arabs, Christian and Muslim alike, in the Holy Land. Ever since the 1st century educated bishops have emerged like Cyril of Jerusalem, his successor John and the Patriarch Sophronius. At the outset of the Arab conquest the Christians of Jerusalem (along with the Christians in the Orient in general) were the bridge that brought Greek thought and philosophy to the Arabs, first through translation and then through their own writings. Historians are in agreement that Arab Christian literature that was prominent from the 8th to 11th centuries, began in the Palestinian desert, in the Mar Saba Convent and in Kharitun. At the end of the 19th century, the Christians of Palestine helped in the renaissance of Arab thought, spearheaded by the Christians of Lebanon and Syria, through writings, magazines, and newspapers that spread in the Holy Land at the turn of this century.

Race

This subject is hard to go into because of its obscurity and the difficulty of clarifying the origins of the Christians of Jerusalem today. This is because more than one nation has passed through this region, occupying and settling the land, and leaving their racial fingerprints behind. No one can tell where the Christians of Jerusalem today came from. There have been Jewish converts, Arab desert tribes who converted beginning in the 2nd century, the Romans, Byzantines, and the Arab conquest beginning in the 7th century, to the Crusaders, Mamluks, Turks and British. One thing is clear: whatever the distant racial origins of the Christian presence in Jerusalem are, they have considered themselves Arabs in language, history, culture, life style, reactions, hopes and suffering for over 1000 years.

Legal Status

In this area as well, the Church has lived more than an ebb and tide throughout its long history.

1   Right from the beginning the Church was persecuted by the Jewish community because it broke away from it. Under Roman rule it was also persecuted for three centuries, just like all Christians were.

2   During the Roman era the Church enjoyed freedom of worship as granted by the Galerios Pact (311): 'Religious freedom should not be restricted, and every one shall be allowed free loyalty in religious affairs according to the dictation of their conscience.' This was before the more famous Milan Pact of 313.

3   In the Arab Islamic era the Covenant of 'Umar (638) stipulated: 'The Christians, their money, their churches and their crosses, are granted protection.' In the era of Harun al-Rashid, Christians were given rights dealing with the protection of their Holy Places as well as funds for their maintenance.

4   The Fatimid, Mamluk and early Ottoman eras had no clear legal cover. The first Ottoman Covenant guaranteeing religious freedoms for non-Muslim residents was the 'Sharif Jalkhana Pact' of 1839. In it the sultan says: 'Full guarantees will be given to our citizens where it concerns life, honour and money.' After that came the 'Hamayon Pact' (1856), which stipulated: 'Effective steps will be taken to guarantee its full implementation.' Before that, the system of *les capitulations* had been enacted to protect foreign Christians primarily, and then Arab Christians. Such agreements were reached with France (1535), Britain (1579), and Russia (1718, 1774). In 1852 the *Status Quo* system was enacted, putting an end to the Christian sectarian conflicts over ownership of the holy sites.

5   During the British Mandate, Article 13 of the Mandate said that Britain's role was to guarantee 'the protection of civil and religious rights for all the residents of Palestine, regardless of race or creed.'

6   In Jordanian times Christians were granted the status given by the Jordanian Constitution: 'Citizens enjoying the same rights and obligations as all other citizens.'

In summary, the legal status of the Christians of Jerusalem went through a situation of persecution in Roman times to a status of *dhimma* under Muslim rule, then a status of *millat* under the Ottoman Turks to the Israeli occupation since 1967.

Present

Whoever enters Jerusalem today finds a sure and unique Christian presence. And what is said about Jerusalem goes for Palestine as a whole. In terms of numbers the presence is humble. I can't give accurate statistics about the number of Christians in the Holy Land. The most credible numbers are somewhere between 250,000 to 300,000 Christian Arabs in Jordan, Palestine and Israel, or about 2.5 to 3 percent of the population. But the strength of the Christian presence in Jerusalem today does not come from its numbers (in Jerusalem there are only 10,000 to 12,000 Christians) as much as it comes from living churches that are active in many areas of life in the city and country. The Christian presence continues and is distinguished in schools, colleges, institutes, universities, centres, spiritual and ecumenical activities, social affairs, and civil and political development.

In recent years the Christian presence has stood out. The Church in Jerusalem has shared the suffering of the Palestinian people, it went along side by side with the people in their struggle for freedom and took leading and courageous stands in the national and international arenas, which is inspired by its past, living present and its hope for the future.

The Future

I would like to end my talk by taking a look at the future. I talk about the way I see the future of the Christian presence in Jerusalem. As a son of this Church, I would like to discuss some of the traditional questions we are asked. Although these questions are well-intentioned they show simplistic thinking. The following are some of those questions:

> Will Christianity in Jerusalem one day become no more than a number of museums because of the continuing emigration of Christians?
> Will Palestinian Christians live under Arab rule with a Muslim majority?
> Will Palestinian Christians be able to co-exist with the tide of Islam approaching from Algeria, Sudan and Iran?

To Answer

1   The local Christian presence in Palestine has existed for 2,000 years, and will continue. Our assurance comes from our faith in the will of our Lord for us, and from the lessons we learn from history, as well as from the will power of our people who know very well what they say and what they do.

2   The Christian presence in Palestine has passed through more difficult times, when they were fewer in number, with less respect for their rights, when they suffered from material, intellectual and spiritual poverty, but were able to withstand.

3   The Christian presence within the Palestinian society derives its strength and its influence from the common stand and common expression of the different Churches, from their openness to one another, from honest, frank and free dialogue among all believers and all righteous people.

When our Christian brothers and sisters in the West ask what is required of them, we say:

1   To pray for the Church of Jerusalem.

2   To consider themselves true spiritual sons and daughters of this the Mother Church.

3   To look at the *human being* in this country as the cornerstone. On this matter, allow me to quote the principle laid down by Patriarch Michel Sabbah for pastoral care. This was expressed in his address, upon his appointment, to all the nuns and monks in the Patriarchate: 'The glory of the Holy Land comes from the mystery of God's presence in it and from the human being who abides in it.' He adds: 'In our

service of the Holy Land, we have to remain objective and focus on our reality, in order to see the believer in his/her context—as they are—so that they will not be overlooked, or their image in anyway changed, through pressure put upon them to suit the desire of the faithful of the world for them. It is true that the Holy Land has a universal perspective because of the message of faith that emanated from it to the whole world, but this universal aspect should not be allowed to destroy the identity of the people who remained faithful to this Land and to our Lord Jesus Christ.' (from *Baha' as-Salam,* 1988, 52-53).

In practical terms, this means getting to know the language of the people of the land, their mentality and customs, and then, to live and work accordingly. It means spiritual and moral support (visits, pilgrimages and worship with the local Christian communities) also material support for educational and social institutions that bear witness to the Christian presence and its universal message.

This conference, undoubtedly, falls along these lines. It bears witness to the true concern for the individual of this Holy Land. Your presence with us is proof that you have chosen the right path to get to know the Palestinian Christian at close range. This in itself is sufficient to remove the barriers and provide an opportunity for genuine and deep co-operation in the search for God's will for all of us, here and now.

8
PATHWAYS TO CHRISTIAN UNITY I
Kevork Hintlian

To talk about pathways to Christian unity in the land where Jesus was born and preached is quite paradoxical and even absurd. To allow disunity to prevail is a denial of the overpowering message of our Saviour. When we discuss issues of Christian unity globally, I tend to think of the experience of the World Council of Churches which started as a formal body in the 1960s. I will not dwell on what was realised world-wide in unity efforts for 1.5 billion Christians but rather look at our immediate experience here in the Holy Land. In my paper I will use Jerusalem as an icon for the Holy Land. The Christians of Palestine cherish Jerusalem because of its historical location and importance.

Unity entails the levelling of many cultural and linguistic differences which, on the other hand, contribute to the richness of the religious experience. The Church of Jerusalem was born and forged mainly in the desert between Bethlehem and the River Jordan. In its formative centuries, the desert was the abode of tens of thousands of austere monks. There, in the arid patches of the desert, the teaching, theology, monastic rules, hymns, feasts and calendar of the Church crystallised. After 451 AD, the church gradually began moving towards the city. This was the beginning of a new hierarchy which fostered power struggles. This was to be compounded by christological controversies ushered in by the Council of Chalcedon. The desert monasteries withstood all these seismic waves and the non-hierarchical system prevailed as before.

The second earthquake which shook the Jerusalem Church on its foundations was the Crusades. The Greek Patriarch of Jerusalem was exiled to Cyprus for about a century. The scars of the sack of Constantinople by the Fourth Crusade have not yet healed in the Orthodox mind. The intensified evangelising activities by Catholic and Protestant groups in Palestine brought inter-church relations to its lowest ebb in the 19th century, compounded by frequent friction in the Holy Places.

We cannot comprehend the attitudes and mentality of the Christians of Jerusalem without understanding their past. Christians have considered their ultimate objective in the Holy Land the preservation of the holy sites, almost their holy *raison d'être*. To achieve this has not been an easy undertaking considering the length of time and the frequency with which the rulers have changed. Over time, a local wisdom has developed of accommodating rulers, with varying degrees of success. Christian survival was possible, by a combination of steadfastness with diplomacy and enormous financial sacrifices.

When Christians in the Holy Land celebrate Jerusalem 2000, they can confidently talk about a success story, whereby they are capable of transmitting to future generations a heritage of devotion, sacrifice and centuries old rich architectural heritage. One of the healthy aspects of inter-Christian life in Jerusalem is that for a combination of reasons, there is little theological discussion compared with what takes place abroad. Jerusalem is not a great forum of theological discourse. The local Church has consciously delegated this activity to its brethren overseas. Avoiding theological debate has greatly reduced local friction. As opposed to some other places where theological harmony is seen as a criterion or index of genuine rapprochement, understanding or ecumenical progress, Jerusalem has its own unique and inherent elements which foster and favour a climate of ecumenical Christian fellowship.

Jerusalem possesses overpowering Christian symbols which transcend community affiliations. What unifies the Christians is the Tomb of Christ, the Grotto of the Nativity, the Tomb of Mary, the Mount of Ascension and the River Jordan, to mention just a few. The holy sites are rallying points for the Christian spirit and devotion. There is a cult of veneration of holy sites which is truly ecumenical.

John the Baptist and the apostles, their successors, the early Christians, and the desert fathers have all left their imprint on the land, laying the foundations of a local spirituality which has grown over the centuries. What unifies the Christians is the land where the major miracles of the Christian faith took place. Here, the Church communicates constantly with its martyrs and saints through their tombs or through prayer. In this land Christians unite through prayer. In this land Christians feel that intercession is more immediate because one can pray at the Tomb of Christ and Mary. What unifies the local Christians are the myriad Christian monuments—the domes, the belfries, the *symandras*, the ruins of ancient churches, the caves where the hermits dwelt, and the graffiti of the pilgrims.

Numerically, Christians do not constitute the dominant group in the city of Jerusalem. More than any other component of their identity, religion has been, to a great extent, a determinant factor in their personality and self-image. Their self-conception and vision has much to do with their collective past experiences and status. In this part of the world, Christianity has been tolerated, but tolerance has not granted all the advantages of the majority groups. So Christians have developed a collective ego, and though they partake of the culture of the dominant group's values, they behave and consider themselves as a sub-culture.

Despite inter-religious tensions in the world and the region, the city of Jerusalem (within the walls), has, throughout history functioned quite harmoniously. Few places in the world with such a high measure of religious intensity can pride themselves of standing the test of time. Virtually most sites of the three religions are intact and have survived the vicissitude of a turbulent history. There is a *modus vivendi*[1] between the religions, a mutual tolerance which flows from a wisdom tested by history.

Another important obligation which Christians assumed and shared

---

[1] Way of living or coping.

was the preservation of the holy sites. The churches can pride themselves of the superhuman feat of being able to maintain continuous liturgical life every night and day since 335 AD at the holy sites of Christianity. This has required enormous human perseverance, sacrifice and financial resources.

Living through turbulent history, the Church has developed a collective memory which unifies its ranks. One lasting factor which has created an organic link with the Christian family abroad has been pilgrimage. Since the early days, the days of the desert fathers, the church has seen the accommodation and hosting of pilgrims as one of its primary spiritual duties. Pilgrimage has always had an invigorating and regenerative influence on the local community. Since 1967, the Eastern churches have been deprived of the spiritual blessings of pilgrimage over land from countries of the Middle East.

So what disrupts the unity of the Church which has survived two millennia of adversity and perils to its existence. I would single out the 19th century as a catalyst. The Greek Orthodox Church, numerically the dominant church, saw in the influx of the Protestant and Latin Churches a colonising effort. The Western Churches which came in full strength after the 1840s relied heavily on European diplomatic support. So diplomatic support was meant to modify the *Status Quo* in the Holy Places, while the Western Churches had their ranks swollen through missionary activity among the Greek Orthodox. The establishment of an extensive network of schools by the Catholic and Protestant Churches reinforced phobias of a systematic onslaught by Westerners, attempting to marginalise or reduce the influence of the Greek Church.

The confrontation between the Western and the Eastern Churches which climaxed in the 19th century came to an end naturally with the First World War. The British administration which replaced the Ottoman regime ignored all European diplomatic interventions and thus broke the vicious circle. Furthermore, it upheld scrupulously and in a non-partisan way all previous undertakings and arrangements for the Holy Places. Instead, the British administration tried to concentrate its efforts on the preservation of the fabric of the city, specifically the ancient monuments and Holy Places. The restoration works in the Holy Sepulchre can be seen as a consequence of a sustained British effort.

Today, it is almost more than three decades since the renovation of the Holy Sepulchre began. The technical bureau which was set up by the three custodian communities, Greeks, Latins and Armenians provides an official forum to iron out problems, both major and minor. Originally meant to resolve technical details arising from restoration work, it soon enveloped all issues which involved relations in the Holy Places. New mechanisms and patterns of daily communication have replaced suspicion, rendering hostile posturing in Holy Places archaic and irrelevant. Through constructive and creative thinking many potential conflicts have been resolved. This reconciliatory spirit has created new mechanisms for containing confrontational issues and established irreversible facts on the ground.

Perhaps it was the first time in recent memory that Christian communities were solving issues through team-work. Suddenly consultation replaced friction, and compromise was the norm instead of defiance. What was once considered insurmountable could be regulated in harmony. The issues of the Holy Places which once widened the gap between the communities has become the bridge.

The changing times and growing solidarity between the communities added to the absence of European diplomacy, transformed confrontation into co-operation. But for the international media and tourist guides, it is still fashionable to dwell on 'bickering Christians' who continue to fight on every inch in this land of liturgy. This 19th century myth is being perpetuated in books about Jerusalem which try to entertain their public rather than convey the present picture. Unfortunately, as a colleague put it 'most authors on Jerusalem copy the mistakes of their predecessors.'

Today, we witness growing signs of liturgical sharing, and even instances of concelebration, as organised by the Coptic Archbishop, Anba Abraham, with the participation of Greek, Armenian, Coptic, Syriac and Ethiopian clergy. The Week of Prayer for Christian Unity every January is one of the most important manifestations of this family spirit. With the multiplicity of Christian events, meetings, conferences, it has become so natural to pray together. In Jerusalem, Christian liturgy is no more an absolute domain belonging to one rite. Many processions of different communities are attended by all Christians, creating a sense of unity in Christian liturgy. Common and shared prayer among Christian Churches is being rooted into the Christian fabric, and becoming an irreversible reality. While on the grassroots level, common worship is a regular event, less structured but more spontaneous and natural. Intermarriage between couples of different Christian communities is no longer frowned upon by the community or by the hierarchy.

Yet, the churches in Jerusalem, are also earthly institutions, with their earthly problems, with their separate administrations, emanating from diverse cultures and sometimes with their old and new agendas. There are churches with their inner tensions, and inter-church tensions, spheres of influence, ambitious churches which maintain high profiles, others a low profile and churches with less financial and human resources problems, others with more chronic problems. In short, there are major and powerful churches, and there are minor ones with less financial possibilities and human resources. There are the ancient or what is called the 'historical' churches. There are the 'ones' who came later in time to the Holy Land. Pluralism and diversity permeate every aspect of the Church's life. Structural differences are not easy to bridge but what can be created is family solidarity. There is a growing sense of common destiny which is being reinforced by the sense of shrinking numerical presence.

Coming back to the term Church Unity. If we try to judge the accomplishments from the self-assessment of the World Council of Churches, it seems quite an ambitious objective. It is premature to homogenise in an absolute manner, cultural, linguistic, theological, historical and geographical differences within a few decades. Our aspirations for more uniform patterns of thinking and acting can be achieved through enhanced communication, mutual tolerance and desire for cohabitation. In the Holy Land, we have to use other yardsticks, and measure progress through local criteria.

I wish to interject a personal example. In the early 1960s when I was a student at the Frere College in Jerusalem, our catechism book still qualified the non-

Chalcedonian churches i.e. the Armenians, Copts, Syrians and the Ethiopians, as heretics of the Church. Today, we are miles away from these attitudes both in spirit and action.

During the last decade, the *intifada* had a galvanising effect on the churches. The church leaders came out with joint statements, defining their positions on human rights and political developments. One could detect a political tone, which continues until today. The memorandum signed by eleven Jerusalem churches 'On the Significance of Jerusalem to Christians' shows that the churches are acting as a group with well-defined orientation and objectives. Though not interfering in the decision-making process of final status talks on Jerusalem, they make sufficiently clear that they have vested interests and wish to be part of a deal whereby their rights and privileges are internationally guaranteed.

The celebrations for the year 2000 will provide the biggest challenge and test of good will and close co-operation. It is a unique occasion for the global church to think about and express its solidarity with the local church. On the other hand, the local church should allow the lay people more say in decision-making. In the minds of the leaders of the churches, it is the hierarchy which represents the churches. This attitude is leading to alienation among the lay members of the church. The celebrations of 2000 could be an opportunity for clergy and lay to overcome their mutual reservations about their respective roles in community life. The realisation of a project presented by a colleague on the establishment of a House of Heritage by the year 2000 will create a new area of co-operation for Christians of the land, emphasising the sense of one family.

The world Christian community can do more to enhance Christian unity by showing genuine care and concern for the multiple problems and welfare of the local churches. Thus the local Church will see in itself a true extension of the Universal Church. The Jerusalem Church in its actions has always gone out of its way to act as representative of its brothers and sisters abroad without receiving their much needed support.

The role of the local church as representative of the Universal Church can be reinforced by a massive and unreserved support of all branches of world Christianity. To this end, more publicity should be made about the work of the local church.

Much progress has been done in communication between the churches of Jerusalem in the last five decades. The fact that there is a permanent body of Jerusalem bishops who meet regularly every month is a source of joy and hope.

The mortal enemy of Christian unity in the Holy Land will be the reintroduction of power politics of the type of the 19th century. It is timely that the Western Church should acknowledge and appreciate the historical role of the Eastern churches in the formative period of the church in Palestine. While Easterners should appreciate the welcome reinforcement and strengthening of the infrastructure of the local church through the arrival of their Western brothers in the 19th century.

The unflagging commitment by all churches to act on the belief that all Christians are, indeed, brothers and sisters in the Body of Christ is the guarantor of a greater measure of unity.

9
PATHWAYS TO CHRISTIAN UNITY II
Jean Zaru

When people learn that I have been involved in the ecumenical movement and theology, they react in several different ways. Some are amused, some are simply scornful, while others are embarrassingly indifferent.

I try to explain that I am as concerned with the human condition in general, as I am with specific conflicts which often represent only the tip of a pyramid of anguish and violence. I say that I am concerned with all the pain and confusion which impedes our unfolding and fulfilment. My understanding of the ecumenical movement is as a movement of the Spirit: one that unites and reconciles us. The Spirit transforms us into a caring and sharing people, breaking down the walls that separate us. The Spirit empowers us in our struggles for justice and peace.

Let me describe my background as a Palestinian Christian in order to give you some insight in understanding our situation. My two grandfathers were brothers. Their family name was Mikhail—a Christian name—and, with the rest of their brothers and sisters, they were members of the Orthodox Church. In the late 18th century, many missionary movements came to Palestine. Each, for one reason or another, wanted a presence in the Holy Land. Most of them built new churches and served the people who joined their churches.

The Society of Friends had a different interest. They did not build a church. They started a school for girls in Ramallah at the request of that community. Many decades later, they built a church and a boys' school. When people applied to become members of the church, thinking that they would benefit from a Friends education, they were most often refused. Quakers believed that they were Christians to start with and were not interested in rearranging Christians into different denominations.

My grandfather on my mother's side lost his wife at a very early age, leaving him with four girls and four boys. He remarried soon after. He was well-to-do and decided to give more freedom to his children to compensate for the loss of their mother. My mother asked to go to the Friends School because that was where her friends were going. My aunts chose to go to St Joseph's School; two of them later joined the Order of St Joseph and became Catholic nuns. My mother was supposed to marry her cousin and, since the Orthodox Church would not perform the ceremony, she chose the Society of Friends (Quakers) and was married under their care. Three of my uncles attended the Anglican School in Jerusalem and, on marriage, shifted to the Anglican tradition. The fourth married an American Baptist missionary and joined the Baptists. This ecumenical family is an example of a diversity that is not theological but situational. When we meet together we have most things in common but our separate existence in different denominations has led us to different experiences.

My family is an example of most of the Christians in Palestine. I dare say very few were converted from other faiths. Most of us were just rearranged, and often estranged, from one another.

This is the soil from which we grew but it needs to be purified. Our challenge, as churches and as Christians, is to turn to the living God. Our division has distorted the Christ whom we proclaim. Our proclamation sometimes hides what it meant for Jesus to do the will of God. It is a challenge, as well, to turn away from such idols as personal security, material goods, or exclusivity in the church, and others, and to seek the will of the living God.

If we accept that we can communicate the Gospel by the way we live together as Christians, what sort of witness is given by our church, our ways of doing mission, our styles of leadership, and our worship and celebrations? The living God calls us to: confess together God's name; seek prayerfully together God's will; discover together what could be done in a particular place by sharing our mutual resources and by uniting our efforts in common actions. In a deeply divided and broken world, our common witness and unity is urgently required if we are to be effective in preserving and transmitting our faith today.

As Christians we are heading to the year 2000. What gift can we bring to Christ for this celebration? As churches and as local congregations we are called to further God's kingdom on earth by offering signs of that kingdom for our time. We are called to make spaces for the participation of all God's sons and daughters in a place where all barriers are broken down. We are challenged to unity because divided communities and churches are contrary to Christ's way. We are challenged to live according to the gifts that God provides us through the Holy Spirit. At every level of the life of the church, God calls us to healthy and mature relationships in faith to Jesus Christ. The forms and agenda cannot be determined once and for all. We must be responsive within each particular context and at each specific moment.

At this moment the time has come to review the Church divisions and the controversies that we have inherited from the 4th, 16th and 18th centuries. Our challenge is to reach back into the scriptures and creeds of the early undivided church so that we can express our common Christian identity as disciples of Christ, members of the first church of Jerusalem—the mother church of all Christians—rather than identifying ourselves with mother churches in Rome, Athens, England, Germany and the United States.

Many might say I am a woman, a lay person and not a theologian; I should not mess with these complicated matters. Yes, I do confess that I am not a theologian. But theology is not something eternal. It is the encounter of the world of God with the worlds of people in the realities of their lives. Where Christ is present, human, historical and theological barriers are being broken. The church is called to convey to the world the images of a new humanity. There is in Christ no male nor female (Galatians 3.28). Both men and women must discover together their contributions to the service of Christ in the church. The church, likewise, must discover the ministry which can be provided by women as well as that which can be provided by men. This is another challenge and another inherited controversy which has kept women aside.

If you travel in Palestine, you will hear many of us singing songs of hope: hope for bread; hope for release; hope for justice and peace; hope for freedom from religious and political persecution; hope for deliverance from infirmities of body and mind; hope for a new community of women and men; hope for cultural authenticity; hope for a responsible use of power, science and technology; and hope for a more visible unity of the churches. Can we sing, teach, speak, pray and act together? Yes, we can, for our nature is founded in God. It is this that is real, true and eternal. Everything else is transitory, for God is all. Nothing that appears contrary to God has life or meaning. Our existence has significance only insofar as it reflects and expresses God.

Our relationship with all others must be guided by this transcendent fact. We are joined to each other through the divinity of our nature and must always direct our actions so that this may be manifest more completely.

Paul takes the illustration for unity from the human body. That the different parts of the body need each other is obvious. In themselves the individual parts or functions have no value whatsoever. It is not that the gifts exercised by the different members enrich and complement one another, which, of course, they should. But what Paul wants to make absolutely clear is that these gifts are worthless unless they become an integral part of the total body. The spirit of God unites, holds the body together, provides mutuality and co-operative effort, reconciles us with each other, with our neighbours and with God.

I would like to end with a prayer from the World Council of Churches' Salamanca Consultative:

Father of our crucified Lord
We remember with sorrow
That we can stand before you as members of the churches that for
    centuries have been cutting themselves off from one another.
We confess that our struggles to understand your truth
And tell of your love have all too often
Had the tragic results
Of shameful rejection and mutually impoverishing misunderstanding.
We are just too sure of ourselves, Lord,
In claiming to know the only way
While vainly praying for the unity You will;
Often we hesitate,
Fearing to upset links with secular powers
And so refuse all change, all newness;
Often we content ourselves with a superficial unitedness and fail to see,
    and fight against,
The sufferings and schisms in our falsified world
Because we pay more heed to our differences
Than to Him who is the centre of us all,
Jesus Christ our Lord.

'Come, Holy Spirit, renew the whole creation.'

10

CHRISTIAN-MUSLIM RELATIONS IN HISTORIC PERSPECTIVE

John L Esposito

Although I have spoken at many conferences over the years, I can think of few concerns that are more important and pressing religiously and politically than the 'Significance of Jerusalem for Christians and of Christians for Jerusalem.' Moreover, who cannot stand awe-struck in Jerusalem, a city so central and symbolically important to Christianity and indeed all of the children of Abraham. The Church of the Holy Sepulchre, the Wailing Wall, and the Dome of the Rock along with so many other religious shrines and schools are reminders of the centrality of Jerusalem for Christianity, Judaism, and Islam.

I address you today as someone born and raised Roman Catholic. For more than two decades, I have studied and written about Islam, the Muslim world, and Christian-Muslim relations. Although I am not a specialist on Jerusalem, I will focus on a perspective that is important for the political and religious future of Jerusalem, that is the issue of Christian-Muslim relations both past and present. Within this context, I will explore how Jerusalem could become a symbol for future interfaith relations.

For much of its history, the meaning and significance of Jerusalem has been both religious and political. While it has been a major centre and pilgrimage site for the three great monotheistic faiths, it has mostly been the scene not of dialogue but of conflict and confrontation extending from the time of the Crusades to the 1967 Arab-Israeli war, and until the present peace negotiations between Palestinians and Israel. As such, Jerusalem reflects the extent to which religion can be a source of identity, culture and nationalism.

For many believers, religion is a way of life which often legitimates the intermingling of faith and politics. The 'liberation of Jerusalem' is therefore both a religious and political issue. Reflecting on these issues today is especially important, for we live in a world which is experiencing a global religious resurgence in which religion, politics, and society are often intertwined. For many in the West, understanding the struggle of Palestinians today, the issue of the future of Jerusalem and the survival of Palestinian Christians, is compounded be several factors:

1   the close relations of America and many European powers with the State of Israel.

2   the equation of the Palestinian struggle with terrorism.

3   Western ignorance of Eastern Christianity in general and the history of Arab

Christianity in particular.

4   The increased tendency in the post cold war period to speak of an Islamic threat or an impending clash of civilisation between Islam and Christendom or the West.

At this critical period in the history of Jerusalem and of the Arab Christian Community, it is important to acknowledge our past and then to explore the future of Christian-Muslim relations.

Historical Background

The history and memory of Muslim-Christian relations has been difficult and contentious. Despite common theological roots and centuries long interaction, Islam's relationship to Western Christendom, like that of the Muslim world and the West, has often been marked less by understanding than by mutual ignorance, stereotyping, and conflict.[1]

Ancient rivalries and modern day conflicts have too often so accentuated differences as to completely obscure the shared theological roots and vision of a Judaeo-Christian-Islamic tradition, as well as points of co-operation and tolerance. This conflict orientation has focused solely upon differences, reinforcing and polarising rather than uniting these great inter-related monotheistic traditions.

Islam's early expansion and success constituted a challenge to Christendom, theologically, politically and civilisationally, a challenge which proved to be a strong stumbling block to understanding and a threat to the Christian West. Both Islam and Christianity possessed a sense of universal message and mission which in retrospect were destined to lead to confrontation and conflict. The rapid rise and expansion of the Islamic empire and the flourishing of Islamic civilisation posed a direct danger and threat to Christendom's place in the world (ascendancy) both theologically and politically.

The theological similarities of Christendom and Islam put the two on a collision course. Each community believed that its covenant with God was the fulfilment of God's earlier revelation to a previous community that had gone astray. Each believed in the history of God's revelation and that its message and messenger marked the end of revelation and prophecy. Thus, while Christians assumed a position of superiority and therefore had little problem with their supercessionist views towards Judaism, a similar attitude and claim by Muslims *vis-à-vis* Christianity was unthinkable and, more than that, a threat to the uniqueness and divinely mandated role of Christianity to be the sole representative of God and the only means to salvation. Islam was viewed as at best a heresy preached by a deluded or misguided prophet and at worst a direct challenge to Christian claims and mission.

---

[1] I have drawn in this presentation from my work, including: *Islam: The Straight Path* (New York: Oxford University Press) and *The Islamic Threat: Myth or Reality?*, rev. ed. (New York: Oxford University Press).

Both Christianity and Islam claimed a universal mission; each was a transnational community based upon common belief and a vocation to be an example to the nations of the world, the vehicle for the spread and triumph of God's kingdom. However, the challenge of Islam was not simply at the level of theological discourse and debate. The success of Muslim armies and missionaries was experienced as a force which seemed to come out of nowhere to challenge the very existence and foundation of Christendom. Although Muslims were initially a minority in the conquered territories, in time, they became a majority due largely to mass conversations of primarily local Christians. In addition, those who remained Christian were Arabised, adopting Arabic language and culture.

The response of Western Christendom was, with few exceptions, defensive and belligerent. Islam was a danger to be reckoned with. A seemingly impregnable Roman empire had buckled and risked being swept away during the 7th and 8th centuries. Moslem armies overran the Byzantine and Persian empires, conquered Syria, Iraq, and Egypt and swept across North Africa and Europe where they ruled Spain and the Mediterranean from Sicily to Anatolia. Ancient historical and theological affinities went unnoticed as the Christian West, the Church and the state, faced the onslaught of an enemy which it found easier to demonize and dismiss as barbarian and infidel than to understand. The battles of the Crusades and in particular contention for control of Jerusalem epitomised the depth of the clash between Islam and Western Christendom.

Challenge and Response

The litany of conflicts and confrontations between Christianity and Islam, the Muslim world and the West, have been many. These experiences have included the Ottoman 'threat' to Europe, the impact and legacy of European colonialism on much of the Muslim world; it was compounded by the creation of the state of Israel and the cold war in the 20th century. There is little need or purpose to review them here.

In the post cold war, there are those who present Islam as a political, civilisational and demographic threat from government leaders in the Middle East and the West to political analysts and the media. The media headlines and images are all too familiar, articles and media programs with titles like: 'Roots of Muslim Rage', 'The Clash of Civilisation', 'Islam's War With Modernity', 'Islam May Overwhelm the West', 'Jihad in America'.

It is for this very reason that the Center for Muslim-Christian Understanding was established at Georgetown University in 1993. Its manner of creation reflects the new realities and possibilities of the 21st century. The Foundation for Christian-Muslim Understanding, based in Geneva and chaired by Hasib Sabbagh, a prominent Palestinian businessman, approached Georgetown University about the possibility of establishing the Center. The Foundation itself reflects the new ecumenical possibilities. Its members are Arab Christian and Muslim business people. These are Christians and Muslims who have lived and worked side by side in the Arab world. They understand and respect the long standing relations (religious, social political, and economic) between Christian and Muslim communities in the Arab world and with the West. They are concerned that stereotypes and over reactions to the actions of the few or to isolated events do not undermine the relationship of Islam and Christianity and the Muslim world and the West in religious and international affairs. Others have joined in their support for the mission of the Center such as those who established the Malaysia Chair for Islam in Southeast Asia.

The Center's vision and mission respond to the realities of the 21st century in which the role of religion in international affairs has become more prominent. We live in an increasingly global interdependent world: politically, economically, culturally. Mass communications report on and reinforce this linkage every day. There is indeed a global religious resurgence, affecting all of the world's great religious traditions and regions. For some, it is a return or greater re-appropriation of religious identity and practice. Others have a more holistic vision which emphasises the social dimension of religion and thus they seek to implement religious values in communities and societies, from a re-emphasis on family values to movements for social justice. Liberation theologies and movements may be found in Christianity, Judaism, and Islam as well as Buddhism, and Hinduism. The name of the organiser of our conference, Sabeel Liberation Theology Center, reflects this theological world view.

Approaches to Muslim-Christian Relations

There are many ways to approach Muslim-Christian relations: dialogue sponsored by religious bodies or organisations (internationally, nationally, and locally); the development of ecumenical theologies; teaching and research at academic institutes and centres; situational, the inter-action of Muslims and Christians in their neighbourhoods and society.

In the 20th century, great strides have been made. We all know of the pioneering efforts of the World Council of Churches, the National Council of Churches, the Middle East Council of Churches and the Vatican's Pontifical Council for Inter-religious Dialogue. However, what is important to note is that these activities (ecumenical dialogues, conferences, contacts, and exchanges) have in many cases increased and now trickle down, penetrate and spread across our societies. We must move beyond the old divisions of the past in which many countries or societies witnessed religious communalism and separatism rather than pluralism. New paths of mutual understanding and co-operation must break down and barriers of our theologies, neighbourhoods and minds.

Any equitable resolution of the future status of Jerusalem will require all its major religious communities to affirm a pluralistic theology of inclusiveness and religious tolerance in which there are no masters and servants but rather a society in which all citizens recognise their equal status and rights before God as children of Abraham. Therefore, despite important religious differences, all are heirs of a common Judaeo-Christian-Islamic tradition, neighbours and servants of God.

The issue of religious pluralism also exists today in the West, in Europe and

America, where Islam has become the second or third largest religion, requiring a new more inclusive vision of religious pluralism that extends beyond that of talk of Judaeo-Christian-Islamic tradition. Here the work of religious leaders and organisations must be sustained by new theological interpretations and visions. This intellectual movement has occurred to a remarkable degree although much, I emphasise, much more needs to be done.

A significant factor is bringing about change is education. Increasingly in the past two decades in America for example, we find an explosion of interest in religious studies. Religion is not only taught in seminars today but indeed far more pervasively in colleges and universities and increasingly in our primary and secondary schools. While there are many problems in initiating such changes, if done well, the study of religions equips our next generations to better understand and hopefully respect, live, and work with others.

The growth and work of centres for Muslim-Christian relations today with multiple missions and tasks reflect our changing realities and possibilities. Centres should provide an awareness of, and respond to the spiritual, political, and demographic linkages of our world. Through teaching, research, publications, exchange and public affairs programmes, Centres have the opportunity to develop and disseminate new visions and contribute in diverse ways not only to mutual understanding but also to resolving conflict.

We are all aware of the important work today of centres across the world from the Duncan Black Macdonald Center at Hartford Seminary, the Centre for the Study of Islam and Christian-Muslim Relations at Selly Oaks, and here at Sabeel and Tantur to name but a few. They do not compete with but rather complement each other, pursuing diverse paths that in some cases coincide and in others parallel each other. Some are primarily concerned with theological dialogue, others with academic training and public affairs. I can speak best about the Center that I am closest to and how it seeks to address the diverse and complex realities of Christian-Muslim relations.

The Center for Muslim-Christian Understanding, History and International Affairs, focuses on the study of the historical, theological, political and cultural encounters of Islam and Christianity. The Center is designed to have a major impact not only in Georgetown University and in Washington DC, but also to engage the broader American and international community. Faculty members teach courses for students both in the school of Foreign Service and the University, at both undergraduate and graduate levels. We are a place where scholars and leaders from Muslim, Christian, and other religious communities can meet and work together. This is reflected in our faculty, fellows, and programmes.

The Center includes three full time faculty members, John O Voll, Amira El-Azhary Sonbol, and myself, Senior Fellows like Irfan Shahid, and visiting professors such as Yvonne Haddad, Samir Khalil Samir SJ, and Fathi Osman. Our visiting scholars and researchers come from Lebanon, Iran, Bangladesh, Malaysia, Tajikistan, etc. We are global in our understanding of Christianity and of Islam and thus, for example, we look at Christianity in the Arab world as well as the West and Islam in South, Southeast, and Central Asia as well as in the Middle East.

The scholarship and impact of the Center are visible in seminars, colloquia, and international conferences at Georgetown, with the participation of Center faculty in conferences and symposia, their lectures and meetings with religious leaders, university faculty and students, government officials, corporate leaders, and the media around the world. The themes of our programmes reveal the scope of our concerns: 'Muslim-Christian Relations in the Twenty-First Century', 'Children of Abraham', 'The Political Future of Jerusalem', 'Political Islam: Its Regional and International Implications', 'Political Participation and Pluralism in Islam and the Muslim World', 'Daughters of Sarah and Hager', and 'Jerusalem and the Future of Arab Christianity' which consisted of Arab Christian leaders from the region, some of whom are here today.

The outreach and impact of the Center is further realised through our faculty and Center publications and our linkages with centres and universities in Europe, the Middle East, and Asia.

In addition to dialogue sponsored by religious organisations, the development of ecumenical theologies, the work of academic centres, there is perhaps the most important factor: the everyday interaction of Muslims and Christians in their neighbourhoods and societies. It is when Christians and Muslims meet, work, and struggle side by side that the greatest opportunities, not only for conflict, but also for co-operation are present. Realisation that we share common human concerns as parents, children, citizens, professionals, and neighbours can be a powerful source for 'humanising' rather than the 'demonizing' of others. Thus, for example, Palestinian Christians and Muslims have been united in their struggle for national liberation and the liberation of Jerusalem. Of equal importance is recognition that, despite important differences of belief and practice, there is shared heritage of faith and value: belief in God, the prophets, revelation, moral responsibility and accountability, divine reward and punishment, and social justice can be a strong source of mutual respect and co-operation.

Any vision of the future of Christian-Muslim relations, to be honest, must not only be aware of the problems of the past but also of the difficulties and injustices of the present. The actions of some governments and organisations in the name of religion or religious nationalism, religious persecution, the plight of women and minorities, and the violation of human rights in many societies remain major challenges. Many still need to recall that God's revelation does not create communities with an exclusive possession of the truth, that equality before God is for all not just for those who believe that they are somehow a chosen community. All are challenged to rethink and internalise an inclusive rather than exclusive global vision which is truly pluralistic and tolerant and to fight those who in the name of God or religion engage in terrorism and intolerance. For if we are all children of Abraham and, despite real and important differences, share a common Judaeo-Christian-Islamic tradition, we also then belong to a global religious and human community that requires freedom and social justice for all. Nowhere has this been more of an issue than in the struggle for Palestine and remains a question with regard to the future of Jerusalem.

The Christian struggle for Jerusalem today is a twofold struggle for peace, justice, and reconciliation that:

1   challenges all Christians to a unity that transcends the divisions of West and East, Orthodox, Catholic, and Protestant for the life (indeed survival) and safety of the mother church of Christendom and its sacred city, Jerusalem

2   requires that all, Christians, Muslims, and Jews avoid the exclusiveness and intolerance of the past and embrace an inclusiveness, based upon recognition of a shared heritage, which will enable all the children of Abraham to say Jerusalem is 'ours' not just mine.

The future of Jerusalem and survival of the Christian community in Jerusalem is dependent upon the strengthening of mutual understanding and trust among Christians and Muslims. The danger is that without a common (Palestinian) nationalist struggle, religious communities can revert to the religious sectarianism and communalism that has reared its head in the past and more recently in Sudan, Lebanon, Bosnia and the Philippines.

We cannot forget our past histories and memories of conflict and injustices. However, I would argue authentic Christianity and Islam (as well as Judaism) challenge us all to move forward, to work together for a united and pluralist Jerusalem built upon mutual understanding and co-operation. As this conference has revealed, such a Jerusalem will require an ongoing commitment to action, a linking of centres and organisations here and internationally, to foster global recognition of the significance of Christians and Muslims for Jerusalem and of Jerusalem for Muslims and Christians.

11

A VISION FOR
CHRISTIAN–MUSLIM RELATIONS

Geries Khoury

Jerusalem is important for Christians because of the presence of the Church of the Holy Sepulchre in it, because of the presence of Christ through his life and teachings, and because of what is written about it in the Old and New Testaments. Jerusalem has a special status. It is a holy city, the city of resurrection, the city of life, of renewal, of charity, love, sacrifice and redemption. This is the spiritual meaning of Jerusalem. For us Palestinians it is important not only because it hosted the Prophet on his celestial journey, but also because over the years, it has become, in terms of our heritage, spirituality and literature, a symbol for the achievement of the legitimate rights of the Palestinian people. It is in Jerusalem that Palestinian selfhood is realised, and where Palestinian being and conscience are fulfilled. It has thus become the spinal chord of Palestinian identity.

Jerusalem is the city that preserved and continues to preserve our spiritual heritage, the Holy Sepulchre and the Dome of the Rock. This is Jerusalem, and it is hard for me to look at it only from the Christian point of view, because that would mean distancing myself from the mystery of the city, its inclusivity and totality. It would be like dividing its holiness, its history and its unity with a sharp knife. That would mean doing injustice to the city, the holiness of the city. What is holy cannot be divided. What is holy cannot be categorised, one time for me and another time for someone else. What God makes holy and whole, cannot be divided by human beings.

I feel it is sinful to speak about the importance of Jerusalem from a Christian point of view only. What if an earthquake shakes Jerusalem and destroys the Holy Sepulchre; or the earth opens and swallows up its sites and churches; would Jerusalem still be important to me as a Christian or not?

As a Christian, when I talk about Jerusalem and its importance to me, I take two equally important issues into consideration. This is because of Jerusalem's history and because of the reality of my existence:

1   The faith dimension from a Christian point of view.
2   Muslim presence.

Because I am both Palestinian and Christian, I cannot talk about one dimension without the other. In other words, because of the history of the region, I think that Jerusalem and the Holy Sepulchre would not be of the same importance, had it not been for the Muslim presence. Also, had it not been for the resurrection and Christian history, Muslim history would not be as important. In Jerusalem, Christianity was reborn with the entry of 'Umar ibn al-Khattab and Islam, which manifested its message and its tolerance when 'Umar met Sophronius with love, approval, respect and covenant, the covenant of God and the covenant of person to person. Ever since that time, it is difficult to separate the two histories. One was embodied in the other, and the two became one. They are of the same essence, with different natures that complement each other, Christian and Muslim. That is why, my vision of Christian-Muslim relations, begins with this history and views this history very seriously.

The future has a base of more than 1,300 years. Our future as Christians is closely connected to our relationship with our Muslim countrymen, our brothers and sisters. It is also related to the extent of our participation in building our one homeland, in demanding our legitimate rights and democracy. It also depends on the extent of our respect for Muslim religious sensitivity as we respect our own. Respect of religious sensitivity requires hard work from everyone of us and on the part of the Palestinian Church. This can take place through education and a genuine and objective understanding of Islam and Muslim heritage based on the Qur'an and Sunna (teachings of the Prophet).

Quite honestly, I would say, we are ignorant of Islam. Even those who claim to know Islam, are ignorant of much of it. It is our primary obligation to study this religion and its rich spiritual heritage. We should respect its followers and accept them according to their faith and creed, and not as we would like them to be. Once we have full knowledge of Islam, we can criticise perverted practice by some Muslims rather than judge Islam itself, through the actions of some parties or individuals. It is damaging to generalise, for wisdom lies in uncovering the truth. Only then will the Church be in a position to demand that Muslims understand Christianity as it is, and as Christians understand it; not the way sectarians and trouble-makers write about it.

We have a day-to-day relationship which is religious and social. Our dialogue is not on paper nor between one article and another; it is rather a daily encounter on the street, at school, in the store, at work, at home and in our neighbour's sitting room. Our future is one. We Christians should not give in to attempts made, every now and then, to change the problem of Jerusalem from a national right to a religious one. I believe that the demand of national rights includes the recognition of religious and other rights, while satisfaction with religious rights does not guarantee national rights. We have to differentiate between the two, and stand together both as Christians and Muslims for our legitimate national rights. Jerusalem is important to me as a Christian when I walk hand in hand, down the Via Dolorosa with my Muslim brother, with our eyes set on the realisation of our national rights, national conciliation and mutual respect for all religions; and as we work together to foil every attempt aimed against our national unity and continued strength n the Holy City.

Jerusalem is not the only place of resurrection. Christ's resurrection is in every sanctuary where Christians come together to pray and celebrate the resurrection of Christ. Christ said 'Love ye one another so that the world should believe that I sent you' (John 13: 34).

Palestinian Christians must insist on two matters so that the world might believe our message concerning Jerusalem:

1   The proclamation of Jerusalem as the capital of the Palestinian State, and integral part of the occupied territories, which means, all international laws apply to it.

2   Palestinians should carry the above mentioned message to the capitals of the world in protest against their stand on Jerusalem. They should erect a protest tent in all of those capitals, where clergymen, in particular, should stay night and day, until the world believes that Jerusalem is important to us.

I will only be convinced that Jerusalem is important to us, Palestinian Christians, when bishops, patriarchs, and clergymen hold hands with the mufti, the sheikh and the qadi, and together travel to Western capitals to talk about the importance of Jerusalem for Muslims and Christians, and of their stand on Jerusalem both from a national and religious point of view.

Challenges

There are many challenges facing national unity, national affiliation and coexistence between Palestinian Christians and Muslims in the Holy Land. I should mention at this point, that relations between the children of the one nation are good despite all the challenges. I think that the reason for these good relations is the fact that we find ourselves in the same ditch, whether under Israeli occupation, the British Mandate or Turkish rule, etc. Today, on our way towards liberation, it is our duty to find ways that will strengthen relations between Palestinian Christians and Muslims and maintain national unity and full participation in the building of the Palestinian state. Following are some of the challenges that face us in our relationship as sons and daughters of the one country:

A   Our Ignorance of Ourselves as Christians

1   Our knowledge of our religion and theology is superficial and almost non-existent.

2   Our knowledge of the history and spiritual heritage of our Churches is minimal.

3   Palestinian Christians, in general, do not have any religious education. Where it is found, the percentage is very small.

4   Christian education in most of our schools and churches is still very basic, lacking in ecumenical spirit, unsuitable for present times or the context in which we live.

5   Palestinian Arab Christians are ignorant of their history and their Christian Arab heritage.

6   Palestinian Christians are ignorant of the history of the Church.

B   Our Ignorance of Others

Palestinian Christians are not only ignorant of themselves, but also of the religion of others. We are ignorant of Judaism and of Islam. We know almost nothing of other religions. In this paper, I would like to concentrate on our ignorance of Islam and Muslim history. Understanding Islam does not mean knowing some verses from the Qur'an or some of the Prophet's sayings that we repeat at every occasion. We Palestinian Christians, or I should say, Christians in general, face a real problem, which we should admit and work to solve. It is our ignorance of Islam which I shall sum up as follows:

1   We are ignorant of Muslim faith, Muslim law (Shari'a) and the teachings of the Prophet (Sunna).
2   We are ignorant of Muslim history, Muslim culture and tradition as well as Muslim heritage.
3   Our religious education of Islam is superficial and unsuitable for the purpose of coexistence.
4   Our ignorance of the nature of Muslim society adds to the difficulty in communication between the followers of both religions.
5   Perceptions and stereotypes of the other, acquired through our upbringing, are distorted and unrealistic. These images have been acquired through our ignorance of each other and coloured by historical residue that we read, without seriously investigating. They are mostly negative images that have had negative impact on our relationship.
6   Western media distort Islam and describe it as a religion of terror and violence. It is mostly Westerners that are influenced by this propaganda, but we too are affected by these negative perceptions which are deliberate, and have political and economic motives.

C   The Ignorance of Palestinians of the West, and the West of Palestinians

Our ignorance of the West and its ignorance of us is one of the main challenges to peaceful co-existence between Christians and Muslims in this country. It is a hindrance to good and positive relations. This is so, because I believe that the West bears some of the responsibility when it comes to the quality of relations between Christians and Muslims in this land, in the East in general and in the world in particular. The reasons for this ignorance and this strained relationship is the following:

1   The East usually regards the West as being Christian. In fact, it is not so; but people do not know that the percentage of believers and those who actually practice their religion is very small. Another matter that people here do not realise, is that

religion in the West comes at the bottom of their priorities. It falls behind economics, social services, as well as culture, education and politics. Talk about religion and its role in Western societies gets weaker every day. In our society, religion still plays a major role, something that is totally unknown to the West.

2   The West regards the Arab world as a Muslim world. It is ignorant of the Christian presence and sometimes disregards it completely. It is ignorant of our Christian history, heritage, spirituality and knows very little about our Christian denominations, our role, our message or our Christian witness. For the West, Arabs are Muslims, and Islam is projected to Westerners as a belligerent religion that was spread by force, by the sword. It is portrayed as a religion that supports terrorism and the violation of human rights. A religion that oppresses women and denies their rights; a religion that brings to mind strange and negative images. We know that these images are caused by the ignorance of us and Westerners, of Islam and its history; but they, nevertheless, influence relations between East and West; and between Muslims Arabs and their Christian brothers and sisters. I would also like to point out that the war in Bosnia, and the treatment of Muslims in Germany and other European states has often, negatively, influenced co-existence in Palestine.

3   The West has a condescending attitude towards us; as masters to slaves. They believe they have all the knowledge and that our role is to acquiesce, or face disaster as in the case of Iraq.

4   The West is ignorant of the nature of relations between Arab Muslims and Christians. It is ignorant of our common past which is 1,360 years old. It is ignorant of the shared participation of the children of the same people in building all facets of Arab culture; philosophy, theology, medicine, geography, history, etc. The West is ignorant of the dialogue that Muslims and Christians engaged in over the ages, of the thousands of books they wrote and translated, of the schools they established together until the time of Plato and Aristotle, when together they transferred these translations to the West.

D   Religious Intolerance

Religious intolerance is one of the biggest challenges facing societies that respects pluralism, freedom, democracy and equality. In Palestine, the Holy Land, there are many fanatic and extreme Jewish groups that see only themselves. There are also fanatic and intolerant Christian groups who came from the West, from Europe and America and settled specifically in Jerusalem. They would like to see only Jews living in this Holy Land. These groups are antagonistic towards Palestinian Christians and Muslims. They are against the peace process and the legitimate rights of the Palestinian people. One has only to look at some of the literature of the International Christian Embassy in Jerusalem and follow its activities and programmes; especially the building of settlements for Jews. In facing this religious intolerance, we have to know how to deal with it in order to weaken it and draw its members to us. We have to communicate with them and do our best to make our voices and point of view reach them. Our voice should be prophetic, loud and clear in its demand for truth and justice.

E   The Building of the Palestinian State

We are in the process of building a Palestinian state and its institutions. We should tread very carefully so that our Christian-Muslim relations would not be threatened by a wrong move here or there, a wrong word or ill-advised stand. We are asked to comprehend what is negative and to get to know each other. We are called to promote trust amongst the children of the one nation and support democratic principles in the Palestinian state, something we all desire, Christians and Muslims alike.

Future Vision from a Palestinian Christian Perspective

As I address this conference which is attended by a big number of Christian Church leaders, theologians, scholars and officials of Church institutions, I would like to declare quite openly that future Christian-Muslim relations in the Holy Land, and a life of reciprocal love, trust and security can be maintained if we endeavour to do the following:

1   Palestinian Christians, especially those living in urban areas should stop repeating sayings that we hear every now and then, such as: we are better educated and more civilised, our homes are cleaner and our families are smaller in number. This false vanity leads to a closed Christian community that will eventually be marginalised, and could breed intolerance towards them. We should warn against this dangerous phenomenon.

2   We should reform our Christian message and look into the content of our Christian witness. In other words, our faith should be rooted in our land and civilisation.

3   In order to understand the content of our message and witness, we have to have a good knowledge of our faith, our history and our spirituality. At the same time, we have to know the other; Islam and Muslims, their creed, their law (Shari'a) and their spirituality.

4   A good and true knowledge of each other is the only guarantee for giving up stereotypes and preconceptions in dealing with the other, and seeing them as they are. A good knowledge of ourselves and of the other leads to mutual respect and acceptance.

5   A genuine participation in the national struggle and real sacrifice for the sake of building a democratic state.

6   Christian clergy and lay people should raise their voices on the issue of Jerusalem. They should declare that Jerusalem is ours and the capital of our Palestinian state. As a Palestinian Christian, I would say quite frankly that Jerusalem is important to me not only because the Church of the Holy Sepulchre is in it, but rather because it is mine, my homeland and the capital of my state. So the importance of Jerusalem is twofold and I will not be satisfied with its religious importance or with religious freedom. The way I view Jerusalem differs from the way most Christians around the world view it. For them, what is important is its spiritual significance and their concern is religious freedom. I believe their view will lead to

the burial of the local Church.

To conclude, I believe our duty as local Christians and as Christians from around the world, is to strengthen interfaith dialogue and in particular Christian-Muslim dialogue. Our spiritual and theological discourse should act as a bridge between nations and faiths. Our voices should be prophetic, whether in our communities, our states or our institutions. We are asked to co-operate in order to spread love among the different nations and the followers of the different heavenly faiths; we need to work together in order to be among the makers of a just peace, and in order to grant Jerusalem, the Holy City, the city of peace, its natural role, the role that God desires for it.

So in the name of the whole of humanity and for the sake of all humanity we pursue peace, especially for those who are oppressed, destitute and humiliated. The peacemakers in our Holy Land do not represent only themselves, but the desire of all those who are threatened by different forms of oppression and fear. Our cry for justice and peace for Jerusalem is a rumbling cry for justice and peace in the whole world, not on the basis of balance of power or selfish interests; but rather on the basis of divine and human values. Those values, that distinguish human civilisation to which God gave a home in Jerusalem.

May there be peace inside your walls, and safety in your palaces.
For the sake of my friends and companions,
I say to Jerusalem, 'Peace be with you.' (Psalm 122: 7-8)

12

THE SIGNIFICANCE OF JERUSALEM FOR MUSLIMS

Antonie Wessels

Current discussion on Jerusalem cannot be seen apart from the meaning that this city has, not only for Jews and Israelis, but also for Christians and Muslims, both within as well as outside the State of Israel. This includes, most certainly, the Arab Christians and Muslims who have lived in the city for many years.

As is well known, in 1947 the United Nations passed a resolution which stated that Jerusalem was to be 'internationalised', Jerusalem was still seen as a *corpus separatum* in this 'resolution of division'. However, as early as 1949 Israel declared that Jerusalem would be the capital of the newly proclaimed state and the seat of the government. After the conquest of the eastern part of the city in the June War of 1967, Israel annexed East Jerusalem. Israel did not receive any international recognition for this decision. The annexation was rejected by the General Assembly of the United Nations in 1967 and an appeal was made for a return to *status quo ante*. For that reason most foreign embassies are to this day not to be found in Jerusalem but in Tel Aviv, although the United States Congress passed a resolution in October 1995 to move the United States Embassy eventually to Jerusalem. In December 1995, the United Nations once more declared that they did not recognise Jerusalem's changed status. The ultimate status of (East) Jerusalem, which the Palestinians consider to be the future capital of their independent state, will be discussed in negotiations between Israel and the Palestinian Authority scheduled for May 1996.

In this article we will look at the last 1400 years of Jerusalem, in which this city became significant for Arabs and Muslims.

The history of Islamic Jerusalem can be divided into three periods. The first period began with the conquest of the city by the second successor (caliph) of Muhammad, 'Umar ibn al-Khattab (d. 644) and ended at the beginning of the 13th century. This period is marked by the building of the Dome of the Rock and the Crusades (1095-1291). In the second period Jerusalem became a provincial city, though it was also considered—by Muslims as well—to be a Holy City. The heart of the old city outside the Haram al-Sharif (the Noble Sanctuary), where the Dome of the Rock and the Aqsa mosque can be found, as it appears today, originated during the Mamluk period (1247-1517). After the Seljuks had marched into Anatolia, the Ottoman Turks conquered what was left of the Byzantine empire, conquered its capital Constantinople, and even extended their power into Eastern Europe. During the Ottoman period (1517-1917) Jerusalem belonged to the Ottoman empire. Sultan

Suleiman I, the 'Magnificent' (1495-1566), left behind the most permanent stamp on the city. Between 1537-1541 the city wall was built, the Dome of the Rock renovated and the four magnificent public fountains designed. The many pious benefactions made by him and his wife contributed to the welfare of the city. In the Haram museum one can still see the great enormous kettles of the soup kitchen, with the list of recipients, which were given by the sultan's wife, for the feeding of the poor and the students. Well-known families in Jerusalem, such as the Khaladi and the Husseini gained their prominent status during this period.

The third period, that of 'modern' history, began in 1831 with the conquest of the city by Ibrahim Pasha (1789-1848), the *wali* or vice-regent of the Ottoman regime in Egypt. From 1831 to 1840 the city was occupied by the founder of the Egyptian royal house, Muhammad 'Ali (1769-1849). The reforms that were initiated under Ibrahim Pasha, the adopted son of Muhammad 'Ali, could not be undone by the Ottoman Turks who gained control of the city again in 1840. The limitations that had been imposed on non-Muslims were lifted and the improved living conditions encouraged many religious people to settle in Jerusalem. In the course of the 19th century, Christian influence in the city grew and after the Crimean War (1853-1856), the prohibition preventing non-Muslims from entering the Temple square was removed.

Western influence was strengthened by the Crimean War. France, Austria, Prussia, Russia, Sardinia, Spain and the United States opened consulates in Jerusalem. The flags of the Christian powers were now raised on Sundays and holidays in the Holy City, and on the birthdays of their kings and presidents 21-gun salutes were fired, a privilege that Jerusalem had until then reserved only for Islamic holidays and 'the birthday of the Prophet' (*mawlid al-nabi*). Church bells could also be rung. Initially, Muslims tried to prevent this but in vain. It was Christians primarily who profited from these changes. About 1880 the Jews even constituted the majority of the population! 1881 saw the beginning of a considerable immigration of Jews. The struggle between the Arabs and the Jewish immigrants strengthened the traditional connectedness of the Muslims with Jerusalem.[1]

This article is arranged as follows. In order to understand the significance of Jerusalem for the Muslims, the connection of the Prophet Muhammad (ca. 570-632) to this city should be discussed first: Jerusalem as the place to which prayer was initially directed and as the place of the nightly journey (*isra'*) and the heavenly journey (*mi'raj*). Next, I will discuss the Arab conquest of the city, after which I will describe the construction of the two most important Islamic shrines: the Dome of the Rock (Qubbat al-Sakhra) and the Aqsa Mosque ('the furthest mosque') in the time of the Umayyads. Following that, I will look at the new significance Jerusalem has acquired for Muslims in connection with the Crusades,[2] which has been inspired by their reaction to them. Finally, I will take up the question of what the consequences of this are for the current status of the city.

---

[1] Cf. the entries 'al-Kuds, Kibla', 'Sakhra', 'Isra', 'Mi'radj', 'al-Masjdid al-Aksa' in the *Encyclopedia of Islam*, new ed.
[2] Sivan, E, 'Le caracterè sacré de Jérusalem . . .', *Studia Islamica* XVII, 1967, pp. 149-82.

Muhammad and Jerusalem

At first glance it seems strange to refer to the Prophet Muhammad for the significance of Jerusalem for Muslims, because the word 'Jerusalem' does not at all appear in the Qur'an.

The earliest Islamic name for Jerusalem is *Iliya' madinat bayt al-maqdis*. *Iliya'* is an Arabicisation of *Aelia,* the name given to the city by the Romans. When Jerusalem was destroyed by the Romans, the city was rebuilt as a Roman colony in 135 CE with a new name, Aelia Capitolina, in honour of the gods of the Capitol and the emperor whose full name was Titus *Aelius* Hadrianus (76-138). A temple to Venus was built on Golgotha. The Romans called the country Palestina or Syria/Palestina. *Falastîn* is also an Arabicisation of this Roman name. During the Crusades, the name Palestina, which had been used since the time of the Romans, fell into disuse. The Crusaders preferred to speak of the Holy Land and the 'kingdom of Jerusalem' instead of Palestina. Earlier Islamic writers called Jerusalem *Bayt al-maqdis,* 'the holy house.' This referred to the Temple and is the translation of the Hebrew *Bet ham-mikdasj*. Whereas *Bayt al-Maqdis* refers to the whole city, the Temple area is called al-Haram. The most usual Arab name for Jerusalem is, in brief, *al-Quds,* 'Holy.'

Qur'anic expressions, which are considered to be allusions to Jerusalem by Islamic commentators, are *masjid al-aqsa,* 'the furthest mosque' (Qur'an 17: 1), *nubawwa siq,* 'the reliable dwelling place' (Qur'an 10: 93), or the *al-ard al-muqaddasa* 'the holy land' (Qur'an 5: 21 (24)). The last designation corresponds to Jewish and Christian use, i.e., a name for Jerusalem that extends to the whole country (Qur'an 7: 137 (133)).

There are clearly two reasons why Muhammad is connected with Jerusalem. First, there is a connection because of the direction (of the prayer, *qiblah*) in which he initially performed his (ritual) prayer (*salât*) and, secondly, because Jerusalem is viewed as the place of Muhammad's nightly journey and heavenly journey. In both cases Jerusalem is not explicitly mentioned in the Qur'an.

When Muhammad prescribed the ritual prayer to his followers, the direction in which they prayed was still Jerusalem and not Mecca. Only in 624, in the second year after the emigration (*hijra*) from Mecca to Medina (the Islamic reckoning of the years begins in 622), is the direction of the prayer changed (cf. Qur'an 2: 142-45 (136-40)).[3] Muhammad followed Jewish custom in the direction of his prayer. The prayer with which King Solomon dedicated the Temple in Jerusalem speaks about prayer in the direction of this holy place (I Kings 8: 44). It is said of the prophet Daniel that he prayed in the direction of Jerusalem (Daniel 6: 11).

In addition, there is still a second reason why the 'house of the holy place' was known to the Prophet. In Qur'an 17.1 it is said that God had his servant (Muhammad) travel (*isra'*) by night from the holy mosque (*Haram*) in Mecca to the 'furthest mosque'. The tradition quickly identified *al-Masjid al-Aqsa* with the Temple

---

[3] These verses are inscribed under the ceramic arch in the porch of the Chapel of the Dome of the direction of the prayer.

in Jerusalem. The addition 'of which we have blessed the circumference' probably refers to a place in the Holy Land, Jerusalem.

According to the story, Muhammad is said to have slept one night in the neighbourhood of the holy house, the Ka'ba, in Mecca or in the house of Umm Hani. He was awakened by the angel Gabriel, who led him to a winged horse called Buraq. Muhammad mounted the horse and went to Jerusalem, where he met Abraham, Moses, and Jesus. Together they performed the ritual prayer, in which Muhammad took the lead.

Exegesis quickly connected the nightly journey and the heavenly journey. A ladder to heaven was first mentioned (cf. Jacob's Ladder in Bethel, Genesis 28: 12). God is called 'God the Lord of the Stairways' (*Dhu 'l-Ma'arij*) (Qur'an 70: 3). This was seen as a visionary experience and brought into connection with 'the vision' (*ru'ya*) (Qur'an 17: 60 (62)). Primarily mystics and philosophers preferred this last allegorical explanation.

The Arab Conquest of the City

It goes without saying that the significance of Jerusalem increased for the Muslims after it was conquered by the Arab Muslims some years after Muhammad's death. The Arabs conquered the south of Palestine at the battle of Ajnadayn in the summer of 634 or, as the classical expression reads: the country was 'opened' (*fath*) for Islam.[4] In 634, though Jerusalem itself was not besieged, the aged patriarch of Jerusalem, Sophronius (ca. 560-638) expressed his sorrow in his Christmas sermon at the fact that it was impossible to travel from Jerusalem to Bethlehem because of the thieving Arabs. A few days later, on the feast of Epiphany, he mourned the bloodshed, the destruction of monasteries, the plundering of cities and the burning of villages by the Saracens, 'who boast that they will conquer the whole world.' It was still four years before Jerusalem fell (638) after the decisive battle of Yarmuk in 636. This battle marked the beginning of the Islamic domination of Palestine, interrupted only by the Crusades (1099-1244) and in our century by the British Mandate (1920-1948) and the conquest of East Jerusalem in June 1967 by Israel.

One of the most important Byzantine theologians, Maximus the Confessor (580-662), was distressed at the time of the Arab conquest of Jerusalem over the fact that the Arabs 'trampled a strange country underfoot as if it was their own.' These words make one think of what the high priest Simon said after the Maccabees had defeated the Seleucids in 164 BCE:

> We have neither taken other men's land, nor are we in possession of other men's property, but of the inheritance of our forefathers; it was wrongfully held by our enemies at one time, but we, grasping our opportunity, hold firmly the inheritance of our forefathers.

---

[4] It is in this way that the 'conquest' (*fath*) of Mecca in 630 is spoken of, as well as with respect to Egypt when it was 'opened' for Islam. The name of the Palestinian resistance movement *Fatah* is an acronym, but the Islamic associations with the word also play a role.

In his turn, Saladin would write to Richard the Lion-hearted (1157-1199), who intended to retake Jerusalem from the Muslims during the Third Crusade, the following letter in which the Islamic claim to Jerusalem was evident:

> Jerusalem is much more ours than yours. In fact it is of greater significance to us than to you, because it is the seat of the ascension of our Prophet and the place where the angels gather. Do not think that we can ever give it up or waver on this point. This land was ours originally, whereas you have just arrived and have taken it over only because of the weakness of its Islamic inhabitants at that time. God will not permit you to build one stone in this land as long as the war lasts.

There are different stories about what exactly happened when the Arab Muslims conquered Jerusalem. These stories betray a certain tenor. In the 10th century the Egyptian Christian Eutychius (Sa'id ibn al-Bitrîq, 887-940, the Melchite patriarch of Alexandria), wrote that 'Umar refused to pray in 'the church of the resurrection' (*kanisat al-qiyama*), as the Arabs call the Church of the Holy Sepulchre, praying instead on the steps to the entrance. 'Umar wanted to prevent the Muslims from later changing the church into a mosque on the basis of his example. He is said to have given the patriarch Sophronius, who took him on his first tour of Jerusalem, a document to this effect. After that, they are said to have gone to the place where the Temple had once stood and had in the meantime become a refuse dump. At his request Sophronius then indicated the Rock as a suitable place for a mosque.

The tenor of this story is patently obvious. This Christian author wants to confirm the inalienable rights of Christians to the churches by appealing to the authority of no one less than the caliph 'Umar himself.

The Islamic authors, however, have a different version of the story. The caliph is said to have finally arrived at the Temple square, which he himself is said to have recognised as the place of Muhammad's night journey!

The traditions agree in that 'Umar had already instituted a place of prayer in the Temple square. It was primarily a practical solution, because the caliph just came up with a holy place without coming into conflict with the privileges given to the Christians.

Eutychius' story is probably not historical, and could have been concluded from another story, in which he relates that Muslims of his time acted contrary to the 'Umar's arrangements and took possession of half of the outside court of the Church of the Holy Sepulchre and built a mosque there, because 'Umar had prayed there. For that reason it was called 'Umar mosque (*masjid*) to emphasise to the Christians that 'Umar had prayed there!

The conditions under which the city surrendered, for that matter, to 'Umar were mild for the Christians. Some relics in the Church of the Holy Sepulchre were lost in the Arab conquest. The cross went to Constantinople and the spear to Antioch. The Christian inhabitants received guarantees for the safety of their lives and properties, churches and crosses, whereas no Jew could live among them! The church buildings were not to be used as living quarters, destroyed or made smaller. The Christians retained their freedom of religion, with the understanding that they had to pay head tax (*jizya*) and help in withstanding the Byzantine troops and robbers.

After the Arab conquest of Jerusalem Muslims from Medina moved to Jerusalem. A saying of the time was: 'The building of Jerusalem is the destruction of Medina.'

In the first period after the Arab conquest Jerusalem retained its Christian character. The Christian feasts also determined the rhythm of the year for the Islamic population. Pious Muslims came into contact with the hermits who lived in the mountains and with other forms of Christian asceticism.

Al-Aqsa Mosque and the Dome of the Rock

Two years after the fall of Jerusalem Mu'awiyya ibn Abu Sufyan, first governor of Damascus and later the first caliph (661-80) of the dynasty of the Umayyads, was appointed commander of the Islamic army that operated in Palestine and Syria. Jerusalem was the place where two important events occurred in his life. In Jerusalem Mu'awiyya was honoured at the beginning of his reign as caliph in 661. It is said that he prayed on Golgotha, in Gethsemane and on the grave of Mary on this occasion.

The Muslims now took over the Herodian Temple square. The Aqsa mosque of the Umayyad period was the first mosque of the city. According to some, the Umayyad caliph 'Abd al Malik ibn Marwan (684-705) built this mosque, but if this mosque originated from the church of the Byzantine emperor Justinian (527-565), then he in fact, against 'Umar's instructions, changed a church into a mosque. He probably gave the order for the construction, which was carried out by his son al-Walid in 705.

One of the important activities of 'Abd al-Malik was that he had a dome built over the Rock—the oldest remaining monument of Islamic architecture—where the Prophet was to have placed his foot before his heavenly journey. The plans for the building of the Dome of the Rock already existed in Mu'awiyya's time but were carried out under 'Abd al Malik, his successor. The date indicated in the dome for the construction is 691, the year of the completion of the building of the shrine.

As far as its composition is concerned, the Dome of the Rock belongs to the tradition of Byzantine architecture, represented by monuments such as those in Ravenna (Italy), in Bosra (Syria) and the Church of the Holy Sepulchre and the Church of the Ascension in Jerusalem. It is almost certain that the builders and designers were Christians of Syrian or Palestinian descent. The lack of any depiction whatsoever of a human figure points to a conscious Islamic tradition. The ornamentation in the mosaics, which have been preserved almost in their original state, do not contain a single depiction of a living being, animal or human.

The original purpose of the building can, aside from the remembrance of Muhammad's night journey and heavenly journey, also be brought into connection with the idea of presenting the new faith in the city of Judaism and Christianity. The establishment of the Dome of the Rock was certainly religiously motivated. By choosing this place, Islam manifested itself as the exclusive inheritor of Judaism and Christianity. The building of the Dome of the Rock was also clearly intended to be a rival of the Church of the Holy Sepulchre and to celebrate the triumph of Islam over Christianity. The Dome therefore had to exceed the Church of the Holy Sepulchre in beauty. The Dome of the Rock thus played a role in the 'symbolic appropriation of the country' by Islam.

The inscriptions betrayed the objective of a clear Islamic message to the Christians. As in so many mosques there is the crucial text: God . . . who has not begotten, and has not been begotten/and equal to Him is not any one' (Qur'an 112: 3). Although the original intention of this passage was directed more at Arab paganism (the idea that God would have children, primarily daughters), it is also read as a denial that God could have a son. Whereas the prophethood of Jesus is emphasised, it denies that he is the 'son of God' (Qur'an 4: 169-71 and 19: 34-37). The phrase 'God has no partner' is repeated five times on the interior of the Dome of the Rock. Also cited is the prayer: 'Pray for your prophet and servant (not son) Jesus.' These texts emphasise the oneness of God.

Jerusalem as the Third 'Holy' City after Mecca and Medina

'Abd al-Malik took a further step in the heightening of the prestige of Jerusalem. It has been suggested that he is to have disallowed Syrians from going on pilgrimages to Mecca out of political considerations, making the pilgrimage (*hajj*) instead to Jerusalem. In this he could have appealed to a tradition of the Prophet Muhammad, in which he is reported to have said that Mecca, Medina and Jerusalem were of the same importance as places of pilgrimage, and even that Jerusalem was the most important. Jerusalem, which can be reached so easily from Damascus, is said to have been presented as an alternative to Mecca and Medina. At present the historicity of this reading is contested. It does not seem right that the Umayyads would have disallowed the pilgrimage to Mecca, given that they themselves also, after all, went on that pilgrimage.

Nevertheless, it is not impossible that the Umayyads played some part in the propagation of the tradition that strengthened the holiness of Jerusalem. The tradition that made Jerusalem a third holy place next to Mecca and Medina stemmed from the 1st century of Islamic reckoning and was generally recognised during the 2nd century. Devout pilgrims made the circumambulation (*tawwaf*) of the Dome of the Rock in Jerusalem. In this circumambulation, for that matter, the pilgrims avoided identifying it with the circumambulation of the Ka'ba. Theologians, who were against this *bida'* (something new that went against the custom or Sunna of Muhammad) felt themselves called to campaign against the ceremonies that the pilgrims practised by the Dome of the Rock.[5]

---

[5] Goldziher, I, *Muslim Studies,* London, 1971, p. 45, nt. 1, and pp. 287, 288.

The Crusades

Under the rule of the Fatimids (909-1171) Jerusalem had to suffer much from the Bedouins. The local problems were overshadowed by the general persecution under Caliph al-Hâkim bi-Amr Allah (996-1021). The apex was the destruction of the Church of the Holy Sepulchre in 1009. Because of his cruelty against the Christians he was sometimes called the 'Egyptian Nero'.[6] After 1038 the church was rebuilt by the Byzantine emperor 'by treaty', but it was forty years before the building was restored.

There were both political and religious reasons for the Crusades. After the defeat of the Byzantine army in 1071 in Asia Minor, Jerusalem fell into the hands of the (Seljuk) Turks, who took Jerusalem from the Fatimids. These events caused panic in Europe, although it was disputed how right and well-founded the fear was. In any case, the Byzantine emperor asked the pope for help in 'liberating' the Holy Land. After the uprising of 1076 the population was murdered. The reconquest of the city in 1096 by the ninth Fatimid caliph al-Musta'lî (1074-1101) was followed on 15 July 1099 by the triumphant entry of the Crusaders.

On 27 November 1995 it was precisely nine hundred years ago that, in Clermont Ferrand (France), Pope Urban II called the people to what would become the First Crusade. The word 'crusade' makes one think of 'taking up of the cross' (cf. Matt. 10: 38). Hearing the pope's summons, many, under the banner of 'God wills it' (*Deus le volt*), travelled in one of at least eight Crusades from Europe to the Holy Land to 'liberate' it from the Muslims. Ultimately, it is only the First Crusade that can be called successful as Jerusalem was conquered. For that matter, it is possible that the pope in his appeal in Clermont Ferrand never mentioned the name Jerusalem. He is also said to have displayed no interest at all in the conversion of the Muslims, although others believe that it was not the case.[7]

The anonymous author of *Gesta Francorum*, a Christian eyewitness of the attack on Jerusalem, wrote:

> Our men followed, killed, and slaughtered even in Solomon's Temple,[8] where the slaughter was so great that our people waded up to their ankles in their blood.[9]

An Islamic historian, Ibn al-Athîr (1160-1233), states concerning the conquest of Jerusalem by the Franks:

---

[6] Atiya, A S (ed.), *Crusade, Commerce and Culture,* New York, 1962, p. 39.

[7] France, J, 'The First Crusade and Islam', *Muslim World* 67, 1977, p. 247. 'It was not until January 13, 1099, that a part of the crusader army, under the command of Raymond of St Gilles, began the long march south to Jerusalem. It was only under intense pressure from the poor and their sympathizers that the count set out, and it may well be that he had no real intention of going to Jerusalem at this stage' (253). Cf. also France, J, 'The First Crusade and the Idea of Conversion', *Muslim World* 58, 1968, pp. 58, 59.

[8] The Crusaders believed the Dome of the Rock to be the temple from the time of Jesus and called it *Templum Domini*. The Aqsa mosque was known as *Templum Salomonis*. These names are often encountered upon old illustrations.

[9] Atiya, 1962, p. 62.

In the *Masjid al-Aqsa* the Franks slaughtered more than 70,000 people, including a few imams and Islamic scholars, devout and ascetic men, who had abandoned their homeland to live in pious isolation in the holy place. The Franks stripped the Dome of the Rock of more than forty silver candelabras, each weighing 3600 drachmas, and a large silver lamp, weighing 44 Syrian pounds, as well as 150 small silver and more than 20 gold candlesticks, and much more booty.[10]

Around this city and the other conquered cities—Tripoli (in what is now Lebanon), Antioch and Edessa (in Turkey)—four states were established which together would form the 'the Latin East.' After a turbulent history the last crusaders were literally driven into the sea in 1291 at Acre (in the north of Israel). The fall of Acre would later be celebrated as a great victory for Islam.

The Nature of the Crusades and the Islamic Reaction to Them

During the first centuries of Islam (the 7th and 8th centuries) one province after another of the Byzantine empire was conquered: Syria, Palestine and Egypt. Islam spread across North Africa, Spain and Sicily. These conquests led to large-scale conversions to Islam. The Crusades between the 11th and 13th centuries can be explained as a counter-attack that was temporarily successful in the 'Holy Land' and more permanently so in Spain because of the *reconquista*.

During the 12th century the 'armed pilgrimages' of European Christians for the defence of the Holy Land were considered to be 'just wars' against the unlawful occupation of the country by the Islamic 'infidels'. The notion of the 'just war' had already been invoked against the Muslims in Spain and Sicily, and even earlier in the Carolingian expeditions against the pagans and Saracens.

The idea of the Crusades did undergo different metamorphoses over the course of time. In the beginning it was practically a collective act of faith, in which Western Christianity attempted to liberate the earthly Jerusalem by the sword, while mysticism desired to reach the heavenly Jerusalem. Although the religious factor did not disappear, a new stage appeared after the conquest and the establishment of the kingdom of Jerusalem.

What had been begun in order to help the Christians ended in inciting the Muslims to a counter-crusade against the whole of Christendom.[11]

Initially, the Muslims had no idea of the *religious* motivation that lay behind the Crusades. The Muslims of Syria, who had to endure the assaults of the Crusaders,

---

[10] Gabrieli, F, *Arab Historians of the Crusades: Selected and Translated from the Arabic Sources,* London, 1969, p. 11.
[11] Atiya, 1962, p. 157.

first thought that the Byzantines (*Rumi*) had again invaded their area. When they realised that this was not the case, they began to call them 'Franks' but never Crusaders! The term 'Franks' was not only intended to refer to those who came from what we today call France but Germans and English people as well.[12] A century later an Arab historian described the first invasion ('crusade') as a part of the general expansion of the Frankish empire that had begun with the conquest of Muslim Spain (*al-Andalus*), Sicily and North Africa.[13] During the two centuries that the Muslims were in close contact with the Franks, they had not developed the least interest in them.[14] With one exception, the Islamic historians did not attempt to connect their story with information about the area from where the Crusaders came and to discover what lay behind this movement.[15]

Characteristic for the situation is that for the term 'crusade' no Arabic equivalent existed in the time that they occurred. The term used now in modern Arabic literature for the Crusades (*Hurub al-salibiyya*) was, remarkably enough, unknown to the Arab authors contemporary with the Crusades. Only in the time of the Turkish Ottomans did this appear to become common currency and only for the first time under the influence of French culture in Christian circles.

Saladin and the Reconquest of Jerusalem and the Consequences

It is astonishing that the conquest of Jerusalem by the Crusaders, lasting decades, did not invoke any strong reaction by the Muslims. This indicates that the Islamic reverence for the Holy City had not yet received the significance it would later receive. However, the Muslims slowly became conscious of the nature of the Christian threat through the establishment of Frankish kingdoms in Islamic territory and the periodic reinforcement by troops from Europe and the invasions.

> The Marquis, the ruler of Tyre, was one of the most cunning and experienced of the Franks, and his was the chief responsibility for, luring the crowds of Crusaders from overseas. He had a picture of Jerusalem painted showing the Church of the Resurrection, . . . Above the tomb the Marquis had a horse painted, and mounted on it a Muslim knight who was trampling the tomb, over which his horse was urinating. This picture was sent abroad to the markets and meeting-places; priests carried it about, clothed in their habits, their heads covered, groaning; 'O the shame!' In this way they raised a huge army, God also knows how many . . .[16]

Primarily in the second half of the 12th century a change in the Islamic

---

[12] Cf. Gabrieli, 1969, pp. 209, 213, 267.

[13] Cf. Gabrieli, J, 'Historiography of the Crusades', in Lewis, B, and Holt, P M (eds.), *Historians of the Middle East,* London, 1962, pp. 98ff.

[14] Watt, W M, *The Influence of Islam on Medieval Europe,* Edinburgh, 1972, p. 81.

[15] Lewis and Holt, 1962, pp. 116, 117.

[16] Gabrieli, 1969, pp. 208-09.

attitude towards the Crusaders came about. The spirit of defeat which reigned in 1099 after the fall of Jerusalem had dissipated. The period of this new approach is connected with the reconquest of Jerusalem. In 1187 Salâh al-Dîn (1137/8-1193), called Saladin in Europe, succeeded in reconquering Jerusalem from the Frankish kingdom. After his victory at Hattîn (July, 1187) Saladin went to Jerusalem. The Islamic historian Ibn al-Athîr tells of the message that the Franks sent:

> They decided to ask for safe conduct from the city and to transfer Jerusalem to Saladin. Saladin's answer was: 'We shall deal with you precisely in the same way as you dealt with the population of Jerusalem, when you occupied it in 492/1099, with murder and slavery and other similar cruelties!'[17]

On 2 October 1187—the day of Muhammad's heavenly journey—the city surrendered upon payment of an agreed ransom.[18]

When the Muslims entered the city on Friday, some of them climbed to the top of the Dome of the Rock to remove the large decorated cross placed there by the Crusaders. When they reached the top a great cry sounded from the city and beyond the walls. In their joy the Muslims called *Allahu akbar* ('God is greater'), the Franks groaned in dismay and sorrow. The cry was so loud and penetrating that the earth shook. Saladin ordered that everything be returned to its former state.[19]

This conquest greatly increased the significance of Jerusalem for Muslims. The city lost its Christian character and traces of the Christian occupation were removed. Many Christians, however, received permission to stay. Only the Eastern Christians (not the European, primarily French) stayed. Jerusalem quickly took on the character of a city dominated by Muslims. The Islamic shrines were given back and many Christian buildings were used for Islamic purposes. The Church of the Holy Sepulchre was given back to the Christians but pilgrimage there was discontinued until 1192. Saladin closed the Church of the Resurrection even as a place of refuge for Christian visitors.

Saladin ordered that the Aqsa Mosque be restored and had it cleaned.[20] In 1187 the Aqsa was rededicated as a mosque. He had the ornamentation of the prayer recess (*mihrab*) and the long inscription of the *qibla* wall re-affixed. A handsome pulpit, *minbar*, was given to the mosque, having been made in Aleppo on the order of Nûr al-Dîn ibn Zangî (1146) for the conquered city, of which he said: 'We have made this in order to place it in Jerusalem.'[21]

As to how important this event of the reconquest of Jerusalem was can be seen from the remark of an Arab historian from the time of the occupation of

---

[17] Gabrieli, 1969, p. 141.
[18] Gabrieli, 1969, p. 142.
[19] Gabrieli, 1969, p. 144.
[20] Gabrieli, 1969, pp. 145, 164.
[21] Gabrieli, 1969, p. 145. The same pulpit was destroyed by fire on 21 August 1969. The fire had been ignited by a Christian from Australia who had lit a fire in the Aqsa Mosque.

Jerusalem by Sultan Saladin. The historian speaks of it as a second *hijra*. According to him, it would be better to date history from this year.[22] For that matter, this reconquest was also very important for the Eastern Christians. It was seen as a significant event in the history of the Copts. For them it made it once again possible to go on pilgrimage to the shrines in Jerusalem, a privilege that had been lost under the Latin government.[23]

The significance Jerusalem received in 12th century Arab literature and Islamic thought is best expressed in a Friday sermon, in which a qadi tells about the retaking of Jerusalem from the Crusaders by Saladin:

> It [Jerusalem] was the dwelling-place of our father Abraham, the place from which your blessed prophet Muhammad rose to heaven; the direction of the prayer (*qiblah*) to which you turn to pray at the beginning of *Islam*, the dwelling-place of the prophets; the place visited by the saintly, the burial place of the messengers [an Islamic burial place east of the *Haram*]: the place where the divine revelation descended and the commandments and prohibitions were sent down; it is the land where humankind will be gathered for the day of judgement; the ground where the resurrection of the dead will occur . . . It is mosque in which the messenger of God performed his prayer and greeted the angels.

The Latin chronicles of the events are unanimous about the chivalry of Saladin, his humanity, and generosity, and the Arab chroniclers emphasise his devotion, justice, asceticism.[24] The Muslims speak of Saladin, 'the liberator (or servant) of Jerusalem' in the following way:

> His city radiated light, his person emanated sweetness, his hand was employed in pouring out the waters of liberality and opening the lips of gifts; the back of his hand was the *qiblah* of kisses and the palm of his hand the *Ka'ba* of hope. [When Saladin died, Baha' ad-Dîn said:] The day of his (Saladin's) death was a day of grief for Islam and the Muslims, the equal of which they had not known since the days of the 'right-guided' caliphs.[25]

The significance of the reconquest of Jerusalem appears from the assertion that the victory of Islam was clear, and was thus the death of unbelief. It was called a striking concurrence that the conquest of Jerusalem was the anniversary of the Prophet's heavenly journey. The world of Islam was ready and adorned for a festival celebrating the fall of Jerusalem. Its merits were illustrated and described and the duty

[22] Khalidi, T, *Arab Historical Thought in the Classical Period*, Cambridge, 1994, p. 182.
[23] Atiya, A S (ed.), *The Coptic Encyclopaedia,* New York, 1991, p. 1536.
[24] Atiya, 1962, p. 80.
[25] Gabrieli, 1969, p. 251.

to visit it explained and precisely reported to everyone.[26]

Islamic Pilgrimage to Jerusalem

The pilgrimage to Jerusalem was not seen so much as a *hajj* but as a visit (*ziyâra*). Books for the purpose of this 'pilgrimage' (*kutub al-ziyârât*) and propaganda writings called *Fadâ'il al-Quds* arose. The latter were a genre that came into being at the beginning of the 11th century.[27] There were originally inhabitants of Jerusalem who praised 'the virtues' of Jerusalem in their books (*Kutub al-Fadâ'il*). In the book *Fadâ'il al-Sham* ('The Virtues of Syria') the claim is defended that Syria (in which Palestine is included) contains nine-tenths of the wealth of the world. It is, moreover, the land of resurrection.[28] The performance of the pilgrimage is no longer considered as limited only to Mecca and Medina: a complete pilgrimage must be extended to the most prominent shrines and graves of the prophets of the two monotheistic religions: Judaism and Christianity. One of the authors claims that a single prayer in Jerusalem—*al-Quds, Bayt al-Maqdis*—is equal to a thousand prayers elsewhere. The conclusion from these works is that the Muslim was obligated not only to visit these places but also to protect and defend them against the Crusaders, who were considered to be 'unbelieving Christians', actual 'pagans' and 'polytheists' whose presence defiled the shrines.[29] The treatments in the *Fadâ'il* make the following distinction: the *hajj* is one of the basic duties of Islam, the visiting of Jerusalem (*ziyâra*) is *recommended*. The order of importance is expressed in the following tradition: 'A prayer in Mecca is equal to two thousand prayers, those in Medina a thousand, and in Jerusalem five hundred.'[30]

Jihad *for Jerusalem*

As a consequence of the Crusades, there arose in the time of Saladin certain books which glorified the merits of Jerusalem and Palestine, literature (poetry) in which the *jihad* ('holy war') was praised. The Christian propaganda for the Crusades in the West met an Islamic counter-propaganda for the *jihad* in the East. It was the 'wars of the cross' that awakened the slumbering spirit of the *jihad*. One of the important consequences of the Crusades was the rediscovery of the old theme of *jihad*. This new consciousness came to expression in the development of a propaganda intended to mobilise Islamic troops in a jihad against the 'infidels.' In 1144 it was the prince of Mosul/Aleppo, Zangî, who said after the conquest of Edessa from the Franks that the foremost goal of the war was Jerusalem. He was the first who spoke clearly of the necessity of liberating the city and gave it a primary place in the *jihad*. His son and

[26] Gabrieli, 1969, pp. 156, 160, 161
[27] Cf. Sivan, 1967, pp. 152, 153, 157f.
[28] Atiya, 1962, p. 134.
[29] Atiya, 1962, p. 133.
[30] Sivan, 1967, p. 68.

successor Nûr al-Dîn (d. 1174) would discharge the task further. His express goal was, he declared in a letter to the caliph, to banish the worshippers of the cross from the Aqsa Mosque and to conquer Jerusalem.[31] The topic of *'jihad* for Jerusalem' was developed and with Saladin, who took over the spiritual inheritance of Nâr al-Dîn, reached its apex,[32] Al-Yunînî (d. 1326), a religious scholar and historian, saw the attack upon Acre not as purely a war between the armies of the sultan and the Christian West but as something that involved the whole Islamic community. In the mosque in Damascus, the Friday prayer was given as the summons for conquest. Al Yunînî appears to have considered the attack upon Acre as a true *jihad*.[33] Jihad was quickly seen by Islamic jurists and commentators almost as a sixth pillar of Islam.[34]

The Muslim fighter for the faith, the *mujahid*, should unite the believers in a 'holy war' to drive the soldiers of the cross from the Holy Places. The *jihad* was propagated in a way comparable with the role the mass media plays today in the stimulation of war. The theme was also presented at the time in the preaching in the mosque. In modern Arab poetry a high place is still accorded to Saladin, 'the hero and liberator of Islam' in the 12th century. Walîd Khâlidî, a member of a well-known Islamic family from Jerusalem, speaks somewhere of *al-Quds* as 'a magnet': 'Jerusalem drew on every romantic legend and tradition and was the pivot of popular religious consciousness.'

One of the consequences of the establishment of the Crusaders in Palestine was that there was a major refugee problem. The majority of the non-Christians fled to Syria, Egypt, and some even fled to Khûrasân. The refugees played a prominent role during the 12th and succeeding centuries in their new cultural environment, as well as in political affairs (as in Egypt). The medieval Islamic biographies refer to a large number of scholars who originally came from Palestine. These scholars provided a major contribution to the area of tradition (*hadith*), law (*fiqh*), grammar, *belles lettres,* poetics and music. The refugees contributed also in the area of the military.[35]

Conclusion

If one surveys history, it becomes clear that political conflicts have influenced religion. The Crusades, which themselves emerged from religious as well as social and political motivations, have undoubtedly contributed to the increase in the significance of Jerusalem for Muslims. In our time as well, one sees interaction between religion and politics. Thus the fire in the Aqsa Mosque in 1969 became the occasion for holding a top *Islamic* conference in Casablanca (Morocco).

In the preceding, a fair amount of attention has been devoted to the role of

---

[31] Sivan, pp. 154, 155, 157.

[32] Atiya, 1962, p. 80; Sivan, 1967, p. 159.

[33] D'Souza, A, 'The Conquest of 'Akka (690/1291)', *Muslim World* 80, 1990, pp. 239-40.

[34] Atiya, 1962, p. 131. (Islam knows five pillars: the creed, the prayer, the giving of alms, fasting and pilgrimage.)

[35] Dajani-Shakeel, H, 'Displacement of the Palestinians During the Crusades', *Muslim World* 68, 1979, pp. 158, 173-75.

the Crusades on the Islamic significance of Jerusalem. In certain Islamic, and particularly fundamentalist, circles, the colonial period is spoken of as a second Crusade period. Sayyid Qutb, the well-known ideologue of the Muslim Brothers in Egypt, who was executed by President Gamal 'Abd al-Nasser, quoted a story too well known to the Arab East:

> General Allenby was nothing more than typical for the habit of mind of all Europe when he entered Jerusalem during the First World War and said: 'Now the Crusades have come to an end.'[36]

After the outbreak of the Gulf Crisis, a mufti from Amman even declared in August 1990 that the *third* period of the Crusades had begun. Such expressions are congruent with those uttered by Muslims who have spoken of Westerners and Christians as 'Crusaders' as such. The term *salîbi* (Crusader) then means Christian in general and *al-salibiyyah* is used as a reference for Christianity and the modern West. The idea of the Crusades has for centuries been the pivot of the struggle between East and West, Islam and Christianity. Modern colonialism is seen as a new disguise of the notion of Crusades to destroy Islam.[37]

'Crusaders' is not, however, only intended to refer to Christians but also to Jews. The Muslim Brothers in Egypt speak in connection with the struggle with the Zionists, even of a 'Jewish Crusade.' Terms such as European Crusades *(al-salibiyya al-urabiyya)* and Jewish Crusades *(al-salabiyya al-yahudiyya)* are used interchangeably.[38] That is, of course, absurd, considering the history of the term and that of the Jews themselves in Europe. It indicates both in the present as well as in the past how conflicts between East and West lead to a 'fundamentalisation' and polarisation of the mutual religious relations.[39]

This misuse of religion can also be counteracted whenever, and to the degree to which, political solutions are found. Even the conflict-filled history of the Crusades shows examples of this. On the one hand, Europeans (at the instigation of Pope Innocent III) who believed that 'the cross' alone could triumph through the sword, waged war against the Islamic 'infidels' while the brother of Saladin, Al-'Âdil al-Sayf, the sultan of Egypt and Syria (1200-1218), conducted a *jihad*. On the other hand, we hear that the conditions in the Levant, following the Third Crusade, taught a new lesson to the Christian Prince Henry of Champagne, King Aimery of Jerusalem (1198-1205), and the Musilm al-Kamîl (1218-1238), the same who had the famous meeting with Francis of Assisi (!), a lesson that each of them attempted to pass on to their successors, namely that a continuous conflict between both sides would be mutually destructive. *Negotiations* could, in contrast, prevent much unnecessary bloodshed. This policy was supported by Italian merchants, because it led to much economic and social advantages. This formula stimulated the growth of

---

[36] Mitchell, T, *The Society of the Muslim Brothers,* London, 1969, pp. 229-30.
[37] Cited by Smith, W C, *Islam in Modern History*, Princeton, 1957, p. 106.
[38] Mitchell, 1969, p. 229.
[39] Lewis and Holt, 1962, p. 148.

Egypt and Syria during the beginning of the 13th century.[40]

The occasion for the current attention for Jerusalem in Israel—the foundation by King David, which primarily emphasises the connectedness of Jews with the city—can also be the occasion for the creation of a sphere of claims and counter-claims. But that can also be used for the creation of a sphere in which there is opportunity for the respecting of one another's feelings with respect to this 'Holy City' and the finding of political solutions by negotiations. It is good to know why Jews, Christians and Muslims—and in particular Israelis and Palestinians—feel connected to the city of Jerusalem. The causes of the enmity must be recognised and hopefully dismantled, so that the cohabitation of Jews, Christians, and Muslims in Jerusalem will not remain an eschatological hope.

---

[40] Nierman, J H, 'Levantine Peace Following the Third Crusade: A New Dimension in Frankish-Muslim Relations', *Muslim World* 65, 1975, p. 118.

13
JESUS AND JERUSALEM:
NEW TESTAMENT PERSPECTIVES
Peter Walker

> *O Jerusalem, Jerusalem! Would that you knew today*
> *the things that belong to your peace! (Luke 19: 41)*

To assess the proper significance of Jerusalem within scripture, Christian history and
contemporary politics is a mammoth undertaking. In this paper a contribution to this
task will be offered through focusing expressly on Jesus and the New Testament
writers. Can we discern their attitude towards Jerusalem? If so, how should it
influence our thinking today?

In principle, for Christians of all persuasions, such a focus should be a primary
concern. Even if some deny the New Testament a position of ultimate authority, the
vast majority would acknowledge that it is necessarily foundational for constructing
a Christian theology. Yet a good case could be made for suggesting that Christians
on both sides of the current controversy (whether they identify with West or with
East Jerusalem) have been failing to give it the attention that it deserves.[1]

Christian Palestinians in particular need to know whether the New Testament
supports Christian Zionism. This latter position works on the assumption that
Jerusalem retains to this day the theological role that it held in the Old Testament
period, that promises associated with 'Zion' may at last be fulfilled in our own
generation, and that the Jewish people have a natural, even divine, right to the city.
In this paper it will be argued that the New Testament gives no endorsement to this
whole construction. Instead the New Testament bears witness to an important and
dramatic shift within God's purposes. The continuity is broken. Thus, those who
seek to be guided in their thinking by the whole of the biblical witness, must read
the Old Testament in a distinctively Christian way, in other words, in the light of the
New Testament.

The case for this New Testament re-evaluation of Jerusalem has been argued
at a scholarly level elsewhere.[2] In their different ways, all the major New Testament

---

[1] Some reasons for this will be noted below in section 3.

[2] See my forthcoming, *The Holy City: New Testament Perspectives on Jerusalem* (Eerdmans, Nov.
1996). The seven major contributors to the New Testament are covered in Chapters 1 to 7.
The arguments presented in this present paper are argued in more detail in the final Chapter
8. The most obvious texts for observing this re-evaluation of Jerusalem are Galatians 4: 25,
Hebrews 12-13, Revelations 11: 8 and the whole treatment of Jerusalem in Luke and Acts.
All biblical references taken from New International Version.

writers offer a new understanding of Jerusalem as a result of the coming of Jesus: they see it as the former holy city which has now opposed God's purposes in Jesus, its Temple as effectively redundant, and its role within Israel's prophetic hopes as now fulfilled in her Messiah. The restoration for which many longed has indeed come to pass, but in a most surprising way.

It is argued here that this critique of Jerusalem is rooted in the teaching of Jesus himself and that this whole new understanding of the nature of God's purposes is validated by the Resurrection. In other areas of theology (such as the inclusion of the gentiles within God's people, or the revelation of God as Trinity) Christians are familiar with the fact that the New Testament, for all its inherent continuity with the Old Testament, also reveals new truths about the purposes and nature of God. In those instances too, this shift in understanding is legitimated by appealing to the teaching of Jesus and the far-reaching implications of the Resurrection. The same applies here.

Thus those who would wish to argue that the geographical entities of the Old Testament (most importantly, the Temple, the City and the Land) retain precisely the same significance as they had before the coming of Christ are, we suggest, failing to note the radical consequences of Jesus' Resurrection and the authority which Jesus possessed to move the scriptural tradition into new paths. On one hand, Jesus clearly identified with the Jewish assumptions about the Old Testament's authority (and therefore about Jerusalem as having been the central place within God's purposes up till that time). Yet, at the same time, he took that tradition in a new direction which was yet paradoxically, so he claimed, its true fulfilment. Thus it is Jesus himself, we suggest, who gives us the warrant to view Jerusalem in an entirely new light.

Jesus and Jerusalem

How then did Jesus view Jerusalem? For ease of presentation this enormous question is dealt with here under seven headings.[3] In the light of the above, it will be noted in what follows that one of the common threads will be the way in which Jesus simultaneously both affirms and subverts the Jewish tradition of his day.

Jesus the Palestinian Jew: Affirmation but Subversion
Jesus clearly identified in principle with his contemporaries' longings for God to act on behalf of his people. He also affirmed the authoritative validity of the Old Testament. This would necessarily have included the scriptural assumptions concerning Jerusalem. He described it as the 'city of the great king' (Matthew 5: 35) and its Temple as his 'Father's house.' The centrality which Jerusalem had in Jesus'

---

[3] Frequent reference is made to the works of Tom Wright. His various articles and books are to be highly recommended, especially his chapter entitled 'Jerusalem in the New Testament' in Walker, P W L (ed.), *Jerusalem Past and Present in the Purposes of God,* Paternoster Press, UK, 1994.

ministry reflected a real centrality which the city had had within God's whole purposes towards Israel and thereby to the world. Thus he had no hesitation in correcting the Samaritan woman's preference for Mt Gerizim: Jerusalem had indeed been the 'place where one must worship.' (John 4: 20, 22).

Yet in that same conversation he indicated that something new was about to take place ('a time is coming and has now come'), something which was integrally related to the arrival of his own person and which would have a 'levelling effect' on Jerusalem: 'you will worship the Father neither on this mountain nor in Jerusalem' (4: 21). Jesus evidently believed he lived in a time when dramatic changes were afoot and indeed that his own coming would have significant consequences for Jerusalem.

Jesus The Prophet: 'Judgement Is Coming'

In the Synoptic Gospels Jesus frequently warns the nation of Israel that it was now entering upon an unparalleled era of judgement, that a disaster was coming, and that Jerusalem would itself soon be destroyed. This 'threat-tradition,' whilst open to the charge of being invented *post eventum*, is increasingly being accepted as an integral part of Jesus' message.[4] It is also plain that, whilst these warnings of judgement have applications in any generation, their primary reference was originally towards the regime of Jesus' own day which was centred on Jerusalem.[5] Moreover, the scholarly temptation to dismiss these warnings as needlessly anti-Semitic fails to note that within Jewish sectarianism pronouncing judgement upon the present regime was not unusual, and that this in turn drew upon an accepted tradition of such criticism in the canonical prophets.

> On the contrary, it was a sign of deep loyalty to Israel's true God, and to deep distress at the corruption which seemed endemic in the national life. Jesus' solemn announcements were completely in place within the world of first-century inner-Jewish polemic.[6]

Thus Jesus pronounced upon Jerusalem and the Temple: 'Behold your house is left to you desolate' (Luke 13: 35); 'The days will come upon you when your enemies will build an embankment against you and hem you in on every side . . .' (Luke 19: 41-44). 'Not one of them will be left on another; every one of them will be thrown down' (Luke 21: 6). 'The time will come when you will say, "Blessed are the barren women" . . .' (Luke 23: 29 ff). Jesus made it quite plain that a significant act of God was about to take place, encompassing Jerusalem and its Temple.

Jesus the Critic: 'You Slay the Prophets'

Why did Jesus announce this coming judgement upon Jerusalem? Throughout the Gospels there are clear indications that Jesus was pinpointing some specific failures in

---

[4] See e.g. Borg, M J, 'Conflict, Holiness and Politics' in *The Teachings of Jesus,* Edwin Mellen Press, New York, 1984.
[5] See N T Wright, 'Jesus, Israel and the Cross', *SBL Seminar Papers,* 1985, pp. 78-83.
[6] N T Wright, *Jesus and the Victory of God,* (forthcoming, SPCK), chapter 8.

Jerusalem. Not for nothing was he compared to Jeremiah (Matthew 16: 14), who had similarly announced the impending destruction of the city because of its departure from God's true purposes. History had repeated itself and Jerusalem could now be described ironically as the place which characteristically 'slew the prophets and stoned those sent to her' (Luke 13: 34). Indeed, in a vivid use of maternal imagery, she is then portrayed by Jesus in this verse as behaving to her 'children' like a false mother, luring them away from the safety which Jesus claimed could be found under his 'wings' alone. If Jesus truly represents Israel's God then Jerusalem, in keeping its children from accepting his embrace, was effectively acting against God's purposes and functioning thereby as an idol.

Jesus' interaction with the Temple authorities likewise reveals some important criticism of the current regime; the incident in the Temple speaks in different ways of the false practices which are debarring true worship from being offered there, and the cursing of the fig tree implies that such worship is in fact barren in God's sight. The 'tenants' clearly are no longer concerned with the master's business. Jerusalem would therefore be judged for the way it was opposing God's purposes.

Jesus the Political Realist: the Invincibility of Rome

Yet, looked at from a quite different point of view, this announcement of judgement was in part a simple piece of *Realpolitik,* a straightforward calculation of what would soon happen if the Jewish people continued to foster rebellion against Rome:

> . . . it did not take much political wisdom to extrapolate forwards and to suggest that, if Israel continued to provoke the giant, the giant would eventually awake from slumber and smash her to pieces.[7]

If Jerusalem became the focus for an independent Jewish nationalism, it would lose. Many of his contemporaries longed for the over-throwing of the pagan yoke, but Jesus warned that this would not bring about the salvation that they hoped. Indeed down that road lay disaster.

Jesus' Self-Claim: 'Destroy *this* Temple'

The Gospels are shot through with Jesus' audacious claims for his own person: the long-awaited Messiah anointed by God, the 'Son of Man,' the true 'King of Zion'. All of these are vitally significant for understanding the relationship between Jesus and Jerusalem. Yet of particular importance are those claims of Jesus which show his unique relationship with the Jerusalem Temple.

As with the *city* of Jerusalem (above), there is no denial of the significance of the *Temple* in the past. Jesus can apply to this Herodian Temple the words of Yahweh in Isaiah referring to the Temple of that earlier period as 'my house' (Isaiah 56: 7 in Mark 11: 17); indeed he says it is 'my Father's house' (John 2: 16). Yet he clearly

---

[7] *Ibid.*

predicts its forthcoming destruction, without suggesting (as popular understandings of the Messiah's role would have expected him to say) that this destruction would be followed by a more splendid Temple of the last days. Yet in addition to the reasons offered above for this forthcoming judgement, it is clear that the removal of this Herodian temple has something to do with the arrival of Jesus.

First, Jesus now claims to be the *locus* of divine forgiveness. Previously, the official, divinely-sanctioned means of forgiveness was through the appointed Temple sacrifices. Jesus, however, quotes the dictum of Hosea 6.6 (Matthew 9: 13; 12: 7): 'I desire mercy, not sacrifice.' He shocks the assembled 'teachers of the law' by declaring to the paralytic that 'the Son of Man has authority on earth to forgive sins' (Mark 2: 10). He declares to the surprised crowds around Zacchaeus' house, 'today, this man is a son of Abraham!' (Luke 19: 9).

> If one was with Jesus, one did not need the restoration into covenant membership which was normally attained by going to Jerusalem and offering sacrifices in the temple. The force of such sentences is lost unless it is realised that, in making such pronouncements, Jesus was implicitly claiming *to do and be what the temple was and did* . . . His offering of forgiveness and restoration undercut the normal system; in modern terms, it had the force of a private individual offering a passport, thus bypassing the accredited office. Jesus was offering just such a bypass.[8]

Secondly, Jesus was making the claim to be the focus of the divine presence. Previously, the Jerusalem Temple had been the place of the Divine Name, the place of the *Shekinah* glory, portraying symbolically God's presence *with* his people. Jesus now appropriated this language to himself. 'One greater than the Temple is here' (Matthew 12: 6). 'When two or three come together in my name, there am I with them' (Matthew 18: 20). 'I am with you always to the end of the age' (Matthew 28: 20).

> It is not enough to say, within a normal Western-Christian mode of thought, that he was 'claiming to be God.' What he was claiming to do was to act as the replacement of the temple, which was of course the dwelling-place of the *Shekinah*, the tabernacling of God with his people.
> When Jesus came to Jerusalem he came embodying a counter system. He and the city were both making claims to be the place where the living God was at work to heal, restore and regroup his people. Though many people still say that the Old Testament had no idea of incarnation, this is clearly a mistake: the temple itself, and by extension Jerusalem, was seen as the dwelling-place of the living God. Thus it was the Temple that Jesus took as his model, and against

---

[8] N T Wright in P W L Walker (ed.), 1994, p. 58.

whose claim he advanced his own.[9]

The Johannine presentation of Jesus as the true 'tabernacle' (John 1: 14) and the new 'temple' (2: 19 ff) is therefore quite in keeping with the enormous claims found within the Synoptic Gospels. In Jesus' person the reality to which the Temple pointed forward was revealed. John's interpretation of Jesus' cryptic statement, 'destroy this temple and I will raise it in three days' (John 2: 19; cf., e.g., Mark 14: 58) is therefore far from fanciful. In this brilliant aphorism (remembered but misunderstood by his accusers at his trial) Jesus was simultaneously indicating both the forthcoming destruction of the physical Jerusalem and his own Resurrection, the raising of the quite different 'temple of his body' (2: 21). He was also indicating that there was some integral connection between these two events. Inevitably the appearance of Jesus, and especially his resurrection, spelt the end of the Temple. Jerusalem could never be the same again, now that Jesus had come.

Jesus' Resurrection: the Prophesied 'Restoration'

Jesus' contemporaries were longing for the 'redemption of Jerusalem' (Luke 2: 38; cf. v. 25). Some of the Jewish people had indeed returned after the Babylonian exile in the 6th century BC, but this hardly matched the extravagant promises of 'restoration' in the exilic prophets. Surely something more was in store? These prophetic hopes then fuelled the political Jewish nationalism that was prevalent from the time of the Hasmoneans through to the era of the New Testament.

Jesus, however, criticised such political and religious nationalism and pointed to a quite different way in which the scriptural promises would be fulfilled. In speaking of his own 'rising on the third day' as being in accordance with the scriptures (Luke 24: 46), he was almost certainly alluding to Hosea 6: 2, which had spoken of Israel's being 'revived' and 'restored'. In other words, Jesus was claiming that his Resurrection was the true fulfilment of that restoration hope: 'the resurrection of Christ is the resurrection of Israel of which the prophets spoke.'[10] The divine vindication had come! Yet it had not been for Jerusalem in some form of restoration, but rather for Jesus himself in his Resurrection. The exile was over! Yet it had been accomplished not through a political Messiah (as many supposed) but through a suffering Messiah who had entered into the divine judgement and then emerged victorious. In a mysterious way, as the 'Son of Man' who was the true representative of Israel and embodied her destiny, Jesus had taken Israel down into death, fulfilling her role as the 'suffering servant' and experiencing her judgement, and had then been restored to life on the third day. In this way, that judgement could be removed, Israel 'restored' and the exile truly brought to an end.

Jesus and Jerusalem: a Clash of Identities

The location of the passion within Jerusalem is therefore no accident. Only here

---

[9] *Ibid.*, p. 66.
[10] Dodd, G H, *According to the Scriptures*, James Nisbet, UK, 1961, p. 103.

could Jesus make good his Messianic claim; only here could he claim to be Zion's true king; only here could he demonstrate his unique relationship to the Temple; only here, at Israel's heart, could he with integrity make his prophetic denouncement of Israel and its leaders; only here could he address four-squarely the issue of Jewish nationalism and its ultimate political consequences; only here could he reveal himself as the true representative both of Israel and of Israel's God; only here could he point his contemporaries beyond Jerusalem and demonstrate the new loyalty that would now be required of them. Then (as now) the identity of Jesus could thus only be understood when set in a vital relation to Jerusalem and all that it stood for.

And so the city associated with God in times past would now reject him who was God's true representative, 'not knowing the hour of its visitation' (Luke 19: 44), thereby failing in its fundamental destiny and proving itself not the herald of God's purposes in the world but rather an obstacle to those purposes. Jerusalem would therefore be destroyed, but Jesus would be vindicated even though first he would taste on the cross the very judgement which he had predicted against the city.[11]

In all these ways one senses not just Jesus' historical critique of the city, but a fundamental and inherent clash between Jesus and Jerusalem at the level of their deepest identities. They stood for opposing things. Or rather, Jesus was now offering in reality what Jerusalem had only offered in shadow, and which now she was failing to offer. Jesus, not Jerusalem, would now become the central 'place' within God's purposes, the place around which God's true people would be gathered.

New Testament Reverberations

The shock waves and reverberations of these unique, dramatic events in Jerusalem can then be felt in the pages of the New Testament. Given the enormity of the changes that were afoot, we may reasonably suppose that it may have taken a little while for the full ramifications to be understood and for the ripples to settle down.

Restorations

From the evidence in Acts it is clear, for example, that the issue of 'restoration' was not immediately understood. This was a critical issue for 1st century Jews. Not surprisingly therefore, when Jesus shows signs of departing, this is the question at the top of their list: 'Lord, are you at this time going to restore the kingdom to Israel?' (Acts 1: 6-8). They presume the Messiah will now finish his appointed work and give Israel that political independence for which she longs.

> Jesus' answer is usually taken as a 'not yet': 'it is not for you to know times and seasons.' Yet Luke surely intends us to read it as a 'yes, but not in that way': 'you will receive power . . . and you will be my witness . . . to the end of the world.'[12]

---

[11] See further, N T Wright, 1985.
[12] N T Wright, in P W L Walker (ed.), 1994, p. 68.

The way in which the Messiah will exert his rule will not be through Israel's independence, but rather through the proclamation of his Gospel throughout the world.

When the force of Pentecost was then unleashed upon the Church, the disciples' understanding of 'restoration' might have shifted to a belief that vast numbers of Jewish people would acknowledge Jesus as their Messiah. Yet this too proved an unfulfilled hope. When the gentiles began to flood the Church, this would inevitably have raised major questions: was not the 'ingathering of the nations' in popular Jewish hope only meant to occur *after* Israel's restoration? Yet clearly the Jewish people were not yet (in this revised sense) 'restored'. The apostles then met in Jerusalem to discuss this issue, where James gave the definitive ruling. What is significant is that he justifies the entering of the gentiles into the Church by appealing to Amos 9: 11-12, a text which had to do with Israel's restoration (Acts 15: 13-21)! As Chris Wright says,

> The considered apostolic interpretation of events was that the inclusion of the gentiles . . . was the necessary fulfilment of the prophesied restoration of Israel.[13]

In other words, the apostles abandoned their earlier beliefs that Israel's restoration consisted in either political independence or in their coming en masse to faith in Jesus. Instead they now realised that the inclusion of the gentiles, being seen as the 'ingathering of the nations,' signified that, in a profound sense, Israel must evidently *already have been restored in Jesus*.

Thus although they were faced with the very same Old Testament passages as we are today, the New Testament writers did not reach a 'Zionist' conclusion. Instead they reached a distinctively Christian conclusion which affirmed the faithfulness of God to his ancient promises and saw these as now fulfilled, even if in an unexpected way, in the coming of Jesus. Biblical Christians today need to follow their lead. To do otherwise, either denying this fulfilment in Jesus, or seeking for a further, more literalistic fulfilment belittles and misconstrues the greatness of what God has done in Jesus and is ultimately derogatory to the person of Jesus and his uniqueness.

The Temple

Concerning the Temple there is similarly an evident development of understanding within the New Testament period. Despite Jesus' clear predictions concerning its forthcoming demise, it was entirely natural for the first Christians to use this central location (as Jesus himself had done) for teaching and proclaiming the new message of the kingdom (Acts 3 ff). As Nineveh had repented, thus averting the prophesied disaster, so might Jerusalem. And even if commanded to take the message to the 'ends of the earth' Jesus had also clearly called them to be 'his witness in Jerusalem' (Acts 1: 8). Thus, even if the main apostolic band gradually dispersed from Jerusalem, those

---

[13] C J H Wright, in P W L Walker (ed.), 1994, p. 16.

around James felt called to maintain this witness to Jerusalem as long as possible, a policy which inevitably required them to be as loyal to the Temple institution as was reasonably possible. Yet their situation became increasingly untenable and they revealed their ultimate loyalties when at the outbreak of the Jewish Revolt they abandoned the city for refuge in Pella.

The writer of Hebrews, writing to a group of Christians who similarly felt a great instinctive loyalty to the ways of Judaism (albeit probably not in Jerusalem, but most likely in Rome) then makes it plain how Christians should view the Jerusalem Temple. Writing before 70 AD, whilst Jerusalem and its Temple are still standing, he is yet able to see that Christ's death is the fulfilment of the Temple sacrificial system. The whole thrust of his argument is that involvement with rituals which are indebted to this Temple system is strictly now incompatible with their new Christian calling (13: 9-14), an argument with which the inheritors of James' stance might well have found themselves in agreement, albeit reluctantly.

At least fifteen year previously, Paul too had understood the Temple in quite a new way: speaking to his gentile converts in Corinth he boldly declared: 'God's Temple is sacred and you are that Temple' (1 Corinthians 3: 17).

> When Paul used such an image within twenty-five years of the crucifixion (with the actual Temple still standing), it is a striking index of the immense change that has taken place in his thought, the Temple had been superseded by the Church.[14]

That such re-thinking was taking place while the Temple was still standing also led to knotty anomalies in practice. Paul believed that through the Gospel the 'dividing wall of hostility' had been broken down in Christ (Ephesians 2: 14); yet that 'dividing-wall' still stood in Jerusalem and when he entered the Temple he had to leave his gentile converts behind (despite the false charges on this score that were subsequently made against him (Acts 21: 28-9)). Such ambiguities must have fuelled in the apostles a sense that they were living in a strange, interim period: Jesus had predicted the end of the Temple, but as yet its services were continuing unabated. When at last Jesus' words were fulfilled, those anomalies came to an end and the conclusions already advanced by Paul, Hebrews and others were vindicated and laid the foundation for how the Church should understand the Temple.

The Temple was therefore *passé*, and there was no expectation or desire that a further 'third' Temple should be built. Some of the prophecies in Ezekiel (Chapters 40-48) might have fuelled such a hope (then as now), but the New Testament writers clearly saw this prophecy as fulfilled in the person of Jesus (John 7: 37-9) and then in the 'New Jerusalem' (Revelations 21-22), where paradoxically there would be 'no Temple', precisely because (again) Jesus as the 'lamb' was its Temple (Revelations 21: 22)!

From the Earthly Jerusalem to the Heavenly

Another way in which the Spirit led the apostolic generation 'into all truth' (John

---

[14] N T Wright, *ibid.,* p. 70.

14: 26) can be seen in their increased focus on the 'heavenly Jerusalem', something which according to the Gospel accounts Jesus did not specifically address. The combination of the painful experience of being 'dispersed' under pressure of persecution from Jerusalem, whilst seeing how gentiles although far removed from Jerusalem could respond to the Gospel and receive the Spirit, will have further led to a playing down of the practical significance of the earthly Jerusalem. God's purposes had evidently moved out from the 'particular' to the 'universal' and in many ways Jerusalem was now proving to be a bastion of opposition to the message of Jesus. Thus in Galatians (probably his earliest letter) Paul could speak of Jerusalem being 'in slavery with her children' (an amazing statement from one for whom Jerusalem had been his *alma mater*!). Instead Christians were to focus on the 'Jerusalem above' (Galatians 4: 25-26).

The author of Hebrews similarly focused on the 'heavenly Jerusalem', the place where Jesus now reigned and to which all his followers were ultimately called (Hebrews 12: 22-4). This, not the earthly Jerusalem, was to be the core of their identity and the object of their hopes. The earthly Jerusalem was the place which had rejected Jesus and was continuing to be dismissive of his followers. Yet, in powerful imagery based on the Passion narrative, he urged his readers: 'let us go out to him outside the camp, bearing the disgrace he bore. For here we do not have a lasting city, but we are looking for the city that is to come' (Hebrews 13: 13-14). The earthly Jerusalem was to be left behind; the focus was to be on the heavenly, 'enduring' city.

Such thinking comes to its final, canonical fruition in the closing chapters of Revelation where the end of human history is described in terms of the 'New Jerusalem, coming down out of heaven from God' (Revelations 21: 2, 10). This is decidedly not the old, earthly Jerusalem elevated onto a higher plain, but on the contrary a quite 'new' city built by God.

Yet the fact that the city is called 'Jerusalem' indicated that the apostles could sense that, despite the enormous changes brought about for the earthly Jerusalem by the coming of Christ, there was an underlying continuity to God's purposes. Even if the Old Testament prophecies concerning Jerusalem had not met with a political fulfilment in Jesus, there was still a sense in which God would honour that prophetic vision of Jerusalem's glory when he brought in the 'new heavens and the new earth' (Revelations 21: 1). The promise did not evaporate into thin air and was not simply 'spiritualised', but would come into its fullest reality at the ultimate end of time. The visions of Isaiah and Ezekiel were not null and void, but instead were affirmed and given an authoritative interpretation.

Conclusions

Despite differences in experience and expression, the witness of the New Testament on this theme of Jerusalem and the Temple forms an impressive unity. Taking their lead from the teaching of Jesus and led by his Spirit to further reflection, they concur that a dramatic shift has occurred in the light of the coming of Jesus.

Thus the Temple is rendered redundant by him who in his person brings the fullness of God's incarnate presence and by his death offers himself as the ultimate sacrifice; and because of the divine presence of the Holy Spirit his followers from a spiritual Temple. In accordance with Jesus' prediction the Temple comes to an end. Meanwhile with regard to the city of Jerusalem, the rejection of Jesus and his followers belies the city's claim to be 'holy' (Matthew 27: 53). The Christian's focus is therefore instead on the 'Jerusalem above' (Galatians 4: 26). Moreover, the future expectation of the New Testament writers did not include some end-times rebuilding of the Temple or a 'restoration' of Jerusalem, precisely because in Jesus that Temple has been revealed and that restoration accomplished.

Jerusalem Today

In all these ways it becomes clear that within the New Testament Jerusalem has lost its distinctively sacred character. This is an important message which those in both West and East Jerusalem today may be inclined to ignore. On the one side, those sympathetic to modern Israel tend to miss the critical reflection of the New Testament writers, and in particular fail to observe the significant 'twist' which Jesus gave to the whole issue of Jerusalem and its role in prophecy. On the other, those sympathetic to the Palestinian cause may understandably react by being dismissive of the Old Testament, or, alternatively, by giving to Jerusalem a theological status which is unwarranted by the New Testament. The New Testament stands as a corrective to both.

It is important to note immediately, that this is not the same thing as denying the validity of Christian memory and tradition. Because of what transpired there (the Incarnation, Resurrection) Jerusalem is unique, and the historic churches have rightly sought to maintain a Christian presence and witness there throughout the last 2000 years. For reasons of religious association, Jerusalem can never be viewed straight forwardly 'as any other city'.

What it does mean, however, is that exalted *theological* claims for Jerusalem (whereby it is assumed that Jerusalem necessarily has some exalted position in God's sight) may be specious, and may be being used to serve other, more human agendas. The most obvious of these is Zionism, and the above analysis serves chiefly as a rebuttal of *that* position. Yet the argument 'cuts both ways,' calling into question all attempts to give Jerusalem a status which ultimately may lack scriptural authority.[15]

Briefly stated, if the New Testament raises questions about Jerusalem's sanctity or 'sacredness', it cannot deny its 'specialness'. This distinction may seem slight, but it may be of crucial importance. For in any debate it is always good to have the New Testament on one's side. Moreover, such a stance (rightly understood) leads not to a disengagement from the Jerusalem issue but rather to a proper engagement with it. For many of the issues in Jerusalem, if they occurred anywhere else in the world,

---

[15] For a preliminary discussion of how Palestinian Christians may think about Jerusalem in the present, see Naim Ateek in P W L Walker (ed.), *Jerusalem Past and Present in the Purposes of God,* Second Edition, 1995, pp. 125-154.

would be recognised as straightforward issues of justice and of humanity. Seeing Jerusalem for what it is, enables Christians to see more clearly that these should be the issues in Jerusalem too.

Moreover, it means that the appeal to Jerusalem's uniqueness does not become the basis for some 'special pleading' in which God's universal concerns for righteousness, mercy, love and promotion of his Gospel are somehow swept aside as though here God has some quite different agenda. This is important, since belief in the 'sacred' nature of Jerusalem can fuel the conviction that God's purposes here might somehow be different elsewhere. There are no 'special rules' for Jerusalem. The supposed 'sacredness' of Jerusalem may blind people to their ethical responsibilities; by contrast, acknowledging Jerusalem's specialness (its centrality in biblical history) should have the opposite effect. Here, above all, it would be ironic if the biblical message went unheeded, but so appropriate if it was obeyed.[16]

Epilogue

In conclusion, it is appropriate to ask what, to many, might seem like an impossible question. If in the Book of Revelation, the Risen Christ reveals his attitude to the seven churches (Chapters 2-3), is it possible on the basis of the Gospels to detect what the Risen Christ might think of Jerusalem? The following questions might provoke such further thought.

1   It was in the city that Jesus prayed for unity amongst his followers (John 17). Amidst the necessary and treasured diversity of our historic traditions, what level of unity does Christ observe today in his Church in Jerusalem?

2   In Luke 21 Jesus looked beyond Jerusalem to the end times and warned of those who might claim 'in his name' to know it all and have a watertight eschatological timetable. In what ways does the same phenomenon occur today in Jerusalem? In what ways do people claim the name of Jesus for things which he would disown?

3   In Luke 23 he intimated that his own sufferings were integrally connected to those of Jerusalem. What must his attitude be to the place not only *in* which, but *for* which he died?

4   In Acts 1-2 he shared his vision for the 'ends of the earth' whilst promising them the Holy Spirit that they might worship him and proclaim his Gospel despite the inevitable pressures they would face in Jerusalem and elsewhere. In what ways does he discern his people availing themselves of his Spirit in Jerusalem today and acknowledging the world-wide scope of his purposes?

5   Finally, as so often noted, in Luke 19, Jesus wept over Jerusalem and claimed that he was the source of the city's peace. Has anything changed?

---

[16] The practical consequences of this position for Jerusalem today are spelt out in greater detail in my 'Centre Stage: Jerusalem or Jesus?', *Cambridge Papers,* March 1996, 5.1.

14
MARCHING TO ZION: WESTERN EVANGELICALS AND JERUSALEM APPROACHING THE YEAR 2000

Don Wagner

The year 2000 is rapidly becoming a type of time magnet drawing a variety of religious and secular organisations into its magical orbit. Of all the groups engaged in the countdown to 2000 AD, it is the evangelical Christians who are showing a renewed interest in Jerusalem and Israel's 'unique' role in what they understand to be the latter days prior to Jesus' return. Jerusalem plays a vital role in the belief system of many evangelicals, beliefs that are readily converted into a tourist bonanza and an ever expanding base of political support for Israel. Some Israeli analysts estimate that during 1996, over three million tourists will visit the country, a figure that will grow to 10 million per year by the year 2000. One of the Jewish state's largest markets is evangelical Christians. Israeli analysts know very well that as the Jewish population in the United States and many other countries declines each year, the best option for future support lies with the fastest growing sector of Christianity throughout the world: evangelical Protestants.

In this paper I will concentrate on the question of Jerusalem and Western evangelical support for Israel. By way of introduction, allow me to cite four types of programmes that illustrate the level of co-operation between the Government of Israel and US evangelicals. First, 'Jerusalem 3000' celebrations have begun, with a massive Israeli tourism campaign designed primarily for evangelical Christians. Major evangelical ministries are planning Holy Land tours and conventions in Israel, such as the large and influential National Religious Broadcasters, which controls approximately 90 percent of religious radio and television broadcasts in the United States. The NRB will convene a 1996 convention in Jerusalem during the month of October 1996. The program will include tours organised by the Israeli Ministry of Tourism with a political and religious message that matches Israel's agenda.

A second example involves the ministry of Texas evangelist Mike Evans, one of Israel's most ardent supporters in the early 1980s. In October 1995, Evans launched the first of his 'Save Jerusalem Miracle Breakthrough Banquets'. These events combine a message on biblical prophecy, a healing service, and an unabashed political appeal for letters and telegrams to US legislators requesting their support of Jewish sovereignty over Jerusalem and the West Bank. Evans plans a television special titled 'Save Jerusalem' and repeat performances of the 'Banquets'.

The third example involves the best-selling Christian author Hal Lindsey,

Jerusalem: What Makes For Peace!

whose *Late Great Planet Earth* has sold over 23 million copies since its publication in 1969. Lindsey has just published a new book titled *The Final Battle*, which sees Jerusalem as the locus of a final bloody battle between Israel and a militant coalition that includes the Islamic world, China, and a revived Russia. Lindsey attempts to correct previous predictions that were never fulfilled and tries to update his interpretations in his latest volume.

Finally, we note the case of the most extreme Christian Zionist organisation in Israel, the International Christian Embassy-Jerusalem (ICEJ), whose public policy is to oppose the Middle East peace process. The Embassy utilises a variety of programs, publications, and statements by its international spokesman to promote its viewpoint. For example, during the Christmas festivities of December 1995, following the Palestinian Authority's assumption of control over a portion of Bethlehem, the ICEJ called upon Christians world-wide to boycott the celebration of Christmas in Bethlehem. Such a ploy, which was promoted widely in the media, served to place Palestinian Christians in a difficult position with their Muslim sisters and brothers who were celebrating new freedom for Bethlehem's Palestinian community. This incident, like the others cited here, is indicative of the negative images of Christianity Western evangelicals project to the Arab world.

In the following paper I briefly examine four dimensions of this issue. First, the paper will examine the Western evangelical Christian community and briefly describe several of the tendencies within this complex religious movement. Second, I will review the historical development of a specific tendency within the most conservative branch of Western Christian evangelicalism, the movement called Christian Zionism. It is here that Israel has found its strongest allies. Third, I look more closely at certain representative events planned for Jerusalem between 1996 and the year 2000 AD. Finally, I will offer several theological challenges concerning the implications of the Christian Zionists' agenda.

I   Who are the Western Evangelicals?

The term 'evangelical' has been so misunderstood and abused by the secular and religious press that we would do well to respect a five year moratorium on the term, particularly as we approach the year 2000 AD. Faced with the unlikely prospect of such a cleansing period, we are left with the alternative of trying to be more precise in our definition and use of the term 'evangelical'.

Derived from the Greek word *euangelion,* which is translated 'good news', or the verb form 'to proclaim good news,' the term was originally applied to the churches of the 16th century Protestant Reformation (Lutheran, Presbyterian, Reformed and Anglican, etc.). In fact, this is how 'evangelical' is used today throughout Europe and the Middle East. However, in the 18th and early 19th centuries, the phrase was applied to a new generation of Protestant pietistic movements, such as Baptists, Methodists, Quakers, and others. By the late 19th century, particularly from the late 1800s until after the First World War, a variety of more fundamentalist movements arose in British and North American Christianity,

74

which emphasised the following: the born again conversion experience as mandatory for all Christians; a strict and often literal interpretation of the Bible; the literal, future second coming of Jesus; the rejection of liberal theological perspectives and of the ecumenical movement. Today there are between 65 and 75 million evangelicals in the United States,[1] making it the fastest growing sector of American Christianity. While mainline Protestant denominations and the Roman Catholic Church report annual losses in memberships and revenue, the evangelicals are growing, with the most conservative and fundamentalist wings showing the highest growth rate.

Most Christian scholars disagree about who the evangelica the journal The Other Side, Dr Ron Sider's group, Evangelicals for Social Action; and two of President Clinton's religious advisors, Dr Tony Campolo of Eastern Baptist Seminary near Philadelphia, PA, and Dr Bill Hybels of the Willowcreek Church, a mega-church in suburban Chicago. Also, a significant number of college and seminary faculty in the hundreds of evangelical colleges across the United States and Canada would fall into this category. These evangelicals certainly claim the name 'evangelical' and ta the journal *The Other Side*, Dr Ron Sider's group, Evangelicals for Social Action; and two of President Clinton's religious advisors, Dr Tony Campolo of Eastern Baptist Seminary near Philadelphia, PA, and Dr Bill Hybels of the Willowcreek Church, a mega-church in suburban Chicago. Also, a significant number of college and seminary faculty in the hundreds of evangelical colleges across the United States and Canada would fall into this category. These evangelicals certainly claim the name 'evangelical' and take seriously the centrality of Jesus Christ; they generally view the Bible as the inspired word of God but do not adopt a literal form of translation and application of the scriptures, and they generally accept the necessity of a 'born again' experience. However, what distinguishes the 'Left' from the rest of evangelicalism is their commitment to social change as a central dimension of faith and practice. The majority of these evangelicals will support justice for Palestinians and Israelis alike. They may be a numerically small movement but they are very influential in the broad evangelical community.

On the opposite end of the spectrum I would place the evangelical 'Right'. This group would be comprised of two different theological tendencies: the fundamentalist and charismatic. They differ on such issues as the manifestations of the Holy Spirit, such as 'speaking in tongues' or *glossolalia*, which is the hallmark of the charismatic movement but not found among conservative Baptists and other fundamentalists. Within the 'Right' are perhaps 75 percent of the Southern Baptists, the largest Protestant denomination in the United States (over 14 million members), other Baptist groups plus the Missouri Synod Lutheran and most Pentecostal and charismatic denominations such as the Assemblies of God. The Revd Jerry Falwell would be an example of a Baptist leader, while Pat Robertson and most television evangelists are of the charismatic persuasion. These groups tend to interpret the Bible literally; they usually have an emphasis on end-times prophecy, and they view the modern state of Israel as some form of contemporary fulfilment of God's promises to

---

[1] See Watt, David Harrington, *A Transforming Faith*, Rutgers University Press, New Brunswick, New Jersey 1991, pp. 33-48.

Israel in the Bible. Moreover, they often view the modern state of Israel as a present or future instrument that God will use to fulfil the prophetic scriptures. During the previous ten years these evangelicals and fundamentalists have begun to develop sophisticated political organisations. They tend to align themselves with conservative politicians such as televangelist Pat Robertson, a presidential candidate in 1988; Patrick Buchanan, a Presidential candidate in the Republican Party in 1996; Senator Jesse Helms, an advocate of the most conservative political agendas in the US Congress; Oliver North of the Iran/contra scandal, who nearly won a 1994 bid for Congress; and former Republican Vice President Dan Quayle. Their strongest political organisation at the present time is called the Christian Coalition, a movement organised by Pat Robertson and headed by Ralph Reed. Reed has recently claimed that his organisation has 80 million members, a statistic that is rather dubious and is being challenged by several Christian groups. The Christian 'Right' is usually pro-Israel and represents the largest potential political support for Israel in the United States. One could safely say that the evangelical or fundamentalist 'Right' consists of 25-30 percent of the American evangelical community.

The third and largest group is the evangelical 'Centre', constituting perhaps one third to 40 percent of all evangelicals. Many are organised in the National Association of Evangelicals (NAE), an alternative to the National Council of Churches. However, new forms of dialogue are now underway and there are signs of healing this fifty-year-old rift in some quarters of the evangelical 'Centre'. On the political level, most of the 'Centre' and the NAE churches would not align themselves with the Christian Coalition's program. The evangelical 'Centre' tends to be apolitical if anything, but there seems to be a new openness to a variety of domestic social justice issues such as urban poverty, healing racism, and questions of human and religious rights. Some sectors of the evangelical 'Centre' have demonstrated a growing sensitivity to the plight and presence of Middle Eastern Christians, including an awareness of the Palestinian cause. The 'Centre' can be found not only in the evangelical denominations with membership in the National Association of Evangelicals, but many are found in such mainline Protestant churches as the Presbyterians, United Methodists, Episcopalians, and Evangelical Lutherans. All of these denominations have organised fellowships and networks of evangelical pastors and laity, usually representing the largest and most influential churches within their denominations. The Presbyterian Church has both the more moderate evangelical movement, Presbyterians for Renewal, and the aggressive Presbyterian Lay Committee. The United Methodist denomination has the 'Good News Movement'. Increasingly, these evangelical networks or movements are exercising their influence on denominational policy, missions, and financial support of denominational structures. While many of these evangelical groups have demonstrated a balanced approach to the Middle East, a disproportionate number of evangelical pastors participate in Holy Land tours, most of which are decidedly pro-Israel and offer little or no contact with Palestinians, even Palestinian Christians.

Many changes are occurring within the 'Centre evangelical' organisations and churches, some of which are reflected in their largest magazine, *Christianity Today*. Founded by Billy Graham and a group of Evangelical leaders in the mid-1940s,

Christianity Today (or *CT*) has come to epitomise the theological perspective of the evangelical 'Centre'. Within the past decade the journal has increasingly turned its attention to an Evangelical examination of the major social justice questions of our time, including the Middle East. For over forty years since its founding the magazine had maintained a view that was focused primarily on Israel and often reflected a dispensational perspective. During the decade of the 1990s, however, *Christianity Today*, while maintaining its commitment to the centrality of Jesus Christ and a high view of the authority and inspiration of scripture, has now added a deep sensitivity to the political complexities of the Middle East and the historic churches of the region, reflecting a new awareness of Middle Eastern Christians and their complex political context. The May 20, 1996, feature story on 'Will the Jerusalem Church Survive the Peace Process?' is a case in point.[2] However, the evangelical 'Centre' is increasingly ecumenical, and during the 1990s has demonstrated in its publications and its mission organisations a programmatic dimension of thoughtful Middle Eastern projects. Many of the large para-church mission organisations, such as World Vision, World Concern and World Relief, are presently involved in vital relief and development projects throughout the Middle East and are gaining new respect among the Arab churches and in some cases among Muslims. Organisations such as Open Doors, with Brother Andrew, and Venture Middle East (VMI) have been engaged with Muslims for several years. When the Government of Israel expelled alleged Hamas leaders from the Gaza Strip in late 1994, it was Brother Andrew and VMI's Len Rodgers who visited them in South Lebanon and drew hostile reactions from Christian Zionist organisations such as the International Christian Embassy-Jerusalem. In addition, the United-States-based organisation, Evangelicals for Middle East Understanding (EMEU), has been engaged in annual conferences, pilgrimages, and distributing educational information since 1988, with most programmes organised in conjunction with the Middle East Council of Churches or other Middle East Christian organisations. EMEU has not hesitated to address the significant justice questions facing Christians in the Middle East such as Israel-Palestine, factional conflict in Lebanon, and Christian-Muslim conflicts in Egypt and Sudan.

The fourth and final group is one often overlooked by students of American evangelicalism but is extremely important and somewhat open to a more balanced theological and political perspective on the Middle East. This branch includes the African-American churches and denominations and the Hispanic, Korean, and other ethnic minority churches in the United States. While the fundamentalist and charismatic wing has been the fastest growing sector of North American Christianity, we might safely project that due to high immigration and birth rates this fourth sector will be the arena of massive future growth within the evangelical community.

This fact was brought to my attention by a Hispanic pastor who recently described how his urban ministry had been visited by representatives of the Israeli Embassy in Washington, DC. The embassy has promised the Hispanic community over $2 million in desperately needed urban community development funds. In

---

[2] 'Will the Jerusalem Church Survive the Peace Process?', *Christianity Today*, volume 40, number 6, May 20, 1996, pp. 56-62.

addition, the ten leading Hispanic pastors in the United States and their wives were flown to Israel on an all-expense-paid vacation. The pastor was told by the embassy official, 'We are aware that within twenty years your community will outnumber ours in the United States, and we want to be certain that your children will support legislation in Washington that will support Israel.' The pastor told me that many of the Hispanic churches and pastors subscribe to the apocalyptic Christian Zionist theology described above and are predisposed to support the political agenda of Israel. When the 'pot is sweetened' with a free Holy Land tour and funds for a poverty-stricken community, one can see that Israel is doing an effective public relations job that will pay political dividends in the future. However, when I asked the pastor if the visit to the Holy Land included meetings with local Christian leaders in Jerusalem, Bethlehem, or the Galilee, he responded, 'We asked if these could be arranged, but they kept telling us that our schedule was too tight and we did not have time.'[3]

II The Development of Evangelical Christian Zionism

What Is Premillennialism?

Certainly the most active of the Western evangelical groups in reference to Middle East issues is Group I, the evangelical right. Within this group we discover a particular type of theological orientation that will be our focus for the remainder of the paper. The scope of this paper does not allow for a more extensive biblical or historical analysis of this movement so I would refer you to chapters V-IX in my book *Anxious for Armageddon*.[4]

The basic genre of theology that is our focus here is called 'apocalyptic thought'. Briefly stated, apocalypticism envisions a future climax to history and seeks to unlock the secrets concerning the timing, sequence of events and other details leading to the end of history as we know it. Of particular importance are those passages in the Old and New Testaments that might be rendered as having apocalyptic significance.

Apocalyptic thought may have become familiar to the Jews during their time of captivity and exile in Assyria, Babylon, and Persia. The roots of this theology probably lie in ancient Persia and spread later to Assyria and Babylon. We can find several illustrations of this thought in the second half of the Book of Daniel, as well as in portions of Ezekiel, Zechariah 9-12, and various chapters of the New Testament, such as the Book of Revelation. By the time of the Maccabbees (167-155 BC) the movement had grown in influence and usage among the Jews, and continued to be popular in Jesus' era. Thus it is not surprising to see occasional examples of apocalyptic thought in the Gospels, Paul's early letters, and the 'Apocalypse' itself (the Book of Revelation).

---

[3] Interview by the author.
[4] See Donald Wagner, *Anxious for Armageddon*, Scottdale, Pennsylvania: Herald Press, 1995, pp. 48-113.

Throughout Christian history there have been frequent outbreaks of 'apocalyptic' theology. One sees the tendency among Jesus' own disciples in the Acts 1 ascension story. The disciples ask the Master just prior to his ascension, 'Lord will you at this time restore the Kingdom to Israel?' Jesus was rather harsh with the disciples, stating bluntly, 'It is not for you to know the times or seasons that the Father has fixed by his own authority.'[5] The apocalyptic longing for mysterious predictions of the future has led to various prophetic phenomena throughout the history of Christianity, such as the Montanist controversy in Asia Minor (156 AD). As we will see shortly, some televangelists and pastors understand the present 20th century events in the Middle East as the time in which Jesus will return and thus a number of events are being interpreted in the light of Jesus imminent 'Second Coming'.

Dispensationalism

A new school of thought developed in certain evangelical communities in the British Isles after the 1820s and eventually spread to the United States, where it gained a degree of popularity that remains until the present day. The doctrine was introduced by the renegade Irish priest, John Nelson Darby. While there have been expressions of this thought throughout the history of Christianity and Judaism, it was not developed in a systematic or populist manner until the 19th century. Gradually, this school of thought has been called 'dispensationalism'.

Dispensationalism might be defined as a modern Western evangelical approach to biblical interpretation that divides all of history into epochs or eras called dispensations. Dispensationalists believe that the latter days of history will be marked by certain signs pointing to the Second Coming of Jesus and the end of history. Jesus' return would have two distinct phases: the first when the true 'born again' Christians would vanish from history and rise to heaven in what is called the 'Rapture' (1 Thessalonians 4.5-11); and second, when Jesus would return to defeat the Antichrist and establish his millennial rule.[6]

Those who believed in 'dispensationalist' theology eventually developed a systematic approach that became popular among the conservative wing of American evangelicalism in the 1880-1920 period, when there was another period of heightened concern for the last days. The 'dispensationalist' movement combined with premillennial beliefs to forge a new wave in evangelical theology, called 'millenialism.'

Millennialism

This is the belief that Jesus will return to establish a 1,000-year rule on earth. However, there are a variety of interpretations as to when Jesus will return and how this Kingdom would be established. Premillennialism is the school of thought within the evangelical millennial movement that believes Jesus will return before the Battle

---

[5] Acts 1: 6-8.
[6] Watt, *ibid.*, pp. 73-74.

of Armageddon and the establishment of the Millennial Kingdom on earth. There are two forms of premillennialism. First, there is the 'historic premillennialist' school, comprised of those who believe Jesus will return before the millennium as a natural historical process, as hinted in selected biblical texts. This is the older and more historic position of many Christians, and several Church Fathers such as Justin Martyr, the Shepherd of Hermas, and Papias. However, nowhere in church history is there an entire system of theology based on millennialism, nor is there the teaching of the 'rapture' and double Second Coming of Jesus.

The development of this second wave of futurist premillennial theology is traceable to the 1800-1830 period in the British Isles. The American and French Revolutions had given many Europeans the sense that their world was falling apart. New forms of political anarchy, radical philosophical ideas, and a series of destabilising wars led many to believe the 1790s-1820s were the countdown to the last days. Historian LeRoy Froom described the ways in which many Europeans interpreted history in apocalyptic terms:

> After the troublous times of the American Revolution and its aftermath, and especially after the devastating effects of the infidelic French philosophy, men turned again to the Bible for light, especially the prophecies in Daniel and Revelation. They were seeking a satisfying explanation of the prevailing irreligion of the time and to find God's way out of the situation.[7]

The second school of premillennialism, the predictive or 'futurist premillennialist' school began to develop. Its characteristic features included the literal interpretation of Scripture; the projection of certain key biblical texts as having a future fulfilment; developing a sequence of events during the 'Last Days' that leads to a type of prophetic countdown; and in general subscribing to a highly pessimistic view of history and of humanity. In basic terms, the prophetic countdown includes the rise of a mysterious figure called the Antichrist, the development of a coalition of nations who will follow this demonic world leader, and an attack on Israel which will lead to a final battle called Armageddon (at the valley of Megiddo in north central Israel). In this view, the revived Jewish state will become God's primary instrument to thwart the power of the evil coalition and the Antichrist. Just as Israel is about to be attacked by this massive military force, the true believers in Christ will be mystically removed from history in an event called the 'Rapture'.[8] These interpreters predicted that Jesus would then return to defeat the Antichrist and his armies at the Battle of Armageddon, and establish the Millennial Kingdom with Jerusalem as its capital. The Christian Church becomes a non-factor in the premillennialist approach, for it has been removed from history and replaced with the nation of Israel. Most premillennialists see the modern state of Israel, established in

---

[7] LeRoy, Froom, *The Prophetic Faith of Our Fathers*, Washington Review and Herald Press, Washington, Pennsylvania, 1954, p. 137.
[8] 1 Thessalonians 4: 5-11.

1948, as the fulfilment of the prophetic texts and as the community God will use in this end-time scenario.

Among the theological components of the movement are the following points, many of which represent a departure from the basic doctrines of Orthodox, Catholic, and Protestant Christianity:

1   Premillennial dispensationalist theology holds that there are two distinct Covenants and Covenant people: the Jew and the Christian. However, disproportional emphasis is placed on the Covenant with Abraham and Israel in this system. The Covenant with Jesus Christ and the Church are both superseded and rendered functionally irrelevant.

2   In addition there are two separate tracks of history: one Jewish and pointing toward a revived Israel; the other Christian but only transitional, or as Darby calls it 'a mere parenthesis'. The church enters history as an equal or as some Protestant and Orthodox theologies state, as the 'fulfilment' or 'replacement' of Israel, but as an interruption whose role is temporary and limited.

3   Third, the church is literally on the sidelines in the dispensationalist system. As we have seen, with the return of Jesus, the true believers or 'the Saved,' will be translated out of history in what is called 'the Rapture.' Being biblical literalists, this group sees the founding of Israel in 1948 as a fulfilment of biblical prophecy, and the capture of Jerusalem as a sign that Jesus will return soon.

4   This form of thinking divides history into distinct eras or 'dispensations,' which are periods of time based on how God will judge the people. In addition to the work of John Nelson Darby, dispensationalism was given its major marketing boost in the United States by C I Scofield, who published a Bible in 1909 with footnotes and an outline imposed on the biblical text according to futurist premillennial dispensationalist principles. One cannot overestimate the influence that the Scofield Bible has had on American evangelicalism for three generations.

According to Scofield's interpretative principles, which are accepted by most futurist premillennialists, there are seven dispensations:

    a)   Adam and Eve (state of Innocence before the Fall)
    b)   Adam to Noah (judgement comes and Noah is spared through God's covenant)
    c)   Abraham to Moses (Covenant and Promise)
    d)   Moses to Christ (the Law)
    e)   Christ to the Rapture (Grace)
    f)   The Rapture (Christians spared)
    g)   Jesus Returns to Rule (Armageddon, defeat of the Antichrist)[9]

---

[9] See the *New Scofield Reference Bible*, Oxford University Press, New York, 1969, especially pp. 1-20.

We note here that the Church has been removed from history as a vehicle of God's redemption. This is because Israel is understood by dispensationalists as God's primary vehicle in this theological system. There is essentially no need for the Christian church to achieve God's purposes in the historic dispensationalist perspective. Such a theological viewpoint leads to two conclusions. First, it leads invariably to a pessimistic orientation to life, seeing history wind down to a predetermined scenario of genocidal proportions. Second, it tends to make the believer feel futile about the situation in front of him or her. My mother often says, 'Don, why care about the Middle East? The Lord is coming back and anything you do is a waste of time.' In Ronald Reagan's presidency, there were several in his administration who held this view, including Reagan himself. Who will forget former Secretary of the Interior James Watt, selling off large sections of our National Parks in the United States? Why worry about the distant future if Jesus could return at any minute?

III   Historical Overview: Christian Zionism In England

Time will permit only a very basic overview as to how Christian Zionism developed within the British Isles and then came to North America. Three trends of thought converged in Britain by the year 1600. The first trend occurred early in British literature as some early writers interpreted the British people as the 'new Israel'. The earliest work in British literature, *The Epistle of Gildas* (4th century), and the great historian of the 7th century, the Venerable Bede (673-735 CE) in his *Ecclesiastical History,* both used images of the Britons as God's chosen people. Their numerous battles against various invaders from the northern Scandinavian hordes and beyond were viewed as parallel to those of Israel in the Old Testament against the Philistines or other enemies. This hermeneutical principle produced several variations, including one which interpreted the British as the lost Tribes of Israel, the ones to redeem the world. This theme reappeared throughout British literature in such great writers as John Milton, John Bunyan, and Samuel Taylor Coleridge.[10]

The second theme emerged much later, perhaps in the 15th century, when we begin to see references to the Jews returning to the Holy Land as a necessary step prior to Jesus' return and the end of history. This is called 'restorationism,' and is a theme that later merges with futurist premillennialism and then dispensationalism. As the British colonial dream began to expand, Restorationism became a practical possibility. The influential Lord Shaftesbury could argue in 1839 that England must support the return of the Jews to Palestine in order for the empire to be blessed and the millennial reign to be ushered in by Jesus Christ.

The third theme is the 'futurist premillennial dispensationalist' theology that we developed above. It combined elements of the 'British as the New Israel' doctrine and restorationism, but added the dispensational chronology, rapture, minimal role of the Church, and the literal fulfilment of prophetic scriptures in Jerusalem and the

---

[10] See Tuchman, Barbara, *Bible and Sword,* Ballantine Books, New York, 1956, pp. 121-174.

Holy Land. One of the earliest forms that I have come across is the Revd Thomas Brightman's monograph, 'Apocolypsis Apocolypsios' which dates back to 1585. Here he used several of the Old and New Testament apocalyptic texts and claimed there must be specific steps taken to support not only a Jewish return to the Holy Land but an Israeli state. Brightman was forced underground with his views.[11]

One of Brightman's disciples was Sir Henry Finch, who was a Member of Parliament, and who functioned much like the Attorney General does in the United States. In the year 1621 he called for British support of Jewish settlement in Jerusalem and Palestine and brought the matter to Parliament. While he was forced out of office, his writings and advocacy of the position gave it credence. The defeat of the Cromwell experiment and persecution of the Puritans, both preaching various forms of restorationism, millennialism, and British Israelism, placed the movement on the shelf for over 100 years, but it did not vanish.

The events leading up to the year 1800 provided precisely what the movement needed, a sense of catastrophe and the hint that history was moving to a climax. The chaos caused by the French and American Revolutions led many English Christians to turn again to the apocalyptic texts in Daniel and Revelation. One voice was that of the Revd Louis Way, who in 1809 became the director of the foundering London Society for Promoting the Gospel among the Jews. The LSPGJ was a missionary society calling for the conversion of the Jews to Christianity, but it supported a restored Jewish state in Palestine and called upon Members of Parliament to support it. The movement became a hobby of some British literary figures, such as Samuel Taylor Coleridge, and gained significant public support when House of Commons member Henry Drummond became Director. In 1829, Drummond convened a series of prophecy conferences at his estate in Albury, England.

One can see a political dimension of the dispensational movement develop first in England, and later in the United States. In England, we mentioned Sir Henry Finch's bringing before the Parliament as early as 1625 the issue of England's support of settling the Jews in Palestine. The movement seems to have gained support again with Lord Shaftesbury's work, following the publication of his article in *The Times* of London in 1839. Shaftesbury's writings and political work combined appeals to British colonial themes, such as the need of a land bridge to India (across the Middle East), with the restoration of the Jews, and their need for a state in the Holy Land. Incidentally, Lord Shaftesbury was one of the early architects of the campaign within the Anglican Church and Parliament that eventually established St George's Cathedral here in Jerusalem, and sent its first bishop, a Jewish convert to Christianity. There were others who carried Lord Shaftesbury's vision and Darby's theology into high places, such as Lord Laurence Olifant, (1829-88), who was for a time a Member of Parliament and an author who left his work in England to settle in Palestine and write. His volume, *The Land of Gilead,* was a romantic blend of Christian Zionism and British restorationism.

By the time Theodor Herzl and the early Jewish Zionist fathers began to lobby British politicians on behalf of the Zionist dream, they found a ready audience.

---

[11] For a more detailed survey of these themes, see Wagner, *ibid.*, pp. 85-95.

The preliminary work had been done in a theological sense by Darby and his forerunners, and by the tradition of Lord Shaftesbury. When Herzl's successor Chaim Weitzmann began a series of meetings with the influential conservative political leader, Lord Balfour, the die had been cast. Balfour was a Christian Zionist in the Darby-Shaftesbury tradition, and saw himself and England as God's instrument to re-establish the Jews in the Holy Land. Balfour's commitment to Zionism could not be mistaken, as noted in the following statement: 'Zionism, be it right or wrong, good or bad, is rooted in age-long traditions, in present needs, of far profounder import than the desire and prejudices of 700,000 Arabs who now inhabit the land.'[12]

Balfour's views were matched during this important period by Prime Minister David Lloyd George, who was brought up in a Christian Zionist background. He wrote of his education, 'I was brought up in a school where I was taught far more about the history of the Jews than the history of my own land.'[13] The historian Christopher Sykes noted that in negotiations with the French and other powers at the Paris Peace Accords, Lloyd-George could not grasp the current geography and people of Palestine because his mind was fixed on his Sunday school maps and biblical terminology instilled in him since childhood.

Between 1862 and 1877, John Nelson Darby made six missionary journeys to the United States, a contribution that is credited with expanding the influence of futurist premillennial dispensationalism in the United States. Darby became the primary agent of bringing Christian Zionism to America and planting its theology in American evangelicalism. Darby influenced several leading clergymen in mainline Protestant churches, including Presbyterians and Methodists. In addition, he was a major source of influence on evangelists such as Dwight L Moody, the leading US evangelist of his day, and the Bible and Prophecy Conference movement. The prophecy conferences were a major force for futurist premillennial dispensationalism after 1876. Many pastors, university and college professors, and others followed Darby down a path of suspended exegesis.

IV   Countdown to the Year 2000

Let us look very briefly at several of the practical aspects of Christian Zionist expression as we approach the year 2000.

Political Dimensions
Many of the programmes of the Christian Zionists have direct or indirect political implications. An unstated purpose of the various programmes appears to be the enlistment of political support for the state of Israel from within the fastest growing sector of Christianity world-wide, the evangelicals. A second agenda is to increase education in Zionist principles through tourism, which brings us to a third agenda, the outpouring of tourist dollars to Israel itself. These three goals are among the

---

[12] Quoted in Chapman, C, *Whose Promised Land?,* Lion Publishing, Batavia, Illinois, 1981, p. 54.
[13] Sykes, Christopher, *Two Studies in Virtue,* Alfred A Knopf, New York, 1954, p. 254.

benefits that the modern State of Israel will reap in the coming years.

A major focus of recent efforts has been the delicate question of Jerusalem. One of the central issues in the debate is who will have sovereignty over the sites in the city deemed holy by Muslims, Christians, and Jews. Various actions by the Government of Israel when combined with statements by its political leaders indicate that Israel is pre-empting negotiations on the final status of Jerusalem, scheduled to begin after May 29, 1996 (the date set for Israel's national elections). Israeli agencies and their allies in the Christian Zionist networks have spared little time or expense in conditioning the hearts and minds of Western Christendom to support Israeli sovereignty over the entire city of Jerusalem, not only the holy sites.

Consider, for example, the spring, 1995, issue of *Christians and Israel*, a quarterly publication of the Israeli embassies in various Western nations and mailed to key Christian leaders. The cover story on 'Jerusalem' quoted the Christian Zionist Director of the organisation Bridges for Peace, Clarence H Wagner. The author, who is well known for his anti-Arab rhetoric and pro-Israel political perspective, states the following:

> Before Israel negotiates away responsibility for the Christian Holy Places in Jerusalem to the Palestinian Authority, it ought to consider . . . the wider interests of the Christian world.
>
> Christians must be guaranteed freedom of access and worship in Jerusalem, both now and in the future. While various Christian sects may differ on how that might be achieved, many Christians recognize and support Israel as the legitimate custodian of a united Jerusalem.[14]

The writer has carefully stated that his and other Christian organisations are marshalling their resources, plus the ever present support of the various ministries of the Israeli government, to bring about a united Jerusalem under Israeli sovereignty. Israel is well ahead of those who would advocate alternative points of view, such as the division of Jerusalem into an Arab and Jewish city, or the internationalisation of the city. It would appear that the careful efforts of the Christian Zionist groups and many others have planted seeds in Western minds of the Israeli vision of Jewish sovereignty over Jerusalem, a view that will gain the necessary political support throughout the world when the issue is put to a test.

The message of Israeli sovereignty over Jerusalem is underscored in a variety of ways, some more subtle than others. I will leave the issue of tourism to a separate category but allow me to mention the central theme of Israeli tourism for the next five years: 'Jerusalem 3000'. Prominent in the brochures on Holy Land tourism and in virtually every issue of the major evangelical magazines, Jerusalem 3000 projects the image that we are celebrating that Jerusalem has been under Israeli sovereignty for 3000 years. Actually, Jerusalem has been under Israeli or Jewish sovereignty for less than 150 years, but the evangelical community does not seem to be questioning

---

[14] *Christians and Israel,* volume 1, number 2, spring 1995, p. 1.

the concept put forth by the Israeli public relations people.

One of the most blatant examples of a political form of Christian Zionism is a Texas-based pastor by the name of Mike Evans. Evans became visible in the 1980s as a self-proclaimed advocate of Israel, and now he is returning with a series of 'Save Jerusalem Miracle Breakthrough Banquets'. In an August 25, 1995, invitational letter, Evans claimed,

> I am going to unveil the truth behind the sinister plot to steal the very soul of Jerusalem from the nation of Israel. I will take you behind the scenes so you can see the demonic forces that are working in our own government to divide the only city in the world reserved by the Almighty as God's City. I will even give you a private screening of our new television special, 'Save Jerusalem', which will expose this sinister plot against Jerusalem in graphic detail. I wanted to show you what all this means in God's end time plan, then show you how you can covenant with God as a prayer partner in His end time plan. . . The City of Jerusalem plays a central role in God's end time plan of the ages. And during this very special banquet, I am going to show you how we can covenant together to Save Jerusalem and live in a new dimension of the provisional blessings of God.[15]

This is a classic mixture of pro-Israeli politics for Jerusalem and the end-time Christian Zionist dispensational theology. Mr Evans, and thousands of preachers and Bible teachers like him from the fundamentalist evangelical communities across North America, will be articulating this message over and over to their followers, who are now in the tens of millions. Israel is preparing them now for the hour of need, and then they will be called upon to take up political action with their legislators and the president to ensure Israeli sovereignty over Jerusalem.

Tourism

Under the banner 'JERUSALEM 3000', the Government of Israel has begun a massive international public relations blitz in an effort to bring up to ten million tourists to the Holy Land during the 1999-2000 period. A multifaceted venue of cultural, academic, tourist, and primarily religious events began in 1995. The sub-theme is, 'ISRAEL: No one belongs here more than you.' There is a tour package for every age and interest group.

For example, a series of special events kicked off in September 1995, with Beethoven's *Fidelio* produced by the Deutsche Staatsoper of Berlin, directed by Daniel Barenboim. On October 11, 1995, 'Jerusalem, Above My Joy' was a massive pageant in celebration of the 'Jerusalem 3000' theme with dancers, musicians, and groups dressed in historic costumes. It also featured delegates from several countries and floats constructed by the town of Viareggio, Italy. Or consider the March 18,

---

[15] Evans, Mike, Save Jerusalem letter, 25 April 1995; pp. 2-3.

1996, 'KING DAVID'S FEAST', a twelve-course banquet prepared by thirty of the world's great chefs under the auspices of the International Chefs' Association.

However, the cultural events will inevitably take a back seat to the Christian tourist events that have been booked for the 1996-2000 period. In February, 1996, the International Christian Embassy-Jerusalem convened its third World Christian Zionist Congress, modelled after Theodor Herzl's historic 1897 World Zionist Congress in Basle, Switzerland. During that same month, up to one million evangelical Christians, including half a million South Koreans, visited the Holy Land and attended conventions organised by various 'church growth ministries'. Among the featured speakers were Revd David Yonggi Cho, pastor of the largest church in the world, Yoido Full Gospel Chapel of Seoul, Korea. Other featured speakers were Robert Schuller of the Crystal Cathedral and Hour of Power television ministry based in Garden Grove, California; church growth expert C Peter Wagner of Fuller Theological Seminary; and Pastor Jack Hayfort, a televangelist and pastor of the Church on the Way in Van Nuys, California. Convened under the banner, 'Jerusalem Celebration 2000', the promotional brochure includes a photo of Robert Schuller claiming 'Jerusalem Celebration 2000 may go down in the history of Christendom as the most exciting celebration of the birth of our Lord Jesus Christ.'

Even larger and more extravagant events are scheduled for later in 1996 and then monthly until the end of the year 2000. More Western evangelicals will be visiting Israel during the 1997-2000 year period than at any time in history. The majority of the conferences, musical events, and tours will be geared toward the Christian Zionist and dispensationalist orientation, with little or no contact with the indigenous Palestinian Christian community.

For example, a Christian radio broadcaster's tour during May 21-29, 1996, included a four-day convention in Jerusalem and a tour of Israel, featuring the Sea of Galilee, Nazareth, a kibbutz, the Golan Heights and Tel Aviv. I asked a participant, one of the leading evangelical radio voices in Southern California, if those on the tour will be meeting Arab Christians. His response was, 'No, they have not been scheduled.' In checking his itinerary, I noticed that Bethlehem was overlooked, and I asked why. He said the tour organisers, El Al Airlines, told them that Bethlehem was too dangerous now that it is under the Palestinian Authority. Armed with his Israeli Government tourist information, which included an El Al T-shirt and complimentary bathroom travel kit, he will stay at five-star hotels and dine on the best meals the country can offer. Everything is free, paid for by El Al and the Israeli Tourist Bureau.[16] Missing from his itinerary are the living churches, the Middle Eastern Christians, who seem a relic of ancient history and archaeological curiosity.

V   The Ad 2000 Movement and the '10/40 Movement'

Perhaps the major organisational principle for Western evangelical missionary efforts and evangelism on a global basis is the 'AD 2000 Movement'. Its impetus came from

---

[16] Private conversation between the author and the evangelical radio personality, Los Angeles, 16 May 1996.

several para-church agencies such as Campus Crusade, YWAM (Youth with a Mission), Operation Mobilization, and Mission Frontiers. Several conservative evangelical denominations have also been involved, including the Southern Baptist Convention, the Assemblies of God, and the Christian Missionary and Alliance.

In the beginning, the AD 2000 Movement stated that its goal was to preach the Gospel of Jesus Christ to every person in the world who had not previously heard it by the year 2000. Gradually, this goal seemed unrealistic and it was adjusted to reach certain targeted people groups. The name of the movement was also changed to the AD 2000 and Beyond Movement. Within the AD 2000 Movement there arose another organising effort: the 10/40 window, the belt on the planet that lies from 10 degrees to 40 degrees north of the equator, and stretches from West Africa to Japan. The 10/40 window constitutes one-third of the earth's total land area and includes approximately two-thirds of the world's population, or just under four billion people. Included are over 90 percent of the world's one billion Muslims, 800 million Hindus, and 300 million Buddhists. According to the organisers, the 10/40 window includes 97 percent of the world's least evangelised nations.

Guided by the evangelical mission researcher Dr David Barrett, Dr C Peter Wagner of Fuller Theological Seminary, and Ralph Martin of Mission Frontiers, there has been a massive international effort of prayer groups, training in mission and evangelism, and research to facilitate the strategies that are being implemented to reach these populations. The project has caught on in an amazing manner as we draw closer to the year 2000, to the extent that Dr Barrett estimates there are over 10 million weekly prayer meetings with nearly 160 million participants. Most are engaged in training or actual missionary activity.[17] The handbook for the prayer groups which lie at the heart of the movement was written by a Christian Zionist, George Otis, Jr, son of George Otiose, SR, the founder of the Voice of Hope radio station in Israeli-occupied southern Lebanon and backer of Major Sad Hatted, leader of the Southern Lebanese militia that co-operates with Israel in the occupied region. The country-by-country analysis assembled by Otiose evinces utterly no awareness nor interest in the indigenous Arab Christian churches of the Middle East. There is no expressed desire for dialogue, fellowship, or partnership with these fellow Christians. Clearly, there is no concern with how negative will be the impact of these AD 2000 and Beyond strategies on local Christians, particularly from Islamic extremist organisations and the Arab governments in the region. It is obvious that the author(s) have not been in dialogue with the Arab Christians of the Middle East.

The section on 'Israel' is a point in case. Among the factual errors are the following:

1   Jerusalem, not Tel Aviv, is listed as the capital of Israel. The only nation in the world to accept Jerusalem as the Israel's capital is Israel itself.
2   Jericho is discussed as if it were a city of Israel. It is under the jurisdiction of the Palestinian Authority, and was previously in the Israeli Occupied West Bank.

---

[17] Otis, George, Jr. (Ed.) *Strongholds of the 10/40 Window*, YWAM Publishing, Seattle, 1995, p. 9.

3   Christianity is not mentioned as a major religion in the country.

4   None of the Palestinian cities are mentioned under 'major cities', such as Gaza, Hebron, and Nablus.

5   Abraham is discussed only as the father of the Jewish people. The Muslim and Christian understandings of Abraham are missing.

6   The historical analysis repeats an old Zionist myth, that when Israel became independent in 1948, it was immediately attacked by the Arab armies. Knowledgeable Jewish historians no longer repeat this myth and Western Christian writers need to move beyond it as well. Not only is this inaccurate historically, but it ignores the attack on Christian and Muslim communities by the Israeli militias, the massacres, and the eventual expulsion of approximately three-quarters of a million Palestinians from their homes.

It is clear that the section was written by a Western Christian evangelical who has been influenced by the Christian Zionist orientation. Not only does the book reiterate inaccurate information but it nudges the ministries and the readers toward a Zionist analysis. Theologically, there is no concern for the Church of Jesus Christ that has been living and ministering in the Holy Land since the day of the first Pentecost. The only local Christians mentioned in the text are members of the tiny Messianic Jewish community (approximately 2000 people), the majority of whom are Zionist in their orientation. But of deeper theological concern is the following key statement:

> Because of Israel's extraordinary political and religious importance, as
> well as being the focal point of God's redemptive work in the world,
> the nation needs fervent and frequent prayer focused on its many
> problems, needs and hopes. The countdown to the year 2000 will
> bring increased opposition to the peace process and those who
> support it. May God's kingdom come, that Jerusalem might again be
> the joy of the whole earth.'[18]

I have three Christian theological concerns with this statement. First, the modern nation Israel is seen as the 'focal point of God's redemptive work in the world'. This is the classic premillennial dispensationalist position, and is in fact a heresy. Israel is a modern political state and not in a Christian theological sense the focus of God's redemptive work in the world. Second, the Church is absent in the redemptive scenario, for as we know from our early analysis, it becomes a 'mere parenthesis' and thereby disappears from the earth. Third, there is the implication that Jerusalem is the centre of God's redemptive work and that it will have an elevated place in the 'countdown to the year 2000'. Such a position plays into the political strategies of Israel's leaders, who wish to enlist international political support for Jewish sovereignty over the city of Jerusalem. Naturally, local Palestinian Christians and their friends across the world are against this approach, as it will inevitably

---

[18] *Ibid.*, p. 115.

weaken the Christian presence and witness, and hasten the already accelerated process of 'emptying' Christians from the city.

Therefore, we lift up our concerns to the leaders of the AD 2000 and Beyond Movement to consider the delicate position that their sisters and brothers in the Holy Land are facing during this critical period. These Western evangelical leaders of this movement, while well intended, are seriously misguided and will inevitably add to the already insurmountable burdens that Palestinian Christians are carrying. It is long overdue that these evangelicals begin a process of 'listening' to and respecting the needs of the local churches. If their prayers and financial resources could be redirected toward true partnerships and encouragement as equal sisters and brothers in Christ, then the local Palestinian Christians will be able to withstand those pressures on them that are making their lives unbearable. If the AD 2000 Movement is concerned at all about church growth, which is the focus of many of its leaders, they must be apprised that their efforts may be in fact adding to the destruction of the church as we know it today in the land of our Lord's birth and ministry.

VI Conclusion

Implications of Christian Zionism
Israel's strategic alliance with the Western Christian Zionists presents the West with a divine argument for Israeli political sovereignty over Jerusalem, and in some cases, the West Bank. Wrapped in the pseudo-theology of Christian Zionism, with frequent biblical references, the resulting presentation of Israel and Jerusalem to Western evangelicals carries the following theo-political implications:

1   Israeli sovereignty over Jerusalem is the only plausible solution for guaranteeing peace and the future of Christian interests in Jerusalem and the Holy Land. Israel is viewed as a 'protector' and guarantor of Christian interests in Jerusalem, and the Palestinians and the Palestinian Authority, which will undoubtedly come under extremist Islamic influence in the near future, cannot be trusted.

2   As Christian Zionists and Israel interpret Jesus and Christianity, there is a preponderance of references to the Jewish roots and context of Christianity. I and most Christians enthusiastically support the undeniable Jewish roots of our Christian heritage, and affirm our sisterly and brotherly ties to Judaism. However, the modern political ideology of Zionism, which often intersects with Judaism, presents an additional challenge to Christianity. Jesus repeatedly rejected the ethnocentric and reductionist political interpretations of himself and of the Christian message. The overstatement of the Zionist version of Christianity at the expense of Palestinian Arab Christian history and the negation of the universal message of Christianity, presents the West with a justification of Israel as an ethnocentric state, granting legitimacy for Jewish sovereignty over Jerusalem, and prepares the way for Western Christian leaders to submit to the moral and political superiority of Zionism.

3   A further result of the Jewish Zionist representation of Christianity is to imply

either directly or indirectly that Christianity is derived from Judaism, and of secondary status as a religion.

4   The Jewish Zionist representation of Christianity in the Middle East, and the political and strategic impact of the practical implementation of their programmes, causes a split between indigenous Arab Christian communities and Muslims. Muslims begin to see a Western and Zionist version of Christianity that reinforces dangerous trends in European Christianity, such as the Crusades and British, French, and American imperialism, and they fail to separate their local Christian communities from these Western intrusions into their region. The Zionist forms of Christianity could have immediate and long range effects on the local Christians that will accelerate their emigration from the Middle East, thus exaggerating a problem that is already very serious.

Some Practical Responses to the Challenge

1   The present conference on 'The Significance of Jerusalem for Christians and of Christians for Jerusalem' must develop a strong statement to Christians world-wide, and to Western Christians in particular. The statement should reflect the urgency of the hour concerning the threats to Jerusalem as a city for all peoples and religions. While the statement should affirm those churches and organisations that have courageously and sacrificially stood with the Christians and those working for the safeguarding of Jerusalem as a city for all faiths, it should challenge those segments of Christianity that have abandoned the Palestinian Christian community and have allowed Jerusalem to lose its rich historical, cultural, and religious diversity.

2   Two monitoring groups must be formed immediately, one in Jerusalem and the other in the United States. Utilising technology and research methodology, the two groups must undertake to collect and disseminate data concerning the Christian and Jewish Zionist strategies and programs for Jerusalem. In addition, the data must be converted into practical strategies that can educate North American Christians and Middle Eastern Christians, Muslims, and Jews, so as to expose the heretical and dangerous character of these programs.

3   The Presidents of the Middle East Council of Churches, the Heads of Churches of Jerusalem, and Patriarchs and church leaders in other Middle Eastern countries, should be asked to issue a statement of clarification and public rejection of the presence and activities of the International Christian Embassy-Jerusalem. There will be a need for additional statements and their dissemination to councils of churches on every continent as well as to evangelical friends world-wide.

4   The churches in the Middle East should consider an educational strategy for the media, their clergy, seminarians, university students, and the communities at large concerning the heretical theology, nature, and programmes of the Christian Zionists. Such education must be developed in the near future for the Muslim and Jewish

communities, so as to reduce the potential negative reactions toward Arab Christians, who will be viewed as a 'fifth column' for continued Western intrusion into the Middle East.

5   Let us consider one project that has limited chance for success but may be of symbolic value. The International Christian Embassy-Jerusalem has been given for their headquarters the home of the Said family, where the Palestinian American scholar, Dr Edward Said of Columbia University, was born. The home was taken from the Said family during the hostilities of 1948-9. The Palestinian Authority should be urged to demand from the government of Israel, particularly the Labor Party, that the house be returned to the Said family and that the activities of the ICEJ be restricted. The ICEJ is against the current Israeli-Palestinian peace process, and thereby represents a threat to the fragile process that is currently underway in Gaza and the West Bank. But further, the ICEJ is a significant problem for the Palestinian Christian community, and their unity with the broader Muslim majority in the region. A thorough study of the ICEJ and their present status, financing, and residence should be undertaken, with the goal of returning the Said family residence to its original owners. Potential litigation should be considered if necessary.

Theological Challenges
Let us conclude by considering very briefly certain critical challenges that can be drawn from Acts 1 and 2.

1   We see in the Pentecost text in Acts 2 a beautiful vision of the church, as if it were a mosaic that emphasises the universality and pluralism of the Church Universal. As one reads the list of those communities present at the first Pentecost, we note that the Body of Christ was exceedingly diverse in race, colour, and Christian denomination. The first Church in Jerusalem was ethnically diverse and represented virtually every region of the Middle East.

2   The Church began in Jerusalem, and included believers from across the Mediterranean: Egypt, Turkey, Germany, France, and Arabs. The Jerusalem Church was a powerful symbol of pluralism. The pluralism of the Church is a sacred trust passed on to the Church Universal, including the indigenous Arab and Jewish communities in the Holy Land today. The pluralism of the Church in Jerusalem must be safeguarded and articulated today as the challenge of Christian Zionism would seek to reduce the Church to marginal status and ethnocentric doctrines.

3   The last earthly appearance of Jesus, recorded in Acts 1: 6-9, underscores these concerns. In this text the disciples ask Jesus, 'Lord, will you now restore the Kingdom to Israel?' It was as if they were saying, 'Well Lord, we enjoyed the miracles you performed. Your teachings were terrific, and you outdid yourself with your miracles. But now are you about to do the big one? Will you restore the Kingdom to Israel?' This was the Zionist question and Jesus clearly rejected it.

Let us be aware that Jesus was very harsh with the disciples who asked the question. He was neither polite nor diplomatic. Jesus was forthright and very clear. There are times that we need to be direct and even prophetic, and this is such a time with the International Christian Embassy-Jerusalem. This is a heretical cult that is alienated from the indigenous church, yet it claims to represent Christianity. This is not a time for uncertainty but to categorically reject the ICEJ as a heresy.

Further, let us be clear that Jesus rejected the approach to scripture whereby all history, and certainly the immediate history, is viewed according to a literal, futurist chronology. 'It is not for you to know the times or seasons that God has fixed by his own authority.' God is the authority, and it seems that to trust a chronological chart, or even history itself is rejected. Thus Jesus rejects the futurist, premillennial dispensationalist approach, and calls Christians to responsibility for justice.

That call, according to the text, will take us into the most difficult areas of the world, including the United States. The root word for 'witness' is *martyrion,* or faithfulness unto death. The object of their witness is Jerusalem, the city of resurrection but also of death.

It is our call today, against a prevailing despair about the future of Jerusalem and of Palestinian Christianity, to rekindle hope, like the disciples on the road to Emmaus, and return to the cities of death. And we do so with the hope of meeting the resurrected Christ on the way. Amen.

15
A PALESTINIAN THEOLOGY
OF JERUSALEM
Naim Ateek

Introduction

What is a Palestinian theology of Jerusalem? What makes Jerusalem differ from Washington DC, Moscow or Cairo or any other city? What is so unique about this city that it requires a theology? These and many other questions come to mind when we consider a theology of Jerusalem. I will attempt, as best as I can, to articulate a Palestinian theology of Jerusalem stemming out of my Christian perspective.

Historical Background

The city of Jerusalem has developed over the last 4,000 years from being a small village that contained on its outskirts a cultic shrine for a Canaanite deity to a metropolitan city, holy today to three major world religions. On a high place near the ancient village of Jerusalem, a local Semitic god called Shulmanu was worshipped. In those days the mountain towering the village must have looked like a great acropolis.

The name Jerusalem is a composite of two words: *Jeru* or *yeru* which means 'foundation of' and carries the connotation of 'laying a cornerstone'. *Salem or Shalem* which is a shortened version of the name of the god Shulmanu. In the Amarna Letters of the 14th century BC, the town is referred to as *Urusalim* which means the foundation of the god Shalem, in other words, the home and place of this god which gave Jerusalem its name.[1] The Shulmanu shrine was, undoubtedly, visited by Canaanite tribes to invoke the deity for health, fertility, and protection. Hence the connection with the word *shalom* or *salam* which, as we know, carries the connotation of peace, health, and wholeness in Semitic languages. Although Jerusalem's earliest significance was most likely religious, the political character of the town developed as well. So Melchizedek is referred to in Genesis as the king of Jerusalem and a 'priest of God Most High'.[2]

---

[1] *Interpreter's Dictionary of the Bible*, 1962, *s. v.* 'Jerusalem'.
[2] Genesis, 14: 18, New Revised Standard Version (used for all citations).

The earliest biblical name for Jerusalem is Salem or Shalem. In Genesis chapter 14, we read how Melchizedek met Abraham as he was returning from battle, and Abraham gave him a tenth of all his spoils. Many Old Testament scholars argue that the Genesis account of the encounter between Abraham and Melchizedek most likely reflects a post Davidic ideology intended to cement the association of the holiness of Jerusalem with Abraham the patriarch of the people. When David captured the city, several hundred years later, he ingeniously selected it because of its geographic location. Since Jerusalem did not belong to any of the tribes, he hoped it would facilitate the unification of his kingdom.[3] Later he brought the sacred ark into the city thus capitalising on its already existing spiritual significance. Be that as it may, long before Abraham came from Mesopotamia (Iraq) to Canaan, and long before David conquered the city, Jerusalem was a holy place for the Canaanites and specially for its Jebusite inhabitants, as well as the capital of their city state.[4]

A Palestinian theology of Jerusalem must necessarily take into consideration those salient points that characterised this city, its evolution and development since the time of the Canaanites. In other words, any theological reflection on the city of Jerusalem must consider a cumulative history that spans four millennia. Over this long period of time, Jerusalem was impacted by all the civilisations that have come to it and gone. The histories of many people superimposed themselves and affected Jerusalem: the many invaders and conquerors, the various ethnic groups and their cultures; the many times of war and peace; the exiles, deportations, and destructions; the intermingling and intermixing of people of different races and languages.

Every period impacted and influenced the city and its people. Some conquerors attempted to erase and eradicate previous histories in order to establish themselves exclusively and give themselves prior and greater claims only to find themselves eventually rebuffed by Jerusalem. Jerusalem has defied them all. The mighty conquerors have come to it and gone. Jerusalem, however, has embraced and integrated the many people and civilisations that have come and stayed in it. She has embraced them as a mother—the Jew, the Muslim, and the Christian. They are all equally her children. Jerusalem, at the end of the 20th century, offers us itself as the cumulative sum of all of its historic past. It presents us with a rich human mosaic that has taken thousands of years to create. A theology of Jerusalem, therefore, cannot escape taking into consideration all that made Jerusalem what it is today.

If one wants to do justice to this theology, one must include reflections on a long list of topics; theology of conquest and war; theology of occupation and exile; theology of religious fanaticism and injustice; and theology of suffering and hope. At the same time we would have to consider a theology of peace, religious plurality and pilgrimage, as well as many others. Both the religious as well as the political have become an integral part of the theological composition of Jerusalem; it cannot be disregarded.

---

[3] *Interpreter's Dictionary of the Bible, ibid., s. v.* 'Jerusalem'.
[4] *The Standard Jewish Encyclopaedia*, 1959. *s. v.* 'Jerusalem'.

A Theology Of Jerusalem

In this short paper, I would like briefly to highlight three salient points that are essential in a contemporary Palestinian theology of Jerusalem.

I

One cannot think of Jerusalem without thinking of holy space. It is amazing that in the history of humankind, certain places are venerated as holy. These places began to be connected with a deity. Gradually or suddenly, they acquired a sacred character that developed and became transfixed in people's beliefs, emotions and psyche. Such sacredness is amplified when more than one religion claims holiness for the same place. Human beings seem to need holy space.[5]

One such place is Jerusalem. It is one of the very few places in our world that is shared in sanctity by more than one religion. A theology of Jerusalem recognises first of all, whether it suits our own theology or not, the presence of holy space in this city which millions of people have experienced throughout history. Faithful members of the three religions believe that here in Jerusalem, more than in other places, they can be closer to God. Jerusalem constitutes holy space for them. Some Jews would like to make a distinction between the holiness of the whole city of Jerusalem for them versus the presence of Christian Holy Places.[6] It is a futile argument and ultimately leads nowhere.

The fact is that Jerusalem is holy space for the three religious traditions. Some call it the City of God. Jesus referred to it as 'the city of the great kings'.[7] The Palestinians call it 'al-Quds al-Sharif,' the holy, the noble. Whether or not it suits our modern way of thinking, it is difficult to deny the historic religious connection of this city with God. God has been active in this city in a special way whether through a Canaanite deity and peoples who had a very primitive or elementary knowledge of God,[8] or through some of the prophets of the ancient Israelites, or through Muslim beliefs and piety for the last thirteen hundred years, or for us Christians because of the drama of redemption that has taken place in the crucifixion, death, and resurrection of our Lord Jesus Christ. The simple and basic point is this: we cannot deny that the adherents of Judaism, Islam, and Christianity firmly believe that God has in the past and continues in the present to hear them, speak and relate to them actively and authentically in this city. Pilgrims from the three religious traditions come or want to come (political climate permitting) to offer their worship and devotion close to their Holy Places.

---

[5] For a detailed discussion on holy space see White, Susan, 'The Theology of Sacred Space', in Brown, David and Loades, Ann, (eds.), *The Sense of the Sacramental,* SPCK, GB, 1995, p. 36.

[6] Werblowsky, R J Z, *The Meaning of Jerusalem to Jews, Christians and Moslems,* Israel Universities Study Group for Middle Eastern Affairs, Jerusalem, 1978, p. 14.

[7] Matthew 5: 34.

[8] Acts 17: 22-34.

Let me illustrate this from the three religions: in the case of Judaism we know the familiar words from the book of Psalms,

> If I forget you, O Jerusalem, let my right hand wither! Let my tongue cling to the roof of my mouth, if I do not remember you, if I do not set Jerusalem above my highest joy.[9]

In the Hebrew Bible, our Old Testament, the word Jerusalem and its corollary name Zion are referred to approximately 850 times. In the Babylonian Talmud, Jews are encouraged to live inside the land:

> A person should always live in the Land of Israel, even in a city with an idolatrous majority, and should not live outside the Land, even in a city with a Jewish majority, for whoever lives in the Land of Israel resembles one who has God, and whoever lives outside the Land resembles one who has no God.[10]

For Muslims, Muhammad is reported to have said,

> He who goes to Jerusalem for nothing but praying and prays the five prayers, i.e. morning, midday, afternoon, sunset and evening, will be as free from his sins as the day his mother gave him birth.[11] . . . He who visits Jerusalem God rewards him as one thousand martyrs. . . . The prayer in al-Haram mosque is worth one hundred thousand prayers; in my mosque one thousand and in Jerusalem mosque five hundred.[12]

In the Christian tradition, the Church of Jerusalem has been known historically as the 'Mother of all Churches.' From the early centuries of Christianity, and from the different Eastern and Western traditions, the Christians desired to have a permanent presence in Jerusalem because of the city's significance. These included the Copts, the Armenians, the Syrians, the Latins, the Ethiopians, not to mention the Byzantine Christians, and later, in the 19th century, the Anglicans, Lutherans and other Protestant churches.

Admittedly, some of us Christians find it difficult to give a special theological significance to a place. Some of us might agree with Eusebius of Caesarea (260-339 AD), one of the greatest Palestinian scholars that lived in Palestine. Eusebius was a Christian historian. When Constantine espoused Christianity, Eusebius was the

---

[9] Psalm 137: 5-6.
[10] Ketubot 100b, *Babylonian Talmud*.
[11] Amer, Yunis, Jerusalem's Significance in Scripture and Tradition: A Muslim Perspective, in Ucko, Hans, (ed.), *The Spiritual Significance of Jerusalem for Jews, Christians and Muslims*, World Council of Churches, Switzerland, 1993, p. 68.
[12] *Ibid.*

metropolitan bishop of the Province of Palestine with his see in Caesarea. For Eusebius, Palestine was not more holy than other countries.[13] Likewise he did not think that Jerusalem was special.[14] His theology tended to play down the role of the Holy Places and Jerusalem. However, Eusebius was on the losing end of an ecclesiastical struggle.[15] Bishop Cyril of Jerusalem, (220-386 AD) witnessed the coming of St Helena and the building of the Church of the Resurrection among others. Cyril began to develop an elaborate theology of the Holy Places. Whereas Eusebius concentrated on the universal and spiritual truths of the Gospel, Cyril, living in Jerusalem and in close proximity to the Holy Places, focused on the significance of the Incarnation and Redemption.[16] Jerusalem for him was the holy city and the Holy Places were a witness to Christ.[17]

Three hundred years after Cyril of Jerusalem, St Sophronius (560-638 AD) Patriarch of Jerusalem clearly sounded the same tune on the significance of Jerusalem when he said,

> Here, it is Jerusalem we proclaim, where God has lived bringing about miracles. Here we announce Golgotha, where God took the cross upon himself. Here we sing of the resurrection, where God rose from the tomb. Here we preach Sion . . . where Christ appeared risen from the dead. Here we glorify the Mount of Olives from where God ascended to the heavens . . .[18]

A distinction must, therefore, be drawn between the New Testament period and later Christian history, post-Constantine, when the theological significance of Jerusalem is discussed. The New Testament, in effect, de-territorialises the Gospel. Jesus was not at all preoccupied with the issue of the land. He preached the Kingdom of God, thus universalising God's reign. Jerusalem and even the temple lost their significance for Jesus. In fact, he predicted their destruction. The scope of God's activity and concern were not limited to any one country or one people. Therefore, the Gospel must be preached beginning in Jerusalem and to all the nations and to the end of the world.[19] The holiness of the place has been replaced by the holiness of the person of Christ. Christ has replaced the temple.[20] Moreover, believers in Christ have also become temples of God carrying within them the Holy Spirit. The worship of God is no more geographically localised. Jesus said to the Samaritan woman at Jacob's Well in Nablus,

---

[13] Walker, P W L , *Holy City, Holy Places?*, Clarendon Press, Oxford, 1990, p. 10.

[14] *Ibid.*, p. 398.

[15] *Ibid.*, p. xii.

[16] *Ibid.*, p. 402.

[17] In spite of this new emphasis, the See of Jerusalem remained suffregan to Caesarea. It was only at the Council of Chalcedon in 451 that the Bishopric of Jerusalem was granted patriarchal status. The church of Jerusalem, however, was respectfully referred to as the 'the mother of all churches.'

[18] Ucko, 1993, p. 13.

[19] Acts 1: 8.

[20] Davies, W D, *The Gospel and the Land*, University of California Press, Berkeley, 1974.

> . . . the hour is coming when you will worship the Father neither on
> this mountain (Gerizim) nor in Jerusalem . . . God is spirit, and those
> who worship him must worship in spirit and truth.[21]

This, I believe is a basic foundation in the New Testament and throughout the first three centuries of Christianity.

The theological shift began generally in the 4th century, after the conversion of Constantine. By glorifying and highlighting the holiness of space, the new theological emphasis was, understandably, on the Incarnation and Redemption of Christ. God in Christ came to a specific country and to specific places. For Christians the holiness of Jerusalem is not innate or intrinsic. The Incarnation of the Holy One has made the whole land of Palestine holy and the places where Jesus had been Holy Places. Cyril of Jerusalem, therefore, distinguished between the Christian Jerusalem of his day and the Jerusalem which crucified Jesus when he wrote: 'This Jerusalem now worshipped him.'[22] 'The God who loves the whole world in Christ has sanctified it and reconciled it to himself.'[23] The whole world has become sacramental. It is, therefore, legitimate to have a sacrament of geography without diminishing in any way God's activity in every other geography. It is humans who need a sense of holy space, not God. Since we cannot live without holy space, it is justifiable to accept the specialness and holiness of certain places more than others. God has acted in this city in a special way for the whole world.

In concluding this section, I would like to mention two points. Firstly, human sense of holiness should not override ethical consideration. Because something is holy it should not license unethical action. The holiness of Jerusalem does not mean that people in power can, in the name or for the sake of this holiness, commit injustice and get by with it. In the days of Jeremiah, the people thought that in spite of their evil and injustice, the city of Jerusalem will be spared from the invading enemy since the holy temple was standing in its midst. The Prophet Jeremiah did not accept that kind of theology. Rather he warned that the moral and ethical demands of God have priority over the sacredness of the place, even if that place were the temple itself.[24] Subsequently, Jerusalem and its temple were destroyed.

In one of his lectures in Jerusalem, Bishop Kenneth Cragg warned that it is wrong to do things in the name of the holy that violates the ethical. When the claim of the holy usurps the demands of the ethical, we are committing an injustice. The criteria of the holy is to bring about that which is good, just, and honest. In the name of the holy we must say with the prophet Amos, 'Let justice run down like water, and righteousness like an everflowing stream.'[25]

Secondly, before one's mind turns to the political importance of Jerusalem, the religious importance takes greater priority and prominence. The religious and spiritual significance of Jerusalem to Judaism, Christianity, and Islam supersedes the political. Many people legitimately believe that the religious significance cannot be

---

[21] John 4: 21-24.
[22] Walker, 1990, p. 401.
[23] 2 Corinthians 5: 19.
[24] Jeremiah 7.
[25] Amos 5: 24.

complete without political sovereignty.[26] Although the acquired holiness and significance of the city can be independent and separate of its political control, we need the political control in order to guarantee fairness for all. Historically, each of the three religions has, at one time or another during its long history in Jerusalem, experienced the absence of political control and consequently suffered religious discrimination.[27] Theoretically, it is possible to fulfil one's religious duties without having political sovereignty over the city. However, the lack of sovereignty hampers and hinders religious freedom. Palestinians can attest to this fact. It has been their daily experience under occupation. The closure of Jerusalem since March 1993 has prevented Muslims and Christians from free access to Jerusalem. Most people have not been able to enter the city in order to worship in their Holy Places especially on the major feast days. In its attempt to Judaise Jerusalem, Israel has suppressed that which is Muslim and Christian and magnified everything which is Jewish. In spite of all of this, Christians and Muslims cling tenaciously to their significance of Jerusalem.

Jerusalem itself, I believe, will ultimately withstand and defy any attempts to exclusivity. Jerusalem cannot be only Jewish. The sooner Israel recognises that this holy space called Jerusalem must be shared equally, the better it would be for the peace and security of all. In other words, although the religious significance is not totally dependent on the political, the political cannot ignore the religious. Therefore, the best requirement for a just peace would demand the sharing of the political sovereignty. The political must bow down to the demands of the religious.[28] The political sharing of sovereignty must be our human response to the holiness of this space. The arrogance of an exclusive sovereign claim must be resisted vehemently. The world community must approach the issue of Jerusalem from its religious significance rather than from its political. It is essential to comprehend deeply that what makes Jerusalem great is not its political character. Rather, it is its religious character which is equally important to Jews, Muslims, and Christians. This is why it is mandatory for the political sovereignty to be shared. An exclusive Israeli political claim will drastically diminish the equal religious significance of the city for the three religions, therefore giving an unjust edge to one. The political should, therefore, serve the needs of maintaining the religious in the best possible way, guaranteeing the equal rights, privileges, duties, and responsibilities of the three faiths. This can best be achieved through a shared sovereignty of the city.

II

Christians cannot think of Jerusalem without thinking of suffering and resurrection.

---

[26] Ucko, 1993, p. 46.

[27] Under the Crusades, Jews and Muslims suffered. Under Islamic rule, Christians and Jews suffered. Under Israeli control, Muslims and Christians suffer.

[28] I am in no way advocating this as a principle that must be always followed. To the contrary, I believe in the separation of religion and state, but in the case of Jerusalem, and for the sake of peace, Jerusalem's religious significance outweighs its political. The religions need parity of rights, because the three religions should take precedence.

It is in this city that our Lord was crucified, died, and was buried, and on the third day resurrected. The passion of our Lord has become the passion of many oppressed people in the world no less our own passion as Palestinians. Tragedy after tragedy has been our experience. Justice has been our cry. The cry of Jesus on the cross has been repeated by many Palestinians, 'My God, my God why have you forsaken me.'[29] The thirty-nine lashes are the lashes of our people, and his agony our agony. Jerusalem is for us the city of suffering, pain, and crucifixion. It is where the prophet Micah in the 8th century BC challenged the political leaders of his day when he said,

> Hear this, you . . . who abhor justice and pervert all equity, who build Zion with blood and Jerusalem with wrong! . . . Therefore because of you Zion shall be plowed as a field; Jerusalem shall become a heap of ruins, and the mountain of the house a wooded height.[30]

In Jerusalem, Isaiah cried out against the injustice of the leaders when he said,

> . . . cease to do evil, learn to do good; seek justice, rescue the oppressed, defend the orphan, plead for the widow.[31]

Jeremiah could not find on the streets of Jerusalem anyone who did justice and in the name of God he declared,

> . . . Do not let the wise boast in their wisdom, do not let the mighty boast in their might, do not let the wealthy boast in their wealth; but let those who boast in this, that they understand and know me, that I am the Lord; I act with steadfast love, justice, and righteousness in the earth, for in these things I delight, says the Lord.[32]

Indeed, a theology of Jerusalem must address itself to injustice, suffering and oppression. The cross and resurrection of Christ become extremely important in this theology. The cross is the epitome of what evil can do; the justice, mercy and love of God is revealed in the victory of Christ over death, evil, and sin. Jerusalem is, indeed, the city of the *Anastasis* (resurrection). Resurrection becomes the source of strength, hope, and new life for us. As Christians we believe that Christ through his death and resurrection has broken the wall of enmity between people of different races and between us humans and God. He is our peace.[33] Therefore, beyond the pain, suffering, and the agony of the cross and all that it resembles in oppression and injustice, life here in Jerusalem can open itself to all of its inhabitants with new

---

[29] Matthew 27: 46.
[30] Micah 3: 9-12.
[31] Isaiah 1: 17.
[32] Jeremiah 5: 1; 9: .23-24.
[33] Ephesians 2: 14-17.

opportunities and possibilities for a new life of peace and reconciliation.

As Christians we can have an important role to play. We can be a bridge. Our role is to witness to the power of God who can reconcile Palestinians and Israelis together. As we believe that the resurrection of Christ was the surprise and the miracle of God, God can create in this city of the resurrection another miracle where peace based on justice can become a reality and where reconciliation can become a fact of life. We only need to open ourselves to the reconciling power of God who can work in us and through us to bring healing and goodness to all the people of this land. The miracle can happen again in Jerusalem and its fruits would be peace and reconciliation for Israelis and Palestinians.

In his book, *Way Of The Cross—Way Of Justice,* Leonardo Boff ends with the words:

> The resurrection is a process that began with Jesus and that will go on until it embraces all creation. Wherever an authentically human life is growing in the world, wherever justice is triumphing over the instincts of domination,
> wherever grace is winning out over the power of sin, wherever human beings are creating more fraternal mediations in their social life together,
> wherever love is getting the better of selfish interests, and wherever hope is resisting the lure of cynicism or despair,
> there the process of resurrection is being turned into a reality.
> Those who believe in the resurrection are no longer permitted to live in sadness.
> The Way of the Cross,
> the painful journey of the Son of God
> and his brothers and sisters
> through the torments of this world,
> does have a real meaning.
> We are destined and called to live life to the full:
> joyous in our hope,
> confident in our love,
> and reconciled to the world,
> our fellow human beings,
> and God.[34]

III

Christians should not think of Jerusalem without thinking of plurality and inclusiveness. Over the centuries, Jerusalem has evolved as a city for Muslims, Christians, and Jews both foreign and local. It is, indeed, a mosaic. Plurality and

---

[34] Boff, *Way of the Cross—Way of Justice,* Orbis Books, New York, 1980, pp. 126-127.

inclusiveness imply at best acceptance, normal relationships, and life together as good neighbours.

In the story of the Good Samaritan[35] we are faced with three philosophies of life. The philosophy of the robbers who are there to steal, dehumanise, and exploit others. They are the criminals and terrorists who know no middle ground. Life with or next to robbers, who always want to grab more, regardless of the rights of others, is impossible. Their perceived end justifies the means. Nothing stands in their own way to achieve what they want. Next we meet the philosophy of the priest and Levite who, in a lesser fashion than the robbers, see their own interest above all others and seem to have nothing to offer to solve the predicament of the wounded person.

Unfortunately many of our neighbours behave like the priest and the Levite, and we too could act like that. The philosophy of the Good Samaritan, however, is that of a person who is willing to share what she/he has with others even at personal risk, in order to be a good neighbour. The Samaritan theology reflects an openness to the enemy. The enemy is now a friend in need. The enemy is a fellow human being and the enmity must be stripped off. It must disappear and love must replace it. A fellow human being is there to whom love and acceptance must be extended.

In a vision of peace for the future we, as Palestinians and Israelis, we as Christians, Jews, and Muslims, must strive to be like the Samaritan. Unfortunately for many years, we have competed with each other for the position of the victim, who of us is the greater victim, stripped and beaten by the robbers. It is time now, rather, to compete for the Samaritan's place. Only this will ensure healing and life.

Jerusalem, as well as our whole land, is full of mutual enemies where bitterness and resentment run high. At the same time, God in history has created in Jerusalem a mosaic of various people of various backgrounds to live together. God places before us today the possibility of death or life.[36] We have a choice of living as enemies and reaping the tragedy of a life of injustice or live with the ethic of the Good Samaritan. We see Jerusalem as our home where the enemy to each of us must become a friend. Where, even at our own risk, we must accept and include the other. Acceptance must replace alienation. Enmity must give way to friendship. Fear must be supplanted by trust. We should strive to make real a part of the dream of Micah and Isaiah where we beat our swords into plowshares and our spears into pruning hooks . . . and not learn war anymore.[37] Micah saw a vision of an inclusive Jerusalem whose inhabitants were of mixed races and of different religions where ' . . . all the peoples walk, each in the name of its god . . .'[38] Jerusalem becomes a real place of diversity, plurality, and inclusiveness for all of its inhabitants.

What are the practical implications of this theology?

1   We must consider Jerusalem as a *waqf,* religious trust, a trust from God.

---

[35] Luke 10: 30-37.
[36] Deuteronomy 30: 15, 29.
[37] Micah 4: 3; Isaiah 2: 4-5
[38] Micah 4: 5.

Humans have long believed that in this city they encounter God in a special way. God has touched many people's lives here. Regardless of how we have come to interpret it as Jews, Muslims, and Christians, this one fact remains valid: we all witness in our different languages of faith that, in Jerusalem we have an experience of the holy. God has met us and continues to meet us in Jerusalem in a special way. We do not own it. Jerusalem belongs to God. We are placed here by God and entrusted with it to be good stewards and to maintain it in such a way that it would continue to be a place of encounter with God for Muslims, Jews, and Christians. For us Christians in particular, it would always be a place where we would continue to witness to the presence of a living Lord and Saviour.

2   We should insist that political sovereignty over Jerusalem should begin with the acknowledgement of the overall sovereignty of God. As Daniel told King Nebuchadnessar, we need to learn '. . . that the Most High has sovereignty over the kingdom of mortals . . .'[39] For the sake of justice, lasting security, and peace, we need a shared political sovereignty over the city, under God who is ultimately the only supreme sovereign. This means accepting each other as brothers and sisters and, in the name of God, honouring each other by granting equal justice for all. It is our moral obligation and responsibility to witness to the love and mercy of God who has entrusted us with Jerusalem. Jerusalem in its plurality challenges any narrow doctrine of God. The way we envisage a solution for Jerusalem, would indicate whether we hold an inclusive or exclusive understanding of God. It also tests our faithfulness to God in being our brother's and sister's keeper. God offers us Jerusalem with a choice. We can either make it the city of perpetual strife or we can make it a paradigm for peace.

3   So far, might seems to have determined the right in the Israel/Palestine conflict. It is high time to let right guide us so that it may become our might and our strength. It would be indeed tragic if Israel would sacrifice the ethical and moral for the arrogance of an exclusive claim to sovereignty. The city of Jerusalem, I believe, will ultimately rebuff it. The religious significance of the three religions, demands a sharing of the political in order to guarantee the religious.

Conclusion

On his last journey to Jerusalem, Jesus agonised over the city and its people. He accused it for not responding to his passionate love. 'Jerusalem . . . how often have I desired to gather your children together as a hen gathers her brood under her wings, and you were not willing!'[40] This was the statement of a person who felt the pain and hurt of a city and of a people who did not 'know the things that make for peace.'[41] Forty years later, the city was destroyed. Inevitably, those who contradict the ways of

---

[39] Daniel 4: 25.
[40] Matthew 23: 37, Luke 13: 34.
[41] Luke 19: 42.

justice and truth will only reap destruction and cut themselves from the city and land. Sooner or later the bitter end will come.

Towards the end of the 1st century, the persecution of the Christian community by the Romans intensified. The writer of the Book of Revelation describes in visions and symbols both the desperate situation of the people of God as well as looks forward to the ultimate victory of God. The world had become so corrupt with evil and sin that nothing short of a new creation is needed to redeem it. A new heaven and a new earth that would entail new relationships between God and people. A new Jerusalem would have to come down from heaven to replace the old corrupt and destroyed city.

Figuratively speaking, Jerusalem cannot be built on the basis of old mentalities, old concepts, and old covenants. It demands new approaches, renewed mentalities, and new covenants. In the Middle East today, we are presumably in a peace process where the two sides recognise that occupation, oppression, and terrorism will not yield a life of security and peace. The old Jerusalem must die. The Jerusalem that some people want to build exclusively for the well-being of one side must be destroyed in our minds and psyche, in our hearts and memory if we truly long for peace and security in Jerusalem and the land. With the benefit of historical hindsight, any monopoly of Jerusalem by one nation or one religion, inevitably, sows with it the seeds of its own destruction.

Put candidly, the survival of the Jews cannot be guaranteed by constructing a Jerusalem built on injustice. We must, with all our power, prevent it for their own sake as well as for ours. We must construct a new Jerusalem for Palestinians and Israelis for the 21st century. It is possible today to envisage a new Jerusalem coming down from heaven. The Jerusalem that is fit for peace and security must be reinvented and recreated. Its new vision comes from God. Jews can keep Jerusalem, only if they let go of it; that is, they can be a part of it, if they are willing to share it. They can enjoy it if they liberate it from their exclusive control. They must love it without choking it. These words sound folly to people absorbed by the arrogance of power and who never seem to anticipate the possibility of losing that power. Yet such is the folly and absurdity of power. Be that as it may, today if Israelis and Palestinians are ready to be open to each other and to God, who should be acknowledged as the sole owner of the city of Jerusalem, it is possible to receive a new Jerusalem coming down from heaven.

In the 1st century, the earthly Jerusalem was destroyed because it did not know what makes for peace. The present contemporary Jerusalem is being constructed on the same basis. It cannot be permanent because it is not just. God offers a vision of a new holy city of Jerusalem adorned with precious stones whose gates are always open because it is safe and just and there is no danger of any theft, or falsehood, or lies, or shameful or impure things.[42]

God will dwell in it.

See, the home of God is among mortals. He will dwell with them as

---

[42] Revelations 21: 2; 10-27.

their God; they will be his peoples, and God himself will be with them; he will wipe every tear from their eyes. Death will be no more; mourning and crying and pain will be no more, for the first things have passed away.[43]

God is setting a vision before all the inhabitants of Jerusalem today, and especially to people in power. It is an offer from God of a recreated new Jerusalem. A Jerusalem which is more just and holy. A Jerusalem which is more inclusive and pluralistic. We have a chance today to be partners with God in reinventing a Jerusalem that can be a fitting place for the indwelling of God with all of its inhabitants.

The deepest lesson of human life is when a person finds beyond time the secrets of living truly in time. If the city coming down from God can be imprinted in our hearts to become our dream and vision for the future of Jerusalem, God will give us the power to lift our present Jerusalem to that higher vision.[44] God is offering us a new future. If we can envision it, conceive it, dream it, will it, and work for it, it can, by the mercy and grace of God, become a reality.

---

[43] Revelations 21: 4.

16
THE SPIRITUALITY OF CHRISTIAN PILGRIMAGE
Anba Abraham

Since the beginning of Christianity, the Holy Land has been rich in Christian Holy Places. These Holy Places still stand, bearing witness to the wondrous Salvation of our beloved Redeemer. It is written: 'For God so loved the world that he gave his only Son, so that everyone who believes in him may not perish but may have eternal life' (John 3: 16). These holy sites are a physical, tangible proof, and an archaeological, historical witness of the reality of salvation through our Lord Jesus Christ two thousand years ago. Jesus said on the day he entered Jerusalem (Palm Sunday): 'I tell you, if these were silent, the stones would shout out' (Luke 19: 40). The stones of the Holy Places still cry out in witness, as if telling visitors and pilgrims of the Lord's personal salvation for them. Throughout Christian history, many people have experienced salvation through pilgrimage.

St Mary, the mother of Jesus, often accompanied the three Marys and the virgins of Jerusalem and others, to visit the empty tomb which stood witness to the resurrection of our Lord. On Easter Day, the angel told Mary Magdalene and the other Mary: 'He is not here; for he has been raised, as he said: "Come, see the place where he lay . . ."' (Matthew 28: 6). This is a heavenly invitation by the angel to all of us, to come and see the empty tomb, and be sure that he rose from the dead as he said he would, and raised us with him from the grip of Satan, from the power of death and all our sins.

Mary the Copt, who spent her life in sin, was transformed, and her heart softened when she entered the Church of the Holy Sepulchre and saw the crucifix and him who was crucified for us and who bore all the pain and shame for her, as is written: 'And if anyone asks them, "What are these wounds on your chest?" the answer will be, "These wounds I received in the house of my friends"' (Zechariah 13: 6) and also: 'But he was wounded for our transgressions, crushed for our iniquities; upon him was the punishment that made us whole, and by his bruises we are healed' (Isaiah 53: 5). Just by looking at the Crucified and seeing his wounds, four centuries after his crucifixion, she was healed of the wounds of sin that imprisoned her all her life. Mary the Copt was healed by the figure of the Crucified, just as in ancient times when people were healed by looking at the brass serpent. They were healed of the poison of the real serpent which is the temptations of Satan. She changed the direction of her life from one of base passion to one of divine ecstasy, the divine love that poured from the cross. She spent the rest of her life in the wilderness of the Jordan Valley until just before her death, when she met St Suziama who administered the Holy Sacraments to her and to whom she narrated the story of her salvation. He told her story, proclaiming the hope of salvation through the blood of our Saviour Jesus Christ who cleanses us of every sin.

Over the ages, believers have come from near and far, to walk in his footsteps and to see the site of his suffering and the site of the salvation story. They feel sanctified by walking the Via Dolorosa, the path that Emmanuel, our God, walked. The place of God's presence is holy, like the place of the 'burning bush' when Moses heard a voice saying: 'Remove the sandals from your feet, for the place on which you are standing is holy ground' (Exodus 3: 5). So also is the ground on which God incarnate, Jesus Christ our Saviour, walked. It is a land that flows with holiness for those who visit it with simple faith and purity of heart and conscience. Pilgrims are able to live through the events of the salvation story, from the annunciation to the birth of Jesus, his baptism, temptation on the mountain, his miracles, his life-giving teachings that take us away from death into a life of love as only he can love. It is written: 'We know that we have passed from death to life because we love one another' (1 John 3: 14). As pilgrims walk in his footsteps, and as they hear him blessing the poor, they desire to be poor; as they hear him blessing the pure of heart, they yearn for that purity of heart that would lead them to seeing him. A transformation takes place inside them, for they are God's holy temples. They can then see him in a transcendental way, in the heavenly Jerusalem, in eternal life.

In this manner, a believer can live through Holy Week, feeling the joy of being in the same place where all the events of the salvation drama took place. They try to fast as he has fasted, they try to abstain from worldly pleasures and to live a life of piety and worship, especially when they are in the very same places where he was. Many live on bread and salt alone.

After sunset: '[We] share his sufferings by becoming like him in his death' (Philippians 3: 10), and '. . . so that the life of Jesus may be made visible in our mortal flesh' (2 Corinthians 4: 11) for if we suffer with him, we will also share his glory.

1   When we discover that his Holy Tomb lies outside the ancient walls, we remember that they took him outside the camp to crucify him. 'Let us then go to him outside the camp and bear the abuse he endured' (Hebrews 13: 13). This memory will give us the courage to carry the shame of Christ. We will not share in the sins of others or conform with this age, but be transformed by the renewing of our minds (Romans 12: 2). We are then able to bear the insult and pain that witnessing to him could bring. By distancing ourselves from sinful pleasures, we witness to his death.

2   As we visit the grave of Lazarus, who was brought back to life by the Lord four days after his death, we remember that Christ is our life and resurrection, provided we repent, and regardless of the gravity of our sins.

3   As we take part in the Palm Sunday procession and walk the path that Jesus walked two thousand years ago; when children and simple folk met him and cried 'Hosanna' (which means 'save us') we feel a genuine desire to cry out with them for salvation from our heavy burdens.

4   We would like to allow him into our hearts to cleanse them, as he cleansed the temple. When we hear him say: '. . . to pray always and not lose heart' (Luke 18: 1), i.e., until we ourselves become a prayer, as the psalmist says: 'I myself am a prayer,' we ask him to reign over our hearts, our lives and our actions.

5   As we visit the place where the sinful woman wept, where she poured the costly ointment over his feet, in the house of Simon the Pharisee, we are assured that he will come into our homes and our hearts, no matter how sinful they might be. We feel the desire to invite him so that we can pour out all our energy as a sacrifice of love in the service of his children, all his children, so that our good deeds will glorify his name and we will become the sweet scent of Christ.

6   As we hear him curse the fig tree for showing what it is not, for appearing good, when actually it is fruitless; we give up hypocrisy and insist on the truth.

7   As we visit the place where he bent over and washed his disciples' feet, we invite him to cleanse us of pride so that we can serve our brothers and sisters, regardless of how much of the dirt of this world they might have accumulated.

8   As he offers his holy body and his precious blood so that we might live and be cleansed by them, we comprehend the depth of his love. He said: '. . . unless you eat the flesh of the Son of Man and drink his blood, you have no life in you' (John 6: 53). We also comprehend the meaning of his presence for he has said: 'Do this in remembrance of me' (1 Corinthians 11: 24). What Jesus means is remembrance through seeing and not just by mental recollection. This is what the original translation of the word 'remembrance' means.

9   We see him praying in Gethsemane, his perspiration like drops of blood, as he prays to the Father: 'Father, if you are willing, remove this cup from me; yet, not my will but yours be done' (Luke 22: 42). This teaches us to put the will of God before our own, no matter how difficult it is to comprehend at the time. It gives us peace to accept joyfully what God has planned for us.

10   As we see them come with torches to arrest him and take him to his death; as we see him heal the ear of the high priest's servant, we learn to put love into practice even for those who have done us wrong. We also learn from what he told Peter: 'Put your sword back, for all who draw the sword will die by the sword' (Matthew 26: 53). This is a call for reconciliation, love and peace.

11   On the way to Calvary, when the women mourned and lamented for him, Jesus turned to them and said: 'Daughters of Jerusalem, do not weep for me, but weep for yourselves and for your children' (Luke 23: 28). We have to understand the depth of this command in order to be concerned for our salvation and that of our children. According to St. Paul: ' . . . I did not cease night or day to warn everyone with tears' (Acts 20: 31).

12   Simon of Cyrene tried to carry the cross of Jesus but was not able to, because the real cross was not the wooden cross but the sins of humanity that Christ took upon himself.

13   We see him hanging on the cross to give us life through his death and to restore to us the dignity of his image through the shame of the cross that he bore. Adam stretched his hand to pick the fruit of death, but Jesus stretched his arms to pick the fruit of life for us. Adam enjoyed the taste of the delicious forbidden fruit,

but Jesus suffered from the taste of the bitter vinegar. Adam wanted to wear the false crown of divinity, but Jesus wore the painful crown of thorns in order to wipe away our sins. Who could take pleasure in sin anymore or allow his or her body to be defiled after its sanctification through his blood?

14   His body was washed with perfume and sweet smelling ointment, so how could we allow our bodies to be defiled by the stench of sin? His body was laid in a new grave, so let us put him in our hearts that are renewed through repentance day by day until he is resurrected in us and until he raises us with him to eternal life.

Visiting the holy sites helps us to live the holy events of salvation as we see and feel them not only with our eyes and senses but with our hearts and souls. We can then say with St John: ' . . . what we have heard, what we have seen with our eyes, what we have looked at and touched with our hands' (1 John 1: 1). We enjoy the glory of salvation in as much as we can capture the mysteries of God through these holy witnesses—the Holy Places—with the help of our senses and our insight.

17
LOCAL COMMUNITY AND TOURISM
Zoughbi Zoughbi

I would like to begin by reading excerpts from a poem written by Cecil Rajendra
entitled, 'When the tourists flew in':

> The Finance Minister said
> 'It will boost the economy
> The Dollars will flow in.'
>
> The Interior Minister said
> 'It will provide full and
> varied employment
> for all indigenes'
>
> The Minister of Culture said
> 'It will enrich our life . . .
> contact with other cultures
> improve the texture of living'
>
> When the tourists flew in
> we were asked to be 'side walk'
> ambassadors
> to stay smiling and polite
> to always guide the 'lost' visitor . . .
>
> When the tourists flew in
> what culture we had flew out the window
> we traded our customs
> for sunglasses and pop
> we turned sacred ceremonies
> into ten-cent peep shows
>
> When the tourists flew in
> the hunger and the squalor
> were preserved as a passing pageant for
> clicking cameras-a chic eye-sore!

Hell, if we could only tell them
where we really want them to go!

Cecil Rajendra
Contours, vol. 7, no. 2, June 1995, p. 38

Indeed, tourism is a mixed blessing. It is something we both want yet fear.

When we talk about tourism, we certainly talk about the economy. Today, we will not tackle this aspect, rather, we will talk about pilgrimage. I am not advocating visits to holy stones only, but rather the interaction with the *living stones* in order to understand the current rolling stones which is my term for the socio-economic political situation. Yes, what we are eager to see is the positive interactions on two levels as Christians and as Arab Palestinians.

As Christians who consider ourselves the offshoots of the natural branch of the olive tree and in unity with the Christian family all over the world, we would like to be seen as we really are, Arab Palestinian Christians, an integral part of the globe and in sisterly and brotherly relationship with all human beings regardless of colour, race, religion, sex and nationality.

On the Arab Palestinian level, we seek solidarity. The purpose of solidarity is not for material resources only, nor merely to visit archaeological sites and ancient stones of civilisation and Christian heritage, but beyond that; 'to go beyond stereotypes and ideologies to meet Christian brothers and sisters, struggling to bear witness to the risen Lord in the contradictions and creativity of the Middle East.'

Therefore interactions with tourists should give the group first-hand experience and knowledge, instead of indoctrination. Our policy should give tourists a chance to hear from Muslims, Jews and Christians; covering the different political, social, economic and religious spectrums. Most group members come with their own prejudices and biases based on their own information and experience, but after the trip and evaluation period, they are not the same, they are new creatures. Most cannot believe what they have seen.

Many people are unaware that there are Arab Palestinian Christians. I have often had group members ask me when I have converted to Christianity. My response to them is that I have been converted by the hand of a great man and teacher, by the name of Jesus Christ. In another instance a woman in one of the groups was wearing a gold necklace of the Star of David. After visiting the Occupied Territories and the Palestinian refugee camps, she angrily took off her necklace and gave it to me and said sell it and give it to the needy. I told her to keep the necklace as a reminder to seek justice. 'We do not want you to be anti-Israel as much as we want you to be pro-justice, no matter where justice stands.'

I have witnessed many instances where I have seen prejudices and stereotyping break down. Groups visit the Dome of the Rock, the third most holy place for Muslims, and one of the head sheikhs usually meets with our groups. After one such meeting, one man turned to me and said, 'Oh, they [Muslims] are not all fundamentalists.' A favourite speaker is a Jewish survivor of the Holocaust who works for peace and justice for Israelis and Palestinians. He talks about human-rights abuses of Palestinians, and says that what was done to Jews during the Holocaust is no justification for what is being done to Palestinians today. His words have helped many people put their guilt over the Holocaust into perspective and inspired them to work for justice for all people.

Groups sometimes spend two or three days in Palestinian Christian homes. For most people coming from a first world lifestyle, staying with Palestinians is somewhat of a revelation. We often have a shortage of water in the Occupied Territories and we have learned to use it efficiently. One woman told me that she felt she was doing her part by recycling paper in the United States, but when she stayed with her host family and saw how they used the water, she realised how much more could be done. The Palestinian mother first used the water to wash the clothes, then used the water that was left to wash the floor, and then the water was used a third time to flush the toilets. And many group members did not realise what a luxury central heating and hot water were until they spent a night in a home that had neither. I have heard over and over again, please come and celebrate Eucharist with the local Palestinians rather than visiting or passing by a church.

These are what I consider successful stories of interaction, where it becomes a learning and understanding experience rather than just a good time. Such alternative trips are valuable because they enhance education. People learn new things, and unlearn others. As Arab Christians living in the Holy Land, we often feel isolated from the greater Christian community around the world, but meeting all the concerned Christians who show an interest in the local community has made us feel more connected. The prefix once used for Palestinians as terrorists will not be used anymore or be replaced by the word fundamentalist.

Tourists should not look down on any culture. They should rather learn about the differences which enrich the human experience. We are not interested in trivialisation of our regional culture. 'A tourist being photographed on the back of a donkey might be beautiful but it is not the kind of stuff so important or catchy as to represent one's culture.'

As Arab Palestinians interaction always helps us dispel myths and stereotypes. Yes, I have heard it several times; foreigners are not like those whom we see in the movies, plays or soap operas, like 'The Bold and the Beautiful', or 'The Love Boat'. Not all of them are anti-Islam or anti-Arabs. It certainly helps and encourages us Palestinians to reach expatriates much more effectively and to invest in a relationship with them.

Dear brothers and sisters, the scripture says, 'Let brotherly love continue.' Let brotherly and 'sisterly' love continue. 'Be not forgetful to entertain strangers. For thereby some have entertained angels unawares' (Hebrews 13: 1).

This is the call of heaven for each of us not only to entertain tourists but to care for each other and have a lively interaction based or faith, love, care, unity and solidarity.

18

A PERSPECTIVE ON PILGRIMAGE TO THE HOLY LAND

Michael Prior

The notion of pilgrimage is a popular one in much discussion of Christian life, from Chaucer's *Canterbury Tales,* through Bunyan's *Pilgrim's Progress* to George Herbert's *The Pilgrimage*, and there is no end to poetic discussions of the more general phenomenon of journey. The practice of pilgrimage occupies a significant part in the spirituality of many Christians. Since it focuses attention on what religious people do, rather than on what they believe, pilgrimage raises fundamental religious questions.

Does Christianity have a theology of sacred places, in the fashion Judaism and Islam have? While in Islam it is a sacred duty to make the pilgrimage to Mecca (Qu'ran 2: 196; 3: 97), Christianity does not require its faithful to make pilgrimage. In fact, St John's Gospel (Chapter 4) is presented as raising the question of the significance of place in the Christian dispensation, since Christ spoke of worship *in spirit and in truth*, rather than on either Mount Gerizim or Mount Zion. Nevertheless, St Jerome, in commenting on, 'Let us go to his dwelling place; let us worship at his footstool!' (Psalm 132: 7), says, 'The psalmist commands that we worship (Christ) in the place where his feet stood' (Jerome *Ep.*, 46.7).

Recently Christopher Lewis has reopened the question of the place of Holy Land pilgrimage in Christian life. He puts his case stridently:

> The significance of the incarnation is not that God is a God of one place to the exclusion of others; it is that he is a God of all places, active in his world . . . God is to be found especially in people; namely in those in need and in the gathered community of the Church . . . It follows that to set off on a journey to grow nearer to Christ is at best a complex matter. It might be that the true search is among those in need . . . In that case a pilgrimage to Israel in search of places where Christ is present, should concentrate not on Jerusalem but rather on the refugee camps and on the aid which can be given to those who are oppressed. Alternatively, the trail . . . may lead back to the church at home (Lewis 1989: 390-91).

He suggests that for the person sweating round the sites, the appropriate text should be, 'He is not here; he has risen' (Matthew 28: 6), or, 'Why do you seek the living among the dead?' (Luke 24: 5). Lewis disdains the attachment to the empty tomb. Christ is in the breaking of bread and in Beirut.

> No place has a claim on God; if any place does, it is the refugee camp
> or the psychiatric ward, but that is because of the occupants and not
> because of anything intrinsic in the place (Lewis 1989: 392-93).

Lewis offers no evidence for any of his claims, and he seems to presume that pilgrimage is at best a distraction from the real encounter with the Risen Christ, which is to be found among people, especially those in distress. He does not seem sensitive to the possibility that people who go on pilgrimage undergo significant conversion to Christian values and action. Since Lewis carries out his discussion on purely theoretical grounds, without reference to the testimony of any pilgrim from any religion, ancient or modern, his assertion is unconvincing. He does not distinguish between the claims of theoretical speculation, and the results of real pilgrimage. An investigation which is sensitive to the value and results of the practice, both in antiquity and today, is called for.

Pilgrimage is a significant religious enterprise in virtually every world religion, and in all periods. This fact alone should caution one against dismissing it. Antipathy to the practice of pilgrimage and to elaborate rituals in religious services, which is detectable in some of the Reformed traditions of the West, owes much to vestiges of a body-soul dualism, which plays down the function of the body, and to the Enlightenment's advocacy of the primacy of reason.

In classical terms, pilgrimage involves leaving the security of one's own place, with its ritual of preparations and sense of separation. Secondly, it is a journey to a particular place, which is marked by an intensity of holiness. Thirdly, the pilgrim has her/his heart set on some personal purpose, e.g., purification, or forgiveness. Finally, in antiquity at least, such pilgrimages were always accompanied by physical difficulties, trials, or threats of failure (Partin 1967). It is striking how these elements feature also in the exodus traditions of the Israelites,[1] and also in the Gospel. It is likely that ritual has helped to generate the narratives as they now exist. The four characteristics are all features of traditional rites of passage, involving initiation into a new status. The detection of these features in diverse contexts suggests that we are dealing with a universal human disposition.

Jesus on Pilgrimage

Since Christians look to the example of Jesus, it is instructive to consider his attitude

---

[1] One discerns in the literary account of Israel's origins, from the exodus from Egypt to settlement in the land of Canaan, that the Israelites pass through three distinct phases: (i) *separation* (involving the exodus and the crossing of the Sea of Reeds), (ii) *boundary* (corresponding to the forty years of wandering in the desert), and (iii) *reincorporation* (corresponding to the crossing of the Jordan, the conquest and the settlement). While on the journey the Israelites make pilgrimage to a sacred mountain, experience a theophany, receive instruction for the new life, and emerge from the wilderness bonded together.

to pilgrimage. Apart from the one pilgrimage to Jerusalem, on Passover when he was twelve (only in Luke 2: 41-50), according to the Synoptic Gospels Jesus came to Jerusalem only on the Sunday of the final week of his life (Matthew 21-28; Mark 11-16; Luke 21-24). John, on the other hand, has Jesus visit Jerusalem for the Jewish Feasts: first visit (Passover, John 2-3); second visit (Sabbath, John 5); third visit (Feast of Tabernacles, John 7); fourth visit (Feast of Dedication, John 10: 22-39); and the fifth and final visit (Passover, John 12-20). But even the literary construction and content of Jesus' movement from Galilee to Jerusalem betrays some of the classical features of pilgrimage.

It is a feature of Luke's presentation of Jesus' own journey/pilgrimage to Jerusalem. First, we have the *leaving:*

> When the days drew near for him to be received up, he set his face to go to Jerusalem (Luke 9: 51; cf. 9: 53).

The reader is left in no doubt about Jesus' *determination and purpose:*

> Nevertheless I must go on my way today and tomorrow and the day following' (Luke 13: 33) . . . And taking the twelve, he said to them, 'Behold, we are going up to Jerusalem, and everything that is written of the Son of Man by the prophets will be accomplished' (18: 31) . . . And when he drew near and saw the city he wept over it (19: 41) . . . And he entered the temple and began to drive out those who sold (19: 45).

The *difficulty* involved is outlined:

> For it cannot be that a prophet should perish away from Jerusalem. O Jerusalem, Jerusalem killing the prophets and stoning those who are sent to you! . . . until you say, 'Blessed is he who comes in the name of the Lord' (Luke 13: 33-35).

In Luke's literary presentation, the readers are invited to join in the pilgrimage, and to share in the difficulties to be encountered:[2]

> As they were going along the road, someone said to him, 'I will follow you wherever you go.' And Jesus said to him, 'Foxes have holes, and birds of the air have nests; but the Son of Man has nowhere to lay his head.' To another he said, 'Follow me.' But he said, 'Lord, first let me go and bury my father.' But Jesus said to him,

---

[2] It is in the Journey to Jerusalem (Luke 9: 51-19: 10) that we read of the duties and privileges of discipleship (9: 51-10.24), the characteristics of disciples (10: 25-11: 13), the readiness for the coming crisis (12: 1-13: 21), and the cost of discipleship (18: 9-19: 10).

'Let the dead bury their own dead; but as for you, go and proclaim the kingdom of God.' Another said, 'I will follow you, Lord; but let me first say farewell to those at my home.' Jesus said to him, 'No one who puts a hand to the plough and looks back is fit for the kingdom of God' (Luke 9: 57-62).

Now great multitudes accompanied him; and he turned and said to them, 'Whoever comes to me and does not hate father and mother, wife and children, brothers and sisters, yes, and even life itself, cannot be my disciple' (Luke 14: 25-26).

However, the city of Jerusalem was neither the goal of the pilgrimage of Jesus—the sentence, 'the days drew near for him to be received up' anticipates the Ascension—nor the resting-place of the disciples.[3] Jesus' last words to them before He ascended were,

Repentance and forgiveness of sins is to be proclaimed in his name to all nations, *beginning from Jerusalem*. You are witnesses of these things. And see, I am sending upon you what my Father promised; so *stay here in the city until* you have been clothed with power from on high (Luke 24: 47-49).

The Acts of the Apostles, the second volume of Luke's work (Luke-Acts), takes up the story at the Ascension scene, with Jesus charging the disciples,

. . . not to leave Jerusalem, but to wait there for the promise of the Father. 'This,' he said, 'is what you have heard from me . . . But you will receive power when the Holy Spirit has come upon you; and you will be my witnesses in Jerusalem, in all Judea and Samaria, and to the ends of the earth' (Acts 1: 4-11).

Those who with Jesus go up to Jerusalem, whether as contemporary disciples, or subsequent readers, therefore, should hope to be empowered from on high, so that they can be witnesses to the ends of the earth.[4]

---

[3] The pattern is detectable also in that great Christian adaptation of the Exodus-settlement traditions, the Letter to the Hebrews, with its sensitivity to *separation* (Hebrews 11: 15; cf. 6: 2; 10: 22), *sacred place* (11: 10, 16; 13: 14), *determination* (12: 4), and, above all in this context, the *difficulties* to be encountered (3: 12-18; 5: 11-6: 12; 10: 23-26; 12: 4). In the perspective of the Letter to the Hebrews, the Christian life is a pilgrimage in the footsteps of Him who has gone before us. Contemplation of His pilgrimage will enable one to persevere.
[4] See the development of the theme, the universalism of Luke-Acts, in Prior 1995: 48-60.

Christianity and Pilgrimage in Antiquity[5]

While there are clear patterns of similarity in the practice of pilgrimage over a wide range of periods and places, modern studies of the phenomenon over a variety of cultures reveal fundamental differences. Recent work by anthropologists of pilgrimage protest against all attempts to predicate a unity of experience on the part of pilgrims. They argue that such generalisations run in the face of the obvious diversity of perceptions and reactions, and can be seen to be a crude superimposition of a uniform, but false model of pilgrimage on the diversity of its reality.[6]

The question posed by Desmond O'Grady,[7] *apropos* of journeying in general, gets at the heart of the search involved also in pilgrimage:

> Why all this voyaging? What do
> we hope to find beyond those icons . . .
> What are we looking for
> and what shall we do
> if ever we find it?

One wonders, if travel in general broadens the mind, whether pilgrimage to sacred places enlivens the spirit? According to Cynthia Ozick, 'A visitor passes through a place; the place passes through the pilgrim.'[8]

Gregory of Nyssa's famous letter of 379 BC (*Ep.* 2, in *Patrologia Graeca,* J P Migne, (ed.) Paris, 1841-, vol. xlvi, 1012d) is presented as an embarrassment to supporters of pilgrimage. His major critique of the practice is that, in addition to the New Testament's silence on pilgrimage, and the immorality involved in bringing the two sexes together, Christianity has no thoughts on places. Instead it stresses that the core of religion relates to closeness to God and neighbour. Going to places brings people no closer to God, he claims, and hence Christians should stay at home. Moreover, the church in Cappadocia is in better condition than that in Jerusalem.

But that is only part of the picture. Contrary to popular opinion, Gregory was no doctrinaire critic of the *tactile spirituality* one associates with places sanctified by Christ. He recognised that in a profound sense the Holy Land was especially holy for Christians because of the fact that Jesus traversed it. The terrain itself, he says has 'signs of the Lord's sojourn in the flesh.' Gregory's context here is different from the other one. He was reacting against the uncompromising intellectualism of a fellow bishop, Eunomius, for whom the dogmatic exactness of Christianity, couched in the language of a philosophical system was prized above all else. Gregory insisted that Christianity was not a matter of the mind only, but invited participation in sacramental practices and symbols. The terrain of the Holy Places 'received the footprints of Life itself,' and serve to remind one that God once walked the earth.

---

[5] See further Prior 1994.
[6] See, e.g., Eade and Sallnow, eds. 1991. For particular reference to the 'Holy Lands', see Bowman 1995.
[7] *At Sea,* in O'Grady 1977: 34.
[8] Cynthia Ozick 1983: 154, quoted in Wilken 1992: 110.

According to Bishop Paulinus of Nola, 'No other sentiment draws people to Jerusalem than the desire to see and touch the places where Christ was physically present, and to be able to say from their own experience, "We have gone into his tabernacle, and have worshipped in the places where his feet stood."'[9] As if by way of some kind of osmosis, the pilgrim absorbs some of the holiness of the place. This is strikingly true of Jerusalem, for there God manifested himself crucially, quite literally, on Golgotha, which, of all places, therefore, is *charged with the grandeur of God*. For Christians, Jerusalem and the surrounding areas were the scene of the historical origins of their faith. Equally significant, perhaps, was the Christian belief that the Second Coming of Christ would take place in that land.

Fundamental to the notion of pilgrimage is that of a sacred place. For Christians, Golgotha became the centre of the world.[10] Whereas the Jews in the past had focused their attention on the temple, so now Christians focused on the Hill of Golgotha. This emphasis can be seen in *Mappa Mundi* in Hereford Cathedral, which places Jerusalem, and the Crucifixion, at the very centre of the world.

In addition to the associations of the sacred with particular places (timeless and ahistorical), there is also the association with the place in terms of time and history. When one talks of a sacred place within the three Abrahamic faiths invariably one associates it with the manifestation of some aspect of the divinity within history, be it the history of Jews, and/or Christians, and/or Muslims. The Holy Land has a person-sacredness, prior to Jesus. In Jewish perspectives, it is the terrain chosen by God Himself as the dwelling place for his chosen people. For Christians, therefore, it is doubly sacred, and much more than in terms of the sacredness one associates with static, inanimate shrines embedded in the landscape.

While the origins of Christian pilgrimage are obscure, the practice certainly predates the conscious efforts of the emperor Constantine to provide a physical anchorage for the Bible, the Sacred Scriptures of the newly adopted state religion with which he hoped to unify his empire. Melito of Sardis visited the Holy Land in the middle of the 2nd century, *so as to establish accurately the books of the Old Testament,* and to examine the relevant places. He was in search of the biblical past, and is the earliest known Christian pilgrim.

Alexander, a future bishop of Jerusalem, travelled from Cappadocia in the reign of Caracalla, with *the stated purpose of prayer and investigation of the sites.* Origen travelled around Palestine *seeking out the location of events recorded in the Scriptures.* Firmilianus, a Cappadocian bishop, visited Origen, and *was in the Holy Land for the sake of the Holy Places.* Pionius, a contemporary of Origen, also visited the Holy Land. Such examples as these make it clear that Palestine was already a place of Christian pilgrimage before the time of Constantine. The province of Palestine harboured the Christian origins of the pilgrims, and was also the place of the future advent.

---

[9] The letters of Paulinus of Nola are in his *Carmina* and *Epistulae,* ed. G de Hartel (*CSEL* 29-30, 1894).

[10] Writing about the year 160 AD, Melito of Sardis spoke of Christ being crucified in the middle of the city (*On Pascha*), which of course conflicts with the New Testament location of Golgotha as being outside of the city. It is likely that he was unaware of the location of Golgotha within Hadrian's colony.

Immediately after his victory at Chrysopolis in 324, Constantine put an end to all persecutions against the Christians, and ordered the restoration of the church's property in the eastern part of the empire. Presumably, the news that the Holy Sepulchre had been discovered and that the site had been reclaimed and converted into a Christian basilica increased the number of pilgrims to the region. The erection of such buildings with imperial encouragement and ongoing support marks the transition of the Christian community from being an insecure one, to becoming a state-sponsored, publicly worshipping one.

The Bordeaux Pilgrim (333 AD) was away from home for at least a year. His account is little more than a list of places to which he attaches an incident from the Old Testament, or from the New Testament, without any sensitivity to a hierarchy of place. There is no mention of any praying, or liturgies, or of any contact with any people in the land. The journey of Egeria (381-384), too, had as its fundamental basis the desire to visit the Holy Places. It was a feature of Egeria's pilgrimage that services of worship accompanied the visits to the Christian sites, with the central place given to the reading of the appropriate biblical text. Egeria's Bible was her constant travelling companion:

> And it was always our practice when we managed to reach one of the places we wanted to see to have first a prayer, then a reading from the book, then to say an appropriate psalm and another prayer. By God's grace we always followed this practice whenever we were able to reach a place we wanted to see (Egeria 10.7, in Wilkinson 1971: 105-106).

According to the account of St Jerome, veneration of the sacred sites was high on the priorities of two Roman noblewomen, Paula and her daughter. Of her visit to Jerusalem he says,

> She started to go round visiting all the places with such burning enthusiasm that there was no taking her away from one unless she was hurrying to another. She fell down and worshipped before the Cross as if she could see the Lord hanging on it. On entering the Tomb of the Resurrection she kissed the stone which the angel removed from the sepulchre door; then like a thirsty man who has waited long, and at last comes to water, she faithfully kissed the very shelf on which the Lord's body had lain. Her tears and lamentations there are known to all Jerusalem-or rather to the Lord himself to whom she was praying (Jerome's *Letter (108) to Eustochium* 9.1. Extracts in Wilkinson 1977: 47-52).

Paula's motivation, as relayed by Jerome, was to be in the places of the Bible. John Rufus says of Peter the Iberian's pilgrimage to Jerusalem, 'Even if it had to be by night he might have venerated the Holy Places, specially Golgotha and the life-giving Tomb!'[11] He records that Peter had worshipped the Saviour in all the places. The anonymous Pilgrim from Piacenza conveys better than any other writer of the period the variety of his experiences.[12]

Since pilgrimage is a journey to a *sacred place,* with a religious purpose, it is instructive to enquire into the motivation of pilgrims. However, one cannot take for granted the meaning of pilgrimage for each pilgrim, nor even a uniform definition of the phenomenon (Eade and Sallnow, eds. 1991: 3). It is clear from our brief survey of early Christian pilgrimage that a major concern was to visit the places associated with the Bible. With varying degrees of enthusiasm the records we have describe how prayers were said at places associated with the ministry of Jesus, and, in the case of Egeria in particular, we have detailed accounts of her participation in the liturgical ceremonies in Jerusalem. There was an abundance of practices possible for the Christian pilgrims to insulate them from the secular culture that surrounded them, and which intensified their religious sensitivities as they made their way towards the goal of the sacred places. Sensitivity to what was going on in the wider culture surrounding the sacred places is not reflected in the accounts from antiquity.

Models of Modern Pilgrimage

Even where the search for the places associated with Jesus is the focus of pilgrimage, it is not the world of antiquity which the modern pilgrim encounters. Romantic notions of pilgrimage to the Holy Land are quickly dispelled if one is allowed to encounter at least some of the reality of people's lives. For example, while Jerusalem is a Holy City in the piety of the three Abrahamic religions, today its political status is at the heart of the Israeli-Palestinian dispute, with each group claiming it for its capital. Modern pilgrimage to the Holy Land, then, is fraught with complexities, religious, ecclesiastical and political.

No pilgrimage site matches Jerusalem as a centre for attracting people from such a wide variety of nations, and from three religions. Unlike most other places of religious pilgrimage, Jerusalem is a centre of pilgrimage for three religions, and, to add to the diversity, for the different groupings within each of these religions. The Haram al-Sharif, sacred to Muslims, is on what the Jews call the Temple Mount. And in the central shrine of Christendom (the Holy Sepulchre) one encounters the six groups of occupants (Greek Orthodox, Latin Catholics, Armenians, Syrians, Copts, Ethiopians), each jealously guarding its rights. 'Jerusalem does not, in fact, appear so much as a holy city but as a *multitude* of holy cities' (Bowman 1991: 98), and 'there are as many different Holy Lands as there are cultures revering that simultaneously mythical and real place' (Bowman 1995: 290). Moreover, pilgrims to Jerusalem

---

[11] John Rufus, *The Life of Peter the Iberian.* Peter died c. 491 AD, and his life was written by his disciple, John Rufus, (c. 500). The (original Greek) text survives only in a poor Syriac translation, and extracts in English are in Wilkinson 1977: 57-58.
[12] Piacenza Pilgrim, c. 570, 'Travels', in Wilkinson, 1977: 79-89.

engage in a great variety of practices, unlike in Mecca which puts its pilgrims through a set routine of rituals.

The modern phenomenon of pilgrimage to the Holy Land is considerably different from that of antiquity. Most notably, modern ones are much shorter, scarcely lasting much more than a week, as against those of antiquity which in some cases lasted some years. Far from encountering the hazards of the journeys of old,[13] it is possible for the modern pilgrim to 'visit the Holy Land' with such a degree of insulation from the surrounding culture that one scarcely leaves one's home. Taxis to the airport, air travel (typically with unsolicited videos of sport, news and comedy, presumably to perpetuate the fiction that one is still in one's sitting-room), air-conditioned coaches on arrival, the tight eight-day schedule under the control of the Israeli guide, religious services conducted by a spiritual director from home, all conspire to provide a different kind of experience from what obtained in antiquity. For the modern pilgrim, of course, the experience is much cheaper and more widely available than heretofore. In many respects, it resembles a purposeful package holiday.

The distinct interests of different groups are reflected in the following brief survey of modern examples of patterns of pilgrimage. Without denying the individual's experience of a pilgrimage we shall comment on typical forms of pilgrimage, and highlight one type which appears to offer a considerable development of the practice.

1 Verifying the Bible

At the end of the last century a certain F J Bliss published a day-by-day account of a pilgrimage of nine days in Palestine, which was undertaken by one hundred and twenty people, of whom twenty-two were clergymen, including the Bishop of Worcester, Canon Tristam of Durham, and five nonconformist ministers (Bliss 1894). The interests of Mr Bliss, at least, are reflected in the account. Although the term *pilgrimage* is used, the account contains little that one would regard as being characteristic of that religious activity. Mr Bliss seems to regard the lectures as the core of the experience. These were on the following subjects: inscriptions, monuments, the reefs on the Mediterranean coast, and the rose of Sharon; the general character of the country; the geographical setting which could deal competently with the assaults on the Bible by Higher Criticism; birds and plants; pottery, and Roman traces; the geology of the Sea of Galilee; walks about Jerusalem; a learned lecture on the Druzes; the present Walls and Gates of Jerusalem; the Haram; the Mounds of Palestine.

---

[13] 'Pilgrimage could, of course, be a risky business with pilgrims forced to navigate wars and epidemics, as well as the often hazardous routes leading to the Holy Land. Until the seventeenth century, pirates threatened those who came by sea-as did violent sea storms-and many pilgrims' ships sank on the way. One commemorative slab reads: "The pilgrims coming from Constantinople were swallowed by the sea-clergy and lay people, men and women alike. In commemoration, the Patriarch erected a cross for the salvation of their souls and engraved this inscription, so that whoever reads this inscription would say: May God have mercy on their souls"' (Hagopian 1994: 116-17).

The Bishop of Worcester spoke of the uncertainty attached to the different sites, and emphasised the spiritual character of Christianity. While a certain Mr Kelk estimated that there were 40,000 Jews, 8,000 Mohammedans [sic], and 12,000 Christians in Jerusalem at the time, there is no mention of having met any of them. There is no contact with the people of the land. There are two references to Arabs: 'The honey is prized by the Arabs, who catch a bee, gum a tiny fragment of feather to his abdomen, let him go, and follow him to his hidden hive' (p. 104), while the second refers to Arab builders in Jericho (p. 105). Mr Bliss' interests were elsewhere: 'The enthusiasm of the pilgrims for the lectures was most gratifying to those who arranged them. In six days they listened to ten lectures and visited all the sites of Jerusalem besides' (p. 107).

2 Making the Bible Come Alive

Since the Holy Land is for Jews and Christians, and to a somewhat less extent for Muslims, the land of their Sacred Scriptures, there is a 'textual sacredness' about it. Making pilgrimage to the Holy Land, therefore, involves seeing those sites, but not merely for topographical verification. Such pilgrimage primarily focuses on the 'realisation' of the scenes described in the text of the Bible. In the Holy Land, 'the Bible comes alive.' In a sense, the Word becomes flesh.

Although this aspect is associated with pilgrims of the Reformation traditions who were brought up on the Bible, it is not restricted to them. In their home parishes, such pilgrims learnt that salvation comes through Jesus Christ, and that constant reading of the Bible, and especially the New Testament is a major agent of salvation. In general such pilgrims prefer to encounter the unmediated Christ in the Garden Tomb, or in Galilee, rather than in the monuments thrown up by two thousand years of devotion to his memory.

Although, in general, Catholics tend to have a greater regard for the sites associated with the life of Jesus they exhibit a peculiar interest in them. Catholics are less concerned with the sites themselves, than with the significance of the biblical events said to have happened there. 'It is from the significance, not the places, that one draws inspiration, and the places serve primarily as loci where the pilgrims are better able to body forth the subjects of their meditations in their imaginations' (Bowman 1991: 114; 1995: 304). Bowman noticed Catholics with their eyes closed during the Via Dolorosa procession.

3 An Orthodox Perspective

The heart of Orthodox pilgrimage is to be present in Jerusalem for the feasts. At the core of Orthodox faith is the conviction that when one stands within an Orthodox church, whether at home or abroad, with its walls and iconostasis replete with icons and its ceilings ornamented with stars and pictures of the Pantocrator, one is on the verge of eternity, in the company of God, the Virgin Mary, and all the saints.

Orthodox pilgrims, in general, come to the Holy Land to prepare for death, to be present at the life-giving tomb. Such pilgrims are in no doubt that they are embarking on an adventure which they hope is going to change their lives. They set out to shake off the impurities consequent upon the Fall, and prepare for death and resurrection. They confess their sinful past before the journey, and have their feet washed at the port/airport of entry into the Holy Land, and by 'baptism' in the Jordan. They enter 'paradise' itself through collective participation in the eternity imaged in the places where Christ had worked his redemptive mission. However, while each place visited effected its unique part in redemption in the past, the function of each place now is to provide entry into the entirety of the redeemed world. In that respect, at least, the specificity of each place recedes in importance when compared with the overriding function of providing access into the eternal. If Catholics use each site to emphasise a particular part of teaching associated with the site,

> the particularity of Orthodox Holy Places . . . is discarded as soon as it has served to bring pilgrims out of the fallen world and into the risen world manifest within the icon-dense churches built over or next to the memorialised sites: an historical moment is only distinct from others in the light of temporality-in eternity all moments are the same' (Bowman 1991: 110).

4 Meeting the *Living Stones*

A feature of each of the types of pilgrimage surveyed above is the absence of significant contact with the realities of the culture in which the pilgrimage takes place. English Protestant pilgrims were anxious to bring a little bit of home along with them: their own food, tea, potted salmon, bacon and Yorkshire ham, and, on one occasion at least, insisted on bottled beer, which burst in the heat. Above all, they insulated themselves against the local culture, and met none of the 'natives'—they were most anxious to avoid contamination by their superstitious practices (Hummel and Hummel 1995: 3, 13).

Responsible tourism stresses the value of engaging with the socio-politico-cultural context of the region being visited. There has been a corresponding evolution in the ancient pattern of pilgrimage in recent years, which emphasises the value of contact with the indigenous Christian communities, the *Living Stones* (1 Peter 2: 5) of the Land (Prior 1989). The following is a synopsis of the official diary of one such pilgrimage I led in 1992. It will be seen that engagement with the wider local culture, in all its complexity, is an essential element.

'On the day after we arrived in Jordan, we celebrated Sunday Mass in Arabic with the local community in the Latin Catholic Cathedral in Amman, and met the Bishop and representatives of his community afterwards. We then visited Dr Hanna Nassir, the President of Bir Zeit University (West Bank) in his offices in Amman. At that time he was prevented from entering his own country, after he had been deported by the Israeli military authorities in November 1974:

At midnight they asked me to come to the Governor's office
. . .When I got there they handcuffed and blindfolded me, put me in
a jeep, and drove me to the Lebanon borders, where they dropped
me from the jeep. They took all my belongings and left me on my
own at about 7.00 a.m. The military officer there read to me the
deportation order, which was in Hebrew, which I could not
understand. I had to explain to the Lebanese army inside the border
that I was a Palestinian and not an infiltrator. The problem for the
Israelis was that they could not charge me with anything, neither for
being involved in the building of our Palestinian society, nor for
teaching physics or mathematics. So they deported me. Had I done
anything illegal, they could have taken me to court. Deportation for
a Palestinian is much worse than being put in jail for a year or two—
at least you could go back home after the jail period!

'He impressed us very much by his obvious lack of vengeance, and the high
moral character of his position. Questions and answers followed, on the prospects for
the future, and on being president-in-exile of a university.

'On Day 3 we crossed the bridge over the Jordan and went to Jericho, and
later visited the reconstructed 4th and 6th century basilica at Tabgha. We had a
communal reading of Jesus' Teaching on the Mount, on the traditional site, the
Mount of Beatitudes, and visited the Church of the Primacy of Peter, and
Capernaum, and read apposite passages from the New Testament. We took the boat
to Tiberias, and drove straight to Nazareth, where we stayed in the Hostel of the
Sisters of Nazareth. After supper we met Archdeacon Riah Abu El-Assal, an
Anglican priest, active in local and national affairs. His inspiring address combined
Christian hope with political realism. The desire for peace and the sadness of
emigration of Christians were his preoccupations. During question time he spoke of
the difficulties of his own life, and impressed upon the pilgrims the need to become
aware of what is going on in other parts of the global village.

'On Day 4, we visited the Basilica of the Annunciation, and celebrated Mass,
after which we went to the Greek Orthodox Church of the Well. We read from
Isaiah 61 and Luke 4 as we left Nazareth by bus. We by-passed Beth Shean on the
way. As we drove down the Jordan Valley from Nazareth to Jericho the sadness of
seeing the presence of numerous settlements was relieved by the sight of a lone
Japanese Buddhist monk, walking up the Jordan Valley in the direction of Beth
Shean, a solitary figure beating his drum for peace. . . . We visited the ruins of the
Umayyad Hisham Palace, and admired the Greek Orthodox Monastery of the
Temptation of Christ from afar, and after lunch we visited the ancient site of Jericho.
After visiting the Tel we 'swam' in the Dead Sea south of Ein Fascha. Our final visit
for the day was to Qumran.

'On Day 5, we visited our old friend, the Sufi, Sheikh Jamal under the Dome
of the Rock. He spoke to us of peace, and an end to the suffering on his people. "I
pray from my heart for peace." We then visited the Dome of the Rock and the Aqsa
Mosque. On Day 6, we took the bus to the West Bank town of Ramallah to visit the

Trustees' Building of the University of Bir Zeit, and then moved off to visit the campus. We encountered a roadblock of soldiers as we tried to visit Bir Zeit village. One of the leaders addressed the soldiers, "People in England will be astonished to learn that we are prevented from visiting academic colleagues in Bir Zeit University . . ."

'On Day 7, we had an audience with the Armenian Patriarch and visited his cathedral. We went to the Mount of Olives to view the Old City, and thence to the Herodion. In Bethlehem we visited the Basilica of the Nativity, and sang "Silent Night" at the Manger. Then we were brought into Deheisheh Refugee Camp by two young inhabitants. Very soon we were approached by a column of Israeli soldiers, who were in walkie-talkie communication with their commander. They insisted that they should bring us round, "to protect us". We made it clear that we did not want to give the impression that we were collaborating with the occupying forces. To our surprise, they relented, and we spent the rest of the afternoon looking at various aspects of the camp.

'We went to the Shepherd's Field where we celebrated Mass together. Then we had a meeting with the *Rapprochement* in Beit Sahour. The spokesman addressed us:

> We want to tell what it has been like in the curfews. Explain to your people that Palestinians are screaming for justice. We are human beings. Animals in Europe are looked after better than we are. Can you imagine our schools being closed? How could this happen in the 20th century? Even South Africa was never as bad as that . . . How can we celebrate Christmas with so much suffering in each family? Our children are deprived of the joy of celebrating even Christmas.

'Fr Prior recited a poem he had written on his previous visit, having seen the demolished house of a family, whose father was trying to put a roof over their heads:

Beit Sahour

While shepherds watched their flocks by night
a mile away the soldiers
dynamite the inn
of the little family

whose fifteen year old, like David,
threw a stone at the Israeli Goliath
but without David's success.

For this crime against the mighty
the lowly are rendered homeless
and pitch their tent

beside the empty tomb.

The grandeur of the mother
ennobled by suffering;
the two children standing uncomprehending,
and the father with a jaded resignation
begins again to raise a covering
over the foundations.

'Later that evening, back in the Austrian Hospice we had a meeting with the Jewish activist, Gershon Baskin on his view of the present and the future prospects for peace.

'On Day 8, we walked through the Old City to the Western (Wailing) Wall, and visited the Church of the Dormition, the Cenacle, and David's tomb. Unfortunately, being the Sabbath, the Chamber of the Holocaust was closed. We paused in silence outside it, contemplating the mystery of human evil. We visited the Church of San Pietro in Gallicantu, and made our way to the Pool of Siloam. We were stopped by a roadblock of soldiers, but after some delay we were allowed to proceed. At the Pool we had a reading from John 9, and then proceeded up the Kidron Valley to Hezekiah's Tunnel. We completed our walk to the Church of All Nations.

'On Day 9, we joined Archbishop Lutfi Laham and his congregation for the Greek Catholic Liturgy at the Melkite Church near Jaffa Gate. After the service we met the congregation, and conversed with the Archbishop, and the youth of his congregation. We exchanged greetings. On Day 10, we rose early for the bridge crossing to Jordan. We proceeded along the Kings' Highway to Mount Nebo, from where Moses viewed the "Promised Land". We celebrated Mass in the Byzantine basilica. We visited Madaba and Kerak. We ended the day at Petra, where we spent two nights, and flew directly from Amman to London Heathrow.'

The Fruits of Pilgrimage

'Though we travel the world over to find the beautiful we must carry it with us or we find it not.'[14] Each group coming on pilgrimage to Jerusalem, with the exception of those on a *Living Stones*-type pilgrimage tends to return home with its fundamental predispositions confirmed.

Protestant Christians tend to concentrate on the relationship between the place and the Bible. After his four years of Eastern travel, Thomas Cook wrote in 1872, 'A new incentive to scriptural investigation has been created and fostered: "The Land and the Bible" have been brought into familiar juxtaposition' (Davies 1988: 148). Reflecting something of the Reformers' disdain for the practice of

---

[14] Emerson, Ralph Waldo, *Essays*, xii, *Art*, cited in *The Oxford University Press Second Edition Dictionary of Quotations*, Chancellor Press, London, 1985, p. 200, 4.

pilgrimage in general,[15] many Protestant pilgrims are uneasy in the presence of the elaborate liturgies one meets in the Middle East, and prefer to encounter the unmediated Christ in the Garden Tomb, or in Galilee, rather than in the monuments thrown up by two thousand years of devotion to his memory. They find the ceremonies of the Holy Sepulchre in particular to be too boisterous to be authentic. In the case of some, this centre of Christian veneration resembles a defiled place, full of corruption and superstition, which like the Temple in Jesus' time needs to be cleansed of its 'superstitions and fraudful degradation'.[16] They prefer the landscapes and the village scenes, which make Jesus come alive. For such people, the Garden Tomb is a God-send. Even if it has no claim to mark the place of the burial of Jesus, its tranquillity responds to the needs of their particular privatised piety.

For Orthodox pilgrims, on the other hand, the precise identification of sites is largely irrelevant. The whole land, rather than any specific part of it serves as a locus for participation in the divine activity of the liturgy. Catholics tend to regard sites as facilitating the 'composition of place', which helps them interiorise the particular biblical text relating to the life of Jesus.

The reality is that the significance of pilgrimage to Jerusalem means so many different things to pilgrims. Bowman argues, 'The holy city is . . . a place where pilgrims who have inherited or developed certain images of a "Jerusalem" during enculturation elsewhere can embody those images and engage them as aspects of the material world' (Bowman 1991: 99). It is his contention that it is at the sites whence pilgrims set out that pilgrims learn what they desire to find: 'At the centres where they go in expectation of fulfilling that desire pilgrims experience little other than that which they already expect to encounter' (p. 121).

I contend that this is not the case for people who go on a *Living Stones*-type pilgrimage. These pilgrims meet the people, and become aware of the social context in which their pilgrimage takes place. They learn at first hand, and in most cases are profoundly surprised by what they find. They discover that Palestine is not the one democratic State of Israel, stretching from the Mediterranean to the Jordan, and from Mount Hermon to Eilat, which the Israeli tourist maps imply. For them sharp moral issues are not submerged in archaeology or tourism, while the local Christianity is relegated to sentiment and the museum, as Cragg fears for outsiders coming to the

---

[15] 'All pilgrimages should be stopped,' wrote Luther (Davies 1988: vii). True Christian pilgrimage, he insisted, was not to Rome or Compostela, but to the prophets, the psalms and the Gospels. The earlier Luther, however, on his visit to Rome on behalf of his Order in 1510-11, performed many of the rituals of pilgrimage, including climbing the holy stairs on his knees to gain an indulgence for his grandfather. For the 1409 Lollards' tract, *The Lanterne of Light,* there were six manners of pilgrimage: from birth to the heavenly city; going to church; visiting the poor; distributing alms; studying holy writ; and, finally, death. There is no other pilgrimage that may please God (Davies 1988: 91).

[16] Edward E Robinson, professor at Union Theological Seminary, wrote of his visit to Jerusalem in 1838: 'We counted it no loss [missing the events of Holy Week] . . . for the object of our visit was the city itself, in relation to its ancient renown and religious associations, not as seen in its present state of decay and superstitions and fraudful degradation' (Robinson, E E, *Biblical Researches in Palestine, Mount Sinai and Arabian Petraea*, New York, 1977: 239) quoted in Wilken 1992: xiii.

occupation of the West Bank (1992: 235). They see for themselves the extent of the belligerence of the ank, and when they hear the accounts of life under occupation, or as inferiors in the Jewish State (Masalha ed. 1993), in all the cases I have encountered, they are profoundly shocked by what they find.

They come to discover for themselves that for present-day Arab Christians in the Holy Land Golgotha is not a sad memory of a distant past, enshrined in encrustments of Byzantine and Crusader church architecture. It is part of the every day indignity and oppression which they share with all other disadvantaged peoples of the world. Their Via Dolorosa is no mere ritualistic procession through the narrow streets of the Old City, but the fate of being subjugated and humiliated in their own land.

Conclusion

The value of pilgrimage need not be a choice between visiting sacred shrines and encountering Christ in a refugee camp or a psychiatric ward. As we have seen, it is possible to conduct a pilgrimage to the Holy Land with a sensitivity to the circumstances of the region. *Living Stones'* pilgrims come to appreciate the life of witness of the Christian communities in a culture which is redominantly Muslim or Jewish. They see for themselves something of the political contexts in which Palestinian Christians live, either as second class citizens of Israel, or under brutal occupation in the West Bank or Gaza. Such pilgrims allow their moral sensibilities to be seduced neither by home-bred religious sentiment, nor by the excitement of the archaeology of an exotic land.

Such encounters with the contemporary political realities of the Holy Land raise important questions for students of the Bible in particular. The biblical legend of the Israelite victory over the Hittites, Girgashites, Amorites, Canaanites, Perizzites, Hivites, and the Jebusites takes on a new significance when one meets their modern counterparts, the Palestinians. One is, on moral grounds, forced to question whether the Pentateuch continues to provide the figment of divine legitimacy for the occupation of other people's land, and the destruction of the indigenous culture. The commandment that, 'You shall destroy all the peoples that the Lord your God will give over to you, your eye shall not pity them' (Deut 7: 16), and the statement that, 'The Lord your God will clear away these nations before you little by little . . . and you shall make their name perish from under heaven' (Deut 7: 22-24), are seen in a new light. In our society such sentiments, rightly, are regarded as an incitement to racial hatred. Of course, they have been used in the past by the Crusaders in the Holy Land, by the Spanish and Portuguese invaders of South America, and by the Boers in South Africa, as well as being exploited cynically by secular Zionism in our own generation (see Prior 1997). They say in South Africa:

> When the white man came to our country he had the Bible and we had the land. The white man said to us, 'Let us pray'. After the prayer, the white man had the land and we had the Bible.

The Bible had become the white man's ideological instrument of colonisation, oppression and exploitation.

The Holy Land experience confronts young enquiring minds with questions about the nature of a God who is portrayed as supporting colonisation, oppression and exploitation. They are forced into wondering whether at such points the first six books of the Bible (Genesis to Joshua) in particular contain racist and xenophobic perspectives. Like the Black Christians in South Africa, they begin to realise that the Bible itself is a serious problem for people who want to be free, and readily commit themselves to terminate the exploitation of humans by other humans.

Study of the effects of pilgrimage to the Holy Land is not at a developed stage. While there is no shortage of spiritual rhetoric, both in antiquity and today, there is a remarkable lack of sociological investigation of the phenomenon.[17] My experience of many *Living Stones'* pilgrimages assures me that the pilgrims are interrogated by the experience of what they encounter. They do not simply have their prejudices refined. Encountering Palestinian Christians in the place of their daily tragedy is an experience that I have no difficulty in describing as sacred. Religious dispositions, such as admiration of virtue, moral outrage, a determination to work for justice, and a sense of being in the company of the suffering Christ rise spontaneously to the surface of one's consciousness. One begins to appreciate that theophanies occur in the midst of the *quotidian trivialities* of the *suq*, as they do in the formal liturgies of the churches and shrines, and on the heights of numinous mountains.

Living Stones' pilgrims, like all Christian pilgrims to the Holy Land *turn down every byway, roaming the labyrinth of ruins, seeking what they may find, inquiring! inquiring!* They too visit *old stones, desecrated shrines, defaced statues, a scatter of carved fragments, old columns and the drums of columns.* But in their enthusiasm for the remains of antiquity, they do not dismiss the social reality all around them, *the profit and loss, buying and selling and barter—the scruffy scuffle for survival.*[18] In general, *Living Stones'* pilgrims encounter something altogether Other, and in the process appear to be changed profoundly.

> Sometimes, the seeker
> becomes the sought.
> Thereafter, the burden's
> to bear the benediction:-
> as the priest his symbols,
> the poet his vision,
> woman love, the mother
> her child and mortal man
> immortality.[19]

---

[17] See the discussion in Sizer 1994.
[18] From Desmond O'Grady, 'The Virgin at Ephesus', in 1977: 39.
[19] From Desmond O'Grady, 'Initiates', in 1977: 37.

References

Bliss, F J 1894. 'The Recent Pilgrimage to Jerusalem', in *Palestine Exploration Fund Quarterly Statement*, April: 101-108

Bowman, G 1991. 'Christian Ideology and the Image of a Holy Land. The place of Jerusalem Pilgrimage in the various Christianities', in Eade and Sallnow, eds. 1991: 98-121

Bowman, G 1995. 'Contemporary Christian Pilgrimage to the Holy Land,' in O'Mahony, *et al*: ed. 1995: 288-310

Cragg, K 1992. *The Arab Christian. A History of the Middle East*. London: Mowbray

Davies, J G 1988. *Pilgrimage, Yesterday and Today: Why, Where and How.* London: SCM

Eade, J and M J Sallnow, eds. 1991. *Contesting the Sacred. The Anthropology of Christian Pilgrimage.* London/New York: Routledge

Hagopian, Harry 1994. 'The Armenians of Jerusalem and the Armenian Quarter', in Prior and Taylor, eds. 1994: 115-25

Hummel, Ruth and Thomas 1995. *Patterns of the Sacred. English Protestant and Russian Orthodox Pilgrims of the Nineteenth Century*, London: Scorpion Cavendish

Lewis, C 1989. 'On Going to Sacred Places', *Theology* 92: 388-94

Masalha, Nur, trans. and ed. 1993. *The Palestinians in Israel: Is Israel the State of all its Citizens and 'Absentees'?* Haifa: Galilee Centre for Social Research

O'Grady, Desmond 1977. *Sing me Creation.* Dublin: Gallery Books

O'Mahony, Anthony, with G Gunner and K Hintlian 1995. *The Christian Heritage in the Holy Land*. London: Scorpion Cavendish

Ozick, C 1983. 'Toward a New Yiddish', *Art and Ardor.* New York

Partin, H B 1967. *The Muslim Pilgrimage: Journey to the Centre* (PhD Dissertation presented to the University of Chicago)

Prior, M 1989. 'Living Stones: A Retreat with Palestinian Christians', *New Blackfriars* 70: 119-23

Prior, M and W Taylor, eds. 1994. *Christians in the Holy Land*. London: WIFT

Prior, M 1994. 'Pilgrimage to the Holy Land, Yesterday and Today', in Prior and Taylor, eds. 1994: 169-99

Prior, M 1995. *Jesus the Liberator. Nazareth Liberation Theology (Luke 4.16-30).* Sheffield: Sheffield Academic Press

Prior, M 1997. *The Bible and Colonialism. A Moral Critique.* Sheffield: Sheffield Academic Press (The Biblical Seminar)

Robinson, E E 1977. *Biblical Researches in Palestine, Mount Sinai and Arabian Petraea.* New York

Sizer, S R 1994. 'Visiting the Living Stones. An Investigation of the perceptions of British and Palestinian Christians on the subject of Pilgrimages to the Holy Land, with particular reference to their impact on the indigenous Anglican Church in Israel and the Occupied Territories' (Unpublished MTh Thesis, University of Oxford)

Wilken, R L 1992. *The Land called Holy. Palestine in Christian History and Thought.* Yale: University Press

Wilkinson, J 1971. *Egeria's Travels.* London: SPCK

Wilkinson, J 1977. *Jerusalem Pilgrims before the Crusades,* Ariel, Jerusalem

19
PROFILE OF THE CHRISTIAN COMMUNITIES: CHALLENGES AND HOPES

Bernard Sabella

Introduction

The Christian communities of the Holy Land have deep roots in the land and strong affinities to Arab Palestinian society. The great majority of Palestinian Christians are of indigenous stock, whose mother tongue is Arabic and whose history takes them back, or at least some of them, to the early church. At present, the 50,000 Christians in the West Bank and Gaza Strip make up only 2.2 percent of the total population estimated in 1994 at 2,238,000.[1] Arab Christians in Israel were estimated, for the same year, at 125,000 or 14 percent of all Arabs in Israel.[2] Christians in Palestine and Israel make up 175,000 or 2.3 percent of the entire Arab and Jewish population of the Holy Land.

Estimates place the total number of Palestinian Christians, world-wide, at close to 400,000 or roughly 6.5 percent of all Palestinians. Based on these estimates, a majority of 56 percent of Palestinian Christians are found outside of their country. This situation of out-migration resulted from the exodus of 726,000 Palestinian refugees in the 1948 Arab-Israeli war. Fifty to sixty thousand Palestinian Christians, comprising 35 percent of all Christians in pre-1948 mandatory Palestine, were among the refugees.[3] In 1996, these refugees and their descendants are spread over the entire Middle East, primarily in the 60 refugee camps dotting the topography of the West Bank (19 refugee camps); Gaza Strip (8 refugee camps); Jordan (10 refugee camps); Syria (10 refugee camps) and Lebanon (13 refugee camps).

As for Palestinian Christians, refugees and non-refugees, they are found mostly in urban areas of the Middle East but many have opted to leave to far away lands such as the USA, Central and South America, Australia and Canada. The dispersal of Palestinians since 1948 has spared no family or group. The demographics of

---

[1] Palestinian Bureau of Statistics, Current Status Report, Series No. 1, *Demography of the Palestinian Population in the West Bank and Gaza Strip,* December 1994.

[2] These estimates are based on figures for Israel found in *The Statistical Yearbook of Jerusalem,* no. 12, 1993, Jerusalem, 1995 p. 25.

[3] Kossaibi, George, 'Demographic Characteristics of the Arab Palestine People,' in Khalil Nakhleh and Elia Zureik, *The Sociology of the Palestinians,* Croom, Helm, London, 1980, p. 18.

Palestinian Christians is as much shaped by the politics of the Arab–Israeli conflict as is the demographics of Palestinians, in general.

A Tradition of Emigration

Palestinian Christians have experienced a relatively long tradition of emigration since late 19th and early 20th century. Early emigration was motivated by worsening political and economic conditions in the Ottoman empire. A feeling of uneasiness with the atmosphere of backwardness in all spheres of life was strengthened by the fear of conscription of young men to the Ottoman army. Families pulled together their resources in order to enable younger male members to travel to Central, South and North America to start a new life. Once these were established in their new localities, they invited other members of their families to join them.[4]

The factors that affected emigration trends, among Middle East Christians, including Christians of the Holy Land, at the turn of the century, can be grouped into three.

First, there were the prevailing bad socio-economic and political conditions which acted as constraints on the prospects of advancement for communities, families and individuals.

Second, there were the educational and vocational characteristics of Christian Arabs which were in the process of formation as a result of missionary educational activity in the region. These characteristics, blended with an entrepreneurial spirit of Christian villagers such as those in Bethlehem and Beit Jala, reinforced the tendency to leave.

Third, the pull of distant 'Christian' lands was too strong to resist given that in those lands fortunes could be made and, at the same time, the community could be preserved through the translocation of indigenous churches in the diaspora. Emigration was thus made a viable alternative to a stagnant and backward society which offered no hope for a better future.[5]

Palestinian Christians as a Migrant Community

At the end of the 20th century and given the political and economic conditions prevailing in the West Bank and Gaza Strip, the Palestinian Christian community fits well the definition of a migrant community:

---

[4] For explanation of early emigration wave of Christians from the Middle East, see Albert Hourani's 'Introduction,' in *The Lebanese in the World: A Century of Emigration,* Hourani, Albert & Shehadi, Nadim (eds.), The Center for Lebanese Studies in Association with I B Tauris and Co. Ltd. Publishers, London, 1992, pp. 5-6.

[5] Sabella, Bernard, 'The Emigration of Christian Arabs: The Dimensions and Causes of the Phenomenon,' Paper delivered at the Giovanni Agnelli Foundation Seminar on *The Christian Communities in the Arab Middle East: Identity, Current Dynamics and Future Prospects,* Torino, May 8-10, 1995, p. 6.

A community with high educational achievement and a relatively good standard of living but with no real prospects for economic security or advancement will most probably become a migrant community.[6]

An emigration survey, undertaken by the author in 1993 on 964 households in the central area of the West Bank, upholds the relationship between high levels of education and standards of living and intention to emigrate. Among the 239 Christian households interviewed, intention to emigrate was double that exhibited by the Muslim households.[7]

The Christian sample in the 1993 survey had slightly more years of education and better income, on average, than did the remainder of the population. In addition, it was clear that almost all of those intending to leave, among Christians, have immediate members of their families abroad. The bad economic and political situation were primary reasons for wanting to leave: 88 percent of those wanting to leave specified the bad economic situation while 61 percent blamed the bad political situation.

Conditions that will help stop or discourage emigration are primarily the improvement of the political situation, mentioned by 47 percent of all respondents and the improvement of the economic situation mentioned by 40 percent.

Peace and its Importance to Stop Emigration

Another indicator of the importance of the political situation is the response received on a question of whether respondents intent on emigration will still leave, if peace were to take place. It was discovered that 49 percent of those intending to leave would not, if peace were to take place. Among Muslims, 38 percent said they would not leave while among Christians the percentage came close to two-thirds and stood at 65 percent. This is further proof that the political situation is an important push factor and that if this situation improves, emigration among Palestinians will be drastically reduced. Based on this and other findings, it becomes clear that the political factor plays an important role in encouraging Palestinians to emigrate or to stay put in their country.

But Why Do Christians Leave?

But why do Christians leave at a higher rate than the rest of the population? The answer is not simple, as it involves interrelated factors and their mutual effects on one

---

[6] Danilov, Stavro, 'Dilemmas of Jerusalem's Christians', in *Middle East Review*, volume XIII, No. 3-4, 1981.
[7] For all figures and information concerning the Emigration Survey of 1993 see: Sabella, Bernard, 'Summary Results and Discussion: Emigration Survey 1993'. Unpublished.

another. First, the socio-economic characteristics of the Christians make them more likely candidates for emigration. Second, is the fact that emigration is not a new phenomenon for the Christians and that there has been a relatively long tradition of emigration, particularly to distant 'Christian' lands. Third, Christians are more sensitive, than the general population, to bad economic and political conditions, particularly if they perceive that the prospects for advancement are not forthcoming. Regardless of how one explains this sensitivity, it has to do with the Christian demographic, economic, educational and occupational profile.

Some conclusions from the 1993 survey throw light on factors which render Palestinian Christians more prone, than the rest of the population, to take the difficult decision of leaving:

1   There is clearly a relationship between the higher rates of departures and the overall bad or worsening economic and political situation during particular years.

2   The process of emigration for whole families starts when one of the children goes abroad to study, marry and/or work and eventually pulls the whole family to him/her.

3   Those religious communities with higher percentage of household members abroad are more likely to have their members exhibit intention to emigrate than those communities with lower percentages. A closer look at the religious communities with high percentage of immediate family members abroad reveals the following percentages in descending order: Armenian Orthodox 61 percent; Syriac Orthodox 50 percent; Greek Orthodox 32 percent; Latins 28 percent; Muslims 23 percent; Greek Catholics 15 percent and Protestants 8 percent.

When intention to emigrate is examined, the Greek Orthodox, Armenian and Syriac Orthodox exhibit the highest percentage of desire to leave. The Protestants have the lowest percentage while the Latins and Greek Catholics are placed in the middle. One can, therefore, argue that, in principle, the smaller the religious community the more likely it is that its members choose to leave. It is appropriate hence to provide some demographic data and indicators on the size and distribution of the various denominations in the West Bank and Gaza Strip.

Size and Distribution of Palestinian Christians in the West Bank and Gaza

Palestinian Christians are found in over fifteen different localities with concentration in the urban centres of Bethlehem, Jerusalem and Ramallah. Following is the distribution of Palestinian Christians by denomination in the various localities of the West Bank and Gaza.

Denomination	Aboud	Bethlehem	Beit Jala	Beit Sahour
Greek Orthodox	536	2133	4733	5749
Latins	443	2934	1116	919
Greek Catholics	10	480	134	528
Syriacs	0	902	120	44
Protestants	28	110	240	95
Total	1017	6559	6343	7335

Denomination	Bir Zeit	Ein Arik	Gaza	Jenin
Greek Orthodox	918	211	2207	169
Latins	1104	117	210	327
Greek Catholics	39	0	22	41
Syriacs	17	0	0	0
Protestants	80	0	40	0
Total	2158	328	2479	537

Denomination	Jericho	Jerusalem	Jifna	Nablus
Greek Orthodox	256	3500	272	436
Latins	164	3900	369	291
Greek Catholics	81	500	8	64
Syriacs	22	250	0	0
Protestants	12	850	0	250
Armenians★	0	1500	0	0
Copts★	0	0	250	0
Ethiopians★	0	60	0	0
Maronites★	0	100	0	0
Total	535	10910	649	1041

★The figures are inclusive of the West Bank, but the major concentrations are in Jerusalem.

Denomination	Ramallah	Taybeh	Zababdeh
Greek Orthodox	4000	72	631
Latins	1100	872	1302
Greek Catholics	650	166	125
Syriacs	100	0	43
Protestants	600	0	150
Total	6450	1110	2251

The total number of Palestinian Christians is 49,702 distributed among the various denominations as follows:

Greek Orthodox	25835	52.0%
Latins	15168	30.5%
Greek Catholics	2848	5.7%
Protestants	2443	4.9%
Syriacs	1498	3.0%
Armenians	1500	3.0%
Copts	250	0.5%
Ethiopians	60	0.1%
Maronites	100	0.2%

Source: *Christians in the Holy Land,* Prior, Michael and Taylor, William, (eds.), The World of Islam Festival Trust, London, 1994.

Christians in Jerusalem

Jerusalem is the Mother Church but it is also the city which accentuates the problem of dwindling numbers of indigenous Christians. In 1944 there were 29,350 Christians living in the city. At present the number of Christians does not exceed 10,910 or 37.5 percent of what it used to be fifty years ago.[8] One can find no solace in the fact that Christians in Jerusalem have the highest 'church per capita' rate in the world with one church for every 177 Christians. If the decline of Christian numbers continue, we may reach a situation whereby some of the smaller communities, such as the Armenians and the Syriacs, will disappear.[9] The churches and holy sites, left behind, will become a 'Tourist Disneyland' as the Archbishop of Canterbury aptly described the situation after a visit to the Holy Land in the early 1990s. But emigration, especially of younger members of the various communities, leaves its negative effects on the whole community. The average age of Christians in Jerusalem and the West Bank and Gaza is around 32 years while that for the general population is 16 years. Because of the older nature of the Christian community, unemployment rate among Christians becomes quite high and reaches over 30 percent.[10] This is so because of the presence of older people in the Christian communities. The ageing of the Christian community is reflected in the absence of a dynamic community life, among certain denominations.

There is also a general dissatisfaction among Christian employees with their income since it is not sufficient to cover the high cost of living. In Jerusalem itself, the average income of a Christian family is only 58.6 percent of a Jewish family. As for housing, only 18.7 percent of Jerusalem Christians own their own homes.[11] While the figure for those Christians in other parts of the West Bank and Gaza Strip who own their houses is probably higher. Still housing has always been a problem of urban dwellers of the Holy Land because of the relatively high cost of real estate in the cities. In the case of Jerusalem, this is complicated by Israeli municipal and ministerial policies which aim at discouraging housing construction for Arabs in order to keep the Arab-Jewish population balance at 28-72 percent in greater Jerusalem. Jerusalem Christians need to construct 481 dwelling units in order to meet their immediate housing needs.[12]

---

[8] Tsimhoni, Daphne, *Christian Communities in Jerusalem and the West Bank Since 1948: An Historical, Social and Political Study,* Praeger, Westport, Connecticut and London, 1993, pp. 22-23.

[9] Sabella, Bernard, 'Jerusalem: A Christian Perspective', in *Jerusalem Religious Aspects,* Passia, Jerusalem, December 1995, p. 38.

[10] Hyman, Benjamin, *et al., Jerusalem in Transition: Urban Growth and Change 1970's-1980's,* The Hebrew University of Jerusalem and the Jerusalem Institute for Israel Studies, 1985.

[11] According to figures in the Israeli Census of the Population conducted in 1983. In the mid-nineties, the disparity between Israeli and Palestinian average income remains. The recent, 1995, Israeli census of the population should provide new information on the topic but the expectation is that a significant gap still exists in average income of the two national groups in the city.

[12] Figures on the housing situation in Jerusalem are taken from *The Statistical Yearbook of Jerusalem,* Municipality of Jerusalem and the Jerusalem Institute for Israel Studies, 1993.

With the housing situation as it is in Jerusalem, there is fear among Jerusalem's Arabs, including Christians, who hold an Israeli identity card, that they will practically be forced to move outside the municipal boundaries of Jerusalem. This will eventually result in the loss of their identity card and consequently their right to permanent residence in Jerusalem. In such circumstances, Jerusalemites who have lived in the city for generations will find themselves excluded from the city. Already, hundreds of Jerusalemite Christian families are living outside of Jerusalem and some of them have difficulty in reaching the city. This is cause for concern, not simply for Palestinians and indigenous Christians, but also to all those who pray and labour for the peace of Jerusalem and the Holy Land.[13]

Another concern which has caused immense emotional and practical damage to Christians and other Palestinians is the cordoning off of Jerusalem from the West Bank and Gaza Strip by the Israelis for 'security reasons.' This has denied the Christian and Muslim faithful the right to free access to their religious Holy Places in Jerusalem since March 1993. Permits are needed from the Israeli military authorities in order to enable those Palestinians wishing to visit Jerusalem to do so. There are instances of Palestinians from Bethlehem and Ramallah, two areas with relatively large concentrations of Christians, who have not visited Jerusalem since the imposition of the 'security belt'. This not only contradicts religious rights but also severely limits the exercise of other basic human rights such as education, health and the fulfilment of simple family obligations such as attendance at weddings, funerals and other occasions of family importance.[14]

Other Challenges to Palestinian Christians

Despite the amount of property, buildings and real estate which the various churches have in Jerusalem and the Holy Land, Christian communities have not been able to become self-sufficient. Dependency on partner churches elsewhere is a characteristic that is almost universal among the Holy Land churches. If this partnership weakens, there is doubt that local churches can make it on their own. This is difficult to say because the church is a community that is supposed to be self-sufficient. In one sense, the church is a microcosm of society and, as such, should be self-dependent. Emigration, on the one hand, weakens the church and therefore there is a need to address this issue and to find remedies and preventive cures. Emigration, however, is a reflection of political and economic factors on which the church, given the circumstances, does not have power or influence. On the other hand, the Palestinian church is weakened by the fact that different vested interests in different churches pose an obstacle to the adoption of a common strategy to face the challenges facing the churches and their faithful. This should be understood within the context of the churches' witness to the society through educational, health, social and other institutions, activities and enterprises. Some churches are doing the best they can,

---

[13] Sabella, *op. cit.*, p. 47.
[14] Sabella, *ibid.*, p. 48.

considering their limited resources. Other churches, however, have not come to grips with the difficult realities of their community and with the need to revitalise it.

Obligation of Palestinian Christians

We, as Palestinian Christians, have also an important role to play and, I am afraid, we have not done so to date. We need to be faithful to Christ's teachings especially at times when tensions and pressures seem to be impossible to overcome. Unfortunately, we are only human and with mounting pressures, we often choose the easy way out: USA, Canada, Australia, etc. In the final analysis, however, it is really not the easy way out but the most difficult and the most costly to the integrity of our community and our church in the Holy Land. We have an obligation to ourselves and to our children to stay put and to overcome, together with all the inhabitants of this land. We are today still in the midst of political conflict but we can see some concrete signs of changes towards peace-making. We are called upon to bear witness to these changes and to take an active part in them. In spite of all of our shortcomings, as churches and as faithful, we are a proud and hard working group of people. We seek to be in communion with all of you who have come to attend this conference and with your churches and communities. We are not in a position to blame this side or that for the predicament of the Christian communities in the Holy Land. Yet, it is clear that the political situation and the long history of Israeli occupation since 1967 have left their marks on our communities and their dwindling numbers. At the same time, the instability of our region is an important fact which encourages emigration. The challenge is clearly to be able to live in a secure and comfortable environment. The sense of communion with you reinforces our determination to accept the challenge and to overcome the difficulties.

A Message of Hope

A memorandum issued by twelve heads of different churches and Christians communities in the Holy Land in November of 1994, has called on all parties involved 'to go beyond all exclusivist visions or actions, and without discrimination, to consider the religious and national aspirations of others, in order to give back to Jerusalem its true universal character and to make of the city a holy place of reconciliation for humankind.'

Christians, according to the memorandum, 'believe the Jerusalem of the Prophets to be the foreseen place of the salvation, in and through Jesus Christ.' As to the continuing presence of a Christian community, the heads of churches emphasise that 'Jerusalem is the place of roots, ever living and nourishing,' and that 'the local church with its faithful has always been actively present in Jerusalem and witness to the life and preaching, the death and resurrection of Jesus Christ upon the same Holy Places, and its faithful have been receiving other brothers and sisters in the faith, as pilgrims, resident or in transit, inviting them to be re-immersed into the refreshing, ever living ecclesiastical sources.'[15]

It is this spirit, applicable not simply to Jerusalem, but to the entire Holy Land, that should motivate all of us to work for the peace of Jerusalem and for that of Palestine and Israel. Palestinians, Muslims and Christians alike, have paid a heavy price for the creation of Israel. We still suffer from the wounds of the century-old conflict. Some of us are not ready yet to explore reconciliation, others have taken the first steps, still others have gone further.

The future, however, cannot be moulded without the hope which emanates from religious traditions that believe in the One God. These traditions should become a mainstay that would encourage all of us, in this Holy Land, to search for answers to very difficult questions such as the future of Jerusalem, holy for the three monotheistic religions and claimed politically by Israelis and Palestinians. Hope, based on religious heritage, should also help us find ways to accept each other with justice, compassion and willingness to reconcile, regardless of how long and hard the process.

Some may think that speaking of hope is simple pontification that would lead us nowhere. But of hope we should continue to speak, not simply because it is in the essence of Christian witness, but because the alternative to hope is utter despair. Despair spells continuation of conflict, war and disruption of the lives of generations to come. We, as Palestinian Christians, should particularly be speaking of hope because with it we can stop emigration, strengthen our communities and contribute to a different future of this Holy Land. With hope we can be at peace with ourselves, with our neighbours and with our own religious heritage as Christians.

---

[15] The full text of the Memorandum can be found in Jerusalem—*The Diocesan Bulletin of the Latin Patriarchate,* volume 1, year 1, January-February 1995 pp. 20-25.

20

THE SEPARATION OF JERUSALEM FROM THE WEST BANK AND GAZA
The Closure as Economic Policy
Lynda Brayer

Jerusalem has been and continues to be a focus of attention for the Western and Islamic worlds. It is central to Jewish belief and practice despite the fact that the Second Temple was destroyed by the Romans in 70 AD. For Christians, Jerusalem is the site of the Passion of Jesus Christ, as well as a centre of his ministry during his life. The Church of the Holy Sepulchre marks the traditional site of his burial and resurrection and, since its erection in the 4th century by Queen Helena, the mother of Constantine, it continues to be a site of pilgrimage. The church has undergone restorations and additions throughout the centuries, but it remains one of the most interesting architectural sites in the Holy Land. For Muslims, al-Aqsa Mosque and the Dome of the Rock, or the Mosque of Omar, come third in the Islamic hierarchy of Holy Places, following Mecca and Medina. We would also do well to remember that these mosques, especially the Dome of the Rock, are not only amongst the most beautiful examples of Islamic architecture, but are treasures of our human civilisation. The retaining wall of the Second Temple plateau, which borders the Haram al-Sharif, or Temple Mount as it is known by the Jews, is called either the Western or Wailing Wall, and serves as a focus of prayer for Jews from the world over. These central shrines have histories stretching as far back as the beginning of each of these religions and, therefore, it would be both inaccurate and incorrect to attempt a hierarchy of holiness of Jerusalem for the three religious faiths. Each has its own history, context and tradition and no-one can, or should, determine relative values for any of them.

However, since the invention of the Zionist ideology which asserts that Jews have a 'historic right' to Palestine, or the Land of Israel, Jews have been making every effort to both inhabit the city and, since the conquest of East Jerusalem in 1967, to increase the Jewish population, and cause a mass exodus of non-Jews or Arabs out of the city. The former president of the State of Israel, Mr Chaim Herzog, attests to the fact that soon after the 1967 June war, he personally participated in the successful effort to get about 250,000 Palestinians to leave the West Bank and Jerusalem, going so far as to provide the people with transportation to the cease-fire border with the kingdom of Jordan, at the Jordan river. He recalled how Israelis patrolled the Old City and 'encouraged' people to leave the city for weeks following the war.

Jerusalem has been adopted as a war cry by the Zionist state. The slogan

'Never again shall Jerusalem be divided' refers to the division of the city between 1948 and June 1967. An international border separating the new Jewish state of Israel and the eastern rump of Palestine, subsequently incorporated into the kingdom of Jordan, cut through the city starting from the area near the wall of the Old City to the south near the Armenian Quarter and stretched northwards, cutting through the site of Notre Dame de Jerusalem. It then continued past what became known as the Mandelbaum Gate (the private home of a Palestinian family) and then swung around westward away from the Shuafat and the northern villages area. The Zionists became intoxicated with Jerusalem and have insisted now for twenty-nine years that 'Jerusalem is the eternal capital of the Jewish people [sic].' Of course, this is a statement which makes no sense. Capital cities are capitals of states or countries, not of people. Rome, for example, is not the capital of the Catholic people, nor is Mecca the capital of the Islamic people. However, this declaration has proved to be a magnetic rallying point for Israeli Jews, world Jewry and Zionists of all ilk, having tremendous evocative power in the imagination of all Jews, secular as well as religious. The Jewish response is automatic and the chant 'Jerusalem shall never be divided again' is reiterated *ad infinitum*.

This unexamined fascination with Jerusalem is to be found expressed in a statement about Jerusalem, called the Jerusalem Covenant, formulated by former Supreme Court Justice Menahem Elon and signed at the Jerusalem Day festivities marking the 25th anniversary of the 'reunification' of the city. The signatories were: former President Chaim Herzog; Prime Minister Yitzhak Shamir; Knesset Speaker Dov Shilansky; Meir Shamgar, former president of the Supreme Court; Avraham Shapiro and Mordechai Eliyahu, former chief rabbis of Israel; Deputy Prime Minister David Levy (soon to be appointed as Foreign Minister in the government of Mr Benjamin Netanyahu) then Mayor Teddy Kollek; and the late Mr Yitzhak Rabin, Chief of Staff in the Six Day War, among others. The following is a partial text of the Covenant:

> As of this day, Jerusalem Day, the twenty eighth day of the month of Iyar in the year five thousand seven hundred fifty-two; one thousand nine hundred and twenty-two years after the destruction of the Second Temple; forty-four years since the founding of the State of Israel; twenty five years since the Six Day War during which the Israel Defence Forces, in defence of our very existence, restored the Temple Mount and the unity of Jerusalem; twelve years since the Knesset of Israel re-established Jerusalem, 'unified and whole,' as the 'Capital of Israel'; 'the State of Israel is the State of the Jewish People' and the Capital of Israel is the Capital of the People of Israel. We have gathered together in Zion, sovereign national officials and leaders of our communities everywhere, to enter into a covenant with Jerusalem, as was done by the leaders of our nation and all the people of Israel upon Israel's return to our Land from the Babylonian exile; wherein the people and their leaders vowed to 'dwell in Jerusalem, the Holy City.'

Once again 'our feet stand within your gates, O Jerusalem-Jerusalem built as a city joined together,' which 'unites the people of Israel to one another,' and 'links heavenly Jerusalem with earthly Jerusalem.'

We have returned to the place that the Lord vowed to bestow upon the descendants of Abraham, Father of our Nation; to the City of David, King of Israel; where Solomon, son of David, built a Holy Temple; a Capital City which became the Mother of all Israel; a metropolis for justice and righteousness and for the wisdom and insights of the ancient world; where a Second Temple was erected in the days of Ezra and Nehemiah. In this city the prophets of the Lord prophesied; in this City our Sages taught Torah; in this City the Sanhedrin convened in session in its stone chamber. 'For there were the seats of Justice, the Throne of the House of David', 'for out of Zion shall go forth Torah, and the Word of the Lord from Jerusalem.'

Today as of old, we hold fast to the truth of the words of the Prophets of Israel, that all the inhabitants of this world shall enter within the gates of Jerusalem: 'And it shall come to pass in the end of days, the mountain of the House of the Lord will be well established at the peak of the mountains and will tower above the hills, and all the nations shall stream towards it.'

Each and every nation will live by its own faith: 'For all the peoples will go forward, each with its own Divine Name: we shall go in the name of the Lord our God forever and ever.' And in this spirit the Knesset of the State of Israel has enacted a law establishing: the places holy to the peoples of all religions shall be protected from any desecration and from any restriction of free access to them.

Jerusalem, peace and tranquillity shall reign in the city: 'Pray for the peace of Jerusalem. May those that love you be tranquil. May there be peace within your walls, and tranquillity within your palaces.' Out of Jerusalem a message of peace went forth and shall yet go forth again to all the inhabitants of the earth: 'And they shall beat their swords into plowshares, and their spears into pruning-hooks; nation will not lift up sword against nation, nor shall they learn war any more.' Our sages of blessed memory have said: 'In the future, the Holy One, the Blessed, can comfort Jerusalem only with peace.'

From this place we once again take our vow: 'If I forget thee, O Jerusalem, may my right hand lose its strength: may my tongue stick to my palate if I do not remember you, if I do not raise up Jerusalem at the very height of my rejoicing.'

> And with all these understandings, we enter into this covenant and
> write: We shall bind you to us forever; we shall bind you to us with
> faithfulness, with righteousness and justice, with steadfast love and
> compassion. We love you, O Jerusalem, with eternal love, with
> unbounded love, under siege and when liberated from the yoke of
> oppressors. We have been martyred for you; we have yearned for
> you; we have clung to you. Our faithfulness to you we shall bequeath
> to our children after us. Forevermore, our home shall be within you.

This is not the place to analyse this Covenant. I would call it an example of
heresy or even apostasy, but this is not the subject of this particular essay. Rather, the
Covenant has been brought into the body of the text in order for outsiders to know
the basic concepts held by Jewish authorities as well as by ordinary Israeli Jews. In
addition, this Covenant must be seen and reflected upon in relation to the precepts
of religious Judaism for whom the importance of Jerusalem lies in its being the site
of the Temple where sacrifices were made to the Lord in expiation for one's sins.
Judaism, in the *Halacha* (i.e. according to Jewish precepts), is holy not in and of itself,
but only because it is the supreme meeting place of a Jew with his God. (I would
hesitate to say, man with his God, because I think this would not be part of Jewish
thinking.) The daily prayer book of Orthodox Jewry, the *Siddur* (meaning the Order)
used in both the Sepharadi (Oriental) and Ashkenazi (European) Jewish
communities, contains prayers concerning sacrificial offerings. In the morning
prayer, *Shacharit,* in Latin called Matins, there is an entire section devoted to *korbanot-*
sacrificial offerings. Sections from Exodus (30: 17-21) and Leviticus (6: 16)
describing the preparations required by the priests and the actual burning of the
sacrificial animals, are read each day. The purpose of these sacrifices is then summed
up as follows:

> May it be Your will, O Lord, our God, and the God of our
> forefathers, that You have mercy on us and pardon us for all our
> errors, atone for us all our iniquities, forgive all our wilful sins; and
> that You rebuild the Holy Temple speedily, in our days, so that we
> may offer to You the continual offering that it may atone for us, as
> You have prescribed for us in Your Torah through Moses, Your
> servant, from Your glorious mouth, as it is said: . . .

This prayer is followed by extensive recitation from both the Torah (the
Pentateuch) and the Talmud concerning the details, each of which is as important as
the next, of the different sacrifices. While Judaism passed on to synagogue worship
entirely, following the destruction of the Second Temple, it is quite apparent that the
sacrifices occupy a central part of the prayer. There are different schools of thought
among Jews. Some call for a reconstruction of the Temple, with the attendant
necessity of destroying the Islamic mosques on the Haram al-Sharif, while others
would say that the Temple will be rebuilt with the coming of the Messiah. In either
case, the Temple Mount retains its holy status. Many Orthodox Jews refuse to visit

the site for fear of treading on the ground of the Holy of Holies, the inner sanctuary of the Second Temple.

It is against this background that one must assess the inaccessibility and closing off of East Jerusalem from Palestinians living in all the territories occupied since 1967. But before I even do that, I just want to comment on the term 'East Jerusalem.' Before 1948, there was one town, and not a very large one at that, which was called Jerusalem. Following the 1947/1948 war initiated by the Hagana, Jerusalem fell under two opposing armies: the Arab one and the Jewish one. Neither side had the power to defeat the other, and the eventual outcome was the establishment of an international border through its middle, so to speak.

It was from this division that the two appellations East Jerusalem and West Jerusalem arose: the former, the Arab section and the latter, the Jewish city. There was expulsion of people from their homes: nearly all the Arabs living in the Talbieh, Katamonim and Baq'a sections fled across into the Arab controlled area, while the Jews in the Old City were brought into West Jerusalem. Thus each side became more or less mono-ethnico-religious. In this description it must be apparent that the term 'Arab' is a cultural and linguistic term. It has no religiously defining quality. The term 'Jew' on the other hand, only defines religion, and therefore includes people of different races and nations. It is contestable whether there is a Jewish nation: although it is agreed upon that there is a Jewish community. Be that as it may, the division in Jerusalem remains between Arab and Jew.

Moreover, the Zionist evocation of the name 'Jerusalem' has served Zionist ideology without revealing its dangerous and perfidious side. Jerusalem arouses Jewish emotions, but these are totally different from those of the *goys*.[1] Because of the commonality of the city to the three religions, the name 'Jerusalem' also conjures up flights of the imagination for Christians and Muslims. But their understanding of Jerusalem and its importance is different in each tradition: none of them think of Jerusalem with a territorial dimension, other than that of a town within which the holy shrines are located. Jerusalem as a fortress to be conquered, a capitol to be retrieved, a territory to be liberated, a capital to be developed *ad infinitum*, is simply beyond the boundaries of Christian and Muslim religious perception, understanding and significance today. However, these are the modern Zionist ideas and practices.

In Judaism, Zion is only the Temple area: and while David did set up his administration in Jerusalem, it was Solomon who built the First Temple. Ironically, Zionism tends to conflate the biblical[2] political dimension with the religious

---

[1] The term *goy* is actually a Hebrew word meaning 'nation.' It has become a pejorative in Jewish circles and refers to gentiles who are deemed to be of lesser importance than the 'Chosen People', i.e. the Jews.

[2] I have deliberately used the term 'biblical' because it is not synonymous with historical. Zionism insists on a literal reading of the bible of those aspects which it wishes to regard as historical for the purposes of supporting its claim of 'historic rights' to Palestine.
Traditionally, the *Halacha* has been much more circumspect about the actual historicity of events *per se* described in the Tanakh, and the rabbis would not have concerned themselves with the facticity of specific events nor with the archaeological discoveries. For them, the Bible and Talmud are essentially about the relationship between God and the Jews: for Zionism, the crux of the matter is the connection between Jews and the Land of Israel, with the Bible being brought as supporting evidence for this claim.

dimension, forgetting however, that modern Jewry is the inheritor of the religious tradition of the rabbis, a tradition which almost disdains the historico-political aspects of Jewish historiography. Rather, it stresses the Law, or *Halacha*, which it regards as the heart of Judaism, defining as it does the relationship between man and *makom*-place, a surrogate term for God.

Zionism has hidden behind the unspoken differences in conception, understanding and practice between Zionists on the one hand, and Christians and Muslims on the other hand, but has promoted rather the so-called overlapping of religious purpose. It has thus managed to veil the ultimate political intentions of the Jewish state, which is to create a Jerusalem and Palestine free of non-Jews, while at the same time finding for itself allies in the Christian world who support these very policies which aim to empty the Holy Land of its Christians. The support of the 'peace process' itself is a paradigm of such support. One cannot help but be stunned at the irony.

In this essay, I attempt to undertake that very exposure of the underside of Zionist ideology because it has manipulated religious and romantic feelings and attitudes for the most hard-headed of *Realpolitik* goals without ever having to be called to account for policies and their effects. In any other context, these policies would be considered as unmitigated racism and colonialism, which have caused, and are still causing, the massive ravaging of the indigenous Arab population in Palestine, the Palestinians.

The expulsion of this population out of Palestine and the subsequent refusal of the Israeli government to allow refugees back into the country to return to their homes, is a process which has been taking place for about one hundred years. The term most recently invented for such behaviour is 'ethnic cleansing,' first used in the Yugoslavian context, and then most hideously replayed in Africa between Rwanda and Burundi, both examples merely reflect the same policy of the Nazi government of Germany.

Such ethnic cleansing is part and parcel of Zionist ideology and is an integral part of both its theory and its practice. The methods have been varied and changeable, but the policy has been unwavering. Its greatest success was in the 'War of Liberation' or 'War of Independence' as the Zionists describe the catastrophe which catapulted upon Palestinians in 1948, leading to the removal of 90 percent of Palestinians from that part of Palestine taken over by the state of Israel. The war of June 1967, seen by many rabbis as a miracle from God (see Jerusalem Covenant), exacerbated further the situation of those Palestinians living in the remaining rump of Palestine called the West Bank, with nearly 300,000 escaping to save their lives into the surrounding Arab countries. The Palestinian refugees in Lebanon, Syria, Jordan, as well as in other Arab and non-Arab countries in the world, are testimony to this catastrophic destruction of an indigenous community.

Zionism did not succeed fully in its aims of creating a homogeneous Jewish state composed of Jewish citizen-residents only. It is for this reason that there has been, and there continues to be, a continuing drive against Palestinians to get them to leave Israel/Palestine through all manner of means including both brute force and law. Zionists reject Palestinians for two reasons: first of all, Palestinian Arabs are not

Jewish; they are either Christian or Muslim. Second of all, they are the natives of Palestine, and their continued existence in Palestine serves as a reminder of the essentially alien and foreign origin of the Jew. Zionists have proved to be past masters in deception: they have indulged in the art of legality, an art which uses the forms of law to perpetrate violations of human rights and dignity, and when they have found it expedient to do so they have not been beyond resorting to fraud, forgery and theft, relying as always on the trustworthy judiciary to back them up and when necessary, to use physical force violence, and even total warfare.

The closure of Jerusalem, which is also at one and the same time, the closure of occupied Palestine, is part of the continuing policy of ethnic cleansing of Palestine. It is another step in the slow strangulation of the Palestinian population in ever diminishing land-locked locations. But it is not an isolated event. A correct understanding of the closure, blockade, or military siege (all appropriate terms) must include, where necessary, reference to historical Zionist practices in order to correctly assess modern day Zionist behaviour.

Earlier in the article, I referred to the fact that the State of Israel did not allow return of the refugees back into that part of Palestine which became Israel. Only a very few people were allowed back in, precisely because of the Zionist policy of setting up a Jewish state. It is important to see the closure in this light as well. The closure serves as an effective barrier forbidding the influx of Palestinians into Jerusalem. In South Africa, the *apartheid* government used the term 'influx control' and the mechanism of a pass, or permit book, which regulated the movement of Africans from one area to the other. A black person found without a pass was committing a crime for which the punishment was a prison sentence. White areas were placed out of bounds to blacks unless they received a special permit given against an employer's guarantee. The whites needed only a certain amount of blacks to work for them. The government did not import workers although it encouraged the immigration of Europeans into South Africa to try and affect the demographic balance, tilting it more towards the whites, despite the huge disparity of numbers.

The Jewish closure is run on the same basis, except that Israel has brought in foreign workers as well as immigrants to replace Palestinians. Israel uses its own form of pass: it is the identity card or *huwiyya* in Arabic, which controls the movement of its bearer. For instance, Israel has issued two different IDs for East Jerusalem and the West Bank and Gaza, a system still continuing under the Palestinian National Authority. East Jerusalem, with expanded borders, was officially annexed in 1980. Israel, therefore, unilaterally expanded the territory of the Jewish state of Israel[3] but did not automatically grant citizenship to the Jerusalem Arabs. Israel issued special Jerusalem IDs which differ in colour from those issued to the people in the West Bank and Gaza. The difference however, is not merely cosmetic, but substantial. Palestinians with Jerusalem IDs may travel in Israel and in the territories: those with IDs from the territories may not enter either Jerusalem, neither east nor west, and

---

[3] The annexation is in violation of international law and both rejected and unrecognised by the international community but put fully into practice in the Israeli legal system and Israeli administration.

not Israel proper, without permits. The permits are not being issued except under exceptional circumstances. Therefore, through the closure, Israel has effectively expelled hundreds of thousands of people from areas Israel considers to be sovereign Israeli territory. At the same time, Israel will remove the Jerusalem ID from anyone found to have moved to the West Bank or Gaza.

The loss of an identity card and right to reside in Israel or Palestine has far reaching consequences. It causes the break-up of families, the loss of work and businesses, and most important for the Israelis, the loss of the right to inherit immovable property. Such a right was lost by the Palestinian refugees from the 1948 war, and is still continuing today with the loss of identity cards. In both Israel proper, and in the occupied Palestinian territories, Israel has laws and military orders which effectively forbid a foreigner from inheriting property. If property is found to be owned by some people living abroad, then the custodian for absentee property can expropriate such property 'in the interests of the people abroad'. This has been the method used to transfer all Arab property in Israel into Jewish hands. The same method is being used in Jerusalem and the occupied territories.

The reason that Palestinians can 'lose' identity cards, is because they do not have rights of citizenship. They are protected by neither the *ius soli* (law of the soil) which establishes the principle that wherever one is born, one may remain forever with rights of return, nor by the *ius sanguine*, a principle whereby a child inherits the citizenship of its parents. Palestinians are considered resident aliens in Jerusalem and the occupied territories. Thus, if their domicile is determined not to be in either of these areas, then the identity card is removed from its bearer.

Another similarity between the closure and early Zionist practice is to be found in the fact that Israel has almost banished all Palestinian workers from workplaces in Israel. Under the guise of the claim of 'security'[4] the borders have been sealed against Palestinian workers. However, we should remember the practice of *'avoda Ivrit'* which translates into 'Hebrew work' but which served as a euphemism for the practice of denying work to Palestinians and replacing Palestinians with Jewish workers in the early years of the century. These racist practices were at the basis of much of the disturbances between Jews and Arabs in the early years of the Zionist venture. I would like to stress that the general Zionist ideology is against allowing any *goy* to work in Israel. Practically speaking, this is a situation which is impossible to maintain, because there are very few Jewish manual and service labourers.

In actual circumstances, the Zionists have preferred to keep Palestinians locked

---

[4] I do not want to discuss the whole concept of security that is used by the Israeli authorities. Suffice it to say, that this is the justification according to which Israel violates all moral norms and international treaties. In one sense, the use of the excuse 'security' indicates that the Israelis know that if no justification is put forward, then their behaviour would be considered criminal, at least, and crimes against humanity and war crimes, at most. The most rife and horrendous examples of the violation of human rights norms justified by 'security' considerations is to be found in the widespread torture practices of the Israeli government, and in the death squads, known as 'Cherry' and 'Simon' who murder political opponents–all of whom are described as 'wanted' terrorists. Euphemistically this is known as 'extra-judicial killing'. Non-euphemistically, this is called murder and war crime.

up in the occupied territories, denying them work and denying any influx of funds into the territories, and to bring foreign workers from Thailand, Rumania and the Philippines to do those jobs that are not filled by Jews. The reasoning is that these foreigners, while not being Jews, will not be absorbed by the Jewish population, and are preferable therefore to Palestinians, precisely because they are foreign and not native. If Israel has to have non-Jewish workers, then she will prefer anyone, but not the Palestinians. Such foreigners can never assert a claim to the land of Palestine.

This policy has brought about the situation of an estimated 200,000 foreign labourers, most of whom work in construction, who are taking the jobs that Palestinians needed to receive, following the de-development of Palestine under Israeli occupation. That is to say that Israelis have preferred to allow the earnings of the foreign workers to leave the country, rather than have such earnings going into the Palestinian economy.

It is quite easy to see from such an analysis that Zionist ideology can accomplish many goals with one action. It is also easy to understand that such a multifaceted ideology is diabolical in its outreach, and viciously murderous for Palestinians. Having attempted to show the connection between previous Zionist practices and present Zionist practices, in order to provide the overall context for the closure, I would like to concentrate on just a few aspects of it, mainly the political and the economic, elaborating on their effects.

The closure creates at times a two-way blockage: no-one may enter Jerusalem and no-one may leave it, has had, and will continue to have, enormous consequences for the entire Palestinian population. The first long-term instance of this iron clamp-down occurred with the 24-hour curfew imposed on the West Bank, Gaza and East Jerusalem during the Gulf War. This meant that people could not leave their homes for work, education, medical care, or family reasons, etc. With curfew, all life comes to a halt. Curfew by definition involves closure, which is a euphemism for siege. Since 1991, the closure has been more or less in effect, creating a situation which did not really exist prior to that, except in the case of individuals. Suddenly, however, the entire population was forbidden to come to what the Israelis defined as Jerusalem.

On the eve of the Jewish New Year (24 September 1995) two and a half million Palestinian residents of the West Bank and Gaza began their 24-day long imprisonment in the 'land of closure.' The justification brought forward were 'security reasons.' Nevertheless, it was obvious to every Israeli that the real reason for imposing this state of siege on the Arab civilian population under occupation was the wish not to spoil the festivities of Rosh Hashanah and Yom Kippur (the Jewish New Year and Day of Atonement) while glorifying three thousand years of 'Jewish' Jerusalem, by having Palestinians in their midst. Palestinians were forbidden both to enter the territories from Jerusalem, and to leave them to come to Jerusalem.

The political effects include the fragmentation of the Palestinian people into three groups: Israeli Palestinians, Jerusalem Palestinians and West Bank and Gaza Palestinians. The Israeli Palestinians hold Israeli citizenship and are ostensibly as free to move as are Israeli Jews. The Palestinians in the West Bank and Gaza will now be issued with new identity cards issued by the Palestinian National Authority (PNA), granting them the status of quasi-citizens (one can only be a citizen of a state or country and not of an 'autonomous' area). Jerusalem Palestinians, that is those Palestinians who lived in Jerusalem under Jordanian control until June 1967, have a totally unique status: they are 'resident aliens' in the land of their birth. They do not have Israeli citizenship, unless they ask for it, and lately most people have been refused it on the grounds that they 'do not speak Hebrew'. Yet they carry a Jerusalem identity card based on the fact of their domicile. If they live outside of Jerusalem for a certain period of time, and have not renewed their identity cards, they are deemed to have changed their domicile and are no longer a resident of Jerusalem.

However, this is not the whole story. Obfuscated by the obvious racism and unnecessary cruelty, are the economic reasons driving the Oslo 2 *apartheid* strategy. This strategy has been developing since the Madrid Conference in 1991 through the first Oslo Accord and its legal descendants: the Cairo and Taba Accords.

A no less important purpose of the closure, is the destruction of the centrality of the Palestinian city within Palestinian society. A city is not merely a cultural and commercial and administrative centre for the towns and villages in its environs. It is, and represents, the modern world in all its diversity and potential, with the urban population spearheading development within a developing society. The closure prevents free access to and movement between cities and their peripheral areas, of people, ideas, and services e.g. educational and health facilities, commercial and industrial development, and most important of all, prevents the *sine qua non* of civilised society, the possibility of organised political activities and the establishment of political institutions. This policy inevitably leads to increasing social fragmentation and atomisation, and destroys the coherence necessary for individual and social well-being and development. The closure therefore, is undermining and destroying the dominant status and progressive role of the cities, while turning them into a random collection of neighbourhoods. Such destruction of the Palestinian city through its isolation and degeneration is meant to break the backbone of the national political will, resulting in the breakdown of the national infrastructure, thus pushing Palestinian society as far backwards as possible.

Jerusalem is unfortunately the paradigm of this policy. The closure line passes through Jerusalem village neighbourhoods and cuts them into two or even more fragments. The village of Hizme has been atomised into bits of land scattered amongst the illegal Jewish settlement of Pisgat Ze'ev, located to the north of historical Jerusalem. Residents of some parts of Hizme are stuck like glue to the land. In order to 'legally' travel outside their part of their village, they have to 'illegally' leave this area, to get a permit to travel from the military governor. However, to undertake this travel, they will be fined and possibly jailed for travelling without a permit to get a permit to travel. Such divisions also characterise some parts of Abu-Dis and al-Azariyya.

The truncation of Arab village neighbourhoods is part and parcel of the 'reunification of Jewish Jerusalem.' It permits the Jews to annex the land but to dispose of the non-Jewish population. This same policy has led to town planning schemes in the Arab neighbourhoods which not merely freeze residential building, but declare already built houses as illegal and therefore targets for demolition. Such policies have led to the imposition of fines upon Palestinians to the tune of hundreds of millions of shekels if not billions of shekels. The average fine is 100,000 shekels (approximately $US33,000) accompanied by a demolition order. Such planning has led to a shortfall of more than 22,000 Arab homes in East Jerusalem, and this has caused the 'voluntary' exit of Arabs from the Jerusalem area, thus contributing to the ethnic cleansing that is the aim of Zionism.

In the Israeli news broadcast announcing the closure it was also announced that US President Clinton declared the 'autonomy' area a trade and custom free zone. The following day, delegates from the USA, Israel and the PNA signed a series of documents enabling Palestinians to export custom free goods to the USA.[5] The American Trade Commissioner, Micky Cantor, and the Israeli Minister of Trade and Industry, Micha Harish, clarified that the agreement included mainly industrial products. Whoever was unaware that the Americans are not interested in Palestinian agricultural products, learnt in the same broadcast that the American delegate approached his Israeli counterpart in a request to enable American farmers uninterrupted access to the Israeli market.

It is difficult to imagine the USA buying Palestinian agricultural products on the one hand, and then selling its own agricultural products to Israel on the other hand. It is also difficult to suppose that selling American goods in the autonomous areas would somehow affect the American balance of payments deficit. The income of the great majority of the Palestinians is extremely low; only the top echelon will be able to purchase custom free American commodities. If that is the case, then what do the Americans really want to buy from the autonomous areas? Or to be more exact, what does American capital have to gain there? After all, profits, and not charity, is the name of the game.

The only goods available in abundance in the autonomy areas are unemployed workers looking for a job in order to provide for their families. These tens of thousands, if not hundreds of thousands of desperate workers who were kicked out of the Israeli economy under the slogan of 'separation' of the Labour-Meretz government, have been added to the farmers uprooted from their confiscated lands. They are all now awaiting the second stage of the Oslo Accords: the establishment of the 'industrial parks.' Such parks will be built by Palestinian labour with American capital or the capital of multi-national companies relying on Israeli advisors and Palestinian middlemen contractors. An experimental industrial park of this kind is already operating with much success at the Erez Checkpoint in Gaza. This plan is surprisingly similar to the American plan for exploitation of Mexican labour 'NAFTA' (North American Free Trade Agreement). Palestinian workers not only will be exploited in these work camps but Palestinians in general will be prevented from enjoying the fruits of their labour. That is, these products are destined for overseas markets and are expected to create sufficient profit for investors who are interested in investing in the industrial parks.

The first stage of preparing the Palestinians for this plan was forcing their standard of living down to the bare minimum possible, creating massive unemployment in order to make them desperate for work, and thus turning them

---

[5] *Ha'aretz* newspaper, 18 October 1995.

into future obedient and frightened labourers. They will be forbidden from setting up trade unions except for those erected by the PNA. This will limit, if not actually deny, their rights according to the International Labour Organization and is the real reason why Arafat, the executor of this plan, is clamping down on the press, going so far as to arrest and hold in detention editors and journalists. He also floated a proposed law forbidding the erection of associations independent of the PNA, but it appears that sympathisers have warned him off from this tactic. However, Palestinian labourers will be under the control of the manifold Palestinian security and police forces 'without the High Court of Justice and B'tselem' *à la Rabin* to protect them inside the autonomy ghetto, encircled by electric fences, patrols and checkpoints guaranteeing the closure from the Israeli side. The closure is a vital tool for establishing the apartheid regime along with land confiscation, demolition of Palestinian homes inside Israeli Jerusalem, breaking up of families through the prevention of Jerusalem residents receiving permission for their spouses to join them from the autonomous areas, absence of permits to reach Jerusalem for work purposes and thereby forcing Palestinians into their Israeli-made 'Palestans.' The closure serves to detach Palestinians from their economic sources and resources. It is the closure that caused the drop in the standard of living in the Gaza Strip by 60 percent. It is the closure that forces Israeli employers to fire the remnants of Palestinian labourers who cannot work on a regular basis. It is the closure that forces Palestinian labourers in Gaza to humiliate themselves before the PNA to provide them with a number of work days per month in order to enable their children to at least *live* in a state of malnutrition rather than starve.

The closure is also meant to turn the Palestinian farming population into a destitute community. An example are the deliberate hold-ups imposed by the Israelis at the checkpoints in order to cause agricultural produce to rot from the delays, driving the 'Palestan' farmers into bankruptcy. Guy Behor 'the Arab affairs expert' reports in patronising mockery:

> Nashashibi, the Palestinian Minister of Economy, implored the Israeli authorities to facilitate the export of 3000 tons of guavas to Jordan, the only market for Palestinian guavas. He begged them to release the truckloads containing rotting guavas held up at the border in violation of the agreements. The Palestinian farmers cannot bring their produce into Jerusalem: the Jerusalem Palestinian cannot buy Palestinian produce in Jerusalem.[6]

The commercial consequences of the closure are such that the Palestinian merchant, or small factory owner, cannot bring his goods to the Jerusalem market. He will have to get special permission, and this is almost impossible to receive. The Israelis however, are past masters at applying the heinous policy of 'divide and rule'. There are some privileged Palestinians who can get the right to 'export' into Israel. On the other hand, Israeli goods flood the Palestinian markets because there is

---

[6] *Ibid.*, 31 October 1995.

nothing to stop them, except the shopkeepers themselves, who have no access to any other goods. They therefore are a captive market, and the financial benefits are all Israel's.

The closure is accompanied by additional means to hasten the impoverishment of the Palestinians. An economic policy intended to harm the population was revealed in an interview given by 'a top army officer' to Nahum Barnea, a journalist of *Yediot Aharonot (Latest News)* 14 April 1995. In it the apparent subject was the relationship of relatives, affiliates and actual neighbours to those people who have taken up arms in their struggle against the Israeli occupation and conquest. 'We want to deprive them of economic rights; we believe it can be done within the framework of the law.' Arbitrary destruction of homes within the areas in which 'wanted' (Palestinians) are caught, shows that from the viewpoint of the army, every Palestinian falls into one of the three categories, and not least, people who unwittingly get caught in the crossfire.

The closure therefore must be seen as an instrument of war, an instrument whose purpose is to destroy Palestinian society as much as is possible. It is therefore not inappropriate to quote Tacitus' comment on the Romans: 'In every place to which they come, they wreak desolation and call it peace.'

Lynda Brayer is the Executive Legal Director of the Society of St Yves, a Catholic legal resource centre for human rights, established by the Latin Patriarch of Jerusalem, Michel Sabbah, for the purposes of serving the poor and the oppressed. The Society has devoted its energies to protecting Palestinians living under occupation, a situation which unfortunately continues unabated. The Society began its work in an office in the Notre Dame Center of Jerusalem, but with the almost hermetic closure imposed on the West Bank in March 1993, a second office was opened in Bethlehem.

21
THE CHANGING FACE OF JERUSALEM
Ibrahim Matar

Throughout its history Jerusalem was a united city and from the 7th century to May 1948, an Arab city run by a Palestinian Muslim mayor.[1] However, from May 1948 to the present, the city of Jerusalem has been witnessing a process of Judaisation accomplished by the dispossession and uprooting of its indigenous Christian and Muslim Palestinian population and their replacement by exclusively Jewish foreign immigrants.

This displacement of Palestinians from the Holy City has been achieved in two stages. The first stage occurred in May 1948 when the Jews occupied all of what came to be known as West Jerusalem, evicted by force its 60,000 Palestinian inhabitants and physically took over their villages, homes and lands.

The second stage took place after the Israeli occupation of East Jerusalem in the 1967 war, when the Jewish state annexed its eastern part and began a process of colonisation by confiscating private property and building on such lands. Today the Jewish state is in complete control of the city, yet most property and real estate still legally belongs to the indigenous Palestinians who have been living continuously in Jerusalem for centuries.

This paper will expound on the land area usurped by Jews in both West and East Jerusalem and the methods used to displace Palestinians in order to answer the question: To whom does Jerusalem belong?[2] A map will be used to show the border changes that have taken place since 1948, the growing Jewish control of the city and Palestinian property including villages, urban areas, and lands that have been seized and/or confiscated from 1948-1995.

Post May 1948-Uprooting of Palestinians from West Jerusalem

The traumatic events of April-July 1948 turned the 60,000 Palestinians evicted from their homes in what became known as Jewish West Jerusalem into permanent exiles

---

[1] Cattan, Henry, 'Chronology of Jerusalem', in *The Palestine Question*, Croom Helm Ltd, England, 1988, p. 392.
[2] This paper is based on an article by the same writer under the title 'From Palestinian to Israeli: Jerusalem 1948-1982', published in the *Journal of Palestine Studies*, vol. XII, no. 4, Summer 1983, issue 48.

and displaced persons.[3] This civilian Palestinian population was forced to flee its homes by a deliberate wave of terror attacks designed to ethnically cleanse non-Jews from West Jerusalem. The most infamous of these acts committed by Jewish terrorist organisations were the massacre of civilians in Deir Yassin, a small village on the outskirts of Jerusalem, and the blowing up of the Semiramis Hotel in the Palestinian neighbourhood of Katamon in West Jerusalem.

The purpose of this paper is not to describe the Jewish terror acts of 1948 that led to the dispossession of the Christian and Muslim Palestinians of West Jerusalem, but rather to describe the methods used by the Jews to usurp Palestinian property and what use was made of this property.

The seizure of Palestinian property in what came to be known as West Jerusalem was carried out in two phases. Henry Cattan, a well-known Palestinian International lawyer, wrote on this issue:

> Palestinian property which was described as 'absentee property' was seized under the Absentee Property Regulations of 1948 and vested in the Custodian of Absentee Property who was given the power to administer the property, but not to sell it nor lease it for a period exceeding five years. Then in 1950, Israel took the next step, namely the confiscation of this property. This was achieved by the Absentee Property Law (1950) which again vested 'absentee property' in the Custodian and authorized him to sell it at its official value to a Development Authority established by the Knesset (Article 19).[4]

In other words, the Palestinians forced from their homes in West Jerusalem were not allowed to return and then were declared permanent absentees and their property sold by so-called 'custodians' for the benefit of Jews only. This process can only be described as 'legalised theft'. Under these laws, even the Palestinians who were evicted from West Jerusalem in 1948 and today live in 'annexed East Jerusalem' and hold Israeli identity cards cannot claim back their property in West Jerusalem. They are called the 'present absentees'.

The extent of the Palestinian property seized in 1948—be it real estate, agricultural land, or homes in urban neighbourhoods or rural areas—that today lies within the West Jerusalem municipal boundaries, and consequently has been built upon for Jews, is described below and illustrated in the attached map (figure 1). This information is based on site visits by the writer and interviews with dispossessed Palestinians who today live in East Jerusalem.

A brief description of the Palestinian villages seized and depopulated in 1948, the property and lands of which were incorporated into the West Jerusalem Municipality boundaries, follows:

---

[3] John Quigley, 'Old Jerusalem: Whose to Govern?' in the *Journal of International Law and Policy,* vol. 20, Fall 1991, p. 150.

[4] Henry Cattan, *The Palestinian Question,* p. 72.

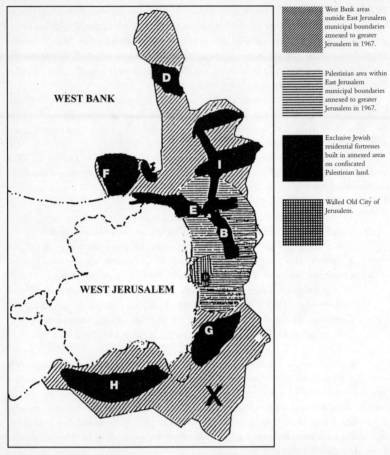

Figure 1: Post 1967 Israeli Settlements in East Jerusalem and Vicinity

First Wave 1968—1,200 acres seized

B   Mount Scopus (Hadassah Hospital and Hebrew University expanded from pre-1967 enclave)

C   Jewish and Moghrabi Quarters (expanded to four times 1948 size, 2,300 Jewish settlers in 1996)

D   Attarot Industrial Park (400 acres tract for Israeli industries)

E   French Hill, Ramat Eshkol, Ma'alet Difna Mt Scopus (first Israeli housing colonies in East Jerusalem, 20,300 settlers)

Second Wave 1970—3,100 seized

A   Neve Yaacov (19,300 settlers in 1996)

F   Ramot (most developed of existing colonies, with a population of 37,900 in 1996)

G   East Talpiot (built on private Palestinian land and in former UN zone, 18,000 settlers in 1996)

H   Gilo (30,200 settlers in 1996)

Third Wave 1980—1,100 acres seized

I   Pisgat Ze'ev (50,000 Jewish colonisers in 1995, construction expanding to increase settlers to 60,000 by end of 1996)

Fourth Wave 1991–470 acres seized

X   9,000 apartments approved in April 1995 for Har-Homa, a new Jewish settlement

Fifth Wave 1992–500 acres seized

J   Ramat Shu'fat (2,100 units to be completed by the end of 1996, 15,000 Jewish settlers expected)

1   Lifta and Sheikh Badr, and all their surrounding agricultural lands to the north of Jerusalem. Land ownership in 1948 in this village was distributed as follows:

Palestinian	7,780 *dunums*
Jewish	756 *dunums*
Public	207 *dunums*
Total	8,743 *dunums*

Note: *dunum* equals 1,000 square metres.

The above figures indicate that Palestinians owned 89 percent of the land, the Jews owned 9 percent and the rest was public.[5]

Today, some of the old homes of Lifta remain abandoned while the newer ones are inhabited by Jews. The village high school building is now used as a Jewish religious site. A number of modern hotels such as the Sonesta and the Hilton are built on the property of Lifta. However, more importantly, most Israeli government ministries are built on Lifta land. This includes the Israeli Knesset building, the Prime Minister's offices, and the ministries of Foreign Affairs and Interior. In fact, the Knesset is built on the private property of the Khalaf family which now lives as 'present absentees' in the Sheikh Jarrah Quarter of East Jerusalem.

2   Deir Yassin and surrounding agricultural lands. The land ownership in 1948 in this village was distributed as follows:

Palestinian	2,701 *dunums*
Jewish	152 *dunums*
Public	3 *dunums*
Total	2,856 *dunums*

The above shows that Palestinians owned 95 percent of the land and the Jews owned the remaining 5 percent.

This small village located in the north-west of West Jerusalem had a population of 900 in 1948. On 9 April 1948, it was attacked by the Jewish terrorist organisation *Irgun Zvai Leumi* led by Menachem Begin. By twelve noon that fateful day, the village had fallen to the attackers who subsequently committed the infamous massacre of the children, elderly, and wounded who were unable to leave the village. Today, the houses in the centre of the village are used as a sanatorium for mentally ill Jews, run by the Israeli Ministry of Health. The village cemetery has been bulldozed and covered by a road leading to a new Jewish residential settlement built on the lands owned by the villagers of Deir Yassin. The stone quarries that Deir Yassin was famous for have now become a Jewish industrial zone. The village's two-room elementary school building is now the home of Chabed Labovitch.

---

[5] For details about the villages, its occupation and depopulation by the Jews see *All That Remains: The Palestinian Villages Occupied and Depopulated by Israel in 1948*, edited by Walid Khalidi, Institute of Palestine Studies, 1993.

3   Ein Karem and surrounding agricultural terraces located to the west of Jerusalem were incorporated into the municipal boundaries of West Jerusalem, as were Lifta and Deir Yassin. Land ownership in 1948 in this village was distributed as follows:

Palestinian	13,449 *dunums*
Jewish	1,362 *dunums*
Public	218 *dunums*
Total	15,029 *dunums*

The Palestinians owned 90 percent, the Jews 9 percent and the rest was public.

In 1948, this village had a population of 4,500 predominately Christian Catholic Palestinians, as Ein Karem is the birthplace of John the Baptist. That year, all the inhabitants of the village were forced to leave. Today, all the village houses are inhabited by Jews. The churches that still exist in the village have become museums without any congregations. The Jewish Hadassah Hospital is built on the lands of this village. Finally, it is one of the major ironies of history, that Yad Vashem, a memorial to the Jewish victims of the Nazis. is built on the terraced land of the dispossessed, exiled, and involuntarily 'absentee' Palestinians of Ein Karem.

This Jewish memorial in Ein Karem testifies to the fact that the Palestinians are in fact the last victims of Hitler, as they had to pay with their villages, lands, and country for the establishment of the Jewish state.

4   El-Malha. After Ein Karem, this was the second largest of the four villages located to the south of Jerusalem. It had a population of 3,000 Palestinians.

Land ownership in 1948 in this village was distributed as follows:

Palestinian	2,701 *dunums*
Jewish	153 *dunums*
Public	3 *dunums*
Total	2,857 *dunums*

The above indicates that Palestinians owned 85 percent, the Jews 13 percent and the remainder of the land was public.

The Palestinians of this village were forced from their homes in April and July 1948. Today, their houses are inhabited by Jews. Where the village mosque stood there is now a Jewish house. Jewish settlements, including the Stadium of Jerusalem and the recently opened Jerusalem Mall, have been built on the village land.

Thus, 90 percent of the land of these four villages that were occupied by the Jews in 1948 and annexed to West Jerusalem Municipality belongs to the Palestinians. Almost 30,000 *dunums* have been built upon by the Jews and today they constitute most of the Jewish residential areas of West Jerusalem.

In addition, Palestinians were also evicted from most of the urban residential quarters of West Jerusalem that came under Jewish control in 1948. These urban neighbourhoods include:

1   Upper and Lower Baqa'a
2   Katamon
3   Talbieh
4   Mammilla and Shama'a
5   Part of Abu-Tor
6   Musrara
7   Part of Rehavia

These residential areas were part of New Jerusalem developed by the Palestinians outside the walls of the Old City, at the beginning of the century. They had mixed populations of mostly middle class Christian and Muslim Palestinians, such as doctors, lawyers, merchants, and civil servants working with the government of Palestine under the British Mandate. These neighbourhoods were fully developed with apartment buildings, modern private residences, villas, stores, offices, workshops and family cottage industries.

In April and May 1948, after the Palestinian population was forced to leave, all the neighbourhoods were completely taken over. Today, Jews live in these Palestinian homes. Palestinian houses were also turned into Jewish religious schools or small private hospitals. In the Mamilla Quarter, part of the Mamilla Muslim Cemetery was turned into the Israeli Independence Park and an outstanding building, owned by the Muslim Awqaf which housed in the 1930s the first Palestinian theatre, is today the offices of the Israeli Ministry of Trade and Industry. The residence of the Israeli president is built on Palestinian property in the previously Palestinian Quarter of Talbieh.

The magnitude of the expropriation of Palestinian property in pre-1948 modern West Jerusalem can be appreciated when it is realised that the Palestinians owned 40 percent of new Jerusalem, the Jews 26.12 percent and the rest belonged to Christian and Muslim religious communities and the government of Palestine.[6]

The present market value of the Palestinian property usurped in 1948 in what is today West Jerusalem is in the billions of US dollars. Thus Palestinians were not only permanently uprooted, but were also severely impacted financially.

From the above, it is clear that most of the areas that lie within the West Jerusalem municipal boundaries belong to the Palestinians, be they the Palestinian villages that were incorporated into the municipal boundaries of West Jerusalem after 1948, or the Palestinian urban quarters that in 1948 formed part of modern West Jerusalem. Furthermore, despite the fact that Palestinians were declared permanent absentees by Israeli law, this property legally still belongs to the Palestinians, as title in land registries is still in the name of the original Palestinian owners.

It is pertinent to point out here that the amount of Jewish-owned land in 1948 in the Jerusalem district, which extended from Jericho and the Jordan River in the east to the Latrun Monastery on the edge of the coastal plains to the west, did not exceed 2 percent of the total, while Palestinians owned 84 percent of the land and the remaining 14 percent was public. This is according to land-ownership records by

---

[6] Henry, Cattan, 1988, p. 253.

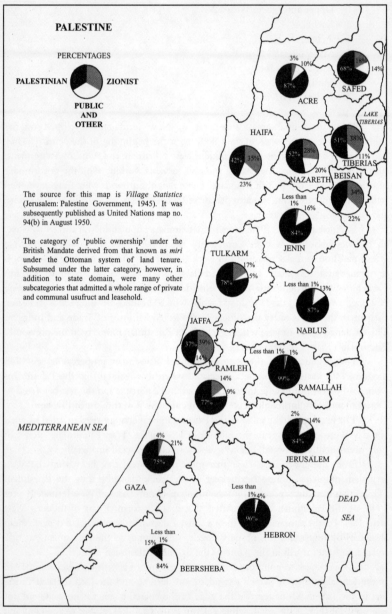

Figure 2. Zionist and Palestinian land ownership in percentages by subdistrict, 1945.

sub-district in Palestine in 1945 shown in the map (fig. 2).

Post June 1967-Annexation and Colonisation of East Jerusalem

The June 1967 War brought the eastern part of Jerusalem including the walled Old City under Israeli occupation. Shortly thereafter, the Jewish state began a series of measures intended not only to maintain Jewish control of the city and its Palestinian population but also to change its demographic character. This was accomplished by moving Jews to the occupied part of Jerusalem and building exclusively Jewish residential fortress colonies on confiscated Palestinian property. What follows is a brief account of the measures and policies adopted by the Israeli government in occupied East Jerusalem since June 1967.

The first measure of the Jewish state was to dismiss and disband the elected Palestinian Municipality of East Jerusalem that had been functioning since 1948. The elected Palestinian mayor, Rohi El-Khatib, was subsequently deported to Jordan for refusing to accept the dissolution of his municipality.

On 22 June 1967, the Jewish state formally annexed occupied East Jerusalem by extending over the city the law, jurisdiction and administration of the State of Israel. Since that time, the Jewish state has continued to Judaise the city and take measures that affect the lives and property of the Palestinian indigenous population of East Jerusalem. These measures include:

1   Walled Old City of East Jerusalem. Shortly after the fighting ended in June 1967, Jewish bulldozers destroyed over 135 homes in the Islamic Moghrabi (Moroccan) Quarter, to make way for a plaza next to the Wailing Wall. In the wake of this destruction 650 Palestinians were left homeless. It is worth pointing out in this context that the Wailing Wall is part of the Western Wall of the Muslim Dome of the Rock compound and belongs to the Muslims. Henry Cattan writes:

> Following the bloody riots in 1929 over an incident at the Wailing Wall an international commission was appointed in 1931 by the British Mandate, with the approval of the League of Nations, to inquire into the rights over the Wailing Wall. The commission found the ownership of the Wall accrues to the Muslims and the pavement in front of the Wall where the Jews perform their devotions, is also Muslim property.[7]

In addition to the destruction of the Moghrabi Quarter, the Israelis evicted Palestinians from their homes in the Old City and replaced them with Jews. Up to the present, over 5,000 Palestinians have been evicted from other Muslim Quarters. As a result of these measures the Jewish quarter of the Old City today is four times the size it was in 1948.

---

[7] *Ibid.,* p. 266.

2   Municipal boundaries of East Jerusalem. The 1967 annexation of occupied East Jerusalem included not only the area of the Municipal boundaries of Arab Jerusalem as these existed in June 1967, but also other parts of the West Bank, specifically areas from the Bethlehem and Ramallah districts. Consequently, East Jerusalem, as it is known today, is three times the size it was in 1967. Furthermore, in drawing the expanded boundaries of annexed East Jerusalem, the Israeli objectives were to maximise land area and minimise the number of Palestinians included within the new boundaries.

A number of Palestinian villages were excluded from the expanded municipal boundaries of East Jerusalem, but some of their lands were included in these boundaries. For example, to the east of Jerusalem, four fairly large villages— Hizma, Anata, Bethany, and Abu Dis—remained outside the boundaries as did two villages in the west, namely Beit Iksa and Beit Hanina. In the north the gerrymandered boundaries extended into the Ramallah district to include the Jerusalem airport but to exclude Dahiet el-Barid and El Ram, and the refugee camp of Kalandia. If these Palestinian neighbourhoods and villages had been included in the East Jerusalem municipal boundaries, a minimum of 80,000 Palestinians would have been added to the Palestinian population of Jerusalem which would have certainly affected the demography of East Jerusalem and tipped the balance in favour of the Palestinians.

The policy of maximising the annexation of Palestinian lands within East Jerusalem has another convenient objective for the occupation authorities, namely to facilitate the usurpation of Palestinian property. Under conditions of annexation Palestinian property can be confiscated in accordance with Israeli law and under the pretext of 'public purpose'. From the Israeli point of view this is preferable to seizing the land on the pretext that it is 'state land' as is the policy in the West Bank, since such seizures can be challenged if the land is cultivated according to old Ottoman laws.

3   Confiscation of Palestinian private property in East Jerusalem. Having changed the boundaries of East Jerusalem to suit its designs, the Jewish state embarked in 1967 on a policy of Judaisation and colonisation of the newly occupied part of the city by seizing Muslim and Christian Palestinian property and building on such land exclusively Jewish residential fortress colonies. This is not only contrary to international law governing occupied territories, but also amounts to a form of apartheid, based on religious discrimination rather than on colour as in South Africa.[8]

Between 1967 and the present, the Jewish state dispossessed the Palestinians of over 24,000 *dunums* of the most expensive real estate in the heart and outskirts of East Jerusalem. This dispossession was achieved by a method that can only be called 'legalised theft'. Private property was seized on the pretext of 'public purpose' in

---

[8] For an analysis of International law and the Palestinian occupied territories, see Playfair, Emma, (ed.), *International Law and the Administration of Occupied Territories: Two Decades of Israeli Occupation of the West Bank and Gaza Strip,* Clarendon Press, Oxford, 1992.

accordance with Israeli laws, since, according to Israel, East Jerusalem was annexed and therefore governed by such laws. The 'public' refers only to the Jewish public and excludes the indigenous Christian and Muslim Palestinian citizens of Jerusalem. The 'purpose' is the construction of Jewish residential fortress settlements on these usurped lands.

Most of the Palestinian property in East Jerusalem was seized in the early 1970s and 1980s, however, confiscations have continued into the 1990s and up to the present (see fig. 1).

In January and April 1968, immediately after the occupation, 1,200 acres in the heart of East Jerusalem were confiscated from the Palestinians for construction of the first Jewish residential colonies in the Holy City. These colonies include French Hill, Ramat Eshkol, and their extensions located on the property of Palestinian owners from the Sheikh Jarrah quarter. In addition, an industrial park was established in Kalandia on the north-west borders of Jerusalem, on the property of Palestinian owners from Kalandia and Rafat.

In August 1970, an additional 3,100 acres of privately owned Palestinian property were seized. On this land, four large fortress colonies were built. They include Ramot in the west, on the property of Palestinian owners from the villages of Beit Iksa and Beit Hanina; Gilo in the south, on the property of owners from Bethlehem, Beit Jala, Beit Safafa and Sharafat; East Talpiot in the east on the property of owners from Sur Baher; and Neve Ya'acov in the north on the property of owners from Beit Hanina.

In March 1980, an additional 1,100 acres were seized for the construction of the Jewish colony called Pisgat Ze'ev in the north-east on the property of owners from Beit-Hanina and Hizma. This colony is presently expanding rapidly as more apartments are currently being built in order to increase the number of Jewish settlers from 30,000 to 60,000 by the end of 1996.

In April 1991, an additional 470 acres were seized from Palestinian owners from Beit Sahour and Sur Baher in the south of Jerusalem for the planned settlement of Har Homa. 9,000 apartments were approved for the construction by the Israeli government in May 1995. The struggle of the Palestinians against the construction of this settlement has not ceased. The land seizure has been challenged in the Israeli High Court. On several occasions, Palestinian land owners have demonstrated in protest against the seizure of their property. Recently, Palestinian owners from Bethlehem also demonstrated in protest against the seizure of more of their lands for a planned road to link this colony with the existing settlement of Gilo.

The establishment of this settlement will create a southern wall that will separate the Palestinians of the Bethlehem area from Jerusalem. More importantly, it will also question the meaning of the peace that Israel has signed with the Palestinians.

In April 1992, an additional 500 acres were seized for another new residential settlement called Ramat Shu'fat on the property of owners from the Palestinian village of Shu'fat. This settlement is presently under construction and approximately 2,100 apartments are expected to be completed by the end of 1996, adding another estimated 15,000 Jewish settlers in East Jerusalem.

In May 1995, an additional 150 acres of private property belonging to Palestinian owners from Beit Hanina and Beit Safafa were confiscated for expansion of Ramot and Gilo settlements. This last seizure was rescinded after protest by the Palestinian owners and the Arab Israeli members of the Knesset who threatened to withdraw their support of the Israel government.

With the completion of Ramat Shu'fat, the Palestinian population of East Jerusalem will be encircled and flanked from the north, south, east and west by Jewish fortress settlements. The only direction that remains free for the Palestinians of Jerusalem is the sky above them. The 157,000 Palestinians of Jerusalem are already outnumbered as the number of Jewish settlers reached 160,000 in 1995, and is estimated to reach 180,000 by the end of 1996. In May 1995, the Israeli government approved the construction of an additional 9,000 apartments in the new settlement of Har Homa on land expropriated in 1991, and 7,000 apartments in the existing settlement of Pisgat Ze'ev and Ramot, on lands expropriated in April 1995. The completion of the apartments will add another 80,000 illegal Jewish settlers in annexed Occupied Jerusalem which will increase their number to over 260,000 by the end of the century.

In addition to moving Jews to the occupied part of East Jerusalem, the Israeli government also moved the Israeli ministries of Housing and Agriculture, the headquarters of the Israeli Police, the Border Police, the Israeli Army Central Command, and the civil courts to East Jerusalem as well. The sum total of this process of Judaisation leads only to one conclusion: the Jewish state from day one of occupation of East Jerusalem had no intention of ever withdrawing from the Holy City.

4   Planning restrictions for the Palestinians of East Jerusalem. Palestinians living in the so-called unified Jerusalem were not only dispossessed and impoverished for the exclusive benefit of the Jewish population, but were restricted in building on their own land as well. This was achieved by limiting the number of building licences issued to the Palestinians, by failing to approve the master plan for the Palestinian neighbourhoods which would facilitate the issuing of licences and, finally, by declaring large areas of Palestinian-owned lands 'Green Zones', meaning that Palestinians are not allowed to build on this land.

Sara Kaminker, a past member of the Jewish Municipality of West Jerusalem, and member of the committee called 'Peace for Jerusalem'—revealed in an article published in the Arab daily *Al-Quds,* 1 August 1993 the following:

1   That the Jewish Municipality of Jerusalem 'paints in green' or creates green zones only to prevent the Palestinians from building on their own land.

2   That these green zones can be conveniently changed when the Jews decide to build on this land. As an example she mentioned that in one of the meetings of the Municipality of Jerusalem, Mayor Kollek announced that a new Jewish neighbourhood was to be built on Palestinian land in East Jerusalem, planted with trees and declared

a green zone! When Sara Kaminker explained that this would entail destroying trees, Kollek answered, 'The only objective of planting the trees is to prevent the Arabs from building on the land until the time comes to build a Jewish quarter.'

Kaminker added in that revealing article what Palestinians have known all along: Mayor Kollek had quietly, over the past 26 years of occupation of East Jerusalem, judaised the city, and that his future plans, as well as those of the present mayor, are to continue this path in order to create islands of Palestinians encircled by a sea of Jews.

Finally, in order to complete the Judaisation and Jewish control of East Jerusalem, on 30 March 1993 the Israelis closed access to East Jerusalem for Palestinians from the West Bank. The impact of this closure on the Palestinian population has been devastating. It has reduced business in East Jerusalem by 80 percent, cut the West Bank into three cantons and limited the access of Christians and Muslims to the holy sites in the city. As a result of this closure Palestinians from the West Bank are not permitted to enter the city of Jerusalem without permits from the Israeli authorities. At first the Palestinians thought that this was a temporary measure. Yet today, this closure of Jerusalem has become permanent and only a handful of Palestinians are given permits to enter the city.

The Israelis declare at every opportunity that the conquest of both West and East Jerusalem is now an accomplished fact, that it is the eternal capital of Israel and that it is 'not negotiable' under any circumstances. However, I have shown that in fact, most of the land and properties whether in West or East Jerusalem still belong to the Palestinian people. Despite the fact that the Jews have seized Palestinian property in West Jerusalem, and confiscated it for 'public purpose' in East Jerusalem, title to all this property still lies with the Palestinians.

In the Declaration of Principles on Palestinian self-government signed in Washington in September 1993, negotiation on the future of Jerusalem has been delayed until negotiations begin on the final status of the Palestinian occupied territories which are planned for May 1996. This delay will only make it more difficult to reach a settlement, as the Jewish authorities are continuing to violate international law and private Palestinian property rights by continuing to expand Jewish colonies and refuse to accept a settlement freeze.

However, continuation by the Jews to create new facts should not distract from negotiating a fair solution to the issue of West and East Jerusalem based on application of international law and UN resolutions. Such a solution should be based on the following principles:

1   Dismantling all illegal Jewish colonies in East Jerusalem built after June 1967, and the return of all confiscated property to its legal owners, including what has been built on the land.
2   Repatriation of Palestinians to their homes, villages and property in West Jerusalem by changing their status from 'absentees' to 'present', or compensation for property for those who do not wish to have their property back.

3   Restore Palestinian sovereignty to East Jerusalem and declare it as capital of the Palestinian State.

Finally and until such a solution is reached, the 157,000 Palestinians of Jerusalem are determined to continue their struggle to liberate themselves from Jewish discrimination, exploitation, and control. They are determined to defend and protect their property rights, and their right to self-determination and freedom.

22
THE MESSAGE OF JERUSALEM TODAY
Munir Fasheh

A Parable/An Analogy

Jesus used parables to illustrate what he wanted to say. It is inspiring to do the same. If a frog falls in boiling water, it struggles to get out. If it falls in water under ordinary temperature, however, and the water is heated, the frog will feel comfortable at the beginning. When the temperature reaches a dangerous level, the frog doesn't even try to do anything. It has already lost its struggle for survival. Similarly, human beings seem to be ill-equipped in sensing and responding to threats to survival when they come in slow and gradual doses.

The Palestinian Situation Today

The real dangers and threats we currently face as Palestinians are subtle and hard to sense. In the short term, conditions may seem to be improving but in the long term the threats are far-reaching. The forms, degree and extent of fragmentation we currently face are unprecedented, not only at geographic and social levels, but at the family and personal levels also. Society is changing as people become more interested in making money and building larger homes. These values are replacing the values, which for example, made it possible for Palestinian society in the West Bank and Gaza Strip to remain civil and viable for six years without any governmental laws or police and despite attempts by the occupying Israeli power to dismantle the society and drive people against each other.

One of the most far-reaching dangers we currently face is the new 'mandate' given to the World Bank for the 'development' of Palestine. The debt which will accumulate together with compound interest will place a huge burden on future generations. This is one of the most dangerous factors in the current 'peace' formula, yet it is the one least talked about. Although part of the money is spent on the much needed salaries for government employees, the bulk is going to unnecessary (even harmful or useless) expenses such as for foreign experts and companies. In spite of the role that the World Bank has played during the past 50 years in afflicting nations by dismantling societies, robbing them of their resources and ways of survival by putting them in almost perpetual debt, the bank has been placed in charge of the development of Palestine! In a very real sense 'aid' through the World Bank is like AIDS: it kills the internal immune system of societies and prepares them for a slow death.[1] It is like the mandate given to Britain after the First World War to help it 'rule' Palestine. Not only did the British leave us without a chance to govern ourselves but also left us without a country. This absurdity points to the first message of Jerusalem today which I would like to emphasise: never trust big powers or international organisations to solve your problems; people have to depend on themselves and their mutual support for one another if they are interested in saving themselves, their future and their planet. Put concisely: whereas Britain stole our past, the World Bank (and associates) is stealing our future.

These slow and subtle dangers take additional forms in the case of Palestinian Christians. Denominational housing projects are one very serious danger, Christian seats in the Palestinian legislative council are another. Emigration is a third. Other forms include: ghettoising Palestinian Christians in terms of their perceptions and language; losing a sense of community and connectedness to a whole, narrowing our thinking and shrinking our dreams, and so on.

In 1967 the Israeli-Arab War stirred in me rebellious feelings against both the fragmentation of Palestinians and the fragmentation of knowledge. I started seeing more clearly the role of dominant discourse and existing institutions (educational, religious and political) in producing this fragmentation. I have continued to rebel against these things since that war. There is a big difference between diversity and fragmentation. Diversity is a healthy colourful integrated whole; fragmentation, at best, is like a broken mirror. Any breaking of Palestinian society along religious or ethnic lines is like breaking a mirror; there is no way to put it back together.

There is no deep meaning to the words we use unless they are connected to our experiences, our lives, the realities we live in, and our perception of the world. This means we often need to look 'underneath the surface' and go beyond the established meanings of words in our search for a meaningful understanding of the words we hear, read or use. The only authentic contribution I can make to the effort of seeking a more collective understanding of Christ and Jerusalem, is to tell you what Christ's words mean and what the message of Jerusalem is for me today as a Christian Palestinian from Jerusalem.

I was born in Jerusalem in 1941 and was expelled along with my family from our home in 1948. Since then, our home has been inhabited by European Jews, whom I was told were 'chosen' by God to live in it, play with my toys, even eat the food we left. That absurdity was one of an ever-increasing number of absurdities, hypocrisies, deceits and injustices of various kinds, which I have been exposed to and have had to live with, since I was a child. What makes things more irrational is the way Western media and scholars still place the blame on 'me', the Palestinian.

Many of the absurdities and hypocrisies I have had to live with are connected

---

[1] A statement by all Africa Conference of Churches, marking the 50th anniversary of the World Bank and IMF and launching the movement 'Fifty years is enough' carries these words: 'Every child in Africa is born with a financial burden which a lifetime's work cannot repay. The debt is a new form of slavery as vicious as the slave trade.' [From a fact sheet produced by the Inter-church Coalition on Africa, which is a Canadian ecumenical coalition of eight national churches in Canada.]

with God. It was very difficult for me as a child to reconcile two Gods in my mind; one in whose name I was expelled from my home, and the other who was revealed in the beatitudes, who is the God of the scapegoats, the persecuted, the dehumanised and the poor. Not only have I never been able to reconcile the two but, over the years, I have watched the God of the deprived and scapegoats slowly retreating and being defeated, especially within official circles, religious institutions, official media, the clergy, scholars and leaders. Today more than ever before, I see the God of the scapegoats disappearing and the God of the hypocrites rising again. A third message of Jerusalem today, is to make sure that the God of the persecuted and the dehumanised is not defeated in our minds, hearts, actions and relationships with one another. Although this sounds like a simple act, it requires courage, intellectual honesty and a sense of social responsibility, all of which are generally absent in those who hold the symbols and means of power in the world today.

Examples of hypocrisies I have been living with are numerous and ever increasing: building a state on the basis of religion; giving priority to a particular group; wiping out villages; killing children; stealing other people's land and water, and restricting the movement of people to closed areas, are some examples. All these are considered crimes and cause outrage everywhere except in the case of Israel. The list of double standards never seems to end, and in the case of Israel, the victim (e.g., 'me')—all along—has been blamed.

Examples of absurdities and dehumanisation are also abundant. For example, on the personal level, I have been unable to get residency rights for my wife and two sons, so they cannot live with me in this country (I have been married since 1967). The refusal of major humanitarian and international organisations to support a study on the effect on Palestinian children of the first two years of the *intifada,* when they were killed, beaten, maimed and their bones crushed by Israeli soldiers is shocking, especially when the same organisations flood Palestine today with plans for the development of Palestinians and their children. However, these 'plans' do not take into account the experiences and authentic voices of the Palestinian children and youth, but instead try to mould these to serve the political ends of others. The so-called Christian Embassy in Jerusalem is housed in a 'stolen' house, ironically the house of a prominent Christian Palestinian, Professor Edward Said. From where I live today in Ramallah, I can see two settlements expanding and encroaching onto lands that belong to the town's inhabitants and this is happening more than two years after the beginning of the peace talks. The so-called Palestinian passports are actually Israeli travel documents carrying the same Israeli occupation identity card numbers, but with a Palestinian cover. Any movement from one major area to another, or from the West Bank to the outside, requires a permit from the Israelis, even though this often only entails a journey of 10 minutes. According to optimistic estimates, more than 80 percent of the West Bank will remain directly in the hands of Israel; the underground water reserve of the West Bank and the Gaza Strip, which is the life line of the Palestinians and which was 'sucked out' by Israel during the past 28 years is not a topic for discussion; and, as a final example of living absurdities, while European Christians created the Jewish problem and European Jews created the Palestinian problem, Islam is blamed! Islam is currently the main scapegoat in the international mass media and among experts on world affairs. (I must also add that I have found absurdities and hypocrisies thriving in other places in the world as well, not just in Israel.)

The continued hypocrisies and accompanying dehumanisation (sometimes in new and more subtle forms) and lack of protection for Palestinians are at the root of the problem. Recent examples of these are: continuing to arrest people under what is called 'administrative detention' without charges or court proceedings; arresting Palestinians on roads between 'townships'; a young Palestinian girl in Hebron was pulled by the hair and killed by settlers, one day after the assassination of Rabin; Israeli bulldozers uprooting olive trees, some hundreds of years old, in order to lay roads and make space for settlements for Jews coming from New York and elsewhere. We cannot hope for a lasting solution and for a better future (for everyone) without dealing with these hypocrisies. A fourth message of Jerusalem today, is the necessity to have the intellectual honesty and social courage to point out hypocrisies in ourselves as well as in others.

The most disturbing fact is that everything which has been built on the basis of the Oslo and Washington agreements can be erased by Israel overnight. What is being built is so shallow and superficial. From what I see happening I believe that Israel is preparing the conditions where it can again put the blame on Palestinians in order to dismantle what has been built. These processes need to be recognised and addressed with honesty. This points to a fifth message of Jerusalem today which is to remind the world that the concept of 'chosenness' is irrational, that people are equal under God and that people can be better than others only through their deeds and relationships.

A Talk with Jesus

The more I experience, the more I see the similarity between Jerusalem today and Jerusalem as described in the Gospels at the time Jesus walked on this land. Christ was most familiar with the situation in Palestine and the influence of Rome on the daily lives of the people living there. Similarly, I find myself most familiar with the situation in Palestine and the influence of the new Rome-Washington DC-on the daily lives of people here. It is not a coincidence, then, that I feel Christ's words, parables and images in a very deep and personal way. I can feel his words vibrating within me as if I hear him in person today. If Christ decided to come to Palestine today for a visit and happened to meet me walking (say on the same road he walked with two of his disciples on their way to Emmaus, a village destroyed by Israel in 1967) we would have a lot to talk about. It would undoubtedly be one of the most fascinating conversations in my life. I am sure that after I tell him about the practices and claims of those in power in the region and beyond, and how the money is used by the 'big donors' his reaction could be something similar to the following:

Jesus: What you have been telling me sounds just like my Palestine of 2000 years ago! What I hated most was the extent of the hypocrisy and the use of money and power to crush people and dismantle communities. Hypocrisy was everywhere, in the words of the Pharisees, in the actions of the moralists and in the attitudes and practices of those who thought they were better than others. I still remember, how Pontius Pilate washed his hands as if to disclaim all responsibility for what was to happen to me and permitted his soldiers to strip and mock me. He was the one who delivered me to the cross. That is why I didn't take his questions seriously and sometimes even just looked at him without saying anything. It is so similar to what you are telling me is happening today. I couldn't stand that hypocrisy and kept pointing it out in people's words and actions. It wasn't easy because hypocrites held the strings of power in the land and I knew it might lead me to the cross, but I did it anyway. I also told people not to judge others, and even turn the other cheek for those who have been victimised and scapegoated like themselves. This does not mean one should remain oblivious in the face of plans to dismantle societies and break the solidarity among people. When you mentioned what the World Bank and others are doing, and how the money is being used, you reminded me of the time I walked into the temple and saw people using money to buy people's future. It is strange how much people misunderstood me. It is true that I turned the other cheek to those who were hurting me, like the soldiers at the cross, and asked God to forgive them because they didn't realise what they were doing, but I never turned the other cheek to those who knowingly used money or power to cause misery to others. I remember that I even used a whip to throw such people out of that place which was supposed to be one of the few places where people could feel safe. I would not hesitate to do the same thing again, and in the same place, with those who are using money today to plant future misery for innocent people.

What you told me of the current happenings to Palestinians reminds me of the time when the devil took me to the mount overlooking Jericho and tried to tempt me by saying he would give me Jericho and beyond, if I go along with his plans. How ironic! The same place, similar promises! I remember I told the devil to go away; that people do not live by bread alone. To be robbed of one's soul and humanity is much worse than to be robbed of one's land. What is at stake here is the humanity of people. If I were in the shoes of the Palestinians today, I would say the same thing to those who are giving you similar promises, including promises of millions of dollars. Tell them, what will it profit them if they gained the whole world but forfeit their life. You can tell the new hypocrites (although that may lead you to the cross) who come to you carrying the pictures of the new Caesars on their dollars, what I told the man who showed me the coin with Caesar's face on it: 'Render unto Caesar the things which are Caesar's and unto the Palestinians the things which are the Palestinians.' The role of the new coin is the same as the old one; to fragment communities, buy people's souls, kill their mutual support for one another, and wipe out long-term forms of survival. We cannot afford to look at any event in isolation; we have to constantly try to see the whole picture. Crushing human beings was a main worry and concern of mine when I lived in Palestine. I defended people against anything that was insulting and humiliating and oppressing to them. I could not just watch and remain silent. I had to say and do what needed to be said and done. We cannot afford to remain silent. If we do, the very stones will speak out. You, yourself witnessed that in 1987 when the world remained silent for decades in relation to your situation, the very stones spoke out.

I: The situation today sounds so similar to that of your day. It is common practice for innocent people to be turned into scapegoats, and there is a huge gap between official claims and what is actually taking place on the ground. We need so much to love and support each other, especially to care for our children, and to become like children. We also need to tell stories (parables) in order to understand the world so we can create a different reality.

Jesus: Don't waste your time and energy on changing symptoms or making symbolic gains. Instead of asking people in power to change the world, join others to create a more desirable world through practising new values, new priorities and new ways of relating to one another. Emphasise collective action, love your neighbour and the people who are like you (regardless of whether they call themselves Christians, Muslims, Jews, atheists, communists, fundamentalists or whatever). This is the only viable and human response to the attempts of separating you from one another and robbing you of your humanity. Don't look at their labels or their words, but, rather, at where they stand in the process of dehumanisation. Your enemy is not the soldier carrying the gun to shoot you, but those whose greed for money, power, profit and control makes them arm that soldier and use him to crush other human beings and set people against one another. Beware of those who honour you with their lips but whose hearts are far from you, for they often have ugly plans in store for you. Carry the 'whip' if you have to, like I did, but your energies should go mainly towards loving one another, caring for and supporting one another and building solidarity networks and a common future together. Take care of your children, the youth and the deprived, for they shall inherit the earth, and remember when two or more gather with this in mind, I will be amongst them. If you see innocent people crucified, don't feel discouraged, for sometimes the only way to save life is for some to lose or give it for the sake of others. This is exactly what happened to me. It is a sad but true fact of life. Although you seem to have worse days ahead of you, do not lose hope. The beauty of life lies in the relationships that exist among people; in living simply and fully, close to nature and each other, and refusing to allow consumerism and jealousy to control your life, values and perceptions. This was the message I gave to the world from Jerusalem 2,000 years ago, from the city that gave me a lot of headaches. It is the same message the people in Jerusalem can give to the world today: it is life and people which are sacred, not cities or places.

I am sure that, in his talk with me, Jesus would be as concrete, simple, warm, humble, sincere, human and as profound about the human condition, and what to do about it, as he was 2,000 years ago. I am sure he would laugh when he hears that we need large expensive buildings in which to pray to the God of the poor. He would definitely laugh at the claim that one needs a degree in theology to understand what he said very simply to people of his day. It could be that what Jesus said is difficult for the 'sophisticated' and those in power, but not for those who have not lost their honesty, senses and connectedness to life. That is why he chose his close friends from the down-to-earth people and why his harshest words were directed against hypocrites and those who abused money and power to crush others.

I am sure I would be able to talk with Jesus as a friend and even invite him to our home. It is possible that my great great . . . grandmother did invite Jesus home to meet her family (I was born less than five miles from where he was). Maybe in places other than Palestine, people would think of Jesus as a celebrity, our ancestors knew Christ as a human being close to people and full of life and internal strength, so there is no reason for us Palestinians not to feel the same way towards him today.

What Does it Mean to Love One Another?

I believe that Christ's call to love one another was the strongest statement he ever made and which led to his crucifixion. His love was manifested in exposing hypocrisy amongst those in power in Jerusalem; expelling those who were playing with peoples' lives from the temple; washing his disciples' feet; and in refusing to differentiate among people. He refused to judge people according to ethnic groups, religion, place of birth or what they did for a living. Instead he categorised people according to whether they were preserving or destroying life, suffering or causing suffering, humanising or dehumanising people. His love was manifested in having the honesty and courage to say and do what was needed, in spite of the Romans, the secret police, prison or courts.

Although Christ cared deeply for the 'spiritual' aspects of life, he was concrete in his words, actions and the positions he took. He was compassionate and biased towards the persecuted. He bound his life and message with the suffering. He cared,

173

loved and respected people deeply and went beyond the obvious and familiar in practising that care. While acting in solidarity with the scapegoats of society, he also carried and used a whip when dealing with money changers in God's house. He was aware of the limitations of the mind and language, and their ability to distort life and reality. That is why he combined words with practice. He did not act as a reformer when dealing with the Pharisees and Scribes, instead he confronted them by saying 'you hypocrites!', while at the same time asking people to look inside themselves, at their own hypocrisies and the way they perceived things which affected their understanding and behaviour. In short, Jesus was biased, not towards Christians, but towards the scapegoats in society. For example, if someone in Gaza is labelled by the world as a fundamentalist, Christ would not be fooled by the label but would look at whether the person was being used as a scapegoat or not. He would be the first person to defend him or her in words and action, regardless of consequences. Jesus looked beneath the surface of things and also within the larger context. His love for humanity and his readiness to defend human beings is unmatched.

The Message of Jerusalem Today: a Summary

When Jesus walked this land, Rome was the only 'superpower'. Christ knew that he could not fight Rome through its own means. In fact, his fight was directed precisely against those means, as well as against the values that accompanied them. His approach was to plant seeds of a different nature, of a different world.

I find myself today in exactly the same situation. As I walk in the same place, Washington is the only 'superpower'. The most I feel we can do is to plant seeds of a different nature. Again, the main actors in planting such seeds are people themselves. The seeds needed to humanise the world today contain three simple principles that Christ taught 2,000 years ago, and which remain true today:

1   Human beings do not live by bread alone (Matthew 4: 4).
2   Love one another (John 13: 34).
3   First take the log out of your own eye, and then you will see clearly to take the speck out of your neighbour's eye (Matthew 7: 5).

The first two principles point to the importance of the spiritual dimension in life; the third points to the importance of fighting hypocrisy in ourselves as well as in others.

This is the message of Jerusalem today. The spiritual dimension and loving one another are crucial to building, not only a lasting peace in the region, but a saner world for everybody. As they were at the time of Jesus, hypocrisy, intellectual dishonesty and using various means (both subtle and not so subtle) to fragment and dehumanise people and communities, are the underlying evils in today's world. Hypocrites always find scapegoats to cover up their evil and deny their responsibility for what is happening. They always appeal to high moral principles to justify their crimes, actions and policies and are usually intolerant of anyone who exposes their hypocrisies. The price of being intellectually honest, of having integrity and a strong sense of social responsibility, of exposing hypocrisy and of trying to bring people together, today as in the time of Jesus, is usually very high; it may lead to the cross. The message of Jerusalem for Christians today is that they have to take a stand, just like Christ did 2,000 years ago.

Indigenous Palestinian Christians are heirs of the first Christian community in the world, and as such, have a tremendous role to play, as we inherit a beautiful and precious dream. We have also been an integral part of a bigger whole: Arab Islamic civilisation. It is up to us either to waste what we have, or keep the diversity and look at what we have as seeds for a more human and happier world. We either fall into the trap of filling our children with fear and giving them 'small dreams' (like having some seats in the 'national' council) or plant in them the seeds of a big dream: joining others in creating a different world. What we aspire for, rather than what we fear, should be the driving force and our source of energy. We can do this by reminding the world again of the everlasting and inexhaustible human resources: creativity, learning, loving feelings and a sense of responsibility towards nature and future generations. These are the elements of building a different world.

Just as Christ did 2,000 years ago, we can remind the world that injustice, dehumanisation and hypocrisy cannot survive for ever; that they cannot sustain life or bring happiness and security to people. We can remind the world of the power of loving feelings and mutual support and of their role in building a different world. Since the number of people who are ready to translate their hope into action seems small, we must remember that Christ started his mission with just twelve friends (one of whom, later, was ready to 'sell' him for thirty pieces of silver!).

The message of Jerusalem today, in particular, is to expose the hypocritical statement that Jerusalem is a holy city. Christ's concern was never the 'holiness' of the city, but the importance of gathering its sons and daughters together, of people caring for and loving one another. Christ was always disappointed and frustrated at the fragmentation of the city's inhabitants. Cities or places may hold special meaning for some people, but that should never be a reason for killing or dehumanising others. The message of Jerusalem today is that a holy city (if we insist on using this term) should be a source of inspiration, of uniting people, of embracing diversity, and *not* of conflict; of religious purity, and *not* of excluding others, especially its original inhabitants, like me. For me, Jerusalem is a very special place. I was born in it, I will always love it, and I will always want to have access to it. Forbidding me from entering it is a crime, irrespective of the reasons offered to justify it, or of which God in whose name I am forbidden to enter it.

Jesus loved to refer to himself as the 'Son of Man'. For him, the ultimate value in life is human solidarity and human community. According to him, if a man says I love God but hates his fellow human beings, he is a liar. For him, love for others is manifested by laying down one's life for one's friends. 'This is my commandment,' he said, 'that you love one another as I have loved you' (John 15: 12). In the final analysis, this is the true message of Jerusalem, today as it was when Christ walked in the city.

23
THE EFFECT OF POLITICS ON ARCHAEOLOGY

Nazmi Al-Jubeh

No city has received as much world attention as the city of Jerusalem. It is probably the city that has more literature written about it than any other place. In spite of this large quantity of publications and the long history of research on the city, its history remains complex due to controversial points of view of historians and archaeologists. It is a city of diverse and contradictory civilisations as well as religious, political and cultural controversies.

It will certainly be an arduous mission to go over the enormous works accomplished by archaeologists on the city of Jerusalem. Those works began almost one and a half centuries ago and led to the production of thousands of books, reports, extracts, surveys and the discovery of items of great value.

It is only natural that the first school of thought that attempted to uncover the history of Jerusalem is the biblical school. There was an urgent need for theologians, especially Christian theologians, to trace the geography of the Bible (the Old and New Testaments). A large number of geographical sites are mentioned in the Bible, and occasionally there are descriptions of the topography of some sites. This attracted biblical scholars to Palestine, and Jerusalem in particular in order to discover and clarify the names and sites mentioned in the Bible.

The policy of Ibrahim Pasha (1831-1840) during the Ottoman occupation of Palestine was to open up to the West. This provided the opportunity for biblical scholars to come to Palestine and start their archaeological digs. Those early pioneers used the Bible as their historical and geographical guide and imposed the biblical reference to identify sites. They were very anxious to discover and learn about the Holy Land, and so were the Western countries, who became anxious to have a foothold in Palestine, particularly in Jerusalem. Those pioneer archaeologists did a tremendous amount of excavation in the most important archaeological sites. Although we are very grateful to them for highlighting various historical and archaeological aspects of Palestine, yet we cannot deny that they have often been at fault.

As you know, archaeology can be a science of destruction as well as a science of discovery, since excavation sites get destroyed in the process and cannot be reconstructed. Therefore archaeologists have one chance only to study the historical mounds before they start their excavation on them, and if they do not do that in scientific and logical ways, without pre-conceptions or bias, it would be impossible for them to re-examine their results.

The limited scientific knowledge in the mechanics and technology used for excavations in the last century and the first half of the 20th century had a negative effect on the work of diggers. What is meant here is not to attack their work but rather to diagnose the difficulties that those early pioneers faced, and how such difficulties and problems have affected us at the present time. The great number of digs that took place then have complicated matters because in that process much valuable information was lost or destroyed, especially since documentation was minimal.

The biblical school focused mainly on the Bronze and Iron Ages, thus information on other periods was disrupted or destroyed either intentionally or unintentionally. The end result was a great loss of information pertaining to the Islamic and Byzantine periods, especially since relics of those periods were on the top layers of the sites that archaeologists carelessly removed without attempting to document them properly, as they were in a hurry to reach to the lower layers pertaining to the biblical period.

Most of the data collected from digs during that period in Jerusalem is considered, from an objective point of view, confusing and cannot be completely reliable. The remarkable development in the process of the history of various archaeological layers has cancelled a great number of past hypothesis, but without actually having the opportunity to rewrite its history.

Critical studies of biblical archaeology surfaced in the fifties of this century and coincided with the developing critical studies of the biblical text (Old Testament). But the effect of this approach remained limited despite developments in the science of archaeology and its mechanism including the biblical aspect of it. Diggers for biblical findings failed to comprehend the continuity and historical chronology of the different periods, They understood the culture of the various and successive periods in this land, as if it were separate and unrelated events, that is, not as a unit of continuous interaction between the people and their environment. The irony of this biblical school is that it offered a large amount of information about man and his environment during the Bronze Age and very little information about the Ottoman period, even though it is much closer to our times and in spite of the abundant sources available concerning that period.

Most studies on Jerusalem prior to 1967 fall under this first category-biblical school. We have no knowledge about serious studies in the field of Islamic archaeology except for that written on al-Haram al-Sharif in Jerusalem, Qasr Hisham in Jericho and partial information on Qasr Miniah on the north western bank of Lake Tiberias. Thousands of Islamic sites were either neglected or destroyed.

The second school of thought is the Israeli archaeological school. (Again we need to be cautious about generalisations that could be understood to include all Israeli archaeologists. Here we refer to the dominant stream of thought.)

The Israeli school of archaeology fell into the trap of nationalism and ideology as of day one, just as the biblical school fell in the trap of the Bible. Israel's priority was to prove a historical right and to affirm a promise by God. Israel's existence is justified on the basis of historical right based on finding scientific proof for divine promise.

Since its establishment, Israel was faced with the issue of legitimacy, and lack of recognition, not only limited to the Middle Eastern countries but widespread. Therefore Israel was continuously trying to prove its legitimacy and gain recognition using both biblical texts and archaeological findings to support its claim.

What characterises archaeology in Israel is that it has been utilised to achieve the political goal of legitimacy and recognition. Therefore digs spread from north to south, from east to west in search of signs or relics to prove the relationship between the Jewish people and the land of Palestine, and to a lesser extent to attract Jewish immigration to the 'Promised Land'. Amidst all this insistence and challenge a lot of sites and findings fell victim to the limited political interpretations. It must be noted here, that this took place wilfully, unlike the first biblical school, for lack of interest in anything other than biblical. Therefore the obliteration of the various findings of different periods and their destruction took place in response to political decisions.

In the city of Jerusalem, where challenges are greatest and the struggle between the parties is deeper, politics continue to be on top of the list of priorities. A large number of digs have taken place in Jerusalem and its surroundings since 1967. But the most important and most intensive of these digs took place in the area surrounding al-Haram al-Sharif, the Dung Gate and the Jewish Quarter. All these digs were basically done with the intention of uncovering sources to prove and assert the rights of Jews in the city and to look for signs and remains of the Second Temple, rather than to uncover historical, archaeological or aesthetic sites in this area, which is distinguished by multi-cultural remains. As a result of such works most of the periods with no links or ties to the Jewish people and history were marginalised. The focus was totally on whatever had any connection with the Jewish people. For example the Jewish Quarter, which was first established in the latter part of the Middle Ages, was transformed into the most important quarter in the Old City. In addition, it encompasses a large number of archaeological gardens, despite the fact that Jewish ownership of this quarter did not exceed 12 percent of its area, the rest of which is owned by Muslims and Christians. The Wailing Wall (Western Wall) is privileged to have the largest open area within the city walls. This is easily noticed by visitors to the city. All this was done at the expense of the Dung Gate area which Israel completely demolished in June 1967. Another archaeological irony is Israel's reduction of the long history of this country to three periods:

a) The First Temple.
b) The Second Temple.
c) 1967.

Despite the long history of the city of Jerusalem, it was arbitrarily made to evolve around these three short historical periods. This also applies to the history of the rest of Palestine, but to a lesser degree. An absurd example of this is the newly erected archway that begins from al-Wad Road to the Wailing Wall courtyard on which is written: 'A similar archway existed here during the period of the Second Temple.' Thus the history of an Umayyad archway has been completely cancelled. This assumption of the existence of a similar archway (God knows) became the absolute truth, whereas the historical truth was abolished. Similarly, there are intensive publications on the period of the Second Temple describing everything that might have existed at the site of al-Haram al-Sharif. While the Dome of the Rock, Jerusalem's jewel, that distinguishes its identity is not at all mentioned.

Another stark and blunt example is the diversion of the path of a main street in Sheikh Jarrah, because of the existence of a tomb that goes back to the Roman period. The grave is not identified but there is a slight suspicion that it could belong to a Jewish person. The diversion of this same street led to the destruction of an Armenian church and monastery facing Damascus Gate that dates back to the Byzantine period. All this is happening despite the importance of this great church that contains magnificent mosaic art work which greatly contributes to the history of the city. It is important to indicate that Israel's Department of Archaeology is performing fundamental changes on the form and existence of magnificent Umayyad palaces that were discovered at the south western side of al-Haram al-Sharif. These palaces made it possible for us to have a clear insight about the city of Jerusalem during the Umayyad period. Israel's claim that the city is unimportant for Arabs and Muslims from their political point of view, does not comply with the existence of these great palaces. Currently, there is an attempt to remove them in order to dig up a street that goes back to the Roman period (Herod's). The story after the discovery of these palaces is of great interest to every archaeologist. In the seventies, when these palaces were verified as authentic Umayyad palaces, the principle excavator there was the Israeli politician Yeg'al Yadeen who gave orders to remove these palaces completely. One of his assistants notified the press about this important discovery, otherwise we would never have heard about their existence of which we have no other information. The significance of the story of these palaces is a clear indication of what is going on in our country under the guise of a civilised science (archaeology). The task of this civilised science is to bind civilisations together in order to prove that integration and interaction is inevitable between different civilisations throughout the ages. Our country's civilisation was never a form of the civilisation in the Arab peninsula. On the contrary it was in constant interaction with the surrounding civilisations.

Since 1967, there has been an ongoing systematic plan to change the features of Jerusalem as well as its historical image. This caused its Arab inhabitants to feel estranged in their own city and environment. Walking through the Jewish Quarter, one notices the great discrepancy between this quarter and the rest of the city. The city has lost its harmony and historical integration through the detachment of this part architecturally, culturally and even demographically.

Going back to the street which destroyed the historical Armenian church, I am astonished how the Israeli Department of Archaeology, the Department of Environment and the 'civilised' municipality of Teddy Kollek agreed to the construction of this 'Bist-Masrab' street that leads to the city wall! This street does not only ruin archaeological sites, but also pollutes the historical city wall. The daily passage of thousands of cars underneath the wall in the area between Damascus Gate and Jaffa Gate is a systematic destruction of Arab heritage in the city. We expect twenty years from now, that the bright white stones in that area will become polluted and dark from car fumes, acids and carbon dioxide.

As soon as the British Mandate assumed authority over Jerusalem, it removed the Ottoman clock from Jaffa Gate, since neither historically nor aesthetically did it fit that ancient wall. When considering scientific criteria for maintaining the cultural heritage, this move is worthy of respect. But today, as the 20th century comes to an end, when scientific concepts and notions with regard to culture and cultural heritage have reached a high level of progress, we never expected Jerusalem's Municipality to construct an ugly concrete bridge facing Jaffa Gate. This bridge ruined not only the historical image of the place, but also its visual harmony. Furthermore, the municipality allowed high-rise building that does not blend with the general landscape on the western side.

With the slackening off of the political struggle brought about by the peace process, we hoped that our Israeli colleagues will rid themselves of their political, ideological, and national obsessions that directed their actions; since these pressing needs have lost their importance and the need to distort history and forge archaeological findings are no more necessary to falsify historical facts to suit Israeli's interest.

Archaeology is a field of science that Palestinians have not fully dealt with. Only in the sixties of this century did they indulge in this field but not within Palestine. Most of them studied and worked in this field in Arab countries: Syria, Jordan, Lebanon, and the Gulf States as well as in the West.

In the mid-seventies, Bir Zeit University took the initiative to establish a Department of Archaeology and was followed by al-Najah University in Nablus and the Institute of Islamic Archaeology in Jerusalem. Yet the accomplishments of these institutions were as modest as their available resources. They lacked, in varying degrees, the basic infra-structure, the investment in which is very costly. It is worth mentioning that conditions in the past were not suitable for developing a Palestinian scientific archaeology. Excavation under Israeli occupation was prohibited by international law. The Department of Archaeology, under the Israeli civil administration was closed to Palestinian experts. Those experts spent years of theoretical study in this field and did not get the slightest opportunity to put their knowledge into practice. We know of about 150 Palestinian specialists in various aspects of this field, only a handful of whom were able to find work before the advent of the Palestinian Authority.

The futuristic outlook for this field of science is not at all gloomy, especially since the Palestinian Department of Archaeology will undertake the serious and grave responsibility of preserving archaeological sites and restoring the due worth and value of many neglected sites in order to enrich our cultural heritage and help our economy.

We demand that our universities take the responsibility of providing our country with well qualified graduates to serve in this field. We hope they avoid the trap which our neighbours set for themselves to intentionally forge historical facts and fake scientific findings.

We Palestinians, consider ourselves descendants and heirs of all peoples and civilisations that passed or lingered in our land, Palestine—Canaanites, Hittites,

Hebrews, Egyptians, Philistines, Greeks, Romans, Crusaders, Turks, Kurds, Moroccans and others.

We relate to all these peoples and find no contradiction between the impact they left on our country and our Palestinian national identity. We should not be biased towards any of those periods regardless of their identity.

We should be proud of all those periods without prejudice, for then and only then, could we talk about the science of archaeology, as pure and unpoliticised: an archaeology based on the policy of projecting human achievements and progress in Palestine throughout the ages.

24
POLITICAL CONFLICT AND ENVIRONMENTAL DEGRADATION IN JERUSALEM

Jad Isaac and Leonardo Hosh

Introduction

Among all the cities in historic Palestine, Jerusalem possesses a special political, economic and religious status for people around the world, especially its residents, Palestinians and Israelis. Such importance has, however, brought political conflicts between its inhabitants which are adversely reflected on the living conditions and the environment of Jerusalem.

After the Israeli occupation of East Jerusalem in 1967, restrictions have been strictly imposed on the development of the city's Palestinian communities. Moreover, infrastructure and services for this group of residents, by the Israeli Jerusalem Municipality, became inadequate for providing a healthy living environment. Overcrowding became the norm and the pressure on Jerusalem's land and natural resources has been devastating as well.

This paper will present several of the main factors threatening the sustainability of the environment in Jerusalem and the environmental safety for the people inhabiting the city.

Present Day Jerusalem

Soon after its occupation of Palestinian East Jerusalem in 1967, the Israeli government enforced several measures which changed the geopolitical boundaries of the city, as well as its legal and physical status, in an effort to facilitate the subsequent Israeli illegal annexation of Jerusalem.

The first measure was the application of Israeli law on the city of Jerusalem. Following this, Israel expanded the municipal boundaries of the city in a jagged manner, enabling it to include as much land as possible while excluding as much of the Palestinian population as possible.[1] The boundaries of the East Jerusalem municipal area were enlarged from 6.5 km² to 70.5 km² which enveloped land from

---

[1] Kuttab, Jonathan, 'The Legal Status of Jerusalem', *Palestine-Israel Journal of Politics, Economics and Culture,* vol. 2, no. 2, Jerusalem, 1995, pp. 52-58.

28 Palestinian villages and towns in the West Bank.[2] Even with this expansion to more than 10.8 times its original size, only 22,000 Palestinian inhabitants were added to the population of Jerusalem. Land from Beit Hanina, A'nata, Abu Dis, and five other villages, for example, were absorbed into the new extended East Jerusalem but their population of approximately 80,000 people was excluded.[3] The Palestinian inhabitants of the city were given blue identification cards (ID) which distinguished them from Palestinians living in the rest of the West Bank, who were and are still obligated to carry orange IDs.

On 30 July 1980, the Israeli Knesset passed a law declaring East Jerusalem part of united Jerusalem, the capital of Israel, and officially annexed the city to the Israeli State. Regardless of the many international and United Nations resolutions condemning this annexation, Israel continued with its discriminatory policies and, moreover, proceeded to judaise the city. Many Palestinian lands within the new municipal boundaries were confiscated, closed or assigned for 'public use'. 'Public use' traditionally implies building housing neighbourhoods exclusively for Israeli Jews. Presently, only 13.5 percent of Palestinian East Jerusalem is available for Palestinians to live on or develop. The remaining land is reserved for the exclusive use of Israeli Jews.

As of today, not a single new Palestinian neighbourhood has been planned in East Jerusalem while more than 15 large Jewish neighbourhoods have been built in Palestinian East Jerusalem and several more are planned. Such policies changed the demography of the city from just a few hundred Jews in 1967 to almost 160,000 at the present[4]—a number almost equal to the number of Palestinians now living in Palestinian East Jerusalem.

Despite cultural, religious and economic attachment of Palestinians residing in the West Bank and the Gaza Strip to Jerusalem, Israel currently denies Palestinians free access to Palestinian East Jerusalem. Since January 1991, Palestinians have been required to obtain special permits from Israel in order to enter the city, whether for worship, visiting relatives, or seeking medical treatment or jobs. Also, historically, the economic base of Jerusalem is its role as a market centre for the rest of geographic Palestine and other neighbouring regions. The closure of East Jerusalem to the Palestinians living in the remaining parts of the West Bank and Gaza Strip has, therefore, greatly affected the trade routes and devastated the city's economy, as well as the economy of the West Bank and Gaza Strip. The closure of Jerusalem has brought a noticeable decline in economic and social standards.

Furthermore, to ensure maximum control over the land, the Israeli government designed a bizarre urban planning scheme for East Jerusalem in which

[2] Tafakgi, Khalil, 'The Geographic and Demographic Distribution of Israeli Settlements in the West Bank' [in Arabic], *Qadayya Filistiniyya,* summer 1995, Gaza Strip, pp. 6-23.
[3] Kothari, Miloon and Jan Abu Shakrah, 'Planned Dispossession: Palestinians, East Jerusalem and the Rights to a Place to Live', *COHRE,* Occasional Paper no. 4, Geneva, September 1995.
[4] Municipality of Jerusalem and The Jerusalem Institute for Israel, Statistical Year Book of Jerusalem 1993, no 12, Jerusalem, 1995.

approximately 86.5 percent of the land came to be out of Palestinian reach.[5] According to this scheme, only a small number of building permits was granted to Palestinians. Even then, there were great restrictions on the size of the construction and the number of floors. In sum, development of Palestinian neighbourhoods has been stunted and the provision of municipal services extremely neglected. Such circumstances have led to several serious environmental problems in the Palestinian side of the city, including among others, the accumulation of solid waste, overcrowding, land degradation, unhealthy housing and living conditions.

The final status negotiations on Jerusalem are expected to last for a maximum of three years. Aspects of Jerusalem to be discussed include: sovereignty over the city, the legal structure, religious freedom, and cultural rights. However, in the meantime, the Israeli government has not stopped its unilateral practices in Jerusalem in which it is creating *de facto* realities on the ground. These *de facto* realities are certainly affecting the outcome of the negotiations on the final status of Jerusalem in Israel's favour, an action that is totally in violation of United Nation's resolutions, particularly 298 and 242, and standing Palestinian-Israeli agreements.

Infrastructure and Services

The provision of infrastructure and civil services for East Jerusalem is currently the responsibility of the Jerusalem Municipality. However, the deliberate procrastination of the Jerusalem Municipality in approving town planning schemes for most Palestinian areas in East Jerusalem has hindered any serious development in the infrastructure and services since 1967. Without planning schemes it has been impossible to open new roads, lay sewerage networks, extend pipeline systems, designate building areas for new schools or public institutions, or develop public parks and gardens. The inadequate network of roads has consequently led to traffic jams, low quality services in trash collection, mail distribution, or even fire station services.

Waste Water Disposal

In East Jerusalem, and according to the Jerusalem Municipality resources, as of August 1994 there were only 15 km of sewerage network lines in East Jerusalem while the need reaches to more than 150.8 km. The new network lines planned for the year 1994 were only 7.2 km.[6]

The only comprehensive effort to develop the sewerage networks in the Palestinian neighbourhoods of East Jerusalem was to replace the old Ottoman sewerage networks in the Muslim and Christian quarters of the Old City. This was necessary due to the touristic importance of these two quarters. Outside the walls of

---

[5] Kaminker, Sarah, East Jerusalem: 'A Case Study in Political Planning', *Palestine-Israel Journal of Politics, Economics and Culture*, vol. 2, no. 2, Jerusalem, 1995, pp. 59-66.

[6] Unpublished Document, Arab Studies Society, Map Centre, 1995.

the Old City, sewerage network maintenance and development was partial and sporadic and currently does not correspond to the increase in water consumption and current population.

According to PASSIA 1996, the current sewerage networks in East Jerusalem reach approximately 60 percent of Palestinian houses.[7] However, our field work demonstrated that major segments of the networks are not fully functional and cover partial areas. For example, the sewerage networks cover only 10 percent of the houses in Qalandia refugee camp, and 25 percent of A'nata neighbourhood.[8] The remaining 40 percent of the Palestinian communities in East Jerusalem use cesspools (an earthen cistern which collects disposed sewage) for sewage disposal.

Although using cesspools may be a relatively hygienic method for sewage disposal, the main problem of sewage disposal is still unsolved. Cesspools are emptied regularly and their contents are dumped in open places and valleys without control or treatment.

At present, most of the East Jerusalem drainage, both runoff rain water and sewage, is emptied into Wadi al-Nar (Qidron valley), located south east of Jerusalem city. The sewage is dumped into the valley in an area outside the city limits, due to sanitation considerations. The sewage flows down the valley to end in the Dead Sea; en route, some of the sewage percolates into the ground.[9] Although the groundwater aquifer is at a deep depth in that location, prolonged percolation of the sewage into the soil may cause the pollution of the aquifer.

Sewage treatment plants do not exist in East Jerusalem. Furthermore, the Israeli Jerusalem Municipality has no plans in the near future to construct sewage treatment plants to serve the East Jerusalem area. However, an international tender has been let for construction and operation of a new sewage treatment plant in Israeli West Jerusalem (Sorek and Refaim), planned to be functioning by 1998.[10]

Moreover, most Israeli settlements in East Jerusalem lack infrastructure for sewage disposal. Sewage from these settlements flows down the fields and valleys and, in most cases, pass near or through Palestinian populated areas or agricultural land.[11] One example is the sewage flowing from Neve Ya'acov settlement, passing through Hizma village land, and reaching Ein Farrah spring, east of the village. Villagers reported that the sewage flow affects the spring water quality and prevents the villagers from utilizing it for any purpose.

Solid Waste Disposal
To date, there are no sanitary landfills serving Jerusalem and thus solid waste services

---

[7] *PASSIA*, Palestinian Academic Society for the Study of International Affairs, Jerusalem, 1996, p. 236.
[8] Environmental Information System Database, ARIJ 1996.
[9] Abells, Zvi, and Asher, Arbit, *The City of David's Water Systems,* The Faculty of Printing Techniques, Hadassah College of Technology, Jerusalem, 1995.
[10] *Ibid.,* 1995.
[11] Environmental Information System Database, ARIJ 1995.

for Palestinian communities suffer from negligence by the Israeli Jerusalem municipality.

The main solid waste disposal site serving Jerusalem is located on a piece of land near the Palestinian town of Abu Dis. The site, totalling 300 hectares, was confiscated by the Israeli government on 2 September 1988 and was illegally declared as state land.[12] The dumping area lies south east of the town centre and is almost a kilometre away from the closest Palestinian houses. The site is currently managed by the Israeli Jerusalem Municipality.

This dumping site near Abu Dis village has no adequate measures to prevent leaking of toxic waste or pollution of groundwater. The site is also unguarded and has no fencing, thus allowing scavengers and people to go into the site, searching for food or recycled material. This set-up increases the chances of spreading disease, especially because medical waste is dumped in this site without proper treatment.

The compiled data about waste collection in Jerusalem indicate that labour, equipment, and vehicles in the Palestinian part of the city are not adequate to provide the appropriate services. The number of trash collecting staff in East Jerusalem areas is approximately 83 employees, while the number of staff needed to properly serve the area should be 125.[13] Solid waste is collected using plastic bags, containers of different capacities (75 litres to >23 cubic metres), compactor trucks, and container collection-vehicles. However, the total number of this equipment is much less than what is actually needed.

Medical Waste

The amount of waste generated from the various medical and health care facilities in East Jerusalem is enormous compared to other areas in the West Bank. This is an indicator of the activity and large number of patients treated in these facilities. However, disposal services for medical waste are inadequate, comprising a serious threat to public safety.

Field survey of health facilities in East Jerusalem, conducted by ARIJ's team, covered six out of the seven existing hospitals and seven private medical laboratories. Site inspection showed that all hospitals surveyed are located in residential areas while medical labs are in commercial areas. The location of these health care facilities, although convenient for patients, is certainly inappropriate considering the threat of contagious diseases generated from improper handling of medical waste.

The quantity of medical waste generated from the surveyed health care facilities in East Jerusalem is estimated at 130 tons per year.[14] The generated waste is classified as biological waste (body organs, tissues, blood, urine, stools, etc.), sharp and pointed objects (needles, lancets, syringes, blades, saws, etc.), and contagious

---

[12] Cohen, Shaul, E, *The Politics of Planting—Israeli-Palestinian Competition for Control of Land in the Jerusalem Periphery,* The University of Chicago Press, Geography Research Papers, no. 236, Chicago, USA, 1993.

[13] Unpublished Documents, Arab Studies Society, Map Centre, 1995.

[14] Field survey conducted by ARIJ in early 1996.

waste (media culture, diapers, swabs, test tubes, cotton, surgical dressings, dialysis tubes, etc.). Despite this large quantity, currently no service exists, private or public, specialized in treating and disposing of medical waste. Medical waste treatment services exist in West Jerusalem, however they do not accept medical waste generated from Palestinian hospitals in the city, except for radioactive waste. Only radioactive waste, generated by Maqassed Hospital, is sent to Hadassah Hospital facilities in West Jerusalem for treatment and disposal.

Although not all medical facilities were surveyed in East Jerusalem, the information gathered on disposal methods of medical waste is more-or-less representative of the remaining facilities. The disposal methods used for various medical waste is outlined in Table 1.

Table 1
Methods of Disposal of Medical Waste in the Jerusalem District

Waste Type	1	2	3	4	5	6	7	8	9	10	Total
Blood samples	53.8	7.7	23.1	0.0	7.7	0.0	0.0	0.0	7.7	0.0	100
Blood tubes	46.1	7.7	23.1	0.0	7.7	0.0	7.7	0.0	7.7	0.0	100
Petri dishes	25.0	8.3	25.0	0.0	16.7	0.0	16.7	0.0	8.3	0.0	100
Urine	66.7	0.0	8.3	16.7	0.0	0.0	0.0	0.0	0.0	8.3	100
Pipet tips	61.5	15.4	7.7	7.7	7.7	0.0	0.0	0.0	0.0	0.0	100
Cups	69.2	15.4	7.7	7.7	0.0	0.0	0.0	0.0	0.0	0.0	100
Test kits	76.9	7.7	0.0	7.7	0.0	0.0	0.0	0.0	0.0	7.7	100
Tongue depressors	61.5	15.4	7.7	7.7	7.7	0.0	0.0	0.0	0.0	0.0	100
Swabs	38.5	15.4	7.7	0.0	23.1	0.0	7.7	0.0	7.7	0.0	100
Syringes & needles	38.4	7.7	15.4	0.0	0.0	0.0	30.8	0.0	7.7	0.0	100
Lancet	33.3	8.3	16.7	0.0	0.0	0.0	33.3	0.0	8.3	0.0	100
Diapers	100	0.0	0.0	0.0	0.0	0.0	0.0	0.0	0.0	0.0	100
Bed sheets	25.0	0.0	0.0	0.0	50.0	25.0	0.0	0.0	0.0	0.0	100
Beds	66.7	0.0	0.0	0.0	0.0	33.0	0.0	0.0	0.0	0.0	100
Infusion set	100	0.0	0.0	0.0	0.0	0.0	0.0	0.0	0.0	0.0	100
Tubes	60.0	0.0	0.0	0.0	20.0	20.0	0.0	0.0	0.0	0.0	100
Syringe	66.7	0.0	0.0	0.0	0.0	0.0	33.3	0.0	0.0	0.0	100
Urine bags	100	0.0	0.0	0.0	0.0	0.0	0.0	0.0	0.0	0.0	100
Stool	66.7	0.0	8.3	16.7	0.0	0.0	0.0	0.0	0.0	8.3	100
Toilet paper	100	0.0	0.0	0.0	0.0	0.0	0.0	0.0	0.0	0.0	100

Numbers are in percent

*

1 = dumped in domestic trash containers without treatment
2 = burned then dumped in domestic trash containers
3 = autoclaving
4 = disposed off in the public sewerage
5 = sterilized by Chlore, Alcohol, or Detol
6 = re-used
7 = disposed off in special containers
8 = treated by special companies
9 = either 2 or 5
10 = either 1 or 5

Therefore, the majority of medical waste generated in East Jerusalem is disposed of without prior treatment or proper handling. In almost one third of the medical facilities that were surveyed, proper precautions were not taken in handling sharp and pointed objects waste, thus increasing the infection risks for garbage collectors and children. Petri dishes which are used for bacterial culture are one of the few types of medical waste treated before being disposed. Surgery waste, from general and maternity hospitals, is collected in plastic bags and disposed of in the municipal garbage.

Health Services
A field survey, conducted by ARIJ's team in early 1996, showed that approximately 150,000 patients refer every year to East Jerusalem's seven hospitals for treatment. A major portion of these patients are from areas outside East Jerusalem or from other districts in the West Bank. The well-equipped and highly specialized medical care facilities in East Jerusalem are, in many cases, the sole provider of medical treatment for thousands of cases. Thus, in this regard, health care in East Jerusalem is an integral and indispensable part of the overall West Bank health system. The Israeli closure of East Jerusalem to Palestinians from other areas is therefore depriving thousands of patients from receiving adequate treatment.

The provision of health services for Palestinians in Jerusalem has been greatly affected by the Israeli closure and, in particular, the recent tightening of the closure which began in early March 1996. On several occasions, and for extended periods, Israel has prevented doctors and medical staff who are residents of areas outside East Jerusalem from reaching their job locations in East Jerusalem. In a letter sent to the previous Israeli Prime Minister, Mr Shimon Peres, dated 27 March 1996, the directors of five major hospitals in East Jerusalem explained that the East Jerusalem hospital activity dropped by 75 percent after the closure and that approximately two-thirds of the medical staff are from the West Bank and Gaza Strip and thus have been unable to get to the hospitals. Al-Maqassed Hospital, for example, was greatly affected by the recent closure as 400 out of its 640 employees were denied from reaching their job location. Augusta Victoria hospital also was deprived of 70 percent of its staff.[15] Consequently, measures should be taken to allow the access of patients to the health facilities in East Jerusalem in a manner that would not be affected by political circumstances.

Fire Fighting Services
A single fire station exists in East Jerusalem, located east of the Old City. This station is responsible for all areas in East Jerusalem, including its northern parts, in regard to fire fighting, investigation of fire incidents and prevention. The station hires 12 employees who alternate in three shifts.[16]

---

[15] 'Jerusalem in the Shadow of the Closure' [in Arabic], *Al-Manar Newspaper,* vol. 6, no. 272, Jerusalem, 22 April, 1996, p. 3.
[16] Unpublished Documents, Arab Studies Society, Map Centre, 1995.

Neither the location nor set-up of the fire station in East Jerusalem is adequate. The station is located on a highly sloping street and opposite to the vegetable market, which does not facilitate the exit of the fire engine in the manner needed in times of emergency. Communication means between the fire station and staff dorms and offices do not exist. Therefore, moving the fire station into a more adequate location is essential, an additional station is also needed to cover the northern parts of the city.

Fire fighting within the walls of Old City is another serious problem. In this overcrowded part of Jerusalem, the narrow streets and stairs do not permit free movement of fire trucks to all parts of the Old City. The number of water outlets which supply water for fire hoses is not enough to cover all parts of the Old City and thus places its inhabitants at serious risk. More water outlets are needed in the Old City and the purchase of special fire vehicles suitable for this area is also essential.

Water Networks
After 1967, the Jordanian-built water network was the main backbone of the water network in the area, where the Israeli Jerusalem Municipality connected to it and added temporary new lines. The temporary lines were laid over the ground and were supposed to be replaced by a new underground water network. Due to lack of approved town planning schemes, many parts of the temporary network are still in use and are inadequate. Being aware of the needs, the Jerusalem Municipality assessed the water supply situation and decided in 1984 to begin replacing the temporary network. As of mid-1995, a new network was laid in the Old City, Bab al-Zahreh, Sheikh Jarrah, and Shua'fat. Only less than 30 percent of the water network plan was carried out. The remaining part of the project remains undone.

Since 1988, Shua'fat refugee camp has suffered from a lack of water supply as the Israeli military government ordered the camp to be disconnected from the water network because of dispute over the cost of water.[17]

Land Use and Town Planning Scheme for Jerusalem
Although 85-90 percent of the land of East Jerusalem belongs to Palestinians, presently, only 13.5 percent of East Jerusalem is available for the Palestinians to build on, live, and develop.[18] The restrictions on Palestinian built-up areas in East Jerusalem have been conducted under the umbrella of the Town Planning Scheme (TPS) which the Israeli Municipality of Jerusalem formulated for Jerusalem.

Soon after the 1967 war, Israel cancelled the town planning schemes that were prepared and approved by the Jordanians in 1966 for East Jerusalem and prevented Palestinians from building in areas without approved schemes. Twenty eight years later, very few Palestinian towns have approved town planning schemes. The process for approving TPS for a Palestinian community is very complicated and requires

---

[17] JMCC, *Water, the Red Line,* JMCC, Jerusalem, May 1994, p. 47.
[18] Kaminker, Sarah, East Jerusalem: A Case Study in Political Planning, *Palestine-Israel Journal of Politics, Economics and Culture,* vol. 2, no 2, Jerusalem, pp. 59-66.

several stages and signatures. Presently, less than 25 percent of the Palestinian neighbourhoods of East Jerusalem have a complete and approved town planning scheme.[19] Moreover, in those few towns which do, major parts of the land were designated as 'Green Areas'. 'Green Areas' are lands designated for public open space or for the preservation of unhindered views of the landscape; they simply cannot be built on. The colour green predominates Palestinian town plans in East Jerusalem (figure 2). Accordingly, building houses for Palestinians in East Jerusalem has been extremely difficult which had led to overcrowding to a point that more than 30 percent of the East Jerusalem Palestinian families live in a density of more than 3 people per living room (figure 1).

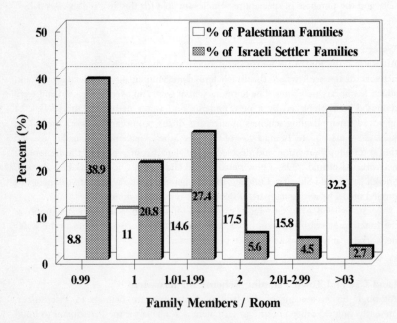

Figure 1: density per room among Palestinians and Israeli settler families of East Jerusalem

Furthermore, restrictions are imposed by the Jerusalem Municipality on construction even when building permits are granted. These restrictions are expressed in the following building codes.[20]

---

[19] Unpublished Documents, Arab Studies Society, Map Centre, 1995.
[20] Kaminker, Sarah, 'East Jerusalem: A Case Study in Political Planning', *Palestine-Israel Journal of Politics, Economics and Culture,* vol. 2, no 2, Jerusalem, pp. 59-66.

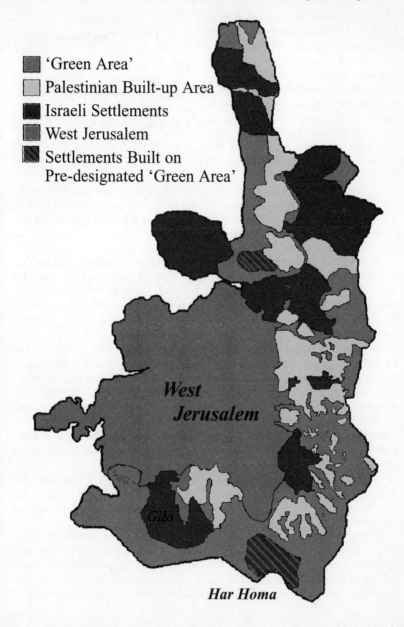

■ 'Green Area'
□ Palestinian Built-up Area
■ Israeli Settlements
▨ West Jerusalem
▨ Settlements Built on
   Pre-designated 'Green Area'

*West
Jerusalem*

Gilo

Har Homa

Figure 2: shows the East Jerusalem land use distribution according to the Israeli-designed Town Planning Scheme.

1   Palestinians are only allowed to build on 15 percent, 25 percent, or 50 percent of the land plot, depending on the zoning and area of construction. In contrast, Israeli Jews building in East Jerusalem settlements are allowed to build on as much as 200 percent flat space of the land.

2   Palestinian buildings in East Jerusalem are confined to one or two stories, whereas Israeli settlements can have buildings up to eight stories.

Table 2
TPS for East Jerusalem

Land use

Israeli settlements	34%
For expansion of settlements	8.5%
Green Areas	44%
Palestinian built-up	13.5%

Source: *PASSIA,* 1995

3   Palestinians owning land larger than 0.1 hectare in size are required to divide the land into parcels of a maximum of 0.1 hectare in order to be granted building permits on such lands. This law is strictly applied even when the land is only few square meters larger than 0.1 hectares.

Such laws are not only discriminatory but induce low efficiency of land use and restrict the number of houses that can be built on the limited area given for Palestinians to develop and inhabit. Since 1967, only 6,440 new Palestinian houses were built in East Jerusalem (12 percent of all newly constructed houses), compared to over than 60,000 new houses which were built by Israeli settlers during the same period of time.[21]

Palestinian houses built without a license have already been, or threatened to be demolished by the Israeli government. As reported by the Palestine Human Rights Information Centre (PHRIC) in mid 1994, the result of the Israeli government policy of denying Palestinians building permits, demolition of unlicensed Palestinian houses, and land expropriation was that approximately 21,000 Palestinian families were either homeless and live in caves and tents, inadequately housed, or are forced to double and triple up with other families[22] (see p. 194). PHRIC has documented over 210 Palestinian homes demolished by the Israeli authorities in East Jerusalem since mid-1986 for licensing reasons.

Palestinian communities of East Jerusalem are becoming overcrowded and cannot handle the population pressure. This policy is adversely reflecting on the Palestinian natural and socio-economic environment, which is further exacerbated by the weak infrastructure and insufficient municipal services.

Furthermore, most of the lands designated as 'Green Areas' in East Jerusalem, which are supposedly left to conserve the beauty of the nature, are neither planted, developed into gardens or parks, nor green. Obviously these 'Green Areas' were selected in places where Israel would like to save the land until the time is ready to build Israeli settlements on them. Sarah Kaminker, a city planner and a member of

---

[21] *PASSIA,* Palestinian Academic Society for the Study of International Affairs, Jerusalem, 1992, p. 235.

[22] Krystall, Nathan, 'Urgent Issues of Palestinian Residency in Jerusalem', *Alternative Information Centre,* 2nd ed., Jerusalem.

the Jerusalem City Council, in one of her articles, quoted Teddy Kollek, the previous mayor of Jerusalem, 'when asked to defend the loss of 1,262 *dunums* of public open space in Reches Shu[a]'fat, Mr Kollek stated that the green paint was originally applied to the map of Reches Shu[a]'fat in order to prevent Palestinian construction on the land until the time was ripe to build a new neighbourhood for Jews.'[23]

The settlement of Reches Shua'fat is not the only one to be built on a pre-designated green area. A forested mountain located at the southern end of the 1967 extended East Jerusalem municipal boundary is another example (figure 2).

Abu Ghnaim, with an area of approximately 2 km², has been forested by both the Jordanians pre-1967 and the Israelis after 1967. It currently hosts around 60,000 pine trees and provides an oasis for several hundreds of precious wild animals and plants. For many years Mt Abu Ghnaim and its surrounding areas, as seen in figure 2, has been designated by the Israeli Jerusalem Municipality as a 'Green Area', thus preventing the expansion of the Palestinian communities in its vicinity. A few years ago, the forest, although largely on private Palestinian land, was confiscated for the purpose of building an Israeli settlement. Using legal channels, Palestinians were able to defer the construction until today. However, after all legal measures were exhausted, construction of the settlement, which will host 6,500 housing units for Israeli Jews, will start in the very near future.

Forests

Afforestation by Israel in the Jerusalem district took more of a political nature. Afforestation projects were mostly concentrated in and around East Jerusalem. This is primarily an attempt to create a green belt around the city and restrict the expansion of its Palestinian communities. Such policy is affirmed by the present TPS for East Jerusalem (see above).

From map analysis, it became clear that the Israeli afforestation in the Jerusalem district is also carried out in areas separating Israeli settlements from their neighbouring Palestinian communities. Such forests create a buffer zone between the two communities and prevent the expansion of the Palestinian communities on lands which are to be saved for the expansion of Israeli settlements. The forests east of Pisgat Ze'ev and Neve Ya'acov are two examples. Similarly, the forests planted around Ma'ale Adumim serve the purpose of securing the land between Ma'ale Adumim and Jerusalem and around the settlement itself.[24]

What's Next

The City of Jerusalem suffers from many environmental problems that cannot be

[23] Kaminker, Sarah, 'East Jerusalem: A Case Study in Political Planning', in *Palestine-Israel Journal of Politics, Economics and Culture,* vol. 2, no. 2, Jerusalem, pp. 59-66.

[24] Cohen, Shaul E, *The Politics of Planting-Israeli-Palestinian Competition for Control of Land in the Jerusalem Periphery,* The University of Chicago Press, Geography Research Papers no. 236, Chicago, USA. 1993.

Adnan Abu Nijmeh applied for a building permit in spring 1991, to build a house on his property in the Wadi Qaddoum area of Jerusalem but was rejected. With no place to live, he decided to build a house on his property without a permit. By the end of the year, the family moved into the house. Several days later, a municipality official told Abu Nijmeh to stop building because the area was classified as a 'Green Area'. After receiving a demolition order in May 1993 Abu Nijmeh hired a lawyer, paid a hefty fine to the Israeli authorities and assumed his house would be safe from demolition. To his and his family's surprise, his house was demolished on 16 November 1993 on the basis that it was unlicensed. Border guards, police and special force units accompanied by municipality officials raided the house without warning. The intruders forced Abu Nijmeh's wife, Nufuth, and her 13 children out of their house without allowing them to remove any of its contents before the house was demolished. The family still lives on an open hillside in two shipping containers, donated by friends, on the site of their demolished house. The municipality has since claimed that the shipping containers are illegal and must be removed. To add insult to injury, municipality social welfare workers threatened to place the youngest children in foster care because the parents had failed to provide a habitable and safe environment for them.

Kothari and Abu Shakra, 1995

contained in this summary paper. A comprehensive profile for Jerusalem is currently under preparation by the Applied Research Institute, Jerusalem (ARIJ),[25] and expected to be published by mid-July 1996. We hope that the research and information will be used by the Palestinian negotiators during their coming negotiation on the final status of Jerusalem and Palestine. The conservation of the environment and its sustainability is as important as any other issues that concern the Palestinian people, and should be dealt with as such.

---

[25] See Applied Research Institute, Jerusalem, world wide web home page at address: http://www.arij.org

25

A BI-MILLENNIAL CELEBRATION IN JERUSALEM: THE HOUSE OF CHRISTIAN HERITAGE

Ruth Hummell

In four years we will be celebrating 2,000 years of Christianity, two millennia of Christian heritage. For all these years Christians of the Holy Land have been and are still bearing continuous faithful witness to the promise of salvation proclaimed in the good news of the Gospels. The Christians of Jerusalem have been a microcosm of the unity and diversity within the Christian family, brothers and sisters with multitudinous differences which often in the past erupted into violent sibling rivalries. But ultimately the brothers and sisters always acknowledge their common parentage in a universal mother Church. For 2,000 years the Christians of the Holy Land, heirs to the mother Church of Jerusalem, have kept their diligent vigil over the Holy Places and welcomed pilgrims from every corner of the earth to partake in what Canon Ateek calls 'the sacrament of geography'.

The following is a blueprint of how to celebrate and commemorate two millennia of Christian continuity in Jerusalem. There will be many conferences and ceremonies in the year 2000 to mark this anniversary of Christianity. But I also propose that the world-wide Christian community consider creating The House of Christian Heritage as a permanent living testimony to the witness of the Church in Jerusalem and an icon of the unity which encompasses the diversity of Christian communions. Let me first give some background on the genesis of this idea and in the process clarify the objectives of The House of Christian Heritage and conclude with a vision of how this living museum could be configured.

The idea was born in the Holy Sepulchre on Palm Sunday 1991, as the Greek Orthodox Patriarch made his second perambulation around the Anastasis (Holy Sepulchre). The hostilities of the Gulf War which had ended but a few weeks before greatly diminished the numbers of pilgrims witnessing this re-enactment of Christ's triumphal entry into the Holy City. This, my first Easter in Jerusalem, provided me with a vivid example of the debilitating misconceptions of each other amongst the different members of the world-wide Christian community.

I stood in relative comfort with my back against one of the Crusader columns encircling the edicule, the rectangular structure of marble cocooning the tomb of Christ. I stood there as a participant and an observer, thinking of the difference between the staid solemn Palm Sunday processions of my Episcopal Church in North

America and this joyous sometimes riotous gathering before me of hardy Greek and Cypriot pilgrims. The ranks of local Christians swelled by these pilgrims vied ardently to catch a piece of an olive branch or a sprig of rosemary cast upon the congregation by this procession.

My reflections were suddenly interrupted by a Mid-Western American asking, 'Do you speak English? Can you tell me what's going on here?' I looked up to see a tall middle-aged man. 'What exactly would you like to know?' I responded. 'Well, what are they doing? Why are all these people pushing each other?' He must have sensed my hesitation because a business card was quickly produced which introduced him as a consultant to several Protestant Christian charitable organisations.

'The Greek Orthodox, Armenians, Syrians and Copts are taking turns re-enacting Christ's triumphal entry into Jerusalem. Each processes three times around the tomb. Now the Greek Orthodox Patriarch is finishing his second pilgrimage.' I stated this with complete authority since I had been briefed several days before by an Armenian friend on the protocol of the Holy Week services.

'Yeah, I know it's Palm Sunday but what does this carnival have to do with religion?' His question was absolutely sincere. For him this was a 'carnival' of shoving pilgrims and embattled prelates trying to push through the crowd. He had come to the Holy Sepulchre for contemplative Palm Sunday inspiration but had found chaos and cacophony.

I was angry that he was disturbing my Palm Sunday meditations and I was angry that I had no ready three-minute cogent argument to explain the antique beauty, the theological rationale or the depths of the belief of the Arab, Greek and Cypriot Orthodox pilgrims.

As the Armenian Patriarch, under branches of an olive tree, began his progress around the tomb of Christ, I continued to think about this man's reaction to the procession of sumptuous robes, banners and enthused Christians brushing past me and I thought about what I was witnessing and my own reactions.

Adjacent to the courtyard of the Church of the Holy Sepulchre is the market of Aftimos, a place of cafes, souvenir and leather shops. Here in a café after the Palm Sunday ceremonies, I sat and watched the pious solemn Protestants coming from the Easter services of the Lutheran Church of the Redeemer (Orthodox Palm Sunday was Western Easter in 1991) mixing with the steady stream of black-clad Orthodox pilgrims coming from the Holy Sepulchre. Two different worlds were brushing against one another, two Christian traditions sharing the same space but not communicating. I realised that I, like so many other pilgrims, was holding up a mirror when I came to Jerusalem. I expected that mirror to reflect my own Episcopalian Christianity. Only after subsequent visits and many encounters with local Christians did Jerusalem become a window for me, and now when I gaze through this window, I see not church hierarchies or sacred geography but the beauty and the strength of the endurance of the indigenous Christian community under adverse and harsh conditions. These 'Living Stones' persevere and remain faithful; this is the Church in Jerusalem.

After this first Easter in Jerusalem I decided to investigate how the West interpreted the celebration of Holy Week in the Holy Land. Being an historian I sought answers in the past. My husband, an Episcopalian priest and ecclesiastical historian, and I merged his interests in the theological theme of the sacramentality of pilgrimage with my interests in the more sociological and personal devotional aspects to write *Patterns of the Sacred: English Protestant and Russian Orthodox Pilgrims of the Nineteenth Century*. The book was our attempt to assist the different Christian pilgrims who visit the Holy Land to better understand not only the origins of their faith but that of their fellow Christians as well.

Patterns explored the different expectations of pilgrims, but much more is needed to build bridges over the divide and, often the chasm, which separates the Christian communities. Initially the idea of a pilgrimage museum where pilgrims could connect with the millions of Christians who preceded them seemed the solution. But as we talked to Sabeel about the idea of celebrating the year 2000 with a pilgrimage museum we quickly realised that mirrors into their own brand of Christianity which Western and Eastern pilgrims expected needed to be counterbalanced with windows into mutually strange and alien traditions. The Christians in Jerusalem represented all these traditions and they were the living link with the Christians making a pilgrimage to Jerusalem.

This museum, The House of Christian Heritage, would be a mirror and a window. Here, indigenous Christians could create a vehicle to express their collective cultural and historical experiences, a mirror of 2,000 years of tradition and continual witness to Christ's message. The majority of books written on Jerusalem concern Christian archaeology, hierarchies and the Holy Places. Disproportionately little space is devoted to the indigenous Christians and their culture. The House of Christian Heritage would rectify this imbalance and provide a platform for the 'Living Stones' of Jerusalem to celebrate their existence and invigorate their mission to welcome all Christian brothers and sisters to their common roots.

Each year hundreds of thousands of Christian pilgrims travel to the Holy Land to work in the footsteps of the Man from Galilee or participate in the major celebrations of the Christian calendar in the places where they happened. The House of Christian Heritage would provide a window on the indigenous Christian communities in Palestine and their long, varied and multifaceted histories. It would be a place of orientation for pilgrims, a necessary prelude to a visit to the Holy Places. Pilgrims expect the Holy Places to reflect back to themselves that form of Christianity to which they adhere to and when the places fail to live up to their preconceived image they become disillusioned and even angry at those whose iconography has come to define the place and interpret the event.

The House of Christian Heritage would help the pilgrim understand where he/she fits into the complex mosaic that is Christianity and would explain the traditions and iconography of other Christians which appear alien. Here the pilgrim could explore two millennia of Christian belief, both its continuities and its discontinuities. The Roman Catholic or Protestant pilgrim, instead of feeling estranged by the liturgical practices and images of the ancient Eastern Churches, would develop a familiarity and a sense of communion with Eastern Christianity and the indigenous Arab Christians. Equally, pilgrims from the Eastern Churches would acquaint themselves with the spiritual aspirations and expectations of the Western pilgrims to the Holy Land. The House of Christian Heritage would help both traditions to acknowledge the contributions and attachment of each to the Holy City and to celebrate that we all are one in the Body of Christ.

What would a tourist find in this museum of living history? If you sit in the Holy Sepulchre for any length of time you might be asked, 'Whose tomb is this?' or hear some tour guides confuse, distort or trivialise the Christian experience and/or the Holy Places. To many tourists Jerusalem devolves into a 'Christian Disneyland' where one sees quaint black-clad monks and nuns floating through churches, brusquely vying with each other for every inch of sacred ground or performing picturesque ceremonies interesting for anthropological or sociological reasons. For example, during the Syrian Holy Thursday washing of the feet ceremony, the bishop sits on a low stool with his sleeves folded up in preparation for the re-enactment of Christ's act of humility. One of the most moving moments of Holy Week in Jerusalem occurs as the bishop then calls each of the twelve apostles' name in Aramaic, the language spoken by Jesus Christ. In the intimate space of St Mark's Syrian Church the acolytes and deacons answering the call assemble around him. Dozens of tourists crowd and shove around the bishop as he begins his task. With cotton wool and Lux soap feet are really washed unlike the symbolic gesture performed in most churches. The smiles of some of the tourists and also some of the consuls sitting in the sanctuary are patronising and uneasy. Because the Syrians have preserved Aramaic in their liturgy for almost two millennia, this ceremony gives unique voice to the Last Supper. But this continuity is lost in the cotton wool and the Lux soap. The House of Christian Heritage would provide new resources for not only the pilgrim, but the tourist, to learn how to experience the diversity and antiquity of the Christian presence in Jerusalem.

What would be in this museum, The House of Christian Heritage? Here is one vision. The historical evolution of major Christian sites and communities would be exhibited by drawings, maps and models. The use of fibre optic and computer technology would create a user-friendly atmosphere accessible to a wide spectrum of interests and linguistic diversity. The iconography of the various sites would also be explicated based on the principles and theology of the community which created and/or now controls the site and its use. The exhibits would have a logical progression and multiple levels of explanation so that hurried and tightly scheduled groups of pilgrims could attain a quick overview and sufficient grasp of the indigenous Christian presence and their own tradition's historical connection with Jerusalem to make their pilgrimage richer and more meaningful. More extensive descriptions and information (for example, five to ten minute videos) would be placed behind the major thematically based material in order to provide an in-depth experience for those with more time or interest.

In the introduction hall the pilgrim or tourist would be immersed into the common seminal events of Christianity celebrated in the Holy Land (birth, ministry, death and resurrection of Christ). Next the pilgrim would survey the history and iconography of Christianity from the 1st century to Constantine. The rituals developed by Christians to mark, commemorate, represent and appropriate the power and grace of these events would then be depicted and explained. Thus rituals, including the central Eucharistic celebrations, the washing of the feet and the Holy Fire, would be explicated within an historical context. Finally the visitor would explore the holy sites chronologically in the order of the biblical narrative including the evolution of the sites' architecture and iconography.

The goal of this museum, is to be a *sine qua non* of every pilgrim's and tourist's visit to Jerusalem. The House of Christian Heritage would provide the Christians of the Holy Land an opportunity to witness their faith and to shape the experience of pilgrims and tourists as they venture out to explore the Holy Land. Christians around the world would consider The House of Christian Heritage the optimal window and mirror on their heritage. The House of Christian Heritage would be one of the most permanent and significant contributions to Christianity's bi-millennial celebration by surmounting years of misunderstanding and creating an environment of mutual understanding and appreciation.

26
APPLICABILITY OF ISRAELI LAW
OVER EAST JERUSALEM:
CONCEPT AND DIMENSIONS
Usama Halabi

Peace be upon you

Introduction

These remarks will deal briefly with the use of Israeli law and courts as a tool to execute Israel's policies toward occupied East Jerusalem in its borders, which have been expanded its occupation in June 1967. We will stop at the concept of Israel's decision on the eve of the occupation, to extend its administration, courts and laws to the city. We will indicate the damage that this decision did to the status and rights of its residents, and that the laws promulgated to give the annexation a legal cover contradict international law. We can talk about this annexation in six stages of legislation promulgated by the Israeli parliament and high court regarding Jerusalem. Most expressed Israel's position, which aimed to change the status and nature of the occupied city to fit this position. We will also deal with the laws and decisions of the Israeli high court.

First Stage, June 1967, Occupation and Annexation[1]

On 25 June 1967 the Israeli government decided to annex East Jerusalem to Israel. For this political decision to have a legal cover, the Israeli parliament—in deliberations which lasted no more than three hours—decided on 27 June 1967 to promulgate three laws:

1   The amendment to the Law of Government and Judiciary Regulations (Law 11) of 1948-5708, adding to the original law Article 11-B, which stipulates: 'The law of the state, its judiciary and administration cover all the areas of the Land of Israel as

---

[1] For more, see Halabi, A, *The Municipality of Arab Jerusalem*, PASSIA, 1994, Jerusalem, pp. 25-32.

set by the government in law.'[2]

2   The Law to Adjust Municipalities Law (Law 6) of 1967-5727, which added Article 8-A, giving the Interior Ministry the authority to issue a declaration expanding the area of a municipality by annexing new areas as set by the aforementioned Law of Government and Judiciary Regulations.[3]

3   The Law to Preserve Holy Sites of 1967.[4]

The day after issuing these three laws, the government issued two directives. The first stipulated that the state's law, judiciary and administration covered East Jerusalem.[5] The other stipulated the expansion of the borders of the West Jerusalem Municipality, adding thousands of *dunums* of Arab land to it.[6] The total amount of land annexed to the jurisdiction of the Jerusalem Municipality was 72,000 *dunums*.[7]

Thus East Jerusalem, from an Israeli point of view and according to Israeli law, became part of Israel and its Arab residents became subject to Israeli law, which gave them rights and imposed obligations in various areas. For example, the residents of Arab Jerusalem became permanent residents of Israel. They had the right to obtain Israeli identity cards, participate in municipal elections, obtain social security benefits, and move freely in Israel, etc. But at the same time the residents of Arab Jerusalem had to pay taxes to the Israeli authority (government and municipality) and their movement in and out of Jerusalem became subject to Israeli law. Their right to build homes became subject to the Israeli Planning and Construction Law and to the policy and decisions of the Israeli authority. For many years the Israeli administration refused to zone Arab areas, thus making residential construction impossible. Meanwhile, it placed plans for Jewish areas and thousands of housing units were built. This has led to a housing crisis for the Arab residents. For example, out of the 9,070 housing units built between 1990 and 1993, one project (5.1 percent of the units) was built in a Palestinian neighbourhood.[8]

It is no secret that Israel's decision to annex Arab Jerusalem was met with condemnation by the UN and international community, because it contradicts the principles of international law, which does not condone the annexation of occupied

---

[2] Published in the Book of Laws #20-499 Sevan 5727 (28 June 1967), p. 121 (in Arabic) p. 74 (in Hebrew). The full text of the law is attached as Annex A.

[3] Published in the Book of Laws #499, p. 74 (in Hebrew). Full text of the law is attached as Annex B.

[4] Published in the Book of Laws #499, p. 75 (in Hebrew). Full text of the law is attached as Annex C.

[5] Collection of regulations #1967-6-28-2064, p. 2690 (in Hebrew).

[6] Collection of regulations #1967-8-28, 2065, pp. 2694-2695 (in Hebrew).

[7] Arafeh, Abu, Rahman, Abdul, *Jerusalem: New Formation of the City,* Arab Studies Centre, Jerusalem, 1985, p. 62.

[8] See B'Tselem report, *Discrimination Policy* (on planning and construction in East Jerusalem) issued in May 1995. A summary was published in *Ha'aretz* of 10 May 1995.

areas to the occupying country, even if the war that led to the occupation was in self-defence, as alleged by Israel.[9]

Second Stage, The Law of Judicial and Administrative Settlements of 1968

To fill the legal gaps created by the annexation of East Jerusalem to Israel, as there was no solution to be found in the laws of the time, the Israeli parliament issued a special law, the Law of Judicial and Administration Settlements of 1968, amended in 1970. This law stipulated that the Law of Absentee Property of 1950 did not cover the holy sites of Jerusalem. But it forced the companies that were operating in the city to register with the Israeli company registrar. The self-employed were forced to register themselves with Israel if they worked in vocations that require registration. This law gave a legal basis for transfer of properties that belonged to the Guardian of Property of the Enemy Jordan to the Guardian of Israeli Property.[10] As an effect of the implementation of Israeli law in East Jerusalem, all land laws, including confiscation and ownership laws, became in effect. Israeli authorities resorted to these laws intensively between 1968 and 1970, when thousands of *dunums* were confiscated for 'public use'. Jewish neighbourhoods were built to surround Jerusalem. They included: Ramat Eshkol and Neve Yaacov in the north, Ramot in the north west, Gilo in the south, and East Talpiot in the east. At the same time the high court issued more than one resolution affirming the annexation of East Jerusalem to Israel. For example we remember Case 69/283, Abdullah Ruweidi vs. Israeli Military Court of Hebron.[11] Justice Haim Cohen was sceptical as to whether the extension of Israeli law and administration to occupied Jerusalem meant annexation, while Justice Vitcon dealt with the annexation as a reality and Justice Yitzhak Kahan affirmed that East Jerusalem was part of Israel.

Third Stage, Basic Law: Jerusalem is the Capital of Israel

To remove any doubt about Israel's intentions from extending its laws, courts and administration to occupied Jerusalem, the Israeli parliament issued a Basic Law: Jerusalem is the Capital of Israel. The first article of this law stipulated that 'United Jerusalem is the capital of Israel.' Besides the media goal of this law, which affirmed a well-known position, it had a practical goal as well. It gave legal basis for extending funds beyond the normal way the government gives local authorities via the Interior Ministry. The fourth article of this law stipulates that the government will set aside special resources to develop Jerusalem. It will also give a special annual grant to the

---

[9] See Halabi, A, Jerusalem: *Effects of Annexation to Israel on the Rights and Status of its Arab Residents,* PASSIA, Jerusalem, 1990, pp. 14–18.
[10] Original law published in 1968 in the Book of Laws of 1968, p. 247. Amended in 1970.
[11] Rulings of the Israeli High Court, volume 24 (I), p. 419, p. 423.

Jerusalem Municipality (Capital Grant) according to the Knesset's Finance Committee.[12] Israel ignored UN Security Council Resolution 478, issued on 20 August 1980, which condemned Israel and considered all the legislative and administrative measures taken to change the nature and status of Jerusalem, including the aforementioned Basic Law, to be null and void.[13] The Basic Law was followed by a major confiscation campaign of Arab lands. In the winter of 1980, 4,400 *dunums* in the north of Jerusalem—belonging to Shufat and Beit Hanina—were confiscated for the construction of Pisgat Ze'ev settlement.[14] In 1982 about 132 *dunums* were confiscated to annex the industrial zone of Atarot, facing the Palestinian town of al-Ram.[15]

Fourth Stage High Court Rulings 1988-1993

The Israeli parliament and government were not the only two branches of authority that played a role in affirming and fixing the annexation of occupied Jerusalem to Israel. In more than one ruling, the high court affirmed the annexation and enforcement of Israeli laws on East Jerusalem. In high court case 282/88, Mubarak Awad vs. the Prime Minister, Interior Minister and Police Minister,[16] Justice Brak said: 'The government decided in the directive of Regulations on Government and Courts No 1 of 1967 that East Jerusalem is part of the Land of Israel and that the state's judiciary and administration pertain to it. East Jerusalem has been united with Jerusalem, and this is the understanding of annexing East Jerusalem to the state and making it a part of it.'[17] So the court rejected the appeal and decided that the right to reside or lose residence rights in Jerusalem was according to the Law of Entry into Israel of 1952[18] and its regulations. Since Dr Awad had left Jerusalem for the United States for a long time, obtained American citizenship, and married an American citizen, he lost his right to reside in Israel (i.e., Jerusalem). So the Interior Minister had the authority to expel him out of the country according to the above-mentioned law. In High Court case 4185/90, Temple Mt Faithful vs. the Government's Legal Adviser et al,[19] former Justice Menachem Elon used the term 'Temple Mount' and said it was sacred for the Jews. He talked about 'liberating the Temple Mount and Wailing Wall in the Six-Day War.'[20] He decided the following: 'The result of imposing Israeli sovereignty over united Jerusalem in general, and on the area of the Temple Mount in specific, is that all the state's laws, including the Planning and

---

[12] Published in the Book of Laws #980, 5 August 1980, p. 186. Full text attached as Annex D.
[13] The Security Council adopted this resolution in session 2245, with a majority of 14 for and 1 abstention.
[14] Israeli Current Events (Yalkot Hafarsomim), 1980, # 2614, p. 1305.
[15] *Op. cit.,* 1 July 1982, #2831, p. 2390.
[16] High Court rulings volume 42 (II), p. 424.
[17] *Op. cit.,* p. 429.
[18] Published in the Book of Laws of 1952, p. 354 (in Hebrew).
[19] Ruling issued on 23 September 1993, published in the High Court rulings (Piskeh Din) vol. 47 (V), p. 221.
[20] *Op. cit.,* p. 246.

Construction Law and Antiquities Law, apply to the Temple Mount.'[21] So the courts position was that the Islamic w*aqf* should obtain a permit, according to the above mentioned laws, before work on renovating or building in the compound of al-Aqsa.

The ruling of the High Court in the case of the Temple Mt Faithful was issued 10 days after the signing of the Declaration of Principles between the Israeli government and the PLO, which took place in Washington on 13 September 1993. According to the agreement, the Jerusalem issue was delayed till the talks on the final status. But the aforementioned court decision affirms the Israeli position that the annexation of Jerusalem, Israeli presence in it, and the measures taken by the Israeli government in it are a 'domestic' Israeli issue. Israel ignores the fact that, since occupying Jerusalem in 1967, there have been many UN resolutions regarding the illegality of the occupation and annexation of East Jerusalem.[22]

Fifth stage: Law to Implement the Gaza-Jericho Agreement (Restricting Activities) of 1994

The Law to Implement the Gaza-Jericho Agreement (Restricting Activities) of 1994[23] was promulgated after the signing of the Cairo agreement between Israel and the Palestinians on 4 May 1994. It prohibited the Palestinian Authority from opening a representational office, or calling for, or holding a public meeting in Israel before obtaining written permission from the Israeli government.[24] The law allows the Israeli government to prevent the PLO from opening or activating a representational office in Israel. The government can order a closure of such an office and prevent a public meeting called for by the PLO.[25] What matters to us is that the Israeli law talked about restricting the Palestinian Authority's activities 'in Israel,' instead of saying 'in Jerusalem' so as not to give the impression that Jerusalem is different from the rest of Israel's cities; i.e., that it is an indivisible part of Israel.

The legislation was followed by a series of Israeli harassments and hunts of the Palestinian institutions working in Jerusalem before the Declaration of Principles and Cairo agreements were signed. The argument was that they had characteristics of being governmental, or that they work for the Palestinian Authority. 'Israeli security officials' wrote an official document listing 13 Palestinian organisations including Orient House, the Waqf Ministry, the Higher Palestinian Health Council, Palestinian Central Bureau of Statistics, Jerusalem University and Land and Water Establishment. The document proposes opening a file to gather as much information as possible

---

[21] **Op. cit.**, p. 281.
[22] For more on international and Arab resolutions condemning the Israeli measures in Jerusalem, see: Jiries, Samir; *Jerusalem: Zionist Schemes, Occupation, Judaization;* Palestinian Studies Institute, Beirut, 1st ed., 1981; pp. 257-280. Also, *Arab Municipality of Jerusalem,* MS, pp. 72-89.
[23] Issued in the Book of Laws of 1994, p. 85 (in Hebrew).
[24] Article 3 of the law.
[25] Article 4 of the law.

about these organisations. The files should be given to legal experts to study the possibility of action against them.[26] All this despite the fact that the Israeli Foreign Minister at the time, Shimon Peres, had signed a letter to the Norwegian Foreign Minister on 1 October 1993 promising that 'all the Palestinian institutions in East Jerusalem—economic, social, educational, and cultural—including the Islamic and Christian holy sites play a vital role for the Palestinian residents and we will do nothing to hurt their activities.'[27]

Israeli authorities continued to work to divide Jerusalem from the rest of the West Bank by imposing a closure and preventing non-Jerusalemite Palestinians from entering the city unless they have written permission usually given for one day. A special committee headed by Minister Moshe Shahal proposed a list of recommendations to Israeli Prime Minister Yitzhak Rabin on 11 April 1995 that would be called 'separation plans'.[28] The recommendations include the need to restrict the immigration of Palestinians to Jerusalem, studying the possibility of revoking the Israeli residency of Jerusalemites who live outside Jerusalem for long periods of time, and placing six checkpoints on the entrances to Jerusalem under the control of the police to control movement in and out of Jerusalem.

The latest land confiscation campaign in Jerusalem was carried out by a law endorsed by the government on 14 May 1995. The land to be confiscated is 535 *dunums:* 335 belong to Beit Hanina to add new housing units to Ramot, and 200 belong to Beit Safafa.[29] The decision was suspended and not executed due to the media row it caused.

If we consider the Declaration of Principles, which postponed negotiating on the status of Jerusalem to the final stage, a bilateral international agreement, then it is subject to the international principles and standards in the Vienna Treaty on Treaties of 1969. One of these principles is the principle of fulfilling commitments in good faith.[30] To go back to the steps taken by the Israeli government in Jerusalem since the signing—mentioned above (especially the continued confiscation of Arab land and construction of Jewish settlements on them, harassing the Arab residents of Jerusalem and Palestinian institutions working there before the Declaration of Principles)—we reasonably conclude that the Israeli authorities have broken the principle of good faith. They are creating a new situation that supports the Israeli

---

[26] A summary of the document was published in *Ha'aretz* of 10 February 1995.

[27] The text of the letter translated into Arabic was published in *Al-Quds* on 7 June 1994.

[28] A summary of these recommendations was published in *Ha'aretz* on 12 April 1995.

[29] To realise the size of the confiscation carried out by the Israeli government in the Arab areas, and the lands annexed to the West Jerusalem Municipality since 1967, the geographic distribution of these lands, the names of the Jewish neighbourhoods built or to be built on the lands, see *Ha'aretz* of 2 May 1995. Israeli journalist Nadav Shargai estimates the confiscated land to be 24,000 *dunums,* with 35,000 housing units for Jews only built on them. Also see Tufakji, Khalil, 'Judaization of Jerusalem: Facts and Figures', *Journal of Palestine Studies,* no 22, Spring 1995, p. 121, 124.

[30] To analyse the legal status of the Declaration of Principles from the point of view of international law, see Halabi, Usama, 'The Declaration of Principles: Duality of Authority and Elections for the Self-Rule Council', in *National Institutions, Elections and Authority,* Muwaten: The Palestinian Institute for the Study of Democracy, 1994.

position and Jewish presence in the city, weakening the Palestinian position and the Palestinian ability to negotiate effectively when the final-status talks begin. This is already a problem because the Israeli side is the stronger, the dominant, while the Palestinian side (and Jerusalem side especially) is under occupation and does not have the ability to create a situation that serves its interests like the Israeli side can.

Sixth Stage: The Law to Implement the Transitional Stage (Oslo II)

On 17 January 1996 the Israeli parliament promulgated this law to give the contents of the Oslo II agreement a legal nature in the Israeli judicial system. One of the Palestinian victories of this agreement was that the Palestinians of Jerusalem were given the right to vote and nominate themselves in the elections for a self-rule council. Until that point, the Israeli position was that the term 'participation' found in the first appendix to the Declaration of Principles, meant the right to vote, but not be nominated. During the negotiations on the Declaration of Principles, the Palestinian side wanted the wording to mention the right to vote and nominate oneself, but it was rejected at the time.[31] It was also rejected in the negotiations (held in January 1995), for an agreement on the autonomy council elections.[32] But this victory remains humble, as Israel was able to restrict voting rights. It prevented free public campaigning. Campaigning could only be carried out in designated, closed halls. Israeli authorities banned a Fateh rally in Jerusalem that was to have supported the Beit al-Makdes Bloc in St George's field.[33] Israeli soldiers prevented Palestinian candidates from entering Jerusalem if their cars had campaign posters on them. They could only enter if they removed the stickers and posters.[34] The agreement designated polling stations and stipulated that no marks would be placed on Jerusalemites' ID cards to show they had voted. The Israeli Justice Minister argued during the discussion of the Law to Implement Oslo II in the Knesset, that giving the residents of East Jerusalem the right to participate in the elections for a Legislative Council does not mean that Israel has given up its sovereignty over Jerusalem. The Internal Security Minister declared a similar position in his meeting on 17 January 1996 with representatives of the Israeli right wing and the mayor of Jerusalem, Ehud Olmert.[35] Since the residents of Jerusalem who were forced to live outside the municipal boundaries of the city as set by Israel were allowed to vote in their areas of residence, we fear that there is a serious danger that their Israeli ID cards will be pulled after the elections, especially if they live in autonomous areas. The argument will be that they live outside Israel, which means they have no right to live in

---

[31] See Singer, Yoel. 'The Declaration of Principles on Interim Self-Government Arrangements', *Justice, The International Association of Jewish Lawyers and Jurists,* no. 1, Winter 1994, pp. 5–6.

[32] See *Al-Quds* of 27 April 1995.

[33] See *Al-Quds* of 14 January 1996. The announcement for the rally was published in *Al-Quds on* 12 January 1996.

[34] See *Al-Quds,* 16 January 1996.

[35] Israeli Channel 1 TV nightly news (Mabat LaHadashot), 17 January 1996.

Jerusalem. The number of such cases is in the tens of thousands, so we are talking about a very important issue. The demographic issue has its weight when it comes to the negotiations on Jerusalem.

What Should the Palestinians Do?

The Palestinian side must demand that the Israeli government stop its settlement activities in Jerusalem immediately, as it must in the other occupied Palestinian areas. Agreeing to delay negotiations on the Jerusalem issue without giving guarantees to retain the *status quo* has created many problems. Israel has a free hand to do what it wants (especially in a place it considers as an indivisible part of itself) until the final-status negotiations are over, or at least until they begin on the third year of the interim phase. There should be some agreement as to what the Declaration of Principles and its accords (the Cairo and Taba agreements) mean in light of international law and the UN resolutions dealing with Jerusalem, which consider all legal and physical changes created by Israel after its occupation of East Jerusalem— including the annexation decision—null and void. Israel must be asked to stop changing the status quo in the city until after the final-status of Jerusalem is agreed upon. The international community must be called in for help, especially the Vatican, because we know Israel signed an agreement with the Vatican to exchange diplomatic representation after Oslo I (the Declaration of Principles).

The continuation of Jewish settlement activity in Jerusalem is one part of Israeli policy. The other part is the purposeful neglect of the problems of Arab residents, the most important being the housing problem. The Israeli government continues to refuse to place zoning plans to solve this crisis, so many Palestinians from Jerusalem have been forced to leave the city and look for a solution outside its borders. Or they build without a permit, making them subject to legal pursuit and house demolition. So efforts should be stepped up and more financial support given to renovate the currently existing buildings and ensure legal defence for those who are taken to court with the threat of house demolition. Also the housing crisis facing the Palestinians of Jerusalem must be publicised, and there should be continuous pressure on the Israeli government to force it to have a more positive policy towards them as proof of its goodwill. The current negotiations should be taken advantage of in this regard.

The Palestinian side must do everything possible to maintain this human resource in Jerusalem and prevent its exodus. It should hold awareness campaigns about their rights to residence, especially since the demographic dimension is extremely important when discussing sovereignty over Jerusalem. The Palestinian Authority should contact the highest levels on the Israeli side to obtain an Israeli commitment not to damage the residency rights of Jerusalemites who were forced for one reason or another to live outside the Israeli municipal borders of Jerusalem, until a solution for them is written into the agreement that will be reached on Jerusalem.

Finally, we repeat what we have suggested time and again, that a National

Agency to follow-up Jerusalem issues be set up immediately to deal with the general daily problems that face the Palestinians of Jerusalem. It should also keep the Jerusalem issue high on the international and Arab agenda, and have a clear strategy regarding Jerusalem, which would be the basis for the Palestinian position during the final-status talks.

27
JERUSALEM: INTERNATIONAL LAW AND PROPOSED SOLUTIONS
Camille Mansour

My presentation will deal mainly with why and how international law is relevant when thinking about possible solutions for the Jerusalem question. However, I would first like to explain how the question of Jerusalem has historically been dealt with by international law.

Historical background

From 1517 to 1917, the Ottoman empire regulated the status of the various churches which were present in the Holy Land. In the mid-19th century, the powers and rights of the churches were known as *Status Quo*. This term was used in the Treaty of Berlin of 1878 which asserted that 'it is well understood that no change can be made in the *Status Quo* of the Holy Places,' thus giving the *Status Quo* an international character. In 1922, the text of the British Mandate of Palestine defined the powers and duties of Great Britain and confirmed that the mandatory power was responsible for the Holy Places and was bound to preserve existing rights.

In 1947, the United Nations Partition Plan recommended the establishment of an entity for Jerusalem—a *corpus separatum*—that would have an international regime and would be administered by a governor appointed by the United Nations Trusteeship Council. However, as an outcome of the war, the eastern part of the city came under Jordanian control, while the western part came under Israeli control and was proclaimed the capital of the state of Israel. Thus, although the *corpus separatum* did not materialise it did keep some of its international character. That is, foreign countries considered Jordanian and Israeli control as *de facto* control and those countries having relations with Israel refused to establish embassies in West Jerusalem, as the mandate of their consulate covered the entire city.

As a result of the 1967 War, Israel occupied the West Bank, annexed the eastern part of the city as well as some adjacent parts of the West Bank by extending the municipal boundaries of the city. From that period until the present an intensive building campaign of Israeli settlements has been taking place, aimed at changing the demographic and spatial character of the city, its vicinity, and further marginalising the Palestinian population. The international community has so far maintained its long standing *de jure* position on Jerusalem. It has also added three new elements: no recognition of the annexation of East Jerusalem; East Jerusalem is an occupied territory and the building of Israeli settlements is as illegal in the city as in the West Bank; and the rights of the Palestinian population of East Jerusalem are the same as the rights of the Palestinians in the West Bank, namely the right to self-determination. Furthermore, after 1967 the consulates in Jerusalem added to their *de jure* mandate for the whole of the city, a kind of *de facto* mandate towards the Palestinians in the occupied territories.

The Oslo Agreement of September 1993 leaves the solution of the Jerusalem question to the final status negotiations, but recognises the participation of the Palestinians of East Jerusalem in elections for a Palestinian Legislative Council. At the end of December 1993, the Vatican and Israel signed a 'Fundamental Agreement.' One of the provisions of the agreement asserts the commitment of the two parties to maintain the *Status Quo* in the Christian Holy Places to which it applies. In October 1994, the Jordanian-Israeli Peace Treaty recognised a role for Jordan in the Muslim Holy Places of Jerusalem.

With this brief survey of the legal history of Jerusalem, it becomes easier to understand how international law is relevant to the solutions that are and might be proposed in the future for Jerusalem.

The Relevance of International Law to Proposed Solutions

When we talk about proposed solutions for Jerusalem in regard to international law, we refer to four different yet interconnected elements. In other words, solutions for Jerusalem are relevant to international law on four bases:

1   Solutions aimed at preserving some kind of international character for Jerusalem, mainly for its Holy Places;
2   Solutions made according to the principles of international law, such as self-determination, non-acquisition of territory by force, and withdrawal from occupied territory;
3   Solutions referring to exceptional or unorthodox concepts of international law, such as shared sovereignty, joint sovereignty, condominium, boundary flexibility;
4   Solutions based on the agreement of the two local actors involved, insofar as one of them is already a subject of international law (Israel), and the other actor (the Palestinian Authority) is potentially an international actor.

I will now look at these four dimensions in greater detail.

Preserving the Character of Jerusalem

The *corpus separatum* idea, i.e. internationalisation of the city, was created to fulfil certain legitimate objectives. If these objectives could be fulfilled without international status, there would be no need for such a status. These objectives are: maintaining the *Status Quo* in the Holy Places; preserving rights and immunities;

putting the three religions on an equal footing, ensuring that one does not dominate the other; and freedom of access for all and to all Holy Places, whether in the east or the west, which means a unified, open city. Only minimal mechanisms, such as interfaith co-ordination, would be needed to resolve disputes. The two parties (Israelis and Palestinians) obviously do not agree on all these objectives, but they seem to agree that the *corpus separatum* concept is not a tool to end their conflict over Jerusalem. I would add that any immunity enjoying an international character for the Christian Holy Places will have to be accompanied by the same kind of immunity for the Muslim Holy Places.

International Law Principles

No solution would be consistent with international law if it did not include the right to self-determination for the Palestinian people (including those living in Jerusalem) as well as Israel's obligation to withdraw from all the territories it occupied in 1967, including East Jerusalem. The application of these two principles entails that East Jerusalem has to be part of a Palestinian state in all the West Bank and the Gaza Strip.

An argument could be made that reality on the ground has changed with the settlements in and around East Jerusalem, and that it is not realistic to go back to the 1967 borders. However, these realities on the ground have been made against the consistent opposition of the international community. The argument requires the Palestinians to forfeit *de jure* which has been forcibly taken from them, while Israel continues to expand its settlements over lands that are still in the hands of the Palestinians in Jerusalem. This is clearly unacceptable. A further argument could also be made that United Nations Resolution 242 is not the correct basis to resolve the question of Jerusalem. Therefore, if neither Resolution 242 or the *corpus separatum* of the United Nations Partition Plan constitutes the correct basis, what does? Let me repeat here that there is no alternative to the principle of self-determination and complete withdrawal when considering possible solutions.

Exceptional and Un-orthodox Concepts of International Law

This leads us to the third dimension of international law relevant to the question of Jerusalem, namely the intent to overcome the difficulties in the second point by referring to exceptional, unorthodox, or evolving concepts of international law. These may include: shared sovereignty; joint sovereignty; condominium; scattered sovereignty; boundary flexibility; and distinguishing between territorial jurisdiction which implies exclusive sovereignty from functional and personal jurisdiction which in turn implies municipal powers for Jerusalemite Palestinians. I, personally, have nothing against creative concepts which would permit a solution to the Jerusalem question. Nevertheless, I would strongly object to concepts that are a cover for Israeli control over East Jerusalem, that are, in other words, sweeteners. If these concepts are to be considered seriously, they have to cover both parts of the city.

Israel and Palestine as Equal Partners

Finally, international law is relevant to the solution of Jerusalem insofar as it involves two international local actors, namely Israel and Palestine. This would express itself in the principle that anything agreed upon by these actors is by definition in conformity with international law, except the provision reassuring Muslims and Christians about their Holy Places. In other words, this could mean that all concessions made by the Palestinian side would be acceptable in terms of international law as long as they have been officially signed by the Palestinian side. I would like to warn against this approach, because it implies forcing the concessions on the Palestinian side in exchange for Israeli gestures in other matters.

I would like to end with a question: if, as a result of negotiations, there is no Israeli-Palestinian treaty what will happen to the proposals regarding Jerusalem?

28
WHO ARE THE CHRISTIANS IN GALILEE?
Sami Geraisy

I wish to welcome everyone: clergy, lay people, locals, and especially our friends who have come such a long way to express solidarity, friendship and support to the Christians in this country, the Holy Land, and specifically in Jerusalem.

We feel that we are privileged to be residents of Galilee. Our lives in this area can be traced back to the birth of Christianity. The city of Nazareth is the site of the annunciation and where our Lord grew up, studied, and developed. He was a teacher and a learner, discussing issues with the wise men of the Jewish faith.

The Gospel of St John tells us a beautiful story about a wedding that Jesus along with his mother Mary and his disciples attended. That was where he performed his first miracle. At that time people did not offer monetary gifts to the wedded couple, instead, they took along wine, meat, chicken, rice and other commodities. When all the wine was consumed, Jesus, upon his mother's request, asked that the six stone water-jars, used for Jewish rites of purification, be filled with water. When the water was drawn, it had turned into the best wine. This miracle took place in Cana of Galilee (which also happens to be my home town. It is about five kilometres away from Nazareth).

The disciples were recruited from Galilee. Two of them came from Cana, some came from Tiberias and other communities around the lake. The Galileans were privileged to be the companions of our Lord, his disciples who spread the Gospel and the teachings of Christianity; we too, feel blessed to belong to the church which started here. We read in the Holy Bible how Christianity began to spread because of the Sermon on the Mount, the miracles of multiplication, the healing of the sick, and the resurrection from the dead. These miracles were signs of the divinity of Jesus. So we people, we Galileans, feel very privileged to be a part of this community where Christianity has its roots and from which it spread.

The Christian people here lived alongside the Jews, and although there were disagreements, they continued to live together. After the arrival of Islam in the 7th and 8th centuries, Christians found a new formula to live next to those converted to Islam, and so the three communities, the three monotheistic believers, Christians, Jews and Muslims lived together. There were of course, ups and downs, like in any country with different communities, but on the whole they found a way to living together. Most of the people lived together, not in separate villages and communities, but in the same village, city or town. They shared and worked in agriculture, fishing and other activities available in those days.

There was little interruption in this way of life until the Crusades destroyed the lives of these communities. Although the Crusaders pretended to help the Christians in this country and to guard the safety of those coming to visit the shrines, they actually did more harm than good to the country and its people. They created a rift between the Middle East and Europe, a rift between Christians and Muslims, and even between Christians and Christians in the same land. Fortunately, that did not last very long. The local Christians suffered no less than Muslims during the times of the Crusades. After the Crusaders, retaliation to avenge the presence and intrusion of the Crusaders took place. The invasion of the Mamluks from Egypt, and the destruction of the Christian shrines and massacres are examples of this retaliation.

This kind of life continued until the Turks became the occupying nation for four centuries in the Middle East. Those were dark ages because there was little education, schools or medical services. The main goal of these rulers was to exploit the peasant population as much as possible. Villagers were sold by auction in the market place so that taxes could be paid to the sultan in Istanbul. In this way many peasants lost their homes and sometimes their lives, in order to pay the very high taxes that were demanded from them by force. Christians and Muslims alike suffered a great deal during the four long centuries under Ottoman rule which ended with the First World War.

At the turn of the 18th century, a new intervention came with the arrival of European Christians. They came here to build churches, medical centres and schools to serve the local population in towns and villages. The Russians and the Greeks were the first to come and, with the help of the local Orthodox Church, built schools in Nazareth, Cana, Rama, Kufur Yasif and throughout the Holy Land. The Catholics in Europe followed. They established educational institutions. The Friars and Dominicans were interested in serving the people sincerely and genuinely without any ulterior motive. The Scottish Church built a hospital in Tiberias, the Edinburgh Missionary Medical Society (EMMS) built the hospital in Nazareth as well as others in Jordan. Schools were also established. The Anglicans and Lutherans from Europe began to assist local people. There was competition between the different churches in Europe as to who could provide better service to the local population.

These services were run by the local Christians in the country who acted as interpreters, the middle people between the Christian West and the local Christian communities. Through these services they gained status and more knowledge about the country. Christians were part and parcel of the local population and the management of these institutions helped them to participate, co-exist, and belong to the country as much as any other.

The biggest rift took place with the conflict over the country erupting in the 1948 war between Jews and Palestinians. The Jewish underground army, unlike the Palestinians, was well equipped and therefore won the war and established the State of Israel. Israel was established as a Jewish state and all other communities were excluded from becoming a part of this new political and social structure. As a result of the fighting, Galilee, as well as other areas were occupied; hundreds of villages were demolished, inhabitants were expelled while others left to seek safety in nearby villages or towns.

Today, over half of the people living in Nazareth are refugees who came from different communities where villages and lands were taken. They became refugees within their own country. About half of the present Palestinian population in Israel are local refugees. This created a challenge for the local Palestinian population because there was no organisation to provide aid for these refugees. As you know, the majority left the country altogether and took refuge in Lebanon, Syria and in northern Jordan. Today they live in the refugee camps of Sabra and Shatila, of Miyyeh Miyyeh, of Ain al-Hilweh and others.

We know we are entitled to equality, peace and a future. We started an organisation ourselves to care for all the refugees, the sick and the illiterate. We contacted organisations in the West and asked them to join us. Although we have a long way to go, we have more hope today. The Oslo Accords and the ongoing peace process have added hope for the future, but we would like to see the peace process move more rapidly than it is at present.

The issue of Jerusalem was left to the final stage of negotiations. Unless a just solution is found for the city there will never be peace; but your presence and the support of all people of goodwill, who want to see Jerusalem as the shrine of unity, and a place for all citizens, provides solidarity for our cause. Jerusalem is the Mecca for all Christians, Muslims and Jews wherever they are. It is the city that could bring unity and hope for everybody, if the right formula for co-existence is found. Jerusalem belongs to everybody that lives there; it belongs to all the followers of the three main religions: Islam, Christianity and Judaism. They have been able to live together in the past, despite all the obstacles and difficulties, and now they need to find a new formula for co-existence and therefore make a better life for everyone.

We are now part of this struggle for a better future for all. We hope that the politicians will bring about justice so that all citizens will have equal rights in a true democratic system. I am sure, that with your understanding and support and the support of peace-loving people, we shall find a way for a better and more secure life. We are determined to continue to live in Israel. Several people have asked the question: 'When Palestine is established would you prefer to go and live under a Palestinian flag?' Our answer is, 'No.' We belong here. We belong to our community. We belong to our shrines and churches. We belong to the places where we were born and raised. We wish to see peace and to see a Palestinian state next to the Jewish state. We wish to see Israel, not as a state for Jews only, but as a state for all, Jew and non-Jew without discrimination. We would like to see Israel as a democracy, not only in terms of the technical process where everybody is allowed to vote and be elected, but in reference to a true spirit of democracy with respect for all citizens, equal opportunities, the right to bring up families, to have secure homes and ownership over land, and also the right to a secure and better future.

Many of the people in Israel—Christians and Muslim—have been deprived of their lands and their belongings. People moved temporarily from one town to another, for example from Tiberias to Nazareth because they could not stand the fighting. Therefore they were regarded as 'absentees' which meant their property, their home, their land and their business were taken away. They were deprived of their livelihood, so how could they continue to support their families?

These are some of the problems which we face, endure, and which we fight legally. We do not wish to resort to violence in order to make changes. Rather, we have hope in the common sense and faith of forces outside the country. There has been a great contribution by the United States, Scandinavian countries and the European Community to build peace between Palestinians and Jews in this country, the Holy Land. We are very hopeful that these forces will continue to do their job and try to bring many faiths together. Things are now much better than before. Since the Oslo Accord we have more hope and more confidence in the future. We hope that this process will continue and we hope that within a year or two, peace will prevail not only in the Holy Land but all over the region.

We, Christians, Muslims and Jews pray for peace. We deserve peace, our children deserve it too. We are not politicians. We are human beings who have no discrimination against each other but we hope that those who have the key to make peace will have the wisdom to find a way to make it. We depend greatly on your understanding as friends who have come a long way to express friendship and solidarity with us. We appreciate your dedication, your commitment to the cause of peace, to the cause of justice and we hope that your visit will be the beginning of more visits in the future. We hope you will be missionaries spreading the word of the need for justice, of the need to find a just solution and we hope that you will keep supporting our local institutions.

Churchill once said, 'Give us the tools and we will do the job.' Give us your support. We depend on your friendship and we are up to the duty. We have stayed here despite all the problems and obstacles that have stood in our way. We will continue to live with hope. The hope that we have in our hearts comes through our faith. Through this faith we believe that wisdom will overcome evil and that our hopes will be realised.

29
FACTORS AFFECTING THE PALESTINIAN CHRISTIAN PRESENCE IN ISRAEL
Ibtisam Mu'allem

Sisters and brothers, greetings to you all, and special greetings to our guests.

Before I begin I would like to mention two things.

First, the Palestinian Christian presence is a human presence, affected by everything around it: natural, political, economic, social, cultural and religious.
Second, the same factors affect the Palestinian presence as a whole, Christian or Muslim. They lead to the same effects on all Palestinians. So most of my talk will be about the Palestinian presence in Israel in general, and this includes the Christian presence.

I begin in 1948, the decisive year in the life of the Palestinian people. That year witnessed the dispersion and division of an entire nation. After expelling 85 percent of the nation—about 750,000 people—the borders were closed around Israel, and about 165,000 Palestinians remained.

The world forgot that some Palestinians had remained, living in the new Israeli state. In the eyes of the world and international agencies, the Palestinian issue became the issue of the refugees in the surrounding countries. As for the Palestinians who remained in their land, they were totally isolated from the entire world and suffered from a media blackout as well. They were prevented from carrying out any political or national activities. The hardest part of this isolation was the division of Palestinian families. Every family that remained lost relatives, sons, or brothers who were kicked out, or who sought refuge in the Arab countries. Not one family escaped the misery of separation.

In 1948, David Ben-Gurion declared the establishment of the State of Israel in the Declaration of Independence, which proclaimed it to be a Jewish democratic state, that respects the rights of all its citizens without discrimination according to race, creed or sex. This was an announcement directed to the world, and it was considered the nucleus of the constitution of the State of Israel. It expressed the values that this state would be built on. What was its fate? What parts of it remained sacred when the time came for its implementation? And what parts were just words to gain international sympathy, to allow the new Israel to join the United Nations? And can a state be Jewish and democratic at the same time?

The most simple definition of a democratic system is that all its citizens are equal before the law, so is Israel a truly democratic state? And are its citizens equal before the law? Let us see from the events since 1948, especially noting the laws that were imposed on the Palestinians in Israel.

The first thing Israel did to the Arab residents was to put them under military law and the Emergency Mandate Laws, allowing Israeli authorities to bring anyone who breaks the law before military courts, where there were no appeals. The law suspended the activities of all their political and social organisations, and turned the Palestinians into a minority. Every attempt to protest any injustice was oppressed. Curfews were imposed and travel between areas was prohibited. An Arab had to get a special permit to move from one city to another, even if he or she had to move daily due to work. This military government lasted from 1948 to 1966.

Israel defined itself as a Jewish state, or a state for the Jewish people. So what does this mean? And how did Israeli laws express this? Before anything else, it means that Israel will be a state with a Jewish majority. But this is not the only meaning. 'Jewish state' means the state was established for the interests of the Jews only. All the state's agencies work to achieve this goal. The interests of the Jews are above all other interests, including democracy. The high court expressed this in the early 1960s, in the case of the Land Group, or the Socialist Movement. Any party or individual which rejects the Jewish nature of the state cannot participate in elections. In other words, no Arab can request political or national rights. If they want to stay on their land, they must know that this state is a Jewish state, not their state. Laws came afterward to underline and stress this position. In Article 7-A of the Knesset's Basic Law, any list denying that Israel is a Jewish democratic state is prohibited from running in Knesset elections.

Let us backtrack. In 1950 the Law of Return was promulgated. This is the only law that blatantly discriminates between Arab and Jew. It gives the right to every Jew in the world, wherever he is, to enter Israel and reside in it and obtain Israeli citizenship with all its benefits. A Jew is defined as one who has a Jewish mother, or who has an ancestor who had a Jewish mother. Moreover, this Law of Return prevented any Palestinian forced out of his/her land and home two years or more before the promulgation of the law, from returning. It allowed hundreds of thousands, or millions, of Jews to come from around the world, clearly expressing the policy of the Israeli state and its goals in taking over most of the land of Palestine to bring in Jews to live on it. Afterwards, about thirty other laws were made allowing Israel to take over most of the land of Palestine.

Most important among these laws are:

1 The Absentee Property Law of 1950, which allowed the state to take over the lands of all the Palestinians who sought refuge in neighbouring states during the war. It allowed the state to take over the land of Palestinians who moved from one village to another, without leaving the country. These people became present 'absentees' according to the law, and their property became government property. This law does not mention the word 'Arab' or define 'refugee' as someone who left the country. But the standards it mentions apply only to Palestinian Arabs. Israel was and still is very careful about overtly displaying racism in its laws.

2 The Take-over of Land (Compensation) Law of 1953, which, along with the preceding law, allowed the state to take over the property and lands of refugees,

'present absentees' and even Palestinians who never left their homes. This would be done in return for miserly amounts of compensation that would be put in their names in the bank.

3   Dozens of laws were promulgated to allow the state to confiscate thousands of dunums of land owned by the Arabs who remained in Israel, or owned by the local Arab town or village authorities who stayed in Israel. So entire Arab villages and towns disappeared, after the vast majority of the peoples' land was stolen. While 70 percent of the Palestinians worked in agriculture on their land in 1947, only 7.9 percent were working in agriculture by 1989.

The aggression towards Palestinians was not limited to land theft, and the denial of political and national rights. There was blatant discrimination against them in all facets of life. Since 1948, not one new Arab town or village has been built, while hundreds of Jewish housing and farming communities have been constructed. Arab municipal authorities obtain one-third or one-fourth of what Jewish municipalities with the same population obtain. The level of education and education services in the Arab sector is significantly lower than that in the Jewish sector. The same goes for the health sector. Not one hospital has been built in the Arab sector since the establishment of the state. The same three Christian hospitals built at the turn of the century are still the only ones providing health services to the entire Arab sector. Job opportunities are narrow for the Arab, especially for those with higher education.

It is impossible to count all the ways and areas of discrimination suffered by the Palestinians in Israel, because discrimination touches all facets of life. So how has Israel managed to hide this discrimination from its legal texts?

Most of the time discrimination is hidden under the guise of military service. In other words, those who do not serve in the army cannot get the benefits of those who do.

Another way for the state to discriminate in services without putting this discrimination in the law is by allowing a major portion of the services—construction, agriculture, industry, education, health, etc.—to be run not by the government, but by Jews via the Jewish Agency and the Jewish National Fund. These two organisations work independently to provide all sorts of services to Jews only. Since they are not considered governmental organisations, they can discriminate in their services as they wish, without making it seem as if the state is discriminating.

The Basic Law: 'Human dignity and freedom' which was enacted by the Knesset in 1992, stipulates that the life of human beings, their freedom, property and privacy are defended from aggression by the authorities. This law also excluded the Arabs by not mentioning equality and by keeping previous laws in effect. What is the use of a law on 'Human dignity and freedom' when this dignity and freedom are monopolised by one part of the citizenry?

These political pressures have turned over time into social, economic and cultural pressures. An Arab head of a household must work double his Jewish counterpart to provide for the needs of his family, because he obtains no subsidies when it comes to housing, free or semi-free university education for his children, and he does not even get the same social security benefits. Arabs in Israel have to struggle many times more than others to survive. They live through all the challenges and difficulties of modern life without having modern institutions to help them.

This situation produced negative and difficult results for the Palestinians in Israel. There is a mass exodus of youth, especially among those with higher education who have concluded that there is no hope of finding a job that fits their qualifications. A major portion of the best of our youth has left the country. This is causing the Palestinian identity, history and language to vanish. Palestinians do not learn their history at school, they are not encouraged to learn about their roots and past. In the Jewish schools, Jewish students are taught that the Arab is the ugliest creature in the world. As for the archaeological remains that bear witness to the Palestinian presence, and especially to the Christian presence, they are destroyed or buried.

What about the Christian presence? I mentioned that emigration was a major result of the conditions. Christian emigration was bigger than that of other communities because entire families are leaving, not only youth on an individual basis. As for religious life, there is a sort of split between Christian faith and the life that the Christian is living. So what is the role of the church and its organisations in our country? They have a major positive role in retaining the Palestinian and Christian presence through the services that they provide to the people in education, health and even in working on the land.

The Church and Christian organisations helped encourage and strengthen the Palestinian and Christian presence. We will never forget the sacrifices of priests, nuns and lay people, but this is not enough under our conditions. In modern countries religion is separated from the state, but we find ourselves living in a state built on religious foundations. So in a state where the individual's rights are determined by his/her religious affiliation, it is not right for our spiritual leadership to be satisfied with a traditional religious role only. It is not enough to baptise children and make them Christians. We must stand by them in the challenges of life that their faith will be confronted with.

In a state that deals with us according to creed, our spiritual leadership must realise its role in deepening love and tolerance, and must stand by truth and justice for fear that sectarian treatment might divide the Palestinians, Christians or Muslims.

In a country where a human's presence depends on his/her physical presence and the presence of their land, not one atom of the land of our churches, trusts and properties must be sold, because what is sold can never be regained.

My last word is for us, the people of this land: there is nothing in our nationality or Palestinian identity to be ashamed of. Our roots are deep in this land, as deep as history itself. If we lose this identity and this nationality we will find no other. We must not allow the day to come when we are colourless, tasteless, scentless. There is nothing in our Christianity to be ashamed of; it is a religion of love, tolerance and openness. Even if Israel and other countries are largely responsible for the conditions we are in, every one of us bears the responsibility to maintain every element of our Palestinian identity, and to maintain a Christian identity which always works for real justice, love and peace.

30
THE IMPORTANCE OF JERUSALEM TO THE CHRISTIANS OF GALILEE

Boulos Marcuzzo

Dear guests,

It is great faith that brought us together as brothers and sisters, although we have never met before. You have come to Jerusalem and Nazareth, two cities, which are not only our home, but the home of all the faithful in the world. We welcome you all.

We read in the Holy Bible a beautiful passage, 'Land of Zebulun, land of Naphtali, on the road by the sea, across the Jordan, Galilee of the Gentiles—the people who sat in darkness have seen a great light, . . . (Matthew 4: 15-16).

This light is Jesus Christ. Today, you are the great light. You are the light of Galilee through your visit and your welcome presence with us in the Galilee of the nations. I welcome you and I welcome the idea of coming together to talk and meditate on Jerusalem. It is good to have you in Nazareth, the place of the annunciation and life of Christ. It is the city of the Holy Family. I also wish to thank you for your desire to visit this country to get to know the local Church. The Church of the Holy Land, the Church of Galilee, the Church of Christ.

My talk will focus on two points. The first is: who are we, the people of the Church of Galilee? The second point is: what do we have to say about the city of Jerusalem, and what do we expect of it? What are our obligations towards Jerusalem?

Who are we? You might regard my answer with scepticism, but in all humility, pride and strength we say: we are the family of Jesus. We are the Church of the Holy Land. We were established here by no other than our Lord Jesus himself. The apostles laid down our foundations. We are the descendants of the first Christians who were Jesus' companions who heard him and saw him perform miracles. We are the descendants of the first Christians who received the heavenly message from Jesus himself. It was from this first group of Christians that the apostles rose and set forth to the ends of the earth, to your countries, and to all the continents. This is how Christianity spread. We are directly related to Christ; we are his first Church. There is a beautiful historic continuity, beginning with Jesus and reaching this day, passing through the first Church made up of exclusively Jewish families and later families of the nations. The Church went through many turbulent times and various hardships, whether political, economic or other changes that this Holy Land went through. The Church of Galilee went through the same hardships as the Church in the rest of Palestine and the Holy Land. In spite of that, we have kept our special identity, our special characteristics and our special vision. We enjoy a great wealth of heritage and ritual. There is the Greek Orthodox Church, the Greek Catholic or Melkites, the Latin or Roman Catholic Church, the Maronite and the Evangelical Church. All of these Churches are not strangers to the land. They belong to the Land. They were born here and have lived here for many centuries. We thank God that they are still here praising God and upholding the Gospel of our Lord Jesus Christ and His Holy Places.

This Church is indigenous; it is Arab and Palestinian. It is the guardian of the Holy Places. Here, I must put in a word of gratitude to the Franciscan Fathers and let us remember the Orthodox brotherhood of the Holy Sepulchre who maintained and preserved the Holy Places over the ages. We owe it to those Franciscan Fathers, and to the Brotherhood of the Holy Sepulchre, that we are able, today, to visit the Holy Places and discover the personal, geographic and historic dimensions of our Christian faith, which is embodied in the incarnation. It was they who preserved those places for the whole world with zeal and responsibility.

The modern day Church is involved in many initiatives. It wants to play its role in this country alongside its Muslim and Jewish brothers and sisters. It is a Church that is connected with the rest of the world and with the Church Universal. This dynamic blend is fruitful, rich and positive. In order to really comprehend the spiritual wealth of the Holy Places, a visitor has to understand this connectedness between the Churches; their heritage, their traditions and their rituals.

I would like to tell you a simple story of a colleague of mine. He was an Italian writer who came to visit this country and was fascinated by it. After visiting the Holy Places he said: 'I would like to stay in this beautiful holy land and write a book about it.' After one month he said: 'One month is not enough, I want to stay here for one whole year in order to understand this country thoroughly. This country is beautiful but complex. Maybe I will not be able to write a book, but I will write an article in a newspaper or a magazine.' He stayed in the country for one whole year. At the end of the year he said: 'I am still fascinated by this country; its beauty, its message; I am truly fascinated, but I must confess that I am unable to write anything about this country. It is so interconnected, so rich, so complex and beautiful that there is no way that I can describe it. One can only experience this country, live in this country and for this country.'

Dear friends, as we have seen, this Church has many exceptional qualities, but its problems are also not few. In Israel, for instance, we constitute three percent of the population, but we do not want to be a minority in terms of citizenship and rights. We are a numerical minority, but we want to be full citizens within the framework of this state and this country. We do not wish to be looked at as a minority, for we try hard to affirm our legal and official status. We do not have to prove our physical living presence, for we have been here from the beginning of time. From this standpoint we can read the agreement that was signed between the Holy See and the State of Israel. This agreement gives the Church and its institutions legal rights as opposed to rights acquired through the *Status Quo*. This Church is firmly rooted in its ancient faith, and tries to incarnate itself in every place and every age. It also seeks renewal in a sound way. Some Churches, especially Catholic Churches, have come together to celebrate a local ecclesiastical pastoral Synod. Through the process of this 'Synod' movement, the Arab Christian Church, the Church in Galilee, in Palestine, in Israel and in Jordan hopes to root itself in this country, in this age, in this conflict and in this framework.

There is a lot to say about this Church. You only have to look around to see the numerous and various Christian institutions in order to understand the vitality of this Church that desires to play its role of charity, love, service of humankind and the interest of peace and reconciliation.

What does this Church have to say about Jerusalem? This is our primary topic. In the Bible, Galilee is closely connected to Jerusalem. In the Bible, especially in the Gospels there are two poles. The north pole which is Galilee of the gentiles; and there is the south pole: Jerusalem and the southern regions.

There is a constant interaction between the two poles, a positive and fruitful interaction. Jesus Christ himself, the Word of God, was incarnated in Nazareth, born in Bethlehem, returned to Nazareth, from where he set forth to Jerusalem to offer himself and to perform his duties like every other believer in Jerusalem. Jesus lived in this holy city for thirty years. He outlined his general universal policy in the cities and villages of Galilee, especially in the vicinity of the Sea of Galilee. From here, he went up to Jerusalem.

The Holy Gospel portrays the life of our Lord Jesus Christ as a continuous ascent from Galilee to Jerusalem, where his life is crowned by his dying on the cross for our salvation, by his life-giving resurrection and by the outpouring of the Holy Spirit on the apostles and the Virgin Mary. Therefore, there is a continuous interaction between these two poles. Galilee and Jerusalem. Jesus said to the women who came to his burial place to visit: '. . . go and tell my brothers to go to Galilee; there they will see me' (Matthew 28: 10). Yes, There is an interaction between Galilee and Jerusalem until this day. Galilee without Jerusalem is not complete, and Jerusalem without Galilee is not a fully Holy City.

Brothers and sisters, how do we view Jerusalem today? What do we want from Jerusalem and what does Jerusalem want from us? We are in complete agreement with all our Palestinian brothers and sisters in our vision of Jerusalem, the Holy City, as believers and as citizens. First: our vision of Jerusalem is not exclusive; it is not a monopoly for Christians. We seek an inclusive, unified, comprehensive vision of Jerusalem from a civil, political and religious point of view. Jerusalem is for all faiths and for all its citizens. I am not only speaking from a Galilean Christian point of view, but from a point of view that is in harmony with the Muslim and sometimes the Jewish side. What we have to say about Jerusalem is first and foremost that we want a united, undivided city. I repeat, a united, undivided city. Jerusalem is not so today. Of course, there is geographic unity, and maybe a unified network of public transportation, but in reality, that is in the hearts of people, there is no unity. One community does not feel that it belongs to the city because another community has control over it. We want a Jerusalem that is one, united and undivided in every aspect, in reality, in the hearts of the people and in their sense of belonging to the city.

Let me refer you, if I may, to a very important document issued two years ago in November of 1994 in Jerusalem. This document was signed by all the patriarchs, bishops and heads of Churches in Jerusalem. They called it 'A Memorandum of the Significance of Jerusalem to Christians'. I feel that this document is a treasure. Our children will, in the future, study this document because it is in fact a decisive stand of the Christian Churches in Jerusalem. It is in line with the Muslim and Jewish stand on Jerusalem. The first point in the document announces that Jerusalem belongs to its people and to the people of the country without excluding anybody, without giving up any right and in beautiful harmony. I love a statement uttered by an oriental Jewish intellectual and writer by the name of Andrei Shuraqi. He wrote: 'Jerusalem is not a city, it is a symphony,' which means a harmony of voices, parties and stands. We should accept Jerusalem in all its diversity, its variety, its harmony and its comprehensives. This is what Jerusalem is about. We have to respect this reality if we really desire a prominent status for Jerusalem in its unique role and message for us and for all people.

In the memorandum, we also say that no party has an exclusive claim over Jerusalem. This is our experience from the past and from history. Jerusalem has three problems. The first problem is that of external intervention in its affairs. The second basic problem of Jerusalem is the control of one of the internal parties over the others. The third problem of Jerusalem, from a religious point of view, is that we do not truly love it, but rather are fanatic about it. In other words, we have a blind love for Jerusalem without any respect for the other, or the Holy Places. Jerusalem is a holy city that we love and are willing to sacrifice for its sake, but this love should be open to all. This is what is written in that beautiful memorandum. We hope, God willing, that this memorandum will be respected and taken into consideration in all deliberations and decisions on Jerusalem. Last summer, another conference was held in Jerusalem on the situation of the city. Cardinal Achigrai, head of the Peace and Justice Committee in Rome said: 'It is impossible to own Jerusalem, Jerusalem owns us. There will never be justice or peace in Jerusalem unless everybody has an equal share of justice and peace.' If peace and justice are not equally shared, then there is neither justice nor peace. Perhaps in Jerusalem today there is justice and peace, but they are not equally distributed.

Dear brothers and sisters, there is no need to mention how much we have been, how much we are, and how much we will always be attached to Jerusalem; but we, in Galilee, have some criticism for certain religious stands over the city. Those are fanatic stands and fanaticism is not love. Let us remember how Jesus cried over Jerusalem because it is the killer of prophets, because it refused peace and because it refused God's visitation. When fanaticism prevails Jerusalem cannot perform its mission. We have to respect Jerusalem and be holy ourselves in order to make it holy. Churches in Jerusalem have to be open to each other if they want to be Churches that love the city in all its holiness.

Only when fanaticism is overcome and only when the above mentioned problems of Jerusalem are removed—external intervention, the domination of one party over the other and having an absolute claim to its holiness—only then will Jerusalem become the city of peace, the gateway to heaven as the Book of Genesis says, as a symbol of the heavenly Jerusalem and as a symbol of the Church. I will end my talk with the words of Tobit, 'How blessed are those who love you! They will rejoice in your peace' (13: 14).

Jerusalem is for us and for all people a city of peace, a centre for world peace and a joy for the whole world.

31

THE PERSPECTIVE OF A
LAY CHRISTIAN FROM GALILEE
ON THE CITY OF JERUSALEM

Johnny Mansour

A Spiritual Perspective

Christians in Galilee are children of God and, as such, they hold other human beings in respect and dignity. They see in their faces a true image of God and expect from them a similar attitude. Unfortunately, the situation today in the Holy Land is different. Galileans have become strangers in their homeland, the land of their fathers and grandfathers; they have become refugees and displaced persons in their own land. They are obliged to look for ways and means to maintain their existence and hold on to the land they were born in and live on.

This has made a Galilean Christian's perception of his/her existence a living witness of their Christian faith, and their faith in the dignity of all human beings. As an Arab Palestinian Christian I also bear witness to my love of my country, my land and my people. This is a legitimate and logical right. It is from the depth of this love that I respect my brothers and sisters who belong to another people. We are all the children of God, regardless of religion, creed or denomination.

Palestinian Christians view the Holy City as having Arab roots that go back 3,000 years before Christ. This human presence was not just a passing coincidence. Through the ages they obviously interacted creating a civilisation, a culture, a heritage of thought and art, culminating in the incarnation of Jesus Christ in my land and country, thus making the message of God accessible to humankind. As a result of this great event, it became a world civilisation.

Palestinian Arab Christians carried and still carry this heavenly message to the whole world, making their historical role a very important one. This fact needs to be explained. We in Galilee consider Jerusalem a spiritual centre from which the message of Christ spread to the whole world. This message could not have crystallised without its deep foundations in Galilee. Thus, we Galileans are proud that Jesus was a son of Galilee and a son of Jerusalem, which creates a close relationship between the two.

The Good News came out of Nazareth and set forth towards Bethlehem, then on to Egypt and back to its roots—Nazareth. This return was not incidental; it emphasises the importance of Nazareth and Galilee, and the connection between this region and Jerusalem, and its interaction within the events of the life of Jesus on earth.

Jesus chose his disciples from Galilee, from Tiberias and its environs. It was there that he prepared himself and them for the hard and unique task, a task which carried the message of peace, righteousness and justice to Jerusalem. In Jerusalem, his task was not an easy one. He had to deal with the great division between religious leaders and the leaders of the people on one hand; and between the leaders and the people themselves on the other hand.

The people were searching for salvation while the religious leaders were holding firm on to the letter of the scriptures; superficial matters that stand in the way of deeper truths and prevent them from reaching the people.

Therefore, Christians believe that Jerusalem is the centre of salvation about which the prophets spoke. Salvation was fulfilled in Jesus Christ. So it is not strange that Jerusalem became the birthplace of the first Christian community in the spiritual and structural sense. Jerusalem is seen as the basis of Christian reference by the whole world.

In this sense, Galilee set the stage by preparing for Christ's message in Jerusalem; a message that overturned the old and obsolete human norms and replaced them with God's true norms that grant liberation from bondage. By setting the stage for this message, Galilee became closely connected with Jerusalem and its destiny, a connection that reached its climax in the resurrection which is the cornerstone of the Church. The Mother Church was established in Jerusalem and spread forth from there, strong and firm, to the ends of the earth.

The resurrection in Jerusalem is the ultimate expression of a new birth and a real annunciation of new life. This expression is connected with Nazareth, the city of the annunciation.

After the resurrection, Jesus told his disciples that he would meet them in Galilee. Perhaps that was meant to give Galilee an important and leading role in spreading the message of salvation just as it was the place of the annunciation.

The resurrection of Jesus brought Jerusalem out of its geographical confines and placed it in the heart of every believer. It became holy, not because of its churches, temples and mosques, but because of the transformation it has made in people's hearts.

Jesus made Jerusalem the base for the message of true peace that spread from there to the ends of the world. Christians in Galilee, like Christians everywhere, do not consider Jerusalem holy to Christians only, but rather a holy city to all monotheistic religions. This was the intention of Jesus. John the Evangelist says: 'Jesus was to die for the nation, and not for the nation only, but to gather in unity the scattered children of God' (John 11: 51-52).

Because of its status, Jerusalem has become a centre of attraction for believers from all over the world. They come to be blessed by its religious and archaeological sites. Jerusalem has a special place as the heart of Christendom, while Christians in Jerusalem see it as their home. In spite of all the difficulties and the volatile situation, there is an active Christian presence in the city. The Church in Jerusalem is not the stones of the Holy Places but rather a living witness through the sense of belonging of local Christians to the Church.

Palestinian Christians were born in Palestine and in it they continue to live.

They draw their inspiration from Jerusalem and their faith in the resurrection and message of salvation.

The Christians of Galilee and the Problems of Jerusalem

A   The Problem of Emigration

Emigration is one of the most serious concerns and problems that face the Palestinian People. Emigration is not voluntary but comes as a result of the Israeli occupation of Arab East Jerusalem and other parts of Palestine. The occupation has accelerated the rate of emigration among Christians from Jerusalem and other areas, like Bethlehem, Beit Sahour, Beit Jala and Ramallah. This phenomenon of emigration is found all over the Middle East, but it affects Christians more than their Muslim brothers and sisters. The reasons are the oppressive measures of the occupation, economic hardship, land and property expropriation and also because of the growing fear of religious fundamentalism.

Emigration has become a deep wound. Palestinian Christians believe it to be the way for solving their problems, especially because most of them have relatives who have already left the country. Some statistics put the emigration of Christians from Galilee at the annual rate of 20 percent, while in Jerusalem at about 50 percent. The latest census shows that there is an emigration pattern among Jerusalem Christians. The number of Christians in Jerusalem today does not exceed 10,000. The question I would like to put to Christians in Galilee is: what would Jerusalem be like without any Christian human presence? How would the world react if only the stones of the Holy Places remain? Is a human Christian presence necessary for a continued witness to Jesus and his message through the ages?

The problem of emigration among Jerusalem Christians is a real concern for Christians in Galilee who feel that ties with their Jerusalem brothers and sisters are fading.

B   The Palestinian Problem

The reality that exists in Jerusalem today is far removed from the natural human rights of its people. Jerusalem is threatened with drastic structural and demographic changes through the confiscation of land, the withholding of building licenses for Palestinians, the military closure of the city as well as the ill-treatment of its Palestinian population. These measures raise many concerns over the future of the city. In reality Jerusalem is the heart of the Palestinian problem. Even when all other issues are resolved, there will be no peace without a just solution for Jerusalem.

Just as Jerusalem is the spiritual, political and intellectual centre for the Israeli Jew, so too is it for the Christian and Muslim Palestinian. A Palestinian Christian does not accept the claim that Jerusalem belongs only to Jews, for it is not a gift from heaven exclusively to Jews. It belongs to the followers of the three monotheistic faiths. Palestinian Christians and Muslims hold Jerusalem at the core of their lives, it is their past and their future, their roots and their heritage. They cannot surrender their natural and legitimate rights to the city.

The saying that Jerusalem is the city of peace has lost its meaning. It is very far away from peace. The main reason is the violation of the rights of the Palestinian people who live in it. Jerusalem, being the meeting place of the three faiths, requires a special political solution. The Israeli solution is unacceptable because it considers the whole of Jerusalem as its eternal capital, which deprives the Palestinians of their share in the city.

C   Jerusalem as a Model for the Believers of the Three Monotheistic Faiths

It is because of historical events that we have a presence of the three monotheistic faiths in this city. It is therefore wise, for the followers of the three faiths, to learn to live together, not only for humanitarian reasons, but also because of the teachings of all three faiths.

God has chosen Jerusalem to provide a unique experience of God's love to humankind and the love of human beings for each other. The conflict over Jerusalem is detrimental to the city and its citizens. The fact that one side is stronger than the other is not helpful but rather has negative effects. This conflict has caused fear, anxiety, tension and hatred. Is this the message of Jerusalem? Certainly not. Christians want to have a more active role and deeper participation in shaping the future status of their city. They call for a serious effort to break down all psychological and hostile barriers, something that will not happen until the Palestinian people get their full rights. The Palestinians are trying to salvage what remains of Arab Jerusalem so that their identity, their presence, their history and their culture would not be eradicated. This is a cry that appeals to the hearts and minds of all the people in the world to take part in preserving the legitimate rights of the Palestinian citizens of Jerusalem.

Giving back the legitimate rights to the Palestinians of Jerusalem would signal the beginning of real coexistence and the removal of barriers. Short of that, we can only have slogans without the real thing.

Every Jewish person should liberate him/herself from the shackles of an occupation mentality and the control of the lives of others. They are called to face reality and participate in the building of a new Jerusalem, one that will have freedom as the key to its existence.

On the other hand, for Palestinian Christians and Muslims, freedom in Jerusalem should mean their acceptance of the other, their acceptance of Jews as brothers and sisters. The way should be cleared for peace to triumph, a peace established on truth, justice and righteousness.

32
THE HOLY CITY AS AN IMAGE OF
A NEW CREATION
Salpy Eskidjian

Overview

'If you only knew today what is needed for peace.' This sentence from the Gospel of St Luke, chapter 19, was the message that brought us here together. It was the challenge that stayed with us throughout the conference related to the City of Jerusalem—specifically its significance to Christians and Christians to Jerusalem.

Against the background of Jerusalem's turbulent, political and legal history and the conflicting opinions on its status, we gathered here to listen to the voices of our indigenous Christian sisters and brothers, to hear their stories, dreams, analysis and aspirations of Jerusalem. We reflected together on Jerusalem's unique significance to the three monotheistic faiths and specifically to Christians.

With the pain of our Palestinian sisters and brothers we cried. We were uplifted with their vision for a just peace for Israelis and Palestinians alike. Our common faith strengthened us and gave us hope. We expressed our Christian solidarity to the people of the Holy City in their search for justice and peace.

In this ecumenical gathering, Sabeel, the Liberation Theology Center, showed us the 'the way' to look at Jerusalem with a multi-disciplinary approach. The rich heritage of this ancient city was shared with us by distinguished speakers and participants alike. Through its history, theology, culture, geography, demography, archaeology and environment, we were once again reminded what this city was, is and what it means to Palestinian Christians. The political and legal realities as well as future perspectives of Jerusalem gave us the different opinions and requirements for a just peace.

However different our opinions might have been in this respect, we were united through our daily ecumenical prayers and Bible studies in the spirit of love. Our prayers were a manifestation of the unity we have as a gift from our Lord and in hope that there will be peace for this city. We prayed together for all the communities of people in Jerusalem. Our deliberations were an expression of our will to build together a peace founded in justice, love and compassion for all. We prayed that they may be seen that way by the people of the three monotheistic faiths, who share devotion to this Holy City.

Concluding Remarks and Challenges

According to the 1993 Declaration of Principles, the year 1996 will mark the negotiations on the permanent status of the West Bank and Gaza, where Jerusalem's Status will be dealt with.

During this diplomatic battle, which will formally begin in the spring of 1996, it may be assumed that disagreements will encompass many thorny questions: e.g., matters related to sovereignty; jurisdiction and powers, in particular to the sphere of security; transportation and access roads, town planning; Holy Places; municipal matters such as water, sewage, roads education, etc; the issue of settlements; land expropriation, building rights; freedom of movement are only a few of the hurdles negotiating parties will have to resolve. There is hardly any subject which could not lead to conflict.

We pray the negotiating parties will find reasonable compromise that encompass justice, in order that Jerusalem may again live up to its biblical characterisation—a City of Peace.

Recognising the significance of Jerusalem to the continuing Middle East peace process, as well as the deep religious, historical and emotional attachments of Christians, Muslims and Jews to Jerusalem, profoundly concerned about the human rights violations and the facts being created on the ground, like the changing demography, etc., we welcome the challenges extended to us by our Christian sisters and brothers. Their call is not only significance but urgent.

Taking the above into account, following are my main concluding remarks:

1   For Christians Jerusalem is the centre of faith and history as stated in the memorandum of the Heads of Churches in November, 1994.[1]

> [It] is the place of the gift of the spirit, of the birth of the Church (Acts 2), the community of the disciples of Jesus who are to be His witnesses not only in Jerusalem but even the ends of the earth (1: 8).
> [For Christians it remains a continuing reference point, as] the first Christian community incarnated the ecclesiastical ideal . . . it is the place of its roots, ever living and nourishing.
> This Holy City is the image of the new creation and the aspirations of all peoples. It is at the heart of the theology and spirituality of Christian pilgrimage.

2   As mentioned in the same memorandum, Christians should recognise Jerusalem's two essential and inseparable dimensions:

a) [That it is] a Holy City with Holy Places most precious to

---

[1] *On the Significance of Jerusalem for Christians,* Memorandum of their Beatitudes the Patriarchs and the Heads of Christian Communities in Jerusalem, Jerusalem, 14 November 1994

Christians because of their link with the history of salvation fulfilled in and through Jesus Christ;

b) [That it is a] city with a community of Christians which has been living continually there ever since its origins.

It is also the native city where Christians, Muslims, and Jews live. All have the right to live there freely, with the same right and obligation without any distinction and discrimination. As Christians, we therefore recognise that Jerusalem is the home and Holy City for all three Abrahamic faiths and recognise their freedom of access of all and rights to worship in their own ways.

3   Religion should foster rather than hamper efforts to achieve peace. Apart from our distinctive identities, we heirs of the Abrahamic tradition have a shared heritage. This shared heritage and belief in one God which sees human beings as God's most noble creation summon all believers to be peacemakers. The claims we make in the name of our traditions must not be mutually exclusive. Exclusive claims over Jerusalem are the causes for the absence of real peace in Jerusalem.

4   At this critical junction, we should be in constant prayer and in acts of solidarity with Christian communities in Jerusalem, with the regional ecumenical council, in order to ensure a continuing vital Christian presence in the Holy City and to strengthen the historic role of these communities and their leaders in promoting open communication, dialogue and co-operation among all communities here. It is up to each and every one of us to make sure this does not become just another conference as it was mentioned many times.

Thank you Sabeel, thank you Naim and each and every one of you who made this conference possible. This week has been an inspiration for me.

We pray that with efforts like this Jerusalem will always be a place of justice, reconciliation dialogue for the two nations and the three monotheistic faiths, in order that its unique character may contribute, nurture and sustain this justice, peace, love, and reconciliation and co-existence and thus become a blessing to all families of the earth.

'Blessed are the peacemakers, for they shall be called children of God' (Matthew 5: 9, New Revised Standard Version).

33

THE MOSAIC OF JERUSALEM

Harry Hagopian

In 1964, His Holiness Pope Paul VI described Jerusalem as 'the earthly point where God came into contact with humanity and where eternity crossed history.'

Indeed, in the past few days, participants at the conference pondered over transcendental and practical issues relating to God and humankind, to eternity and history, as they impact Jerusalem, and particularly its indigenous Palestinian Christian inhabitants.

To start with, we heard the mosaic of Jerusalem as a reflection of its historical plurality and continuity. We discussed its significance as a pathway to Christian unity and as a vision for interfaith relations.

Later came an exegetical unfurling of this city, mirroring our theological standpoints and our understanding of liberation theology, as a movement that is, in its simplest epistemological form, meant to liberate. We discovered the interpretation of Palestinian Christian place upon holy spaces, how that very holiness is compounded by the claims of all three monotheistic religions. We also heard that the Gospel has deterritorialised physical space through the glorious mystery of the Incarnation, with its locus situated in the Crucifixion and Resurrection. We prayed together about the plural and inclusive nature of Jerusalem within the framework of our faith, one that does not deny the other in order to affirm its own identity, sense of belonging or continuity. Speaker after speaker underscored the need to break the cycle of enmity and to work toward reconciliation on the basis of justice, a cornerstone of our faith, but also a prerequisite for lasting peace.

Along the same vein, speakers conveyed also the alarming trend set by some exclusivist and conservative fundamentalist evangelical constituencies in North America who disregard the indigenous Christian message and override its ethos and significance, decrying any link with the local Church and impelling themselves forward on a well-financed pseudo-political platform that strives to replicate the teachings of the Old Testament as if the New Testament has not yet been made manifest!

Hardly had we taken on board the historical and theological perspectives when we were led on a socio-economic and demographic tour of this city where the Palestinian Christian presence and witness ever since the Church of the First Pentecost were underlined in unemotive numbers. Such numbers confirmed the statistical and existential struggles of this people. However, despite the changing face and pace of Jerusalem, the immense difficulties its local inhabitants face, the *Living Stones* (1 Peter 2: 5) are here to stay. Although churches here are not always full and church leadership is not always united or fully in touch with its grassroots concerns, churches are not museums, or worse a Disneyland, for all to watch with tolerant amusement or overbearing curiosity.

The conference then went into political and legal territory, a territory which was at times uncharted and ad-libbed, at others factual and academic. We received a message that Palestinians need to compromise in their political stance, that pragmatism and a sense of urgency are needed in order to push forward a process in search of peace, or, as Afif Safieh put it, a role in search of an actor. Nonetheless, the strength of feeling from the audience underlined that compromise is a two-way street, and that Palestinians aspire for a two-state solution with Jerusalem as its undivided sovereign capital. Legal reality, be it in the application of Israeli laws in Jerusalem or in the precepts of international law, confirmed the creeping Judaisation of the Holy City through deliberate Israeli legal manoeuvres which disregard jurisprudence and international law.

But where does all this leave Palestinian Christians today, as they attempt to strengthen their fellowship and provide a common understanding of the *Significance of Jerusalem for Christians and of Christians for Jerusalem* in both its biblical and contemporary aspects, locally, regionally and globally?

Have the participants managed to reach a consensus, or a common platform? How have they related to this city which outranks all other cities in the Bible in prominence and wealth of sacred associations? What do they make of a city that, under one name or another, appears in nearly two-thirds of the books of the Old Testament and half of the books of the New Testament? What conclusions can be drawn?

Allow me to deconstruct a few thoughts as we wrap up this conference today:

1   The conference emphasised unequivocally the strong sense of belonging participants felt for biblical and contemporary Jerusalem. This, coupled with an equal sense of belonging to one another, came across as a clear commitment that Jerusalem has a tri-dimensional character incorporating Jews, Muslims and Christians.

2   In fact, many participants came to realise—perhaps for the first time—how Jerusalem is considered both sacred and a physical home for indigenous Christians, regardless of their confessional, denominational or tribal background;

3   The conference also manifested clearly that religion and politics in the Middle East are inextricably intertwined. One spills into the other, or is a function of the other, and this applies to Christians in as large a measure as it does to Jews and Muslims. The disestablishment of church from state, or the religious from the secular, is not a clear-cut phenomenon, even when taking on board the large numbers of 'non-religious' people.

4   In this context, the conference affirmed that followers of all faiths (inhabitants of this one city) should learn to coexist: such coexistence should first apply to Christians within their own diverse communities and then to relations between the

adherents of all three.

5   The conference shed light on the difficulties and obstacles facing Christians in Jerusalem, as well as in the larger context of Israel and Palestine. Such discrimination, leading to many practical instances of injustice, explains to a large extent the ever-growing sense of frustration and soul-searching that has wrested control of their daily lives.

6   However, it is often easier to identify such frustration than it is to find ways of tackling it, or better still, disarming it. This frustration, I understand, occurs on two distinct levels. On the one hand, the reality of the Israeli Palestinian conflict in all its religious, political and social connotations is a complex one that does not always lend itself to simple solutions or does not provide easy insights. On the other hand, there is the added complication that a common agenda with a common vision and a common set of priorities does not exist within those communities, both inside and outside, who are often prey to the ever-shifting priorities and interests of powers and principalities.

7   The conference confirmed that advocacy and interpretation are essential tools for improving the situation and enhancing the future of all its local Christians. But such tools, be they in the form of conferences, speeches, alternative tourism, projects or programs, cannot succeed if they lack any consistent and prayerful follow-up that comes through *empowerment*. We all face a tough challenge if we are to be true to our beliefs: we need to be effective messengers taking the message with us home. Whether through regular bulletins, an enhanced communication network, twinnings, political or social activism, we need to pierce through the fudge, obfuscation and double-talk in order to be faithful to ourselves as much as to our sisters and brothers in our one apostolic faith.

Such empowerment becomes so much more powerful when it goes hand in hand with a strong conviction in the *koinonia t*hat binds all Christians together. Only when this bond is firmly established, and Christians inside and outside the Holy Land speak to each other and work together (rather than at each other and independently), that such steps might truly become effective and find resonance with a wider constituency.

Our faith is at a cross-roads, and Christians ought to seize this k*airos*. Can we harness our efforts to make Jerusalem a truly multi-faith mosaic celebrating Jews, Muslims, and Christians alike? Can we hear the psalmist as he invites us all to 'pray for the peace of Jerusalem' (Psalm 122: 6) Let me wish you all a faithful *Salam, Shalom, Peace.*

Appendix

SIGNIFICANCE OF JERUSALEM FOR CHRISTIANS

Memorandum of the Patriarchs and Heads of the Christian
Communities in Jerusalem
14 November 1994

1   Preamble

On Monday, the 14th of November, 1994, the heads of Christian Communities in Jerusalem met in solemn conclave to discuss the status of the holy city and the situation of Christians there, at the conclusion of which, they issued the following declaration:

2   Jerusalem, Holy City

Jerusalem is a city holy for the people of the three monotheistic religions: Judaism, Christianity and Islam. Its unique nature of sanctity endows it with a special vocation: calling for reconciliation and harmony among people, whether citizens, pilgrims or visitors. And because of its symbolic and emotive value, Jerusalem has been a rallying cry for different revived nationalistic and fundamentalist stirrings in the region and elsewhere. And, unfortunately, the city has become a source of conflict and disharmony. It is at the heart of the Israeli-Palestinian and Israeli-Arab disputes. While the mystical call of the city attracts believers, its present unenviable situation scandalises many.

3   The Peace Process

The current Arab-Israeli peace process is on its way towards resolution of the Middle East conflict. Some new facts have already been established, some concrete signs posted. But in the process Jerusalem has again been side-stepped, because its status, and especially sovereignty over the city, are the most difficult questions to resolve in future negotiations. Nevertheless, one must already begin to reflect on the questions and do whatever is necessary to be able to approach them in the most favourable conditions when the moment arrives.

4   Present Positions

When the different sides involved now speak of Jerusalem, they often assume exclusivist positions. Their claims are very divergent, indeed conflicting. The Israeli position is that Jerusalem should remain the unified and eternal capital of the State of Israel, under the absolute sovereignty of Israel alone. The Palestinians, on the other hand, insist that Jerusalem should become the capital of a future State of Palestine, although they do not lay claim to the entire modern city, but envisage only the Eastern, Arab part.

5   Lessons of History

Jerusalem has had a long, eventful history. It has known numerous wars and conquests, has been destroyed time and again, only to be reborn anew and rise from its ashes, like the mythical phoenix. Religious motivation has always gone hand in hand with political and cultural aspirations, and has often played a preponderant role. This motivation has often led to exclusivism or at least to the supremacy of one people over the others. But every exclusivity or every human supremacy is against the prophetic character of Jerusalem. Its universal vocation and appeal is to be a city of peace and harmony among all who dwell therein.

Jerusalem, like the entire Holy Land, has witnessed throughout its history the successive advent of numerous new peoples: they came from the desert, from the sea, from the north, from the east. Most often the newcomers were gradually integrated into the local population. This was a rather constant characteristic. But when the newcomers tried to claim exclusive possession of the city and the land, or refused to integrate themselves, then the others rejected them.

Indeed, the experience of history teaches us that in order for Jerusalem to be a city of peace, no longer lusted after from the outside and thus a bone of contention between warring sides, it cannot belong exclusively to one people or to only one religion. Jerusalem should be open to all shared by all. Those who govern the city should make it 'the capital of humankind'. This universal vision of Jerusalem would help those who exercise power there to open it to others who also are fondly attached to it and to accept sharing it with them.

6   The Christian Vision of Jerusalem

Through the prayerful reading of the Bible, Christians recognise in faith that the long history of the people of God, with Jerusalem as its Center, is the history of salvation which fulfils God's design in and through Jesus of Nazareth, the Christ.

The one God has chosen Jerusalem to be the place where His name alone will dwell in the midst of His people so that they may offer to Him acceptable worship. The prophets look up to Jerusalem, especially after the purification of the exile: Jerusalem will be called 'the city of justice, faithful city (Is 1: 26-27) where the Lord dwells in holiness as in Sinai (cf. Ps 68: 18). The Lord will place the city in the middle of the nations (Ez 5: 5), where the Second Temple will become a house of prayer for all peoples (Is 2: 2, 56: 6-7). Jerusalem, aglow with the presence of God (Is 60: 1), ought to be a city whose gates are always open (Is 17).

In the vision of their faith, Christians believe the Jerusalem of the Prophets to be the foreseen place of the salvation in and through Jesus Christ. In the Gospels, Jerusalem rejects the Sent-One, the Saviour; and he weeps over it because this city of the prophets that is also the city of the essential salvific events—the death and resurrection of Jesu—has completely lost sight of the path to peace (cf. Lk 19: 42).

In the Acts of the Apostles, Jerusalem is the place of the gift of the Spirit, of the birth of the Church (2), the community of the disciples of Jesus who are to be His witnesses not only in Jerusalem but even the ends of the earth (1: 8). In Jerusalem, the first Christian community incarnated the ecclesial ideal, and thus it remains a continuing reference point.

The Book of Revelations proclaims the anticipation of the new, heavenly Jerusalem (3: 12; 21: 2; cf. Gal 4: 26; Heb 12: 22). This Holy City is the image of the new creation and the aspirations of all peoples, where God will wipe away all tears, and 'there shall be no more death or mourning, crying out or pain, for the former world has passed away' (21: 4).

7 The earthly Jerusalem in the Christian tradition, prefigures the heavenly Jerusalem as 'the vision of peace'. In the liturgy, the Church itself receives the name of Jerusalem and relives all of that city's anguish, joys and hopes. Furthermore, during the first centuries the liturgy of Jerusalem became the foundation of all liturgies everywhere, and later deeply influenced the development of diverse liturgical traditions, because of the many pilgrimages to Jerusalem and of the symbolic meaning of the Holy City.

8 The pilgrimages slowly developed an understanding of the need to unify the sanctification of space through celebrations at the Holy Places with the sanctification in time through the calendared celebrations of the holy events of salvation (Egeria, Cyril of Jerusalem). Jerusalem soon occupied a unique place in the heart of Christianity everywhere. A theology and spirituality of pilgrimage developed. It was an ascetic time of biblical refreshment at the sources, a time of testing during which Christians recalled that they are strangers and pilgrims on earth (cf. Heb 11: 13), and that their personal and community vocation always and everywhere is to take up the cross and follow Jesus.

9   The Continuing Presence of a Christian Community
For Christianity, Jerusalem is the place of roots, ever living and nourishing. In Jerusalem is born every Christian. To be in Jerusalem is for every Christian to be at home.

For almost two thousand years, through so many hardships and the succession of so many powers, the local Church has been witnessing to the life and preaching the death and resurrection of Jesus Christ upon the same Holy Places, and its faithful have been receiving other brothers and sisters in the faith, as pilgrims, resident or in transit, inviting them to be reimmersed into the refreshing, ever living ecclesiastical sources. That continuing presence of a living Christian community is inseparable from the historical sites. Through the 'Living Stones' the holy archaeological sites take on 'life'.

10   The City as Holy and As Other Cities
The significance of Jerusalem for Christians thus has two inseparable fundamental dimensions:

1   a Holy City with Holy Places most precious to Christians because of their link with the history of salvation fulfilled in and through Jesus Christ;
2   a city with a community of Christians which has been living continually there since its origins.

Thus for the local Christians, as well as for local Jews and Muslims, Jerusalem is not only a Holy City, but also their native city where they live, whence their right to continue to live there freely, with all the rights which obtain from that.

11 Legitimate Demands of Christians for Jerusalem

In so far as Jerusalem is the quintessential Holy City, it above all ought to enjoy full freedom of access to its Holy Places, and freedom of worship. Those rights of property ownership, custody and worship which the different churches have acquired throughout history should continue to be retained by the same communities. These rights which are already protected in the *Status Quo* of the Holy Places according to historical *firmans* and other documents, should continue to be recognised and respected.

The Christians of the entire world, Western or Eastern, should have the right to come on pilgrimage to Jerusalem. They ought to be able to find there all that is necessary to carry out their pilgrimage in the spirit of their authentic tradition: freedom to visit and to move around, to pray at holy sites, to embark into spiritual attendance and respectful practice of their faith, to enjoy the possibility of a prolonged stay and the benefits of hospitality and dignified lodgings.

12 The local Christian communities should enjoy all those rights to enable them to continue their active presence in freedom and to fulfil their responsibilities towards both their own local members and towards the Christian pilgrims throughout the world.

Local Christians, not only in their capacity as Christians *per se,* but like all other citizens, religious or not, should enjoy the same fundamental rights for all: social, cultural, political and national.
Among these rights are:

1   the human right of freedom of worship and of conscience, both as individuals and as religious communities,
2   civil and historical rights which allow them to carry out their religious, educational, medical and other duties of charity,
3   the right to have their own institutions, such as hospices for pilgrims, institutions for the study of the Bible and the traditions, centres for encounters with believers of other religions, monasteries, churches, cemeteries, and so forth, and the right to have their own personnel and run these institutions.

13 In claiming these rights for themselves, Christians recognise and respect similar and parallel rights of Jewish and Muslim believers and their communities. Christians declare themselves disposed to search with Jews and Muslims for a mutually respectful application of these rights and for a harmonious coexistence, in the perspective of the universal spiritual vocation of Jerusalem.

14 Special Statute for Jerusalem

All this presupposes a special judicial and political statute for Jerusalem which reflects the universal importance and significance of the city.

1   In order to satisfy the national aspirations of all its inhabitants, and in order that Jews, Christians and Muslims can be 'at home' in Jerusalem and at peace with one another, representatives from the three monotheistic religions, in addition to local political powers, ought to be associated in the elaboration and application of such a special statute.

2   Because of the universal significance of Jerusalem, the international community ought to be engaged in the stability and permanence of this statute. Jerusalem is too precious to be dependent solely on municipal or national political authorities, whoever they may be. Experience shows that an international guarantee is necessary.

Experience shows that such local authorities, for political reasons or the claims of security, sometimes are required to violate the rights of free access to the Holy Places. Therefore it is necessary to accord Jerusalem a special statute which will allow Jerusalem not to be victimised by laws imposed as a result of hostilities or wars but to be an open city which transcends local, regional or world political troubles. This statute, established in common by local political and religious authorities, should also be guaranteed by the international community.

Conclusion

Jerusalem is a symbol and a promise of the presence of God, of fraternity and peace for humankind, in particular, the children of Abraham: Jews, Christians and Muslims. We call upon all parties concerned to comprehend and accept the nature and deep significance of Jerusalem, City of God. None can appropriate it in exclusivist ways. We invite each party to go beyond all exclusivist visions or actions, and without discrimination, to consider the religious and national aspirations of others, in order to give back to Jerusalem its true universal character and to make of the city a holy place of reconciliation for humankind.

H B Diodoros I—*Greek Orthodox Patriarch*
H G Archbishop David Sahagin for the *Armenian Patriarch*
H G Dr Anba Abraham—*Coptic Archbishop*
H G Abba Matheos—*Ethiopian Archbishop*
Archbishop Lutfi Laham—*Greek-Catholic Patriarchal Vicar*
Mgr. Augustine Harfouche—*Maronite Patriarchal Vicar*
H B Michel Sabbah—*Latin Patriarch*
Very Revd Fr Joseph Nazzaro—*Custos of the Holy Land*
H G Dionisius Jazzawi—*Syriac Archbishop*
H G Bishop Samir Kafity—*Anglican Bishop*
H G Bishop Naim Nassar—*Lutheran Bishop*
Mgr Pierre Abdel-Ahad—*Catholic Syriac Patriarchal Vicar*